# DENVER

# TIMBERLINE BOOKS

*Stephen J. Leonard and Thomas J. Noel, editors*

**Colorado's Japanese Americans,** Bill Hosokawa

**Denver: An Archaeological History,** Sarah M. Nelson, K. Lynn Berry, Richard F. Carrillo, Bonnie L. Clark, Lori E. Rhodes, and Dean Saitta

**A Tenderfoot in Colorado,** R. B. Townshend

# DENVER
## AN ARCHAEOLOGICAL HISTORY

Sarah M. Nelson, K. Lynn Berry, Richard F. Carrillo,
Bonnie J. Clark, Lori E. Rhodes, and Dean Saitta

FOREWORD BY
STEPHEN J. LEONARD

UNIVERSITY PRESS OF COLORADO

To the Memory of John L. Cotter

© 2008 by the University Press of Colorado

Published by the University Press of Colorado
5589 Arapahoe Avenue, Suite 206C
Boulder, Colorado 80303

Previously published by the University of Pennsylvania Press

All rights reserved

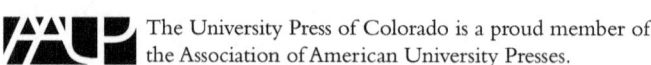 The University Press of Colorado is a proud member of the Association of American University Presses.

The University Press of Colorado is a cooperative publishing enterprise supported, in part, by Adams State College, Colorado State University, Fort Lewis College, Mesa State College, Metropolitan State College of Denver, University of Colorado, University of Northern Colorado, and Western State College of Colorado.

Library of Congress Cataloging-in-Publication Data

Denver : an archaeological history / Sarah M. Nelson . . . [et al.].
    p. cm. — (Timberline books)
 Revised ed. of: Denver / Sarah M. Nelson. c2001.
 Includes bibliographical references and index.
 ISBN 978-0-87081-935-3 (pbk. : alk. paper)  1. Denver (Colo.)—Antiquities. 2. Denver Region (Colo.)—Antiquities. 3. Denver (Colo.)—History. 4. Denver Region (Colo.)—History. 5. Frontier and pioneer life—Colorado—Denver Region. 6. Indians of North America—Colorado—Denver Region—Antiquities.  I. Nelson, Sarah M., 1931–  II. Nelson, Sarah M., 1931– Denver.
 F784.D447D46 2008
 978.8'83—dc22

2008035505

Cover design by Daniel Pratt

CONTENTS

FOREWORD  BY STEPHEN J. LEONARD — ix

PREFACE — xi

CHAPTER ONE — 1
GREATER DENVER AS A REGION OF FRONTIERS AND BOUNDARIES

CHAPTER TWO — 21
GEOLOGY AND ENVIRONMENT

CHAPTER THREE — 61
PREHISTORIC SITES

CHAPTER FOUR — 111
CONTACT, CONFLICT, AND COEXISTENCE

CHAPTER FIVE — 139
HISTORIC ARCHAEOLOGY

CHAPTER SIX — 221
CONCLUSION

AFTERWORD — 229
JOHN L. COTTER

REFERENCES CITED — 243

INDEX — 269

FOREWORD

Teachers tell students to dig into a subject to really understand it. Archaeologists take that advice literally. For more than a century, they have shoveled dirt to reveal Colorado's past. Yet despite all that digging, most Coloradans can claim, at best, only a superficial grasp of the state's archaeological riches. For this we can, tongue in cheek, blame the Ancestral Puebloans at Mesa Verde whose spectacular cliff dwellings have monopolized the public's attention. Few people realize that artifacts found in Golden, near Denver, predate Mesa Verde's Cliff Palace by some 5,000 years. Few know that there are hundreds of archaeological sites within thirty-five miles of the state capitol.

*Denver: An Archaeological History* by Sarah Nelson and her five collaborators fills in some of the blanks by presenting the results of more than seven decades of archaeological work in the Denver area. Here readers will learn not only of ancient sites but also of excavations that illuminate relatively recent nineteenth-century history, such as those at Four Mile House at 715 South Forest Street and at the Tremont House near Speer Boulevard and Auraria Parkway.

A beacon on the proximate and distant past, the volume complements other archaeological studies published by the University Press of Colorado, including Dennis J. Stanford and Jane S. Day's edited volume *Ice Age Hunters of the Rockies* (1992), Mark Stiger's *Hunter-Gatherer Archaeology of the Colorado High Country* (2001), and Robert H. Brunswig and Bonnie L. Pitblado's edited volume *Frontiers in Colorado Paleoindian Archaeology* (2007). It is also a welcome addition to the University Press of Colorado's Timberline Series, which aims to present scholarly treatments of Colorado's people and places.

—STEPHEN J. LEONARD
CO-EDITOR, TIMBERLINE SERIES

PREFACE

This book would never have been written without the interest, encouragement, and downright nagging of John Cotter, and therefore it is dedicated to him. John was a Denver native who graduated from the University of Denver in 1935. He became an archaeologist partly due to the inspiration of Dr. E. B. Renaud, founder of the university's Department of Anthropology. His early experiences in Colorado archaeology included work at the Lindenmeier site. All these facts were reasons for him to request a book about Denver for his series on the Archaeology of Great American Cities.

I first met John (known to his classmates as Jack) at Marie Wormington's house in the 1970s when he was visiting Denver, and later in 1985 when he came to his fiftieth reunion at the University of Denver. He was a delightful person, and with his great charm somehow convinced me to organize this book. I am sorry that he did not get to see the final version, but he did have an opportunity to read and comment on the first three drafts. He was kind enough to write an Afterword for the book, with reminiscences of Denver in the early twentieth century.

I had misgivings about having enough material for a book, because Denver as a city has considerably less time depth than Philadelphia (less than 150 years compared to about 400), and historic archaeology is barely beginning in Denver. On the other hand, the University of Denver has a rich collection of prehistoric materials from Greater Denver, from which few materials have ever been published. The more I learned about these collections the more I knew they should be publicly available, and that somehow I had an obligation to see that they got into print.

The project began in earnest when Bonnie Clark, Lori Rhodes, and I attended the 1994 annual meeting of the Colorado Council for Professional Archaeologists. Bonnie, then a master's degree student specializing in historic archaeology, was keen to begin. Lori already had an MA from our department, and was working in local cultural resource management; she had participated in many recent archaeological projects in Denver. The Colorado Historical Society was giving substantial grants for historic preservation from the Gaming Fund, so we began to see our way clear to serious work on this project. We created an editorial team, adding Richard Carrillo, a well-known historic archeologist in Colorado, K. Lynn Berry, interested in historic Native American sites and another former student with an MA from the University of Denver Department of Anthropology, and Professor Dean Saitta, also in the Department of Anthropology Department. We six became the writers and editorial board.

We began by creating a database from the files of the Office of the State Archaeologist of Colorado and weeding it out to suit our needs. Then we approached a mapping team. Lewis Hyer, University of Denver Geography Department, created the original ARC/INFO GIS database of archaeological sites derived from the Colorado State Historic Preservation Office database of site records for Greater Denver. Francine B. Patterson, University of Denver Geography Department, prepared the Greater Denver study area and site distribution maps as well as the base GIS data layers, which were derived from existing digital data, and digitized hard copy data sources. In the meantime various students helped with the database, which Bonnie Clark supervised. Eric Husman and Matt Morava determined UTMs for sites that had been located only by Township, Range, and Section, expanding the database for all local archaeologists. Cole Early obtained information about the sites from the Historical Society files and as many cultural resource management reports as he could locate. Marcia Tate was very helpful in this data collection phase, lending or giving us copies of her voluminous publications. Donna Bryant located illustrations for the book from the Historical Society files and the Denver Public Library.

In the first year we completed the database and scoured the University of Denver site cards and collections, greatly helped by Lisel Goetz. In addition, we carefully read the "gray literature," site reports in printed form but not made public. During that year, Lori Rhodes, K. Lynn Berry, and Richard Carrillo produced a draft context for the Greater Denver area. The second year we completed four products: a first draft of the full book, a list of C14 dates (mostly Lori's work), a printout of the data base, and all the maps made by Francine Patterson. While we were working on the remaining tasks, however, our group spread apart. Richard was based in La Junta, Colorado; K. Lynn and Lori took jobs in Albuquerque; Bonnie moved to Berkeley, California to pursue a Ph.D., and coordination became more difficult. Input of the many chapter drafts was done by Beth Rudden and Kate Hesseldenz, who are to be thanked for their many long hours in the service of this book. Kate especially was heroic in putting in the time she gave to the final draft.

We assigned responsibility for particular chapters, but anticipated that we would all contribute to the final versions of the chapters. The dispersion of the writers, as well as the fact that each of us had a full-time job, made this difficult. Much of the final editing and text arrangement was left to me, but the other authors have had a chance to make revisions as well.

Several local archaeologists read various drafts of the manuscript. Marcia Tate and Kevin Gilmore were particularly helpful. We would also like to thank the anonymous reviewers whose additional critiques improved our book.

Many thanks to Patricia Smith of the University of Pennsylvania Press for her moral support during this long process. I hope John Cotter is approving of our efforts from the Great Beyond.

The project was generously funded by the Colorado Historical Society, for which we are very grateful. Thanks also to Leo Block, University of Denver 1935, who funded some of the later stages of production.

# DENVER

CHAPTER 1

## Greater Denver as a Region of Frontiers and Boundaries

*Space—like history—is a product of human imagination and more often than not serves as an arena of social competition and conflict.*
—Mark P. Leone and Neil Asher Silberman, Invisible America

This book is written for readers interested in archaeology and in Denver's past, but the sources are *unwritten* history. Archaeological evidence and the evidence of material culture do not merely provide all we can know of the prehistoric inhabitants of the area; they enhance the written record of the historic period as well. The unwritten history of Denver is a story of the relationship of people to their environment on the edge between the High Plains and the Rocky Mountains, a story of frontiers and boundaries. Even in the geologic past the region was characterized by boundaries—sharp transitions—between mountains and plains, the wet and the dry. As a crossroads of cultures for millennia, the Greater Denver area is also an area of frontiers—areas of interpenetration of cultures or environments. It provides a backdrop for understanding the nature of cultural interactions and the processes of integration as well as maintenance of distinct expressions of unique cultural identities. Here many different groups of people have succeeded each other or coexisted.

Denver, nestled up against the foothills of the Rocky Mountains, occupies a place of contrasts in altitude, geology, and climate. These contrasts have contributed to the juxtaposition of different ways of life. So the archaeology of Greater Denver tells a story of many frontiers—and many kinds of frontiers.

The urban core of Denver, the place where the city began, is centered on the confluence of two rivers, the Platte River and Cherry Creek. Since the 1850s this town site has been a confluence of cultures as well (Fig. 1.1), a meeting ground for a variety of economic and social interests, and at times the scene of struggles for dominance and an urge toward expansion. But although the second half of the nineteenth century was a period of particularly great change for Denver, various groups met at the Platte River and Cherry Creek for many centuries and perhaps millennia prior to that. The fact that Denver has been a frontier reflects its natural setting, in which the High Plains meet the mountains, creating a dynamic and unique environment that merges some elements and separates others. Its unique flavor was created by the blending and distinctiveness of the different people who have called it home.

Figure 1.1. Indian tepees and settlers' houses at the confluence of Cherry Creek and the South Platte River. Courtesy of the Colorado Historical Society.

A frontier is often thought of as the interaction of civilized and uncivilized, developed and undeveloped. No such implicit value judgment is intended here. Our concept of frontier includes earlier peoples with varied technologies and adaptations to the different ecological zones that abut in Greater Denver. Our sense of the frontier, then, is that it is a zone of interaction rather than a boundary line. In order to survive in the difficult "frontier" environment, the technologically advanced minority, in spite of their technology, had to borrow from the knowhow of the locally adapted majority and streamline its social order simply to cope with the new surroundings, difficult because unfamiliar. On the American frontier, this simpler mode of life—and all its perceptions of virtue—was short-lived for the Euro-American settlers. Learning from the less technologically advanced Native American populations (and exploiting their lands and resources) rapidly changed into self-sufficiency in Greater Denver.

Patricia Limerick shows that the American west was a meeting ground of cultures. "Happily or not," Limerick points out, "minorities and majorities occupied a common ground" (Limerick 1987:27). This is particularly true of Denver, which was settled later than Salt Lake City and other towns farther west and was thus surrounded by established Euro-American outposts. Land developers in Greater Denver regarded Arapaho and Cheyenne ownership of the land as little more than a bothersome "technicality" (Clark et al.1993). Treaties negotiated with tribes and other interaction with them was largely carried out under the ethnocentric assumption that the Native American should and would succumb to the Euro-American methods of farming, education, commerce, and religion.

This is not to say that the various tribes failed to fight or negotiate for their independence. The purpose of this work, however, is not to document the maintenance of cultural identity and traditions, but to describe the general characteristics of cultural interaction in early Denver. The nature of the contact and conflicts between the two cultures created a particular climate for the developing city. The result was that Denver flourished as a city, but it did so ultimately at the cost of the local tribes. For example, Virginia Cole Trenholm (1970:160) writes, "We find casual mention of 'shameful outrages' to which the Arapaho in the Denver area were subjected. Upon more than one occasion in the winter of 1859–60, one authority tells us, their camps were invaded by brutal, half-drunk white ruffians who overpowered the braves and subjected the women to nameless indignities." It is this type of conflict that created a "frontier" environment (in the worst sense) in the city of Denver and the area around it. The conflicts, however, did not abate with the removal and subjugation of the Native Americans. Other marginalized peoples would replace the Indians in the urban environment.

How can the frontier character of Denver be explored archaeologically? Central to this examination is the concept that a landscape can be considered material culture. Not only can archaeological investigations within a city be concerned with urban issues or frontier typologies, but the city *as a whole* can also be viewed as an artifact. Also guiding this study is the search for social process in addition to pattern. It is the openness of cultures that is of interest here—the interrelated, connected processes of cultures through which patterns either persevere or change.

## THE GREATER DENVER AREA

Denver as a city hasn't been around long, even on the relatively short time scale of American cities. It was founded in 1858 and mushroomed into local importance. Prior to the establishment of the "Queen City of the Plains," as Denver has been called, other groups of people inhabited the plains, mountains, forests, and riversides of the area. These people—Native Americans of various nations, tribes, and bands—did not mark their boundaries on maps, although they must have known the limits of their territories and their habitual trails intimately. These territories were probably both irregular and widespread, fluctuating with the ebb and flow of economic resources and political

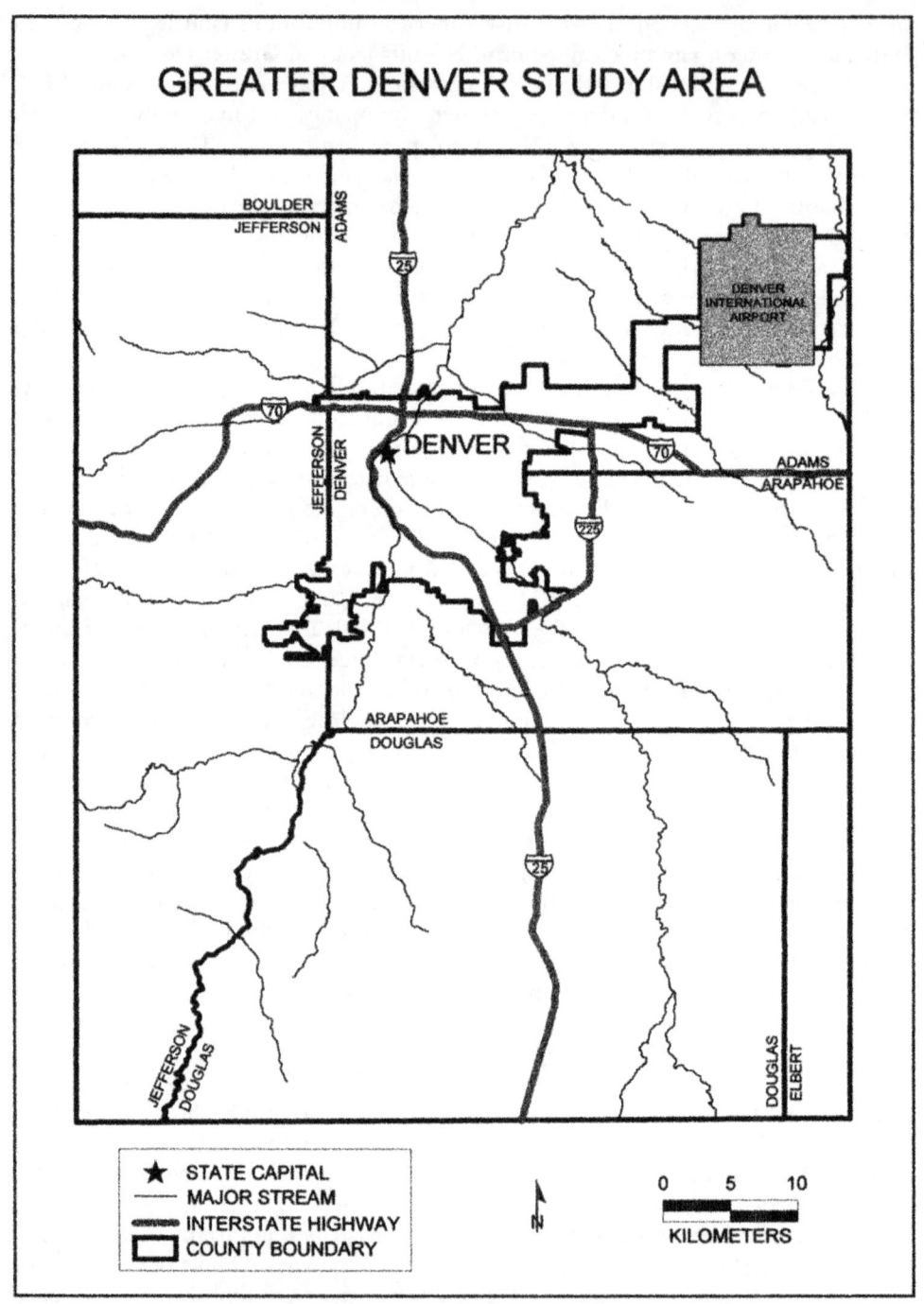

Figure 1.2. The Greater Denver study area, showing county boundaries. Francine Patterson.

alliances, and perhaps overlapping with other groups. But even after the imposition of divisions and borders, networks of interaction stretched beyond the small geographic area that Greater Denver occupies today. The area's inhabitants since the beginning have been involved in broader patterns of settlement, as well as trade and cultural interaction with surrounding areas. However, our project required a defined area. Some boundaries for this book had to be drawn in the interest of maintaining a manageable set of data, and to focus on the central elements of what makes the Denver area unique. A rectangular map proved to be convenient for searching the files of the Office of Archaeology and Historic Preservation (OAHP) and subsequently it was useful for mapping the region (Fig. 1.2). Counties seemed to be unnatural divisions, especially in view of prehistoric sites. At present, suburban Denver stretches about as far as the rectangle we chose. But this rectangle does not cover homogeneous land, so we divided it into four physiographic regions: Hogback, Black Forest, Streams, and Plains. These ecosystems were used differently by prehistoric and historic peoples, but we believe they were significant to all inhabitants. Those differences make intricate patterns on the weave of the urban center. Maps in this book thus reflect these regional differences.

In selecting our study area, the physiographic features of the Denver area provided a logical starting point. The mountains form an inexact but natural boundary to the west, while the foothills are closely related to Denver. Thus the western border of the study area was drawn to include the Hogback area. In the south, Denver's present suburbs stretch past Franktown, so this region needed to be included. The Palmer Divide separates the watershed of the South Platte from that of the Arkansas River. It also separates Greater Denver from Greater Colorado Springs. The higher elevations of the Black Forest catch more rainfall and therefore have different vegetation from downtown Denver, making for alternative uses through time. The riverine environments of the South Platte River and Cherry Creek affect archaeological sites in particular ways, thus we separated this area from the less watered plains. The Plains region to the east has helped to feed Denver with farms in historic times, but prehistoric people moved between the plains and the foothills for their own provisioning. But where in the north and east does Greater Denver end? Since the city of Denver now stretches to the northeast to include Denver International Airport, this new landmark provided a northeast corner for the study.

## The Database

Once the project region was identified, our next step was to compile a total list of sites. The set of site data which we obtained from OAHP included more than 5,000 recorded archaeological sites or areas. Careful examination showed that there were some sites that were inappropriate for our purpose, because they represented isolated artifacts or sites that had no obvious archaeological component. Eliminating these left 1,401 sites, which by the time we added new data gathered during the period of writing grew to 1,517 sites (Fig. 1.3). This database gave us our first view of the range, scope, and density of archaeological resources in the Greater Denver study area. Sites are located throughout and represent a wide range of time periods and site types, from small prehistoric

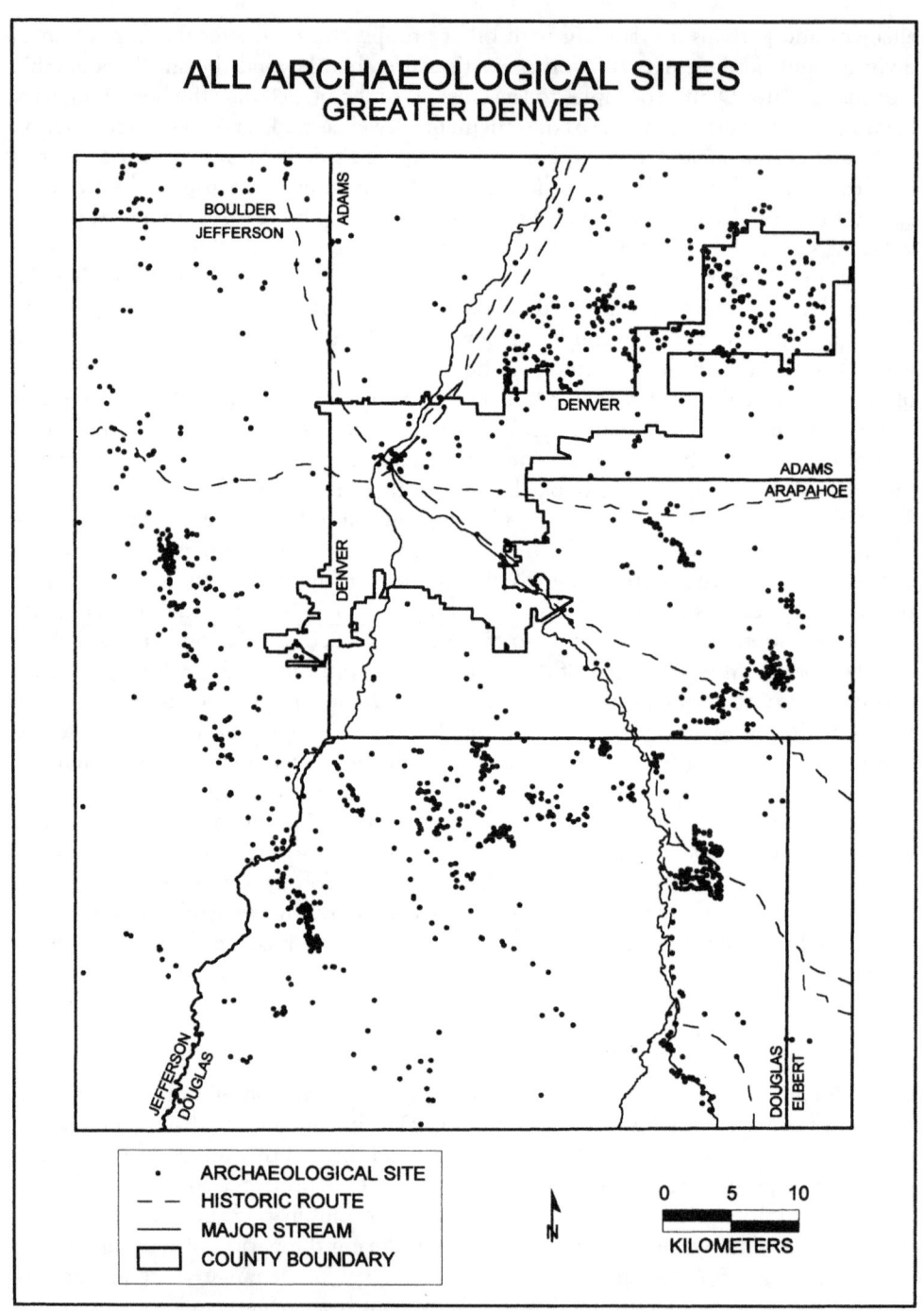

Figure 1.3. Archaeological sites in the study area. Francine Patterson.

scatters of chipped stone, to rock shelters, to historic homes and mines. The database even includes the burial site of a local alleged cannibal, Alferd Packer.

The data as they came from OAHP had to be modified for our project. First, in an effort to group data into meaningful categories, we amalgamated some of the cultural affiliations for dated sites. Sites classified in a number of ways might mean roughly the same thing in the original database. We created larger categories; for example, "Early Ceramic," "Early Woodland," and "Late Woodland" were collapsed into "Early Ceramic."

We used the modified database to run a Geographic Information Systems (GIS) mapping program. By using a GIS system, we were able to map the sites electronically and manipulate them to give information about patterning by time period and site type. The maps located throughout this book are the fruits of that labor.

GIS mapping depends on grid coordinates. The locations of sites in the Greater Denver study area were mapped using the worldwide metric grid system known as Universal Transverse Mercator (UTM). The system works very well with the right types of data, but when we began the project 273 of our sites did not have UTM designations. Locational data, some of which were recorded long ago, needed to be refined as well. In particular, some sites have been located only by township, range, section, and quarter-section, which is not easily used for computer mapping. After analyzing the collections at the University of Denver (the repository for many early Denver area studies) and synthesizing data on sites from numerous sources, we were able to pinpoint locational data on all but 88 sites. These last sites lacked specific locations and could not be mapped.

Another 81 sites that are linear features were not mapped. Linear features presented a mapping problem for two reasons. First, the number of UTM coordinates taken in the field may be inadequate to represent the course of the linear site accurately. Field personnel might record only enough points to roughly delineate the site, not to capture every turn and twist. Second, many of these sites have been recorded a number of times as projects intersect them, but the recorded segments are not readily identifiable as a continuous linear feature. The Highline Canal with site numbers 5AH388, 5AM261, 5DA600, and 5DV840 is a pertinent example, since it runs through four counties with a different number in each. We decided that mapping these features using UTMs was inappropriate and mapping by hand was beyond the scope and intent of the project. The most critical of the linear features, however, such as trails, were hand-mapped and appear on our historic period maps. These sites are the cornerstones of the archaeology of Greater Denver.

In order to have a flow to our narrative, we have put much of the technical information in boxes, which can be skipped, read later, or turned to immediately.

> Box 1A. What Is Archaeology?
>
> Archaeology is a method for learning about the past. While the public perception of archaeological work is often one of glamour, adventure, or romance, the truth is more prosaic. The practice of archaeology requires careful survey or digging and recording the details of the way artifacts are found in the earth and their relation-

> ship to each other and to the soil. The analytical parts of archaeology involve many specialists, from those who study soils to those who analyze plants, pollen, bones, and other materials. From these data, inferences about the lives of earlier inhabitants can be made.
>
> It is customary to divide the work of archaeologists into prehistory and history, depending on whether written records are present. For prehistoric times archaeology is the only direct source of knowledge; written materials provide fuller interpretations of the historic past. Social sciences such as history, sociology, and even cultural anthropology can use methods such as archival research, informant interviews, and direct observation, but archaeology has the advantage of the long view and is in the position to explore topics frequently overlooked by other fields. Archaeology can also focus on the day-to-day lives of ordinary people, allowing a broader as well as a longer perspective.

## THE HISTORY OF ARCHAEOLOGY IN GREATER DENVER

The first professional archaeologist in Denver was not educated as an archaeologist, but came to Colorado to teach French. He made up in diligence and reading what he lacked in training. Dr. Etienne B. Renaud was the founder of the University of Denver's Anthropology Department, in 1922. He and his students scoured Colorado and neighboring states, looking for sites and recording them. They examined the artifacts of collectors and talked to ranchers and farmers about what indications of the past were on their land. Renaud published a series of survey reports (Renaud 1931, 1932, 1933, 1935), of which one specifically pertains to Greater Denver. Some of these sites were reinvestigated over the years, and others have been added to the collections, but the foundations of Greater Denver archaeology were laid by the pioneering work of Renaud and his students. Many of the University of Denver sites were never properly published, so one goal of this book is to make available to the public and the archaeological profession the results of three-quarters of a century of site investigation in Greater Denver. Other sources, especially work done under contract (known as "gray literature"), are also extensively used. Other syntheses of the archaeology of Colorado have been published (Cassells 1983, Stone 1999), but they are of broader scope, including the entire state and beyond. We examine a smaller region in greater detail.

Some of Renaud's students—for example Marie Wormington—were bright lights in local and national archaeology. Others also became well-known archaeologists, such as John Cotter, who had a distinguished career in the National Park Service. When Arnold Withers came to the University of Denver, he inherited Renaud's site cards and site collections. Some of his students became prominent in the profession as well, David Breternitz, Alexander Lindsay, and Alan Olson among them. They worked on various local sites, including Franktown Cave, the only site in the entire area with perishable artifacts remaining. Students from the University of Colorado at Boulder also excavated in Greater Denver, including the Hazeltine Heights burial site. Amateur archaeologists have contributed a great deal through the years, and the responsible archaeological practices of the Colorado Archaeological Society, Denver Chapter, are a model for all paraprofessionals. The definitive work in Greater Denver was done by

Cynthia Irwin-Williams and Henry Irwin, offspring of a dedicated amateur who themselves both became professional archaeologists. Working at both Magic Mountain and LoDaisKa, the Irwins created a stratigraphic record that in its larger outlines still stands. More recently, contract work by Cultural Resource Management (CRM) has added important new details to our understanding of the region.

## Changing Archaeological Practices

The expansion of suburban Denver has had both a positive and a negative effect on archaeology. On the negative side is the disappearance of sites under buildings and parking lots. On the positive side many more sites have been recorded than previously were known, due to federal and state laws requiring archaeological surveys as well as increased local awareness and responsibility. A glance at the distribution map of all sites reveals how few prehistoric sites are recorded in the urban center relative to the total number reported in surveyed areas on the periphery. This does not mean that prehistoric peoples avoided the confluence of the Platte River and Cherry Creek. Rather, the city was built up before an interest in archaeology began, and the relatively rare excavations in the center of the city have concentrated on the historic period.

The map (Fig. 1.3) locating prehistoric sites also makes it clear that surveys have recorded significant numbers of new sites. The heavily dotted areas on the map reflect the locations of those surveys. This map demonstrates the extraordinary density of sites in Greater Denver in areas that have been surveyed, and hint at what may be missing in other areas.

Not only have archaeological surveys and excavations considerably broadened our knowledge of site types and locations, they have increased our understanding and appreciation of local prehistoric people in several ways. Excavations in the most promising of these sites have revealed much that was previously unknown: pit houses and other structures, maize pollen and remnants of wild plants, and sources of lithic tool material to name a few recent strides, all of which add incomparable richness to the database. Both seasonal camps and longer occupations have been found, suggesting that we need a more nuanced approach to Greater Denver archaeology than the simple division into projectile point types that stand for time divisions. Increasing sophistication is evident in recent site reports.

The early work by Renaud and his students was crude archaeology by today's standards, but some of their conclusions have withstood the tests of continued archaeological work. For example, Dale King (1931) wrote his thesis about the eastern Colorado plains, an area that includes Greater Denver. He found campsites the most common type of site, and noted that Black Forest sites tended to be associated with the acquisition of stone for raw material, especially petrified wood. Perhaps more important than the continuing usefulness of generalizations, though, is the fact that some of Renaud's surveys are the only record of sites long since vanished under the expansion of Greater Denver (Downing 1981).

But much has changed in the understanding of Greater Denver prehistory since the early days. One reason for the changes is that most of the area is private property, which can only be surveyed or excavated with the permission of the landowner. Although many sites were known to local collectors, and some were reported to professional archaeologists, vast tracts were unknown, and are only now being surveyed as Denver's suburbs expand. These areas, in changing hands or changing use, require archaeological surveys. It is notable that the attractive places for houses and ranches, where new settlers homesteaded, are also areas where earlier inhabitants found pleasant places to reside, with water nearby, slopes catching sunshine but out of the wind, and often with views of the mountains.

An example of the changing interest in the prehistoric inhabitants, as well as changing archaeological practices, can be gleaned from an area of Arapahoe County along Sampson Gulch and Piney Creek (Fig. 1.4). Comparing early site cards with more recent records reveals that this strip in the Plains subregion had almost continuous sites, especially Early Ceramic villages. The full picture of prehistoric land usage is only beginning to emerge.

Several sites near Smoky Hill road, which was an Indian trail before it was used by settlers from the east, have been recorded at various times. They make an interesting study in changing patterns of archaeology within the region and allow us to obtain a broader perspective on prehistoric land use. Sites on the Davidson, Esser, and Evernut ranches were reported to the University of Denver in 1950 and 1951 by Ernest Kemper, an amateur archaeologist who lived in Denver. His collecting activity was already substantial. He knew the area so well that he located the sites precisely on U.S. Geological Survey quads, noting them as D-1 to D-4 for those on the Davidson Ranch and E-1 to E-2 for the Esser Ranch. A gap in his data between the Esser and Evernut Ranches may indicate an unwilling landowner, but this is only speculation.

The Davidson sites were recorded by the University of Denver during a field trip in the 1970s, but even at that time perceptions of site boundaries differed from Kemper's maps. Whether the apparent boundaries were altered by weather or farming activities, or whether criteria differed, is unknown. For example, on the University of Denver site cards one site appears to encompass both D-1 and D-2, while Kemper's D-1 was perceived as two sites in the later survey. Some of the sites were large enough to be recorded as a "camp or village." The sites appear to be Early Ceramic with cord-marked potsherds, corner-notched points, grinding stones, and stone flakes.

By 1977 this ranch had been developed into suburban homesites. With permission of the new landowner, one site was revisited and surface-collected by a small University of Denver crew, who excavated a shallow test pit. Cord-marked pottery could still be found on the surface, as well as petrified wood, chalcedony, and quartzite flakes. Nothing was found in the one-meter-square pit but mano fragments smaller than 3 cm and a few tiny flakes. Plowing had ground this shallow site literally to bits.

The Davidson Ranch sites were again recorded in the Arapahoe Meadows Survey (Newberry and Tate 1994), when part of the area that had been Davidson Ranch was scheduled to be developed into a golf course. Their work shows that this was an area of intensive prehistoric settlement. Two-thirds of the shovel tests produced cultural materials, including cord-marked pottery, ground stone, and chipped stone. Concentrations of artifacts could still be found, but the artifacts were very near the surface. The differ-

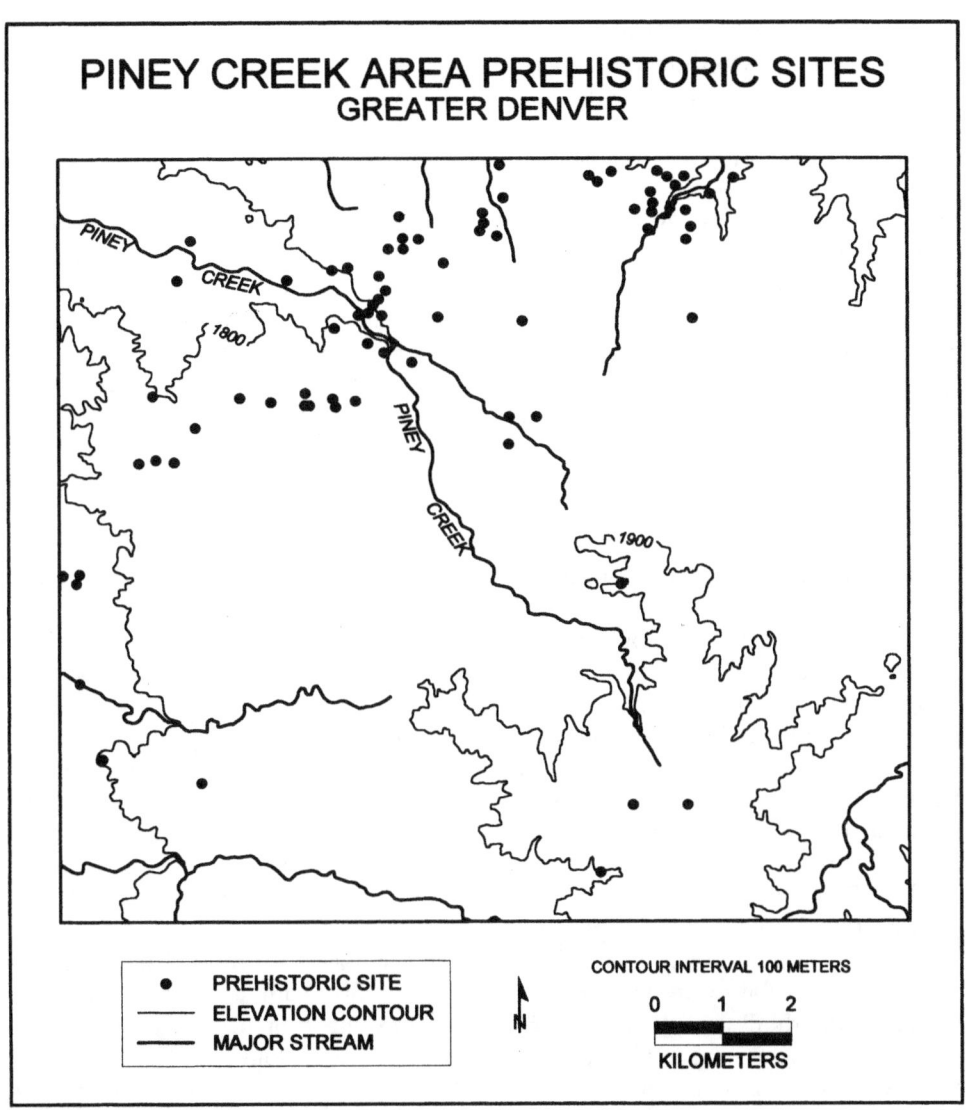

Figure 1.4. Southeastern section of the study area. Francine Patterson.

ence in depth of overburden after forty years may represent soil erosion and the effects of plowing on areas with marginal rainfall.

East of these sites, the Pine Ridge Ranch survey (Mutaw and Tate 1990) revealed additional areas of lithic scatter, covering altogether about 175 acres. This enormous spread of archaeological material lies between the Davidson and Esser sites, and was not recorded on Kemper's map, but part of the area designated as having multiple sites by Mutaw and Tate had been previously noted in the E-470 survey (Joyner 1988). The later crew described one of the sites as much larger than the earlier crew had perceived it.

Moving farther southeast, the Esser sites were given University of Denver numbers, again with disagreements about what constitutes site boundaries. Where Kemper perceived two large sites, both on the northeast of Sampson Gulch, the University of Denver recorders noted five sites, three of them on the southwest side of the gulch. Woodland sherds, bones, flakes and scrapers, manos, and metates were listed as having been observed.

Still trending southeast, farther up the gulch, four large sites at the Evernut Ranch are recorded on the Kemper map, but as they were not recorded by the University of Denver, there is no further knowledge of their content. We do know that the entire strip had intermittent debris from prehistoric peoples, largely from the Early Ceramic period.

What are we to think of such an extensive occupation? Does it represent many years of living along this intermittent stream, repeated occupations at different locations along the strip, or many people at once? There is some indication that Early Ceramic times were cooler and wetter than the present (Gilmore 1991); perhaps the region was better suited to unirrigated crops than it was in the 1890s when settlers from the eastern United States homesteaded the plains. As will be seen in Chapter 2, precipitation in the Denver Basin is erratic, with years of drought and years of floods. Did the Early Ceramic people enjoy good years and then have their own "dust bowl" and abandon the area? This is the kind of question that can only be asked, let alone answered, with a perspective that embraces an entire region.

Some of these sites have been known to archaeologists for more than half a century, and presumably were noted even earlier by the first homesteaders, whose plows turned up the thinly buried artifacts. But the real extent of prehistoric occupation in the area is just beginning to be appreciated. Furthermore, it should be clear that setting site boundaries is more an art than a science. The extent of surface scatter, for instance, may appear to change depending on a number of factors, including intervening surface pickup, recent rains, snow, and winds, ground cover, and various other kinds of surface disturbances. Thus perceptions of what makes a site, and where its edges are, are in the eyes of the beholder.

## THEORETICAL BACKGROUND

Our goal in this book is to create a volume that is useful both to the general reader and to the professional archaeologist, and to avoid a mere recitation of archaeological discoveries. Throughout, we will be looking at open, flexible systems of individuals and societies and how they change over time. These systems are tied together by countless networks of interaction, which themselves come into being, are modified, and change into other systems.

Essential to developing an open model of human society is the obvious notion that local events do not occur in a vacuum; that is, they are not produced by local conditions alone, but are also influenced by broader, external factors. This is true of prehistoric cultures as well as ethnographic or sociological ones. Urban archaeologists Pamela J. Cressey and J. J. Stephens argue that a single area or group within a city should not be studied independently; they propose to view the individual unit of study within a broader framework—"as dependent upon changes within the city as a whole" (1982:44). This logic can be taken a step further, to include the patterns of change within still larger frames such as the region or nation. Eric Wolf begins his book *Europe and the People Without History* by reminding the reader that nations and cultures must be viewed as "bundles of relationships," not individual entities. The only way to understand the forces that guide societies is to understand that "human populations construct their cultures in interaction with one another, and not in isolation" (Wolf 1982:ix).

Often the openness of systems, or the interaction between cultures, is most visible on the "frontiers." At the edges and boundaries of societies, differences become apparent. A clash of ideologies may take place. On the other hand, a mingling of traditions may occur. We might think of the frontier as a cultural ecotone—a transitional zone where two groups meet. In the zone, there are representatives of each separate group and also a third group, one that may be unique to the transitional zone. These interactions and the space they occupy often become *visible*, especially at the boundaries. The next task is to recognize visible parts in the archaeological record, the material culture.

> Box 1B. The Core-Periphery Model
>
> The core-periphery model of spatial and social organization is a useful analytical tool for discussing the interactions that occur on the frontiers of societies. The model is not only about networks of satellite-metropolis *entities* and places, but also about the human relationships between central figures of power and domination and the marginalized individuals who remain at the edges of society. The model opens the discussion for a number of useful questions. Within the city itself, "core" sections of space and population can dominate other zones and people on the margins. If the city is the center of market and social activities, then what roles are played by the people who occupy the peripheral spaces? Land use, transportation, and communication systems link the core to the periphery, but there are structural relationships between the city-center and the edges that allow the core to dominate the peripheral areas (Cressey and Stephens 1982).
>
> The model is especially appropriate for a city like Denver, which was in a sense on the frontier of the nation. It was a satellite of such metropolitan centers as Chicago and New York, from which many goods and services bound for the frontier originated. At the local level, Denver served as the core for such peripheral entities as mining camps, military forts, smaller towns, and eventually the suburbs.

## Material Culture

Material culture is a term used by folklorists, sociologists, anthropologists, artists, pop culturists and others, usually to mean sets of objects people have created. These objects in most cases hold meanings for people, meanings that can be obvious and expressed, implicit, or explicit and implicit at once. Treasured souvenirs of a childhood vacation, a wedding ring, a collection of vinyl records are material culture, as are stone tools, powder for paints, and fruit canning jars. These objects can be studied with archaeological data to explore the ways people organize their understanding of the world, how cultures attempt to keep their separate characters, and the control of economic resources.

Objects have meaning. Each object may be able to reveal something about ideology, politics, social relations, and many other aspects of culture that go beyond function and form. Working with the concept that material items "are simply tools, passive by-products, with little ideological or symbolic component," many people (even archaeologists!) have ignored the potential of artifacts to serve as active agents of cultural reality (Hodder 1982a:196). Recently scholars of several disciplines have come to recognize the role material culture can play in revealing other interpretations of the social fabric.

Studying humans within their built environment can stretch the boundaries of traditional material culture definitions and, in so doing, shed new light on the subject. James Deetz says that material culture is "that sector of our physical environment that we modify through culturally determined behavior" (1977:24). Thus material culture encompasses not just objects but a city streetscape (Deetz 1967) and even noise or air pollution (Upton 1992). These are things that humans create, not in the deliberate way one might sculpt a statue or place Little League trophies in a prominent display case, but in ways that nonetheless reflect and affect the values and habits of the members of the society.

Material culture can be seen as reciprocally affecting and being affected by society. Communication between maker and object exists, but it is not necessarily spoken in unambiguous, clear language. The relationship, or communication, can be interpreted on many levels. To take a common example, a sports car is a means of transportation. Yet it can also be a display of wealth and status. It can also mean youth and vitality to the owner and driver. But there is nothing inherent in the sports car that establishes its meaning—it is strictly cultural. The ambiguities and subtleties of the dialogue between material culture and society do not diminish the importance of material culture, but make it strong and powerful (Hodder 1982a). Material culture has the ability to create values as well as reflect them.

The three examples that follow illustrate some dimensions of the relationship between society and material culture as it creates ideology, establishes power, or maintains cultural identity. They illustrate the utility of archaeological studies in addressing social or political questions.

*Prehistoric Hide Working: An Underappreciated Skill*

Evidence left by prehistoric people is plentiful, but it tends to be limited to hard materials such as stone, pottery, and bone. These objects more frequently become part of the archaeological record than less durable items such as hides or baskets. Thus archaeologists have tended to emphasize technologies such as knapping projectile points and hunting animals, often glossed as male activities. Less attention is paid to "women's work," such as making clothing and tents.

The tools of prehistoric people reveal their technology, both the ways of manufacturing the tools and how the tools are used. For example, traces left on tools may suggest the type of material on which they were used. thus it can be inferred that certain stone tools were used for producing food, clothing, shelter, ornaments, or other tools. An example of an inference often made by archaeologists is that the presence of scrapers implies the preparation of hides. "Scrapers" (the very name we have given these objects implies a function) were presumably used to remove tissue and fleshy remains from the skins of recent animal kills. Studies of wear on their working edges corroborate this use (Semenov 1964). A second level inference, then, is that these prepared pelts were used to make clothing, bags, shoes, shelters, and ceremonial objects. By analogy with historic Native American objects, this inference is strong. Furthermore, archaeologists believe that most ancestors of Native Americans came to the Americas from Siberia, and we know that Paleolithic peoples in Siberia made tailored clothing, because of carvings depicting people in fur trousers and parkas (Okladnikov 1964, Abramova 1967). We also assume that such clothing was necessary for survival in the frozen North. A small piece of tanned leather was found in the lowest level at Magic Mountain (Irwin-Williams and Irwin 1966). Scraps from hide preparation are found at Franktown Cave (see Chapter 3), along with scrapers, thus helping to confirm this string of inferences. In this manner, a picture of the daily lives of prehistoric inhabitants can be built.

We don't know who in the society made the clothing, although ethnographic comparison suggests that women were the tailors. Nor do we know whether their clothes were decorated, although this seems likely. But archaeology can help us begin to appreciate the labor that went into the process, the skills that were needed, and the steps of manufacture. Hides had to be scraped, rubbed with a tanning agent, and staked out to dry. Then the leather was cut to the appropriate pattern using a sharp stone flake. The clothing may have been laced with leather thongs or sewn with thread made from yucca fiber (both are present at Franktown Cave). Needles were found at Lindenmeir in northern Colorado, so fine sewing and decoration were certainly possible. Decorative touches such as fringes, painted designs, or patterns made of shell or teeth were probably added. It is reasonable to suppose that the tailor of the clothing was appreciated by a culture occupying a region of cold and snowy winters. The meanings of stone tools can thus be appropriately extended by inference and analogy.

## Ute Beadwork: Reflections of Cultural Change

The Colorado Historical Society has an extensive collection of beadwork from the Northern and Southern Ute tribes. The beadwork was produced and collected during a tumultuous period in Ute history: one of increased contact with Euro-American settlers. As material culture evidence, how can we understand this beadwork? By the mid-nineteenth century, Ute territory was drastically diminishing due to the encroachment of Euro-American settlers who could back up their "manifest destiny" with help from U.S. soldiers. The Uintah and Ouray Reservation of Utah held the Northern Ute, while the Southern Ute were confined to the Southern Ute Reservation of southwestern Colorado. The objects in the Colorado Historical Society collection reflect the changes as well as the constancy of Ute cultural traditions during this period (1860–1915).

Cultures are not static; they change in many ways. New artifacts might be received through trade or other contact channels. They might be new types made from local materials, whose form was essentially copied from introduced models. They might be made or decorated locally, partly from native materials and partly from imported materials. They could be manufactured through the use of an introduced technique or a native technique similar to the introduced one. Older types of artifacts might still be made, but an imported material was substituted for the local material traditionally used. The artisans may have perceived that the old material was inferior in physical properties, or perhaps it lacked prestige. Perhaps the previously used material became scarce through overuse. Or the only change about the artifact was that new subject matter was introduced. Many of the scenarios described above can be seen in definable patterns, or categories, which can help interpret the dynamics of culture change in Ute beadwork (Satersmoen 1990).

Many examples of cultural change are represented by trade goods received from the new settlers. This should not be surprising, given that vast trade networks existed among tribes long before Euro-American contact and continued even under adverse circumstances. It follows, then, that new materials and new ideas from outside could be, and were, incorporated into a culture's traditions. Not only was this the case among prehistoric and historic period tribes, but also between the tribes and the Euro-American settlers. The continued use of old types of artifacts modified by the substitution of imported materials was widespread (Satersmoen 1990).

A good example of this trend is documented in the presence of glass trade beads among historic tribes. Indeed, when found in an archaeological context, glass beads are often used as a diagnostic tool for the relative dating of sites, that is, glass beads identify post-contact sites. By the mid-1800s glass beads were widely used by many tribes, including the Ute. Styles of beadwork varied, influenced by previous styles of ornamentation, their interactions with the settlers, and the beadwork of other tribes. Plains (Arapaho and Cheyenne) influences on Ute culture are well documented (see Smith 1974, Stewart 1966), and beadwork was no exception.

Artifacts in the Colorado Historical Society collection employing materials of Euro-American origin include beaded moccasins with metal jingles (which can be

Figure 1.5. Beaded moccasins with a design suggesting the flag of the United States. From Carol Sattersmoon, "Cultural Change Among the Northern and Southern Utes as Represented by the Beadwork Collections of the Colorado Historical Society," Master's thesis, University of Denver, 1990.

made from snuff cans, for example); pouches with metal buttons, metal coins, or tokens attached as decoration; and leggings of woolen trade cloth instead of more traditional materials such as buckskin. Designs as well as materials could be borrowed. On one pair of buckskin moccasins the beadwork motif appears to include elements of the U.S. flag (Fig. 1.5). Other traditionally non-Ute symbols, such as a cross, also appear in the beadwork. Some variations on traditional pieces (such as nonfunctional weapons or miniature moccasins) were probably created specifically to sell to a growing number of tourists. Objects unknown to Utes prior to European contact include watch fobs, vests, and knife sheaths, all of which incorporate both native and introduced materials. In all, approximately 46 percent of the 275 beaded items in the collection "manifested some type of acculturation" (Satersmoen 1990:25); by far the most common category of change was that which included traditional artifacts modified by the substitution of imported materials for local materials.

It may be difficult to draw conclusions about cultural change (or constancy) from the above information alone, but that difficulty may point directly to the inadequacies of material culture studies when the emphasis lies more on the "material" than on the "culture." Whether the collectors of this beadwork also collected the histories of its makers (and their reasons for making it) is unknown. It is likely that no one bothered to ask, "Which is more important to you: that you maintained the traditional use of moccasins or that you found a material easier to work with than buckskin?"

To the extent that most artifacts collected were traditional in function and design yet incorporated new materials, it seems likely that the Utes' own perception of cultural identity was not compromised by the introduction of nonnative components. And why should it be? Things change. If a new material is easier to obtain, or deemed superior in quality, and using it doesn't radically alter the way you think of yourself, then using it makes sense. If it alters the way you view your world but you are not uncomfortable with that change, then using it still makes sense. Or perhaps a new object enters your world and you have grown accustomed to its utility. Carrying a watch doesn't make you any less Ute, but wearing it on that beautifully beaded Ute watch fob is a nice touch.

## The City as Material Culture

According to Dell Upton (1992), most material culture studies focus on a triad of "artifact-intention-person"; these studies assume that there is an unambiguous relationship between maker and object that is defined by intent or purpose in the creation of that object. To see the city as artifact, he suggests, would require a new look at the relationship individuals have with their built environment.

It is necessary to move beyond both that assumption and a definition of material culture that only includes the products of "culturally determined behavior." What about things that are created unintentionally or incidentally? People might intentionally alter their environment by dumping garbage in the alleys behind their houses, with a smell as an unintentional byproduct. Upton writes, "Rather than examine the simple relationships between mental intention and physical creation, between a mind and an artifact, the study of the city as material culture ought to investigate the reciprocal relationships among selves and human alterations of the environment; it must take into account both intention and reaction, action and interpretation" (1992:54).

Along these lines, we must remember that people react to and interpret our environment through five senses, not just vision. The noise of police sirens, the smell of a neighbor's yard when she hasn't picked up after her four German shepherds, the taste of serrano peppers, and the texture of the gravel path under your feet as you walk through the garden are ways to perceive our surroundings. Thus the city as an organic whole can become a category of material culture. It is an interrelated montage of the intentional and unintentional, action and reaction.

• • •

The book is organized chronologically. Chapter 2 presents the natural environment of the Greater Denver area, including the natural landforms and subregions that provide the more discrete areas of study. The region is both boundary and frontier because of its geology. This background is important for identifying archaeological resources (which may be more likely to occur in some natural settings than in others) and also for understanding more about people's daily lives. What resources were available? Were those resources scarce or abundant, and could conflict have arisen over access to them? What materials were most popular for making tools? Were they easy or difficult to acquire?

Chapter 3 describes some of the most significant prehistoric sites in the area and what is known or can be surmised about the customs and material lifeways of these early inhabitants. The prehistoric record stretches for roughly 10,000 years—by far the greater part of the time that people have lived in Greater Denver. These people found the juxtaposition of the high plains and foothills, upturned hogbacks and mesas with rockshelters inviting. They create lifestyles through the centuries that also made a frontier of Greater Denver.

Chapter 4 moves to the ethnohistory of the area, or the "contact" period. Much of what happened in Denver is known from historic accounts, not from the perspective of the people who were affected by the Euro-Americans' arrival, though contemporary histories and drawings demonstrate their important presence (which of course continues today). But there has not been a consistent effort to uncover the ways these cultures adapted, modified, or preserved their customs and values. Archaeologists may be frustrated by the paucity of data from this period, but there are a number of interesting areas to consider, especially the potential for corroborating archaeological analyses with documentary evidence. Greater Denver was sometimes a frontier between Native American groups and certainly a location for clashes of cultures.

Relatively little historical archaeology has been done in Greater Denver, so our account in Chapter 5 is restricted, but some interesting inferences about ethnicity and gender can be drawn. We know that Denver maintained a large, diverse population with distinct neighborhoods, business districts, and cultural institutions. The Tremont House, for instance, was a popular gathering spot; investigations at this site have produced some surprising information on the habits of its visitors over several decades. The survey of the Rocky Mountain Arsenal site reveals the work of women in truck farms and "butter and eggs" production. Various frontiers and boundaries appear—urban and rural, urban and suburban—along with the wish to preserve the landscape while using it in various ways.

The final chapter sums up what we know about Denver from archaeological explorations and looks toward what might be learned in the future. Greater Denver has been the scene of much human activity and will continue to provide archaeological sites as it continues to grow.

CHAPTER 2

## Geology and Environment

Although it is not perceptible to someone standing in the middle of the city itself, Denver occupies the deepest portion of a subsurface structural feature that extends from near Colorado Springs north to Wyoming (Fig. 2.1). Termed the "great trough," the Denver Basin is part of the Colorado Piedmont Section, a division of a larger grouping of landforms known as the Great Plains Physiographic Province (Madole and Rubin 1984). The Colorado Piedmont Section encompasses much of eastern Colorado east of the mountains, and is characterized by Tertiary sedimentary rocks that have been eroded by the action of the South Platte and Arkansas Rivers. Most of the Greater Denver study area lies in the Colorado Piedmont Section. The High Plains Section, a second physiographic feature of the same province, includes the portion of eastern Colorado that still retains Tertiary rocks and encompasses the Black Forest region in the southeastern part of the study area. Our study area, although technically mostly in the Great Plains, also includes the eastern foothills of the Southern Rocky Mountains Physiographic Province. This foothill zone is two to three miles (3–5km) wide (Trimble, Scott and Hansen 1984). In order to understand the environmental characteristics of the Greater Denver study area today, we must briefly examine its geological history.

### INCEPTION AND TRANSITIONS

Before about two billion years ago, the record that forms the geological history of the Greater Denver area is sketchy. However, for the past half billion years, it is known that the region was sculpted by a combination of four main natural processes: mountain building; deposition and erosion by oceans, rivers and streams; volcanism; and glaciers (Fig. 2.2).

#### The Colorado Orogeny

Between about 600 and 325 million years ago, the region was a flat, featureless plain covered by several shallow, interior continental seas. About 300 million years ago a geological event termed the Colorado Orogeny (formation of mountains) uplifted the original Front Range. This ancient range was eroded by wind, water, and gravity, and the resulting thick deposit of sand and gravel became the Fountain Formation,

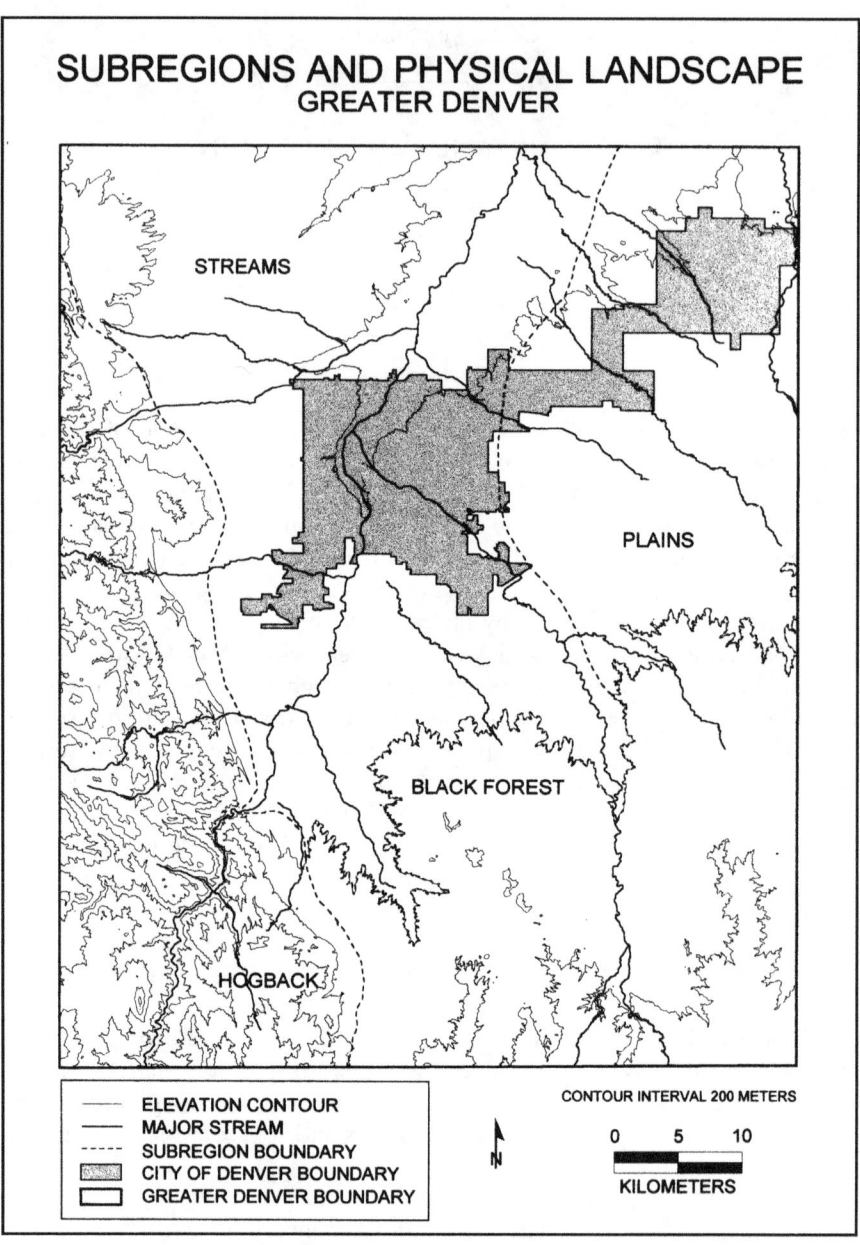

Figure 2.1. Subregions and physical landscape of the Greater Denver area. Francine Patterson. Information compiled from Halka Chronic, *Roadside Geology of Colorado* (Missoula, Mont.: Mountain Press Publishing Company, 1980); Donald E. Trimble and Michael N. Machette, Geologic Map of the Greater Denver Area, Front Range Urban Corridor, Colorado (Washington, D.C.: U.S. Geological Survey, 1979; Ogden Tweto, Ogden, Geologic Map of Colorado (Washington, D.C.: U.S. Geological Survey, 1979).

colorful red sandstone monuments that form such distinctive landscape points as Red Rocks Amphitheater, Roxborough Park, and farther south the Garden of the Gods in Colorado Springs (Sullivan 1992). At the end of the Paleozoic, the sea had moved to the east of Greater Denver, and the Denver Basin itself was a coastal plain.

## The Age of Reptiles

During the next major era, the Mesozoic, several sedimentary rock units accumulated on top of the eroded surface during a series of advancing and retreating seas. The sea that had retreated east of Denver during the Paleozoic advanced again during the Triassic age of the Mesozoic (Fig. 2.2).

The Morrison Formation, from the Jurassic period, contains some of the most productive dinosaur bone beds in the world. Dinosaur tracks and bones are visible in this formation near the town of Morrison, on the western edge of the Greater Denver study area (Lockley 1990), as well as elsewhere the Rocky Mountain region. The physical remnants of camps and expeditions made in the 1870s and 1880s by scientists from as far away as the Yale Peabody Museum, to study and collect these dinosaur remains, are recorded as archaeological sites themselves. Four bone quarries are known to have been worked between 1877 and 1879: three near today's Alameda Parkway and one above Morrison. The site near Morrison is the only one with visible remnants of quarrying into the shale; shale's natural rather quick erosion has covered up evidence of quarrying at the other sites. Some campsites have also been identified that may be work camps associated with dinosaur bone quarrying activities (Black 1994).

The Dakota (Cretaceous age) formations generally were deposited in marshy environments and thus captured the remains of living things of the time, such as dinosaurs, including their footprints. Even the ripples of ancient seas are preserved. As the seas moved toward the mountains, the dinosaurs were driven west to avoid the deeper waters. At Dinosaur Ridge in the Hogback subregion, the Dakota sandstone beds, now tilted at about 45 degrees, are prominent features of the landscape (Stark et al. 1949). Another fossil locality is known in the shales on the east side of the Hogback, where fish scales of an unknown Upper Cretaceous marine species have been collected. Worms and similar creatures from the sea bottom are fossilized along Alameda Avenue.

Finally, ancient plant life also is exposed in the Dakota Formation. What may be the remains of a Cretaceous mangrove swamp or shoreline habitat is preserved in the sandstone layers along the Hogback. A site containing fossil plant remains is located at the crest of Dinosaur Ridge; another, consisting of beautifully preserved fossil leaves in the cliff face and boulders detached from a rock overhang, is recorded just east of Morrison. This rockshelter was used by Native American groups and later campers.

The Mesozoic was an active geological time. For instance, we know of one event during the Cretaceous where mountain building in the Sierra Nevada of California caused hundreds of violent eruptions of dust and ash to spew out and rain down on dinosaurs as far east as the Denver area. By the end of the Mesozoic, the area was again covered by ocean, and mud and limy muds accumulated on the ocean floor to form shale filled with abundant marine life such as mollusks, fish, and marine rep-

| Era | Period | Epoch | Million Years Ago | Geologic Units | |
|---|---|---|---|---|---|
| Cenozoic | Quaternary | Holocene | 0.01 (10,000 years ago) | post-Piney Creek alluvium<br>Piney Creek alluvium<br>pre-Piney Creek alluvium | Eolian sand |
| | | Pleistocene | 1.8 | Broadway alluvium<br>Louviers alluvium<br>Slocum alluvium<br>Verdos alluvium<br>Rocky Flats alluvium<br>Nussbaum alluvium | Eolian sand<br>and loess |
| | Tertiary | Pliocene | 5 | | |
| | | Miocene | 24 | | |
| | | Oligocene | 38 | Castle Rock Conglomerate (White River Fm.)<br>Wall Mountain Tuff | |
| | | Eocene | 55 | | |
| | | Paleocene | 65 | Green Mountain Conglomerate<br>Basalt flows (North and South Table Mtns.)<br>upper Dawson Arkose | |
| Mesozoic | Cretaceous | | 135 | lower Dawson (Denver and Arapahoe Fm.)<br>Laramie Formation<br>Fox Hills Limestone<br>Pierre Shale<br>Niobrara Formation<br>Benton Group<br>Dakota Sandstone | |
| | Jurassic | | 200 | Morrison Formation<br>Ralston Creek Formation | |
| | Triassic | | 240 | upper Lykins Formation | |
| Paleozoic | Permian | | 280 | lower Lykins Formation<br>Lyons Sandstone<br>upper Fountain Formation | |
| | Pennsylvanian | | 325 | lower Fountain Formation | |
| | Mississippian | | 370 | | |
| | Devonian | | 415 | | |
| | Silurian | | 445 | | |
| | Ordovician | | 515 | | |
| | Cambrian | | 600 | | |
| Precambrian | | | 1,800 | Pikes Peak Granite<br>Idaho Springs Formation<br>Coal Creek Metaquartzite | |

Figure 2.2. Geological time and rock units in the Greater Denver area. Information compiled from Halka Chronic, *Roadside Geology of Colorado*; Donald E. Trimble and Michael N. Machette, Geologic Map of the Greater Denver Area, Front Range Urban Corridor; and Ogden Tweto, Geologic Map of Colorado.

tiles, with fossil scales preserved in the rock. A transitional beach deposit followed the ubiquitous sea cover before another return to a nonmarine environment at the end of the Mesozoic. This deposit of beach sands became the sandstone of the Fox Hills Formation. A coastal plain, with lush vegetation, then covered the area and the Laramie Formation was deposited. It too is filled with fossil leaves and wood.

## The Laramide Orogeny

The retreat of the sea and the rise of the Rocky Mountains mark the beginning of the last major geological era, the Cenozoic (in which we are now living). Termed the Laramide Orogeny, it involved an intense period of mountain building 80 to 40 million years ago, and created most of the structure of the Rocky Mountains. The Colorado Front Range, which has a core of rocks more than 600 million years old, was uplifted to its present elevation. During the same event, a band of steeply eastward-dipping Paleozoic and Mesozoic rock formations, consisting of shales, limestones, and sandstones, was downfolded in the Denver area, creating a distinct basin, with the younger rocks in the basin and the older rocks remaining in the foothills and mountains. As the mountains began to rise, streams incised the hard older rocks and material flushed out onto the plains, covering the younger rocks. The Arapaho Formation, as the debris has been termed, is about 500 feet deep under the city of Denver. The rise of the mountains pushed up overlying sediments that created a continuous ridge of eastward sloping hogbacks, which subsequently eroded to form the northern and eastern edges of the basin underlying Greater Denver.

## Volcanos and the Miocene Epoch

Yet another natural force, volcanic action, then came into play. During the late Mesozoic and early Cenozoic Eras, molten lava came to the surface in crevasses in the tilted rocks of the foothills and exploded onto the plains. Some of the lava probably reached the surface through fissures adjacent to Ralston Reservoir north of Golden. The Green Mountain Formation was deposited as layers of volcanic ash and mud flowing from sources west of the Front Range into the basin. (Green Mountain at present is a large flat-topped hill between Alameda Parkway and U.S. Highway 6, with a conglomerate cap hundreds of feet thick.)

Near Golden along the western edge of the of the area, lava flows formed the basalt mesas of North and South Table Mountains (Trimble and Machette 1979). Both Table and Green Mountains were subsequently covered by a layer of loose gravel and soil, known as the Tertiary Pediment for the time period in which it was deposited. The gravel and sand, resulting from the erosion of a surface in the mountains, almost fills the basin to overflowing near the center of Denver.

The geological cycle termed the Miocene Epoch uplifted Colorado as well as much of the western United States to their present elevations between twelve and three million years ago. This uplift rejuvenated streams in the mountains, causing intensive stream cutting. This pattern of alluvial erosion formed the broad, gentle South Platte

Valley, bordered on the west by the Front Range and on the east by undulating grasslands several hundred feet higher. Donald Sullivan (1992) notes that the routes of modern roads follow several of these drainages, allowing for spectacular views along deeply cut, steep-walled canyons for the first several miles into the Front Range from Denver.

## Erosion by the South Platte River

The force of the South Platte River, the major river that drains the Greater Denver area, was the next important factor in shaping the area. The river's course was probably established when its steep gradient captured some of the formerly eastward-flowing streams from the mountains (Scott 1982). This movement of water from the mountains excavated the Colorado Piedmont below the older Tertiary sedimentary rocks that make up the High Plains surface (Sullivan 1992); the resulting lower elevation separates the Colorado Piedmont and High Plains sections. By about one million years ago, the features, attributes, and resources of the Greater Denver study area were much as they are today.

## Glaciers

Changes to the physiography of the area over the past million years have been primarily in the foothills region, the result of glacial action characteristic of the Pleistocene Epoch or "Ice Ages." Snow and ice accumulated on mountain crests and moved in masses downslope, cutting valleys. The heads of most of these glaciated valleys are great semicircular amphitheaters called cirques. The path of a glacier often caused a V-shaped stream valley to become U-shaped as the glacial debris rounded and smoothed the canyon walls. Glacial activity continued until about 2,400 years ago; however, the changes that resulted were primarily in shifting climates rather than terrain modification.

## FEATURES, ATTRIBUTES, AND RESOURCES

Since the last major changes in physiography and terrain, Greater Denver has experienced various microenvironmental changes. Streams continue their downcutting in the mountains through the foothills, to deposit sand and gravel throughout Greater Denver and further east onto the plains. Cycles of deposition and subsequent erosion and downcutting have resulted in a series of terraces in the South Platte River Valley.

## The Subregions of Greater Denver

The environmental factors that may have influenced prehistoric and historic populations in terms of settlement patterns, subsistence strategies, and cultural interactions can be described in terms of four subregions. Each forms a rather distinct ecozone that was significant in the opportunities and constraints offered to prehistoric and historic human populations.

The Hogback subregion constitutes the western edge of the basin, and includes the edge of the foothills characterized by rock formations and the valleys between them

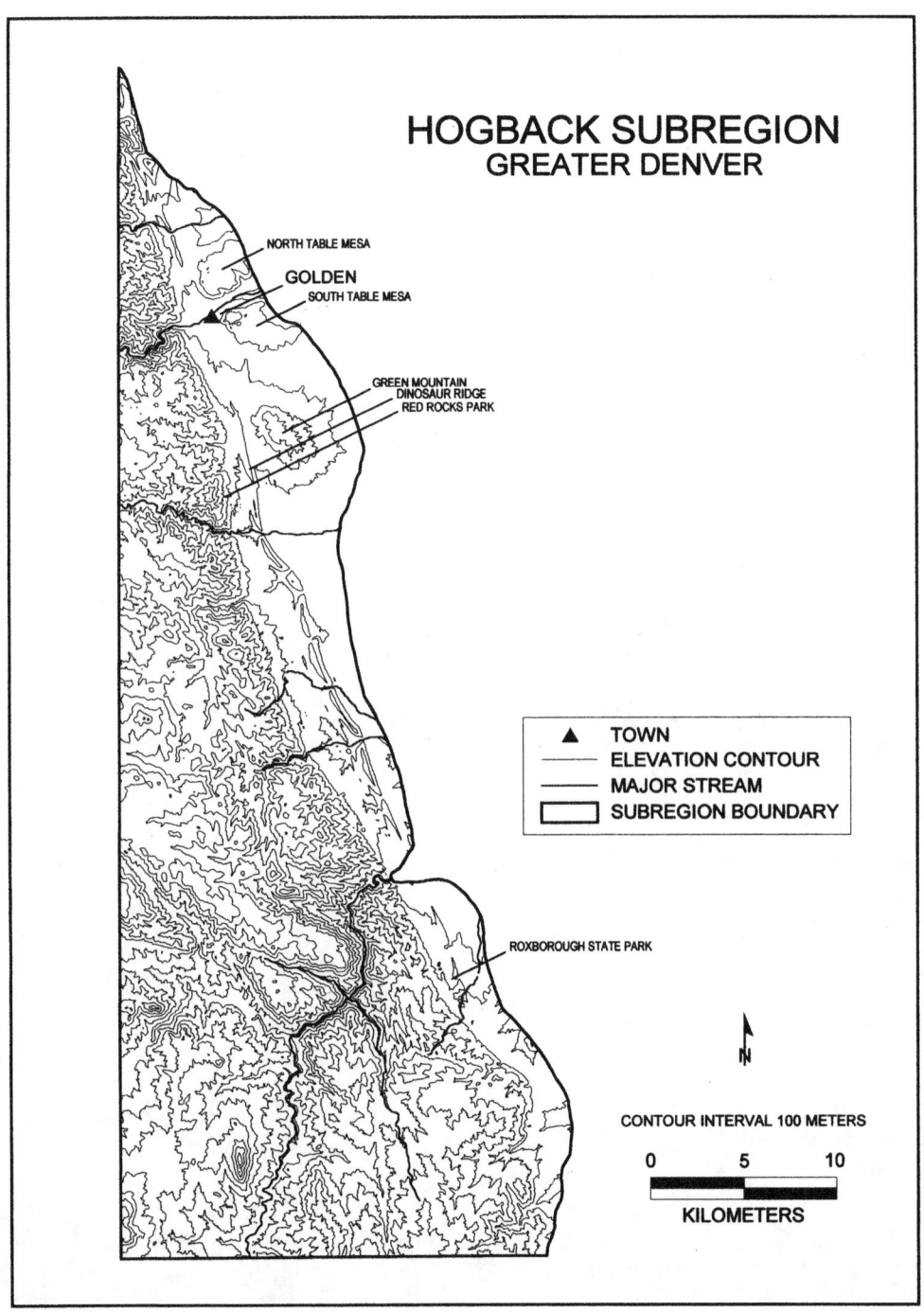

Figure 2.3. The Hogback subregion. Francine Patterson.

(Fig. 2.3). The Hogback Valley on the western edge is narrow, extending roughly 25 miles north from the Sedalia-Deckers highway. It is named for a northwest/southeast trending ridge of the Dakota Sandstone that is itself a distinctive feature, being part of the Colorado Front Range uplift that has remained resistant to weathering (Fig. 2.4).

The tilted sandstone outcrops of the hogback form the eastern boundary of the valley, which has an elevation at the bottom of 5,600 to 5,900 feet. Similar formations occur north and south of the Dakota Hogback. Green Mountain and North and South Table Mountains form large mesa-like features within the Hogback subregion. Internal features such as Red Rocks Park consist of older rocks that have been eroded into unusual shapes. Natural breaks in the hogback at several locations, widened by creeks, streams, and rivers, lead to the interior of the Hogback subregion, which is characterized by montane environments ranging up to approximately 7,850 feet in elevation.

Figure 2.4. Red rocks at Roxborough Park. Photograph on file at the University of Denver.

The combination of Rocky Mountain foothills, the Hogback Valley itself, and the breaks in the Hogback allowing access to the Plains results in a diversity of animal, plant and geological resources (Stone and Mendoza 1994). These are rich in archaeological sites such as rockshelters, camps, and artifact scatters.

A subregion of alluvial soils and rivers, designated Streams, abuts the Hogback on the east for virtually its entire length. This subregion includes the South Platte River, Cherry Creek, and a corridor near their banks (Fig 2.5). The importance of these

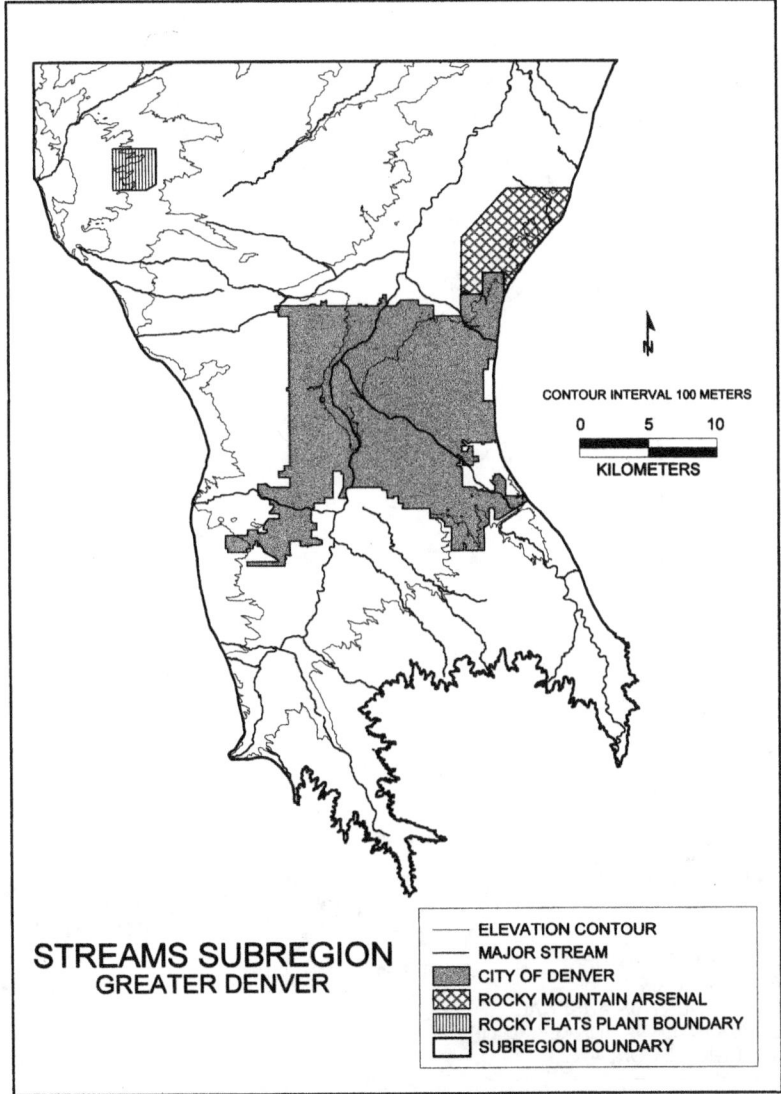

Figure 2.5. The Streams subregion. Francine Patterson

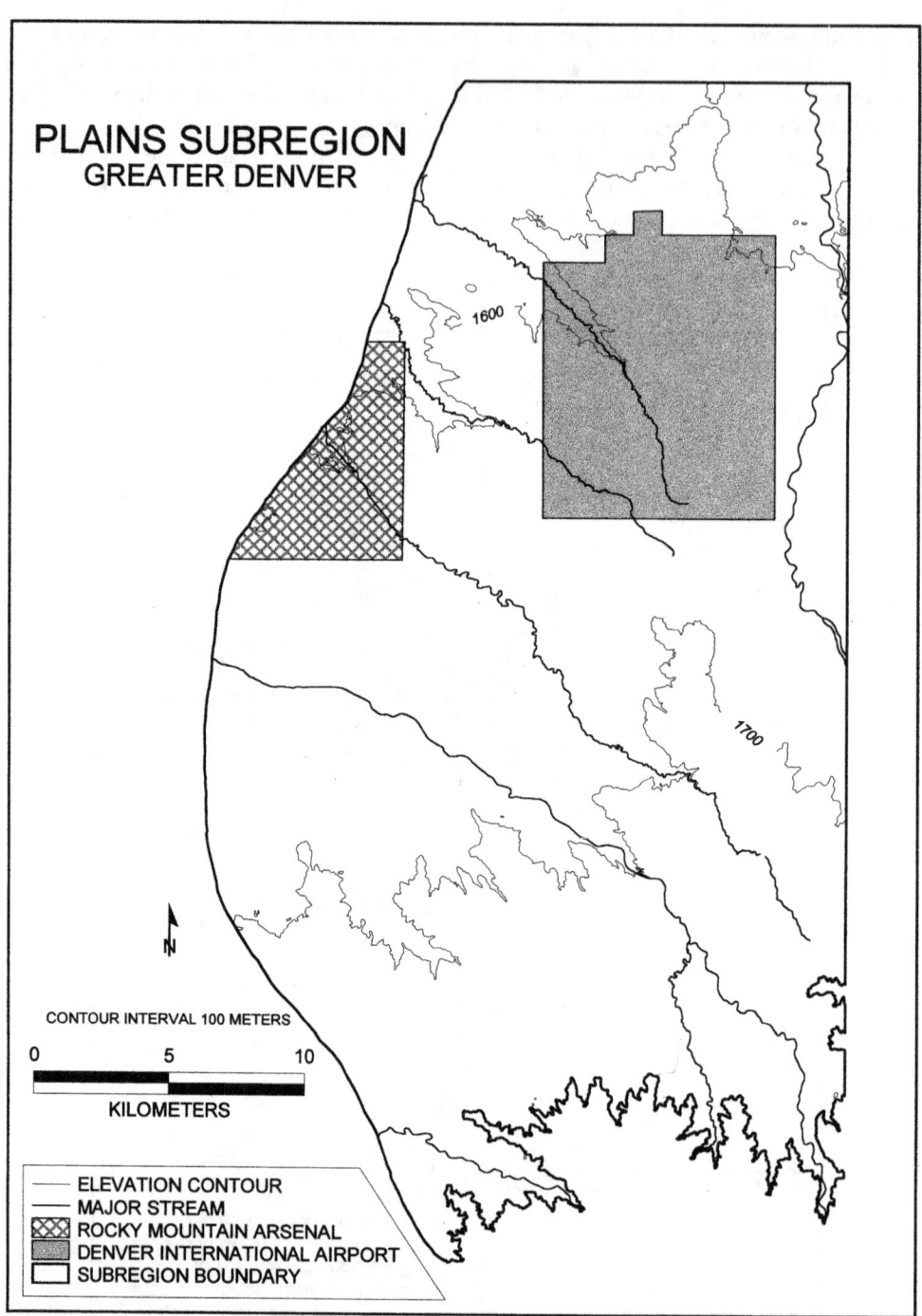

Figure 2.6. The Plains subregion. Francine Patterson.

two streams to the Greater Denver area is clear. The city of Denver developed at their confluence, and major reservoirs, respectively Chatfield and Cherry Creek, were built on the two streams for flood control and recreation. The greater part of the city and county of Denver falls within this subregion.

Between 5,000 and 6,000 feet in elevation, the Streams subregion grades into the Plains subregion on its eastern edge. This subregion is roughly described as lacking major rivers, although smaller creeks abound (Fig. 2.6). It is an area of undulating, gentle hills, with intermittent streams cutting between short grass prairie and semidesert vegetation (Fig. 2.7). Trees grow thickly along these watercourses, and the corresponding riparian vegetation characterizes the stream ecozones.

Figure 2.7. The Plains from the Aurora Dam site. Photograph courtesy of Marcia Tate.

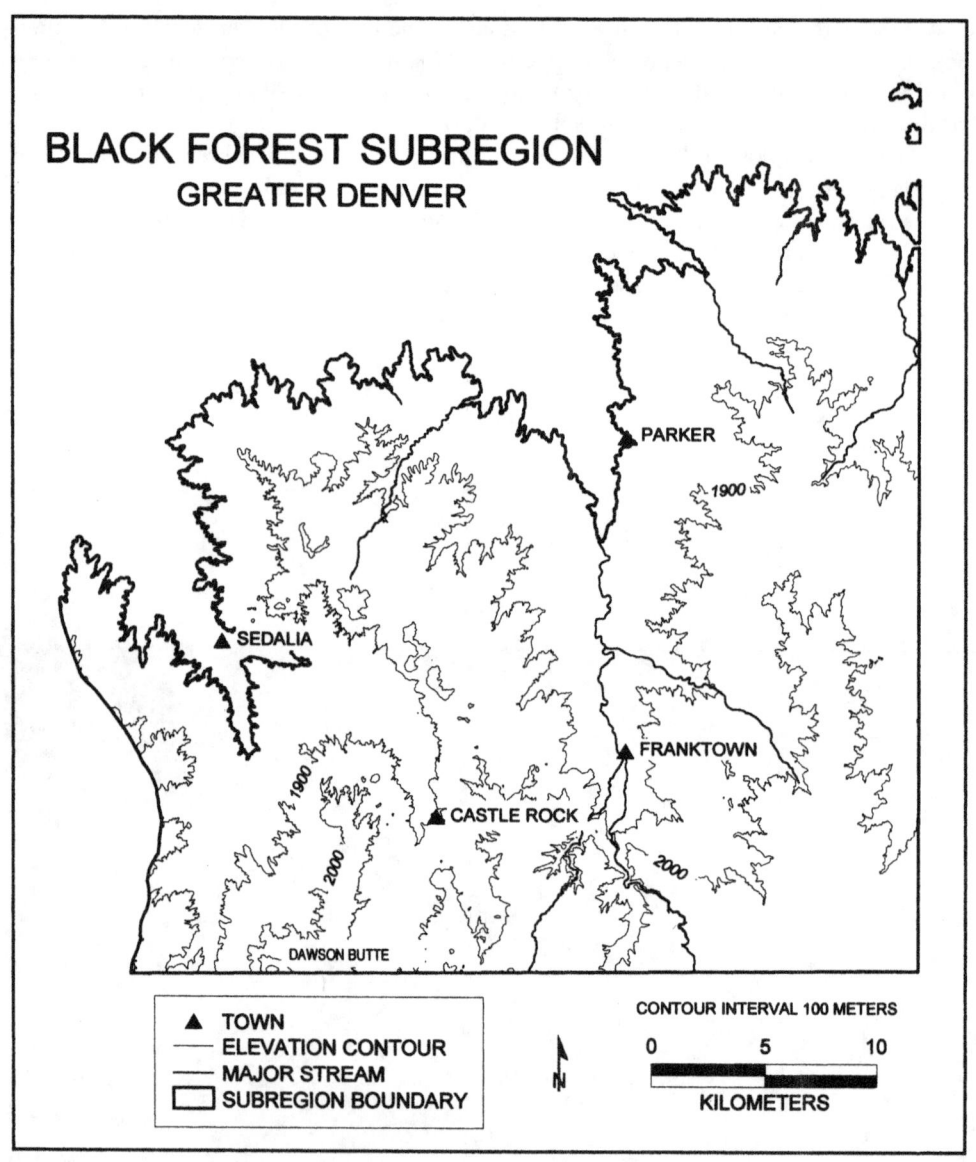

Figure 2.8. The Black Forest subregion. Francine Patterson.

# GEOLOGY AND ENVIRONMENT | 33

Figure 2.9. The Black Forest. Photograph on file at the University of Denver.

The 6,000 foot contour line is used as the boundary of the Black Forest subregion to define where it meets the Plains and Streams subregions and the southern extent of the Hogback subregion (Fig. 2.8). The Palmer Divide on the southern edge is an area of higher elevation that separates the South Platte and Cherry Creek drainages from the Arkansas River drainage. Black Forest is a local term coined to describe its dense stands of pine forest (Fig.2.9). Although elevations on the Palmer Divide as a whole range from 6,000 to 7,500 feet, Black Forest elevations are rather constant, from 6,000 feet at its boundary with the other three subregions and not exceeding 7,000 feet within the study area.

As noted in Chapter 1, our area is a rectangle simply for convenience. The outer borders were defined to facilitate mapping, database manipulation, and other analytical constraints. For example, the northern and eastern borders were established to include Denver International Airport, which is annexed to the city of Denver.

## Geology and Archaeology

Rocks are of great importance to archaeologists because stone tools found on sites are often the major cultural evidence. But they are also important in some cultures as a source of housing materials, and for use as ceremonial objects, raw materials for ceramic temper, sources of pigment, and so forth. The study of geology, therefore, is integral to archaeology as it explains the presence of such resources as outcrops of rock that become a vital resource for tool making, as well as naturally habitable rockshelters.

### *Rockshelters and Outcrops*

Rockshelters are common throughout the Front Range foothills. The dramatic red monoliths of the Fountain Formation crop out at several localities, such as Red Rocks Park and Roxborough Park, along the edge of the foothills in the Hogback subregion. The tilted configuration of these striking formations creates overhangs, rockshelters, windbreaks, and natural alcoves that were used by prehistoric people. Rockshelter sites excavated in the Morrison-Golden area have yielded artifact-bearing levels dating back at least to the Archaic period (Black 1994).

Just east of the Fountain Formation outcrops, fifteen miles southwest of the Civic Center in downtown Denver, a line of Lyons Sandstone foothills form a ridge some 190 feet high and two miles long between Deer Creek and Massey Draw (Bryant, Miller, and Scott 1973). The long ridge of the Dakota Hogback, rising about half a mile to the east of Red Rocks Park and the Lyons Formation, contains many naturally sheltered areas. Many Native Americans took advantage of these rock exposures, using alcoves in cliff faces and on large boulder outcrops as shelters for camping and other activities (Black 1994).

Many of the rockshelters along the Hogback are west-facing alcoves that would not have been selected as year-round habitations because they would offer little protection from the driving winter snows from the west. It has been noted (Black 1994) that in the Dinosaur Ridge area these shelters were not used prehistorically. Eastward facing shelters typically were preferred because they not only offer shelter from storms but also act as solar collectors during the colder months of the year, when the sun shines low in the southern sky. In the Hogback subregion, however, "upslope" conditions also drive the snow from the east into these alcoves. A south-southwest facing rockshelter in the Dinosaur Ridge area was identified by Black (1994) as having been utilized, apparently a compromise between the east and west facing options (Box 2A).

> Box 2A. Rockshelter Use
> 
> According to Kevin Black (1994), the characteristics that define the patterns of utilization of natural rockshelters in the Hogback subregion depend on aspect (the primary direction an archaeological site faces, thereby determining sun exposure, wind, moisture, and view). Rockshelters that face north are too cold in winter but cool and shady in summer, and may have been chosen as midsummer campsites. West-facing rockshelters receive the brunt of wind and rain from thunderstorms spawned in the Front Range, yet they are somewhat sheltered from upslope winter

> snowstorms and may have been used in winter. Rockshelters that face south are too hot in midsummer but serve as excellent solar collectors for cool to cold periods and are sheltered from most storms; they are a common choice for campsites in the fall, winter, and spring. East-facing rockshelters, finally, are sheltered from the driving wind and rain of summer thunderstorms but are exposed to severe upslope storms with winter snow and wind chill. They were probably preferred as summer camps.

Rockshelters also are common in the Black Forest subregion, where they occur between rock formations with different resistances to erosion. Mesas with bluffs are also common in the Black Forest, features that offer protection to a limited degree. Rockshelters are not common in the Streams and Plains subregions, but rock outcrops in these areas were often sought out prehistorically to provide limited shelter and perhaps even for water catchment or grinding.

*Rock Properties and Stone Tools*

Two primary ways of making stone tools are recognized by archaeologists: chipping and grinding. Chipped stone artifacts are shaped into tools such as projectile points, scrapers, and knives by flaking—removing pieces of the rock. Typically this is done by striking a large piece of stone with a harder rock to make a general shape, then finishing the tool by pressure flaking with softer material such as antler and bone. Ground stone tools are made by rough shaping as well, but the finishing process is grinding. Since many of these tools were used for processing softer materials such as grains, seeds, and nuts, they acquired further abrasion in use. Some of these objects are large, heavy, and awkward to carry. It is not surprising that they were typically left at sites.

Characteristics of rocks determine whether they will be used to make chipped or ground stone implements, or shaped for building materials.

*Igneous* rocks, formed when molten material is solidified, compose most of the earth's crust. Those most commonly used in the Greater Denver area include obsidian, rhyolite, andesite, basalt, and granite.

Obsidian is a natural glass. It is dark in color, usually black or occasionally brown and black banded, with a brilliant luster. When struck, obsidian makes a conchoidal fracture, named for its resemblance to a conch shell. The fracture is smooth and can occur in any direction. Obsidian thus breaks in a way that is easier to control and predict than most other rocks, which may break irregularly in undesired directions. Furthermore, the edges of obsidian flakes are extremely sharp. Identifying the precise sources of obsidian has given archaeologists an additional tool for dating sites and artifact assemblages, and also for characterizing cultural interaction and relationships by tracing prehistoric obsidian trade. Obsidian can also be directly dated by a process known as obsidian hydration (see Box 2B).

> Box 2B. OBSIDIAN CLIFF
> Located in northwestern Wyoming near Yellowstone National Park, Obsidian Cliff is one of the best-known quarry sites for obsidian. It is believed by some to be the

> source of obsidian for points east of the Rockies, from the Ohio River Valley and Hopewell core area to the plains of southern Canada (Davis et al. 1995).
>
> Since the mid-1960s, efforts to characterize obsidian instrumentally and quantifiably have been successful in tracing individual artifacts to their exact source and even assigning a date (within a few hundred years) to their period of human use. Obsidian sourcing is made possible through the use of techniques such as x-ray diffraction to determine the unique chemical "fingerprint" of an artifact on an archaeological site. The fingerprint is compared with that of a particular source to ascertain the artifact's origin. Assigning a date to obsidian artifacts can be accomplished by a technique known as obsidian hydration. Unlike any other archaeological lithic material, obsidian has a tendency to absorb moisture in molecular amounts from the environment (a process known as hydration) at rates that can be equated with an established set of bands that measure rates of hydration for the past. Both obsidian sourcing and obsidian hydration studies rely on the collection of samples from a variety of contexts.
>
> The ability to assign such information to lithic materials provides data concerning the cultural affiliation of its users, the antiquity of the artifact's use, and functional use patterns, and allows inferences regarding social and economic interactions between prehistoric populations on regional and interregional scales. Other attempts to directly date lithic materials include techniques such as cation ratio dating, which measures the accretion of desert varnish on the surface of materials that have been left lying on the surface of archaeological sites since the time they were deposited. This technique is still considered experimental by most researchers (Apple and York 1993).

Rhyolites and andesites are both fine-grained rocks, in dark colors of green, red, and gray. Their uniform, fine-grained nature is useful for chipped stone artifacts. Basalt, which is similar to rhyolite and andesite, is even darker in color, ranging from greenish or purplish black to pure black. Basalt can also be glassy and resemble obsidian, in which case it again is differentiated by its edge properties, which are opaque, unlike the translucence of obsidian's thin and razor sharp edges. Granite is not useful for chipped stone tool production, but it has great strength, and because it can be easily cut and polished it is used more than any other stone for buildings, bridges, walls, and so on. This is true for prehistoric as well as modern times, in areas where granite is easily available.

*Sedimentary* rocks are also used for stone tool production. Cryptocrystalline sedimentary rocks provide some of the most commonly occurring and widely used chipped stone materials—chert (or flint), chalcedony, and agate, all of which are found in cavities or nodules of larger rocks, which consist of cryptocrystalline quartz—crystals that are too small to be recognized under an ordinary microscope. They are more like igneous rocks than the remainder of the sedimentary rock group. Chert, like obsidian, is an excellent toolstone because of its property of conchoidal fracture. Formed by water dissolving minerals in limestone and redepositing them together in nodules, it is hard and dense (Stark et al. 1949). It may be white or variously colored. Chalcedony is also often white; archaeologists distinguish it from chert based on its translucent or semitransparent nature and waxlike luster. It may occur in the same formation with chert. Chalcedony often formed in small cavities and is suitable for chipped stone artifacts (Stark et al. 1949). Agate is a variegated chalcedony, and is characterized by colors arranged in alternative stripes or bands or in mosslike forms.

Silicified wood, commonly called petrified wood, was formed when portions of trees buried in sediment were replaced with silica. It may encompass a wide variety of textures and colors, but usually has a waxy appearance. When heated, its texture and colors may change to a dull finish (red in the Greater Denver study area) and it may exhibit pot lid scarring, crazing, and heat cracks.

The textures of typical sedimentary rocks, very unlike cryptocrystalline types, make them unsuitable for chipped stone tools. These rocks, such as sandstone, limestone, slate, shale, and conglomerate, are dense and can be identified by their broken and worn appearance. They are commonly used to make grinding implements such as manos and metates, and for constructing dwellings, paved areas, lined pits, and hearth features.

Rocks that are crushed, heated, or buried for perhaps millions of years only to reappear at the earth's surface during tectonic events are classified as *metamorphic* rocks. They have been substantially changed by heat, pressure, or chemical action. Quartz, made up entirely of silicon and oxygen, is hard and resistant to weathering, and may be colored by different minerals to milky (white), smoky (gray), rose (pink), and amethyst (purple) (Stone and Mendoza 1994). It has a shiny surface, and may be found in crystals or other forms (Stark et al.1949). Quartzite is a very hard metamorphic usually formed from quartz sandstone, and although pure quartzite is white, some forms contain inclusions that may color the material light pink to red. It ranges from coarse- to fine-grained, and the latter types may have a sugarlike finish (Stone and Mendoza 1994). Quartzite, particularly the fine-grained forms, is used for chipped stone tools. Slate, gneiss, schist, and marble, also metamorphic rocks found in the Denver area, may be used for ceremonial objects or ornaments such as pendants, pipes, or beads.

*Tool Stone Sources in Greater Denver*

According to Irwin-Williams and Irwin (1966:55), quarry locations of fine-grained cryptocrystalline silicates, "brown and yellow cherty materials," silicified wood, and assorted quartzites are known in the immediate vicinity of the Hogback subregion (see Fig. 2.10). The Dakota Formation yields an orthoquartzite with color ranges including white, gray, yellow, brown, and red. The Dakota Formation outcrops throughout the Front Range, and quarry localities occur in Roxborough State Park in the Hogback subregion. The Roxborough material is variable in quality. Two specific quarry sites have been identified, both part of a large complex of sites used from the Early Archaic through the historic periods (Tate 1979). They are located on a terrace of the western slope of the Dakota ridge at the extreme southern end of Roxborough Park (Liestman and Kranzush 1987). Another large quarry site is documented on a high ridge of the Dakota Hogback itself. Green Mountain, also in the Hogback subregion, produces a variety of light-colored, fine-grained silicates—a clear to milky white, very fine-grained chalcedony.

Silicified wood is found in many locations near the Front Range. In one locality in the Hogback subregion, the fragments are identifiable as pine, oak and elm (Stark et

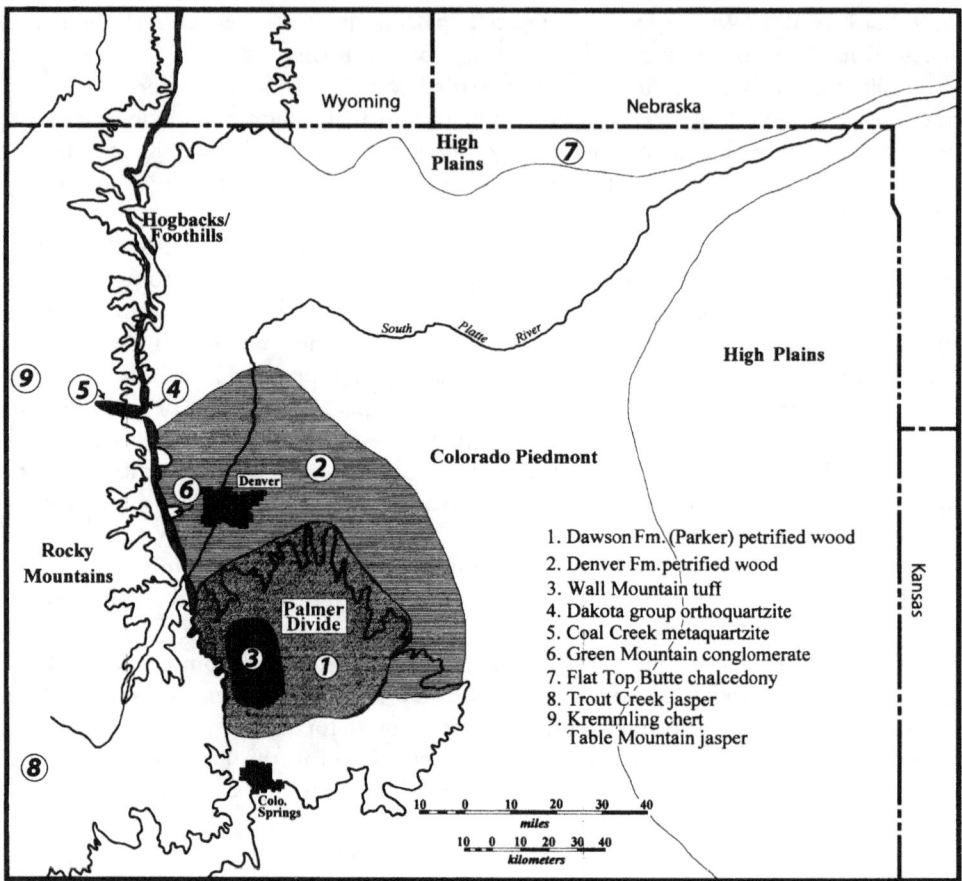

Figure 2.10. Tool stone sources in the Greater Denver area. (1) Dawson Formation (Parker) petrified wood; (2) Denver Formation petrified wood; (3) Wall Mountain tuff; (4) Dakota Group orthoquartzites; (5) Coal Creek metaquartzites; (6) Green Mountain Conglomerate cherts; (7) flat Top Butte chalcedony; (8) Trout Creek jasper; (9) Grand County: Kremmling chert and Table Mountain jasper. Courtesy of Kevin Gilmore.

al. 1949). The Morrison sandstone formation, too, is full of highly cemented or silicified wood. The material is particularly common along Cherry Creek, where it has eroded out of the Dawson Arkose.

The Pikes Peak Granite contains quartz veins, primarily white, which were used prehistorically. Major concentrations of these veins are mapped in the Raleigh Peak area near Buffalo Creek, in the vicinity of Top of the World Campground, and in other areas of the far southwestern portion of the Greater Denver study area, in the higher elevations of the Hogback subregion.

Rhyolite and a variety of other stone materials are found in the Castle Rock Conglomerate of the Black Forest subregion. In addition, near Parker are outcrops of the Denver Formation that contain silicified wood. One of the major lithic sources for the area is silicified wood found in the Dawson Arkose: sandstone, shale, mudstone, and conglomerate with localized coal beds. In fact, the edges of the Black Forest are lined with the Denver Formation. In some areas, complete palm tree trunks lie on the surface of the Dawson Arkose, making this silicified wood easy to obtain. The material includes a dark, yellowish brown type with chert filaments in a clear chalcedony matrix, also a light gray and white type, and a very dark brown wood in a matrix of yellowish brown chert. In addition to the edges of the Black Forest, the Dawson Arkose is exposed at many locations along the Front Range. The formation also crops out approximately one to three miles east of the Dakota Hogback, and usable material, including andesites as well as silicified wood, can be collected from just south of Sedalia to north of Palmer Lake (Liestman and Kranzush 1987). Additional lithic resources at sites throughout the Greater Denver area come from quartzite cobbles occurring in the major drainages (Liestman and Kranzush 1987).

Many lithic quarries on the plains beyond the Greater Denver boundaries were used by the inhabitants of the study area, especially cherts from eastern Colorado in Logan, Morgan, and Weld counties. Flat Top Butte chert, in particular, is found in assemblages in the Hogback subregion (Gilmore 1989:25; McNees 1989:11) and elsewhere.

Other quarry sites near Greater Denver also warrant mention. Chalcedony is found in the Rampart Range, where these stones make the area a favorite collecting place for local rockhounds. Trout Creek jasper has been reported at a site in the upper elevations of the Hogback subregion and also at Bayou Gulch in the Black Forest subregion. This material, which crops out in Chaffee County, Colorado, has very distinctive dark brown mottling that is unevenly distributed throughout the lithic material (Heinrich 1984). It is speculated that this jasper has an unusually good texture for tool manufacture.

*Minerals*

Granite is a source of gold mined historically in Central City and Idaho Springs. Light-colored large ribbons of very coarse crystalline, igneous rock, called pegmatite, are found in canyon walls of the Front Range, injected as molten rock into gneisses and schists. Some of these formations contain gemstones, such as topaz, garnet, amethyst, and amazonite. Amazonite pendants, in particular, have been found in Greater Denver sites. Ocher in various colors, from yellows to reds, was collected by prehistoric people to be used as pigment. Mica flecks occur in the clays that were used for pottery.

## SITE FORMATION AND EROSION

Archaeological materials are deposited on top of geological deposits and through a variety of natural and cultural processes may become encompassed within them. Such sites are most likely to yield sequential information through excavation, as their materials are contained within a matrix that can be interpreted and analyzed. Archaeological materials deposited as people lived under rockshelters, such as in the Hogback and Black Forest subregions, are often buried inside the overhang by weathering of the overhead rock into sand, gravel, and cobble debris or by rockfall. Sites also occur on top of bedrock, either within an overhang that has no sediments deposited on the bedrock floor or in open settings.

## Site Formation Processes

When archaeological materials do not lie directly on top of bedrock, understanding soils and soil formation processes becomes critical to the study of archaeology, since soils constitute the medium in which archaeological sites are deposited and subsequently excavated. Sites become contained in sediment deposits primarily through alluvial, colluvial, and aeolian deposition (Box 2C). Each step in creating an archaeological site can move archaeological materials from their original location. This is characterized as site formation, which may be followed by postdepositional disturbance (Schiffer 1987).

> Box 2C. STRATIGRAPHY
>
> Stratigraphy, or the observation of the relationship of strata (layers) of sediment or rock, is an essential concept for analyzing archaeological sites. Each identifiable stratum represents an individual episode of either human activity or soil deposition, and may be paper thin or several meters thick depending on the nature and duration of the episode. Each stratum is younger than those beneath it and older than those above it. The concept of stratification, when applied to archaeological sites, is not entirely straightforward. For example, a storage pit is associated with the layer in which it originated, or where its top is located, but it cuts through lower strata that were deposited at an earlier time period.
>
> The longer a surface is stable the more complex the soil profile becomes, meaning its thickness, development, texture, etc. Thus, the degree of soil development may be used to correlate deposits of similar age based on such characteristics. In many cases stratigraphic layers may only be visible in a soil profile, a vertical section of soil that displays its layers. Soil profiles may occur naturally, for example as banks where streams have cut into sites, or they may be created during site excavation, when the sides of square, carefully excavated units create vertical faces that expose the layers of sediment surrounding those excavated.

During the early stage of site formation, factors such as occupational trampling and postoccupational and preburial dispersal can move archaeological materials from their original locations. Dispersal can also occur while artifacts are being covered with soil. But even when archaeological materials are securely encased in sediments, the processes that may expose, disturb, or further cover them are still active. Trampling, treading, and scuffage that occurs during the use of a site by its inhabitants varies depending on the texture of the soil and the intensity of occupation traffic (Schiffer 1987). Experimental studies indicate that an occupation "churn zone" is formed in loose soils; loamy soils, which are thicker and better established, may have little churn zone (Gifford-Gonzalez et al. 1985), and soils rich in clay may have no zone at all. Churn zones may blur the occupational surface, particularly in caves and rockshelters that are occupied repeatedly

(Eckerle 1992). But artifacts have a better chance of preservation because they are not removed by intentional cleaning of the occupation surface, so they are thus more likely to be found near their original place of deposition, for archaeologists to uncover and study (Box 2D).

> Box 2D. Deposition of Sediments
>
> Identifying the agent that deposited sediments covering archaeological materials is important for understanding a site, estimating its age, and interpreting its function. Deposition most often is caused by wind, termed aeolian (or aeolian) action, or by water, termed alluvial action. Aeolian sediments include such deposits as loess and dune sand and are most common in arid or semiarid regions. Alluvial materials are deposited by running water and result in such features as dams (where sediment and debris from an overloaded tributary stream may block the channel), fans (an outspread, gently sloping mass of alluvium deposited in an arid or semiarid region where a stream comes from a narrow canyon onto a plain or valley floor), or plains (also produced by deposition of alluvium). Colluvial deposition occurs when the forces of gravity move loose and incoherent deposits (termed colluvium) down a slope to be deposited at the foot. A residual surface, finally, is one that has been eroded down to its original or topographic nature. This term may pertain to rock debris that remains in place when all but the least soluble constituents have been removed by weathering. In archaeological sites, the exposed residual surface often is bedrock, clay formed in place, or desert pavement.

Animals traversing an area, soils washing onto the site from the slope above, and winds are the major causes of postoccupational dispersal. Trampling by animals is the slowest of these processes. Colluvial action, primarily through slope wash, more quickly transports surface archaeological materials to a secondary resting place. Slope wash is caused by a sheet flow layer of water, usually during storms; colluviation may be a more gradual, gravity-driven mode of transport during which heavier and denser materials move downslope farther than lighter, less dense ones (Rick 1976). Wind may move small artifacts during extreme gusts, before they become buried. During the process of burial, artifacts may be moved from their original position. This occurs most often in areas with water action, where artifacts are moved either slowly (during alluvial overbank and sheet wash) or quickly (during channel cutting) based on their size and density (Gifford and Behrensmeyer 1976). Once a site is covered with soil it is still not immune to further impacts. Soil erosion and redeposition may move buried materials. Processes that frequently occur in soils, such as rodent burrowing, plant and tree growth, and freezing/thawing cycles may cause displacement of artifacts.

## Pleistocene and Holocene Deposits

Brown soils are the dominant zonal soil type in the portion of the Colorado Piedmont where Greater Denver is located. Such soils, normally formed under temperate, sub-humid climatic conditions, gradually turn to pale gray calcareous horizons at depths of one to two feet. Parent material is derived primarily from unconsolidated, windborne deposits (Armstrong 1972:22). A late Tertiary alluvium covers the Plains and Streams areas. The higher elevation of the Black Forest is characterized by a mantle of the Denver, Dawson, and Arapaho Formations and the Castle Rock Conglomerate. The Hogback and foothills areas are characterized primarily by woodland lithosols (unzoned shallow soils) (Armstrong 1972:22).

Several late Pleistocene and Holocene deposits that have been described for the Front Range are commonly discussed based on the stratigraphic sequence outlined by Glenn Scott (1963) for the Kassler quadrangle, partially located within the basin. A number of Pleistocene alluvia are identified; the most recent is the Broadway alluvium that occurs along streams such as Cherry Creek, Bayou Gulch, and the South Platte River. It is found under terraces above stream floodplains. (The Broadway terrace is named after a major north-south street in Denver.) The earliest two terrace deposits do not contain archaeological sites because they predate human occupation in the area. Charles B. Hunt (1953) shows the Broadway alluvium on the right bank of the South Platte in the Greater Denver study area, which seems to indicate that the Broadway underlies all younger alluvia in the area of what is today Chatfield Reservoir (Nelson 1979a). Excavations for footings of buildings downtown have exposed loose sand and gravel over bedrock. The alluvium is identified along the banks of the South Platte's major tributaries, such as Plum Creek (Nelson 1979a). A correlating alluvium, the Kersey, overlies the South Platte Valley north of Denver. About ten thousand years ago, downcutting resulted in the isolation of remnants of the Broadway/Kersey terrace. Such remnants are found in the Streams subregion. Scott (1963) assigns these soils an early Holocene age. The soils developed in the alluvium are early Holocene in age, and fossil bones and archaeological material are found there. The Broadway alluvium has been associated with Paleoindian age sites (Montgomery 1984).

Dating and identification of Holocene deposits has proven quite useful in the interpretation of related archaeological remains. Holocene deposits include pre-Piney Creek alluvium, also identified on the Kassler quadrangle. Identified on the second terrace above the South Platte River (Scott 1963), it consists of silt and sand with thin lenses of pebbles, and occurs under terraces intermediate in elevation between the Broadway terrace and the later Piney Creek alluvium. The soil developed on pre-Piney Creek is also early Holocene. An early Holocene aeolian sand occurs as blankets of mostly medium-grained, well-rounded particles, with deposits 3–12 meters thick (Trimble and Machette 1979). Soils in these deposits are similar in development to the Broadway alluvium and are thus correlated to the early Holocene as well (Scott 1963).

## Piney Creek and Post-Piney Creek Alluvium

The Piney Creek alluvium is of great interest to archaeologists. Deposits with the highest potential for intact archaeological sites are the Piney Creek and post-Piney Creek, as well as overlying late Holocene aeolian sand deposits (Newberry and Tate 1994). In fact, it has been noted that archaeological sites in these deposits are often protected if later erosional cycles have not cut into them (O'Neil et al. 1988).

The Piney Creek layer, 1–7.5 meters thick, is late Holocene in age. It is present in the Chatfield Reservoir area on the first terrace above the South Platte River (Scott 1963). It consists of brownish-gray humic silt, sand, and clay forming a flat-topped fill in almost every valley in the basin. The dark gray color, abundance of humus, silty texture, and steep walls in arroyos make it distinctive (Scott 1963:43).

The post-Piney Creek loose humic sand occurs on the first terrace and floodplain overlying Piney Creek. In the Chatfield Reservoir area, it is identified in the floodplain of Plum Creek (Scott 1963). Its thickness is usually 1–3 meters, although it can be thinner. This sediment has been dated alongside cultural occupations, with ages ranging from about 300 B.C. to A.D. 900 at Van Bibber Creek near Golden. A lower unit has been dated by Richard Madole and Meyer Rubin (1984) to 3000–0 B.C. in the northern Colorado Piedmont (Gilmore 1991:45). There is debate regarding the exact age of the deposit, with some researchers assigning it to the Altithermal (5500–3500 B.C.) and others placing it around 800 B.C. Kevin Gilmore, with admirable understatement, points out that these discrepancies must be resolved before the deposits can be truly useful for dating archaeological sites (Gilmore 1991:46–47).

Covering the post-Piney Creek is a layer of aeolian sand and loess of late Holocene age (Scott 1963). These deposits were correlated with cultural materials at the archaeological site of Bayou Gulch, where they are associated with Plains Woodland pottery (Gilmore 1991).

## Water and Archaeology

"Water is presently, and was prehistorically, the critical environmental variable influencing occupation on the Colorado High Plains" (Newberry and Tate 1994:7). The first historic Denver settlement was situated on the South Platte River, virtually at the confluence of that river and the primary tributary within Greater Denver, Cherry Creek. The South Platte River enters the Denver basin from the Hogback subregion, where a major tributary, Plum Creek, joins it from headwaters in the Colorado mountains. The South Platte then flows in a northeastward direction to its confluence with the perennial drainage of Cherry Creek, another north-flowing watercourse that has its headwaters in the Palmer Divide south of Denver and thus flows through the Black Forest subregion as well. After the two join, the South Platte trends generally northeastward toward its confluence with the North Platte River in western Nebraska. Many creeks join both the South Platte and Cherry Creek within Greater Denver.

### Historic Trends and Events

The environment of the area was attractive to Euro-American settlement for several reasons. Perhaps most important was the confluence of the two major watercourses in a semiarid region. Three factors influenced the occupation of Greater Denver from its early historic period to the present: (1) actual environmental trends and events, such as rainfall patterns and temperature fluctuations; (2) human perception of the environment, which sometimes did not reflect reality (Hollon 1966); and (3) the use of technology to alter the environment, either intentionally or accidentally (Lockeretz 1981). All three factors were important to Euro-American migration to the region and greatly influenced local lifestyles.

Climatic effects can have variable durations: a few minutes, such as a hail storm, or several thousand years, such as an ice age. Also, a climatic event can be local (a tornado), or can affect vast expanses of land, as do the changes of the seasons. The results of climatic change often persist long after the episode has passed, and these factors must be considered when reconstructing past climates.

## Droughts

Precipitation is one of the most important climatic variables on the High Plains. Although other factors, such as temperature extremes, wind conditions, and insect invasions, have affected local and regional settlement, drought has been the most critical. "Drought" can be defined in several ways (Bark 1978:11; Felch 1978:25; Riefler 1978:63; Tannehill 1947); here drought is considered a period of less than average available moisture extreme enough to cause cultural adjustment. Frequency of droughts is relatively well recorded for the Greater Denver study area beginning in the mid-1600s.

Great Plains droughts have occurred generally in twenty-year cycles, in the 1850s, 1890s, 1910s, 1930s, 1950s, and 1970s, all of which were drier than average decades (Albert and Wyckoff 1984:1; Bowden et al. 1981:494; Warrick and Bowden 1981:114–15). Particular years or periods within these decades, such as 1894 and the entire decade of the 1930s, were extremely dry. The 1870s period does not fall into the twenty-year pattern, but 1874 in particular was a year of drought conditions in many parts of the Great Plains (Baltensperger 1979:44, 47; Bark 1978:16). The nondrought decades were times of generally average or above average precipitation. Certain years, such 1825–45 (Lawson 1976:30), the 1880s (Baltensperger 1979:44, 48), the mid-1860s to the mid-1880s (Bark 1978:16–17), and 1941 (Albert and Wyckoff 1984:32), were particularly wet years in the Great Plains.

## Floods

Just as the shortage of water causes or contributes to significant hardship, watercourses can also be dangerous and devastating during floods. Historical accounts of flooding in the Greater Denver area are numerous (see the account at the Tremont House Hotel in Chapter 5).

The two major waterways of Denver have both had memorable floods. In 1933 Cherry Creek flooded so severely that it washed out a dam in Castlewood Canyon that has never been rebuilt. In 1965 the South Platte River was swept by a sudden flood that demonstrated its power as an agent of erosion. The flash flood destroyed or damaged property in excess of $508,000,000 and drowned six people (Chronic 1980). H. F. Matthai of the U.S. Geological Survey described the flood:

> The deluge began, not only near Dawson Butte [30 miles south of Denver], but also at Raspberry Mountain, 6 miles to the south near Larkspur. The rain came

down harder than any rain the local residents had ever seen . . . the thudding of huge boulders, the snapping and tearing of trees, and the grinding of cobbles and gravel increased the tumult. . . . Creeks overflowed, roads became rivers, and fields became lakes—all in a matter of minutes.

The flow glutted ravines and from fields and hillsides soon reached East and West Plum Creeks. . . . Large waves, high velocities, crosscurrents, and eddies swept away trees, houses, bridges, automobiles, heavy construction equipment, and livestock. All sorts of debris and large volumes of sand and gravel were torn from the banks and beds of the streams and were dumped, caught, plastered, or buried along the channel and floodplains downstream. A local resident stated, "The banks of the creek disappeared as if the land was made of sugar."
[When] the flood reached the South Platte River . . . the rampaging waters picked up house trailers, large butane storage tanks, lumber, and other flotsam and smashed them against bridges and structures near the river. Many of the partly plugged bridges . . . washed out. Other bridges held, but they forced water over approach fills, causing extensive erosion. (quoted in Chronic 1980:72–73)

In that flood Plum Creek and the South Platte River destroyed 2,500 homes and 750 businesses and resulted in several casualties. Debris was piled in major streets such as South Santa Fe Drive.

In spite of the ever-present danger of flooding, the South Platte River floodplain has been repeatedly built on through the years. Chatfield and Cherry Creek dams were built largely to control floods. Even with the dams, flooding remains a concern.

Other factors also influenced settlement and subsistence patterns on the Great Plains. The year 1874 is remembered for the great grasshopper plague (Baltensperger 1979:47; Bark 1978:16; Dick 1937:203–6), an insect invasion that was a disaster for many farmers: "The grasshoppers alighted in such large numbers on the corn that the stalks bent toward the ground. The potato vines were mashed flat. The sound of their feeding was like a herd of cattle eating in a cornfield. When the insects left a few hours later, the whole country was a scene of vast ruin and desolation. The jaunty waving fields of corn in twelve hours time were reduced to bent over stalks entirely denuded of their leaves" (Dick 1937:205–6).

## THE PALEOENVIRONMENT

The Greater Denver study area epitomizes the transitional nature of the Plains environment as it meets the Rocky Mountains. Lying at the juncture between two major physiographic zones, it cannot be studied as an isolated landform.

The overall climate of Colorado is semiarid continental, characterized by temperature extremes because it is distant from coastal waters that moderate such conditions. In the Greater Denver study area, the mountains on the western edge serve to moderate the range of temperature extremes compared to farther east on the plains (Berry 1968:596; Ruffner and Bair 1985:418). It is not uncommon for the plains to experience daytime summer temperatures above 100°F (37.8°C) and winter temperatures of -15°F (-26°C) (Berry 1968:596). Denver records indicate that on average the city reaches 100°F approximately once every five years. January is typically the coldest month for the Denver region, with an average temperature of approximately 30°F (-1°C) (Ruffner and Bair 1985:418), but temperatures of up to 60°F often occur even in January. The annual average of 15.3 inches (382 mm) of precipitation in Denver is slightly greater than that recorded for the eastern Colorado plains (Ruffner and Bair 1985:420). More than half comes in the form of rain, often downpours; snowfall at Denver averages only 150 cm per year. In the winter, areas near the foothills are often warmed by dry, downslope chinook winds that can make many inches of snow disappear in a few hours.

The early Holocene (7500–5000 B.P.) in the southern Rocky Mountains is a postglacial period, generally characterized as cooler and wetter than our present climate. Benedict (1981, 1985) identifies the Ptarmigan glacial advance (7250 to 6380 B.P.), followed by about 1,000 years of reduced snow and ice and a rise in timberline. The Triple Lakes glacial advance then lasted from 5200 to 3000 B.P.; the first half was apparently cooler than the last half. Between 3100 and 2100 B.P. was another period of rising timberlines and reduced glaciation (Carrara et al. 1984). Finally, according to Benedict (1985), the Audubon glacial advances began around 2400 B.P . The subsequent Sub-Atlantic (2760–1680 B.P.) was marked by wetter and cooler conditions, with perhaps a slight increase in vegetation and animal populations. In Greater Denver the last fifteen hundred years or so have been marked by fluctuations in precipitation and temperature, causing local shifts in bison migration routes on the Plains that affected the human populations reliant on them.

As the environmental setting of the Greater Denver study area subregions is considered, we must keep in mind that our perspective for describing the environment that would have been encountered by prehistoric peoples, and to a lesser degree by more recent groups, is almost certainly skewed by our observations of the environment today. Still, one goal of archaeology is to trace present-day conditions back, finding clues of changes through time that may have affected the way prehistoric peoples lived. These fluctuations in the paleoenvironment, or "old" environment as it is termed, are reflected in such things as the pollen record.

> Box 2E. POLLEN
>
> Pollen analysis is a useful technique for reconstructing past vegetation. The preservation of pollen is a function of habitat, soil type, depth, and other factors. It is often poor in archaeological sites, but better in marshes and wet environments. Pollen is usually collected from a site area as a pollen column, where small samples of soil are taken from regular intervals of a soil profile. When individual pollens are identified they provide an assessment of changing vegetation communities through time, which may then be associated with the archaeological strata from which the samples came.
>
> Interpretation of pollen analysis must take into account the mechanisms for pollen transport and deposition. Pollen can be introduced into sites by natural and cultural means. Windborne pollen can travel for miles, while bee-pollinated plants

> are harder to trace but closer to the plant. Pollen evidence, therefore, is best viewed in conjunction with other evidence of past environments to be truly effective (Apple and York 1993).

Evidence of the earliest humans in Greater Denver dates to about 12,000 years ago, near the end of the Pleistocene. It is commonly accepted that the transition between the Pleistocene and the Holocene was complete by about 10,000 years ago; therefore most human occupation of the Greater Denver study area has been during the Holocene. Colorado's landscape was different 12,000 years ago, containing a combination of animal species, some of which we would recognize today, others not. Mammoth, camel, ground sloth, horse, bison, mountain deer, musk ox, shrub ox, and predators including the giant short-faced bear, dire wolf, scimitar cat, sabertooth, jaguar, lion, and cheetah all were present here prior to about 11,000 to 10,000 years ago (Black 1994).

Tammy Stone and Ruben Mendoza (1994), through a synthesis of paleoenvironmental data assembled by Robert Brunswig (1992), William Butler (1988), Sally Thompson Greiser (1985), and Wayne M. Wendlund (1978), more specifically identify the characteristics associated with changing climatic periods during the late Pleistocene and early Holocene. According to Stone and Mendoza, during the Late Glacial period (about 12,900–10,500 B.P.), ice masses in Colorado resulted in temperatures 16 degrees F cooler than today, with 10 to 25 percent more precipitation, mostly in the form of winter storms. Spruce and pine forest extended down to the western edge of the plains, which were characterized by short and long grass prairies and pine savannas with deciduous woodlands along the rivers. Large animals dotted the plains; white elk, deer, and other large mammals roamed the forested areas (Stone and Mendoza 1994).

## Elevation and Food Sources

According to Sullivan (1992), a good general approach to describing the vegetation, as well as related animal species of the Greater Denver study area, is multitiered and zonal. Boundaries between vegetation zones are rarely distinct, however, as microclimate, slope, and other factors may contribute to variation.

The lowest vegetation zone along the Front Range is the plains grassland and streamside vegetation zone (Veblen and Lorenz 1991). Urban development, cultivation, and livestock grazing have disturbed vast amounts of the original grasslands in the Greater Denver area. Remaining primary grasses include blue grama, buffalo grass, big and little bluestem, and needle-and-thread. Prickly pear and several types of sagebrush are also common, while cottonwoods, willows, and box elder are found along stream courses. The Streams and Plains subregions were characterized in early historical times by this shortgrass prairie/riparian ecotone, although modern urban landscaping has largely replaced native vegetation throughout much of Greater Denver. Grassland is found less commonly in the Black Forest subregion. At least 21 species from the plains grassland and lowland riparian zones are known to have been used by indigenous groups for food or medicinal purposes (Stone and Mendoza 1994). Plants such as chokecherry, wild onion, cattail, wild currant, prickly pear, and yucca would have provided food throughout the year because many possess edible shoots, stems, leaves, seeds, and fruit known to have been used by various Native American groups (Harrington 1967).

In the Chatfield Reservoir area wheat grass and needle grass join the assemblage of the more common blue grama and buffalo. Cottonwood and willow trees grow profusely along streams, and in one remaining area of floodplain in the Chatfield Reservoir area, an understory within the cottonwood forest is present, which includes poison hemlock, western snowberry, golden currant, woodbine, and wild grape. Cattails and bulrushes also are found in moister areas. Identified along Plum Creek are wild roses, yucca, prickly pear, and scrub oak (Nelson 1979a). Excavations at the historical archaeological site of Four Mile House along Cherry Creek revealed a majority of seeds identified as Russian olive, a historic transplant to the Denver area. Bulrush, thistle, and cottonwood, all natives, are next in frequency. Several yucca seeds were found in various contexts, indicating that cottonwood, bulrush, and yucca were the local flora when Four Mile House was inhabited in the 1800s.

Bison were the dominant native faunal resource on the plains until their near extinction at the end of the nineteenth century. Today they are still present in small, managed herds. Until the early 1970s there was a fenced-in bison herd near Cherry Creek Reservoir, but it had to be relocated when suburbia began to surround the park. Pronghorns are common on the plains, as are mule deer and black-tailed prairie dogs, which may be found in large colonies in the grasslands. Burrowing owls and greater and lesser prairie chickens (an endangered species) are part of the prairie grasslands, while eagles, hawks, and prairie falcons are important predators (Sullivan 1992). At Rocky Flats mule deer are common, and smaller mammals such as white-tailed jackrabbits and desert cottontails also occur. Coyotes, red foxes, striped skunks, and long-tailed weasels are common, as are various rodents such as pocket gophers, meadow voles, and mice. Birds include western meadowlarks, horned larks, mourning doves, great horned owls, and hawks. Bull snakes and rattlesnakes lurk for the unwary, and western painted turtles and western plains garter snakes can be found in ponds and moist areas. Streams, ditches, and ponds yield black bass, fathead minnows, bluegills, and crayfish (Dames and Moore 1991).

In the Streams area, mammals include mule deer, red foxes, raccoons, skunks, white-tail deer, beavers, cottontails, muskrats, and mink (Nelson 1979a). Some of these creatures still inhabit the less dense suburban areas. From earlier times, bison and mule deer are the most common bones found in the Piney Creek alluvium, while horse, mammoth, and camel have been found in older deposits (Scott 1963). The Streams subregion also reports fish, in "poor to fair" numbers depending on the precipitation. Fishing is presumed to have been good during warm and wet cycles, and mussel shells have been found at archaeological sites overlooking Plum and Deer Creeks (Nelson 1979a).

The transition to the montane vegetation zone occurs at about 1,800 meters, an elevation approximately that of the Dakota Hogback and Red Rocks Park in the Hogback subregion. Montane vegetation zones also occur, though less frequently, in the Black Forest subregion. Ponderosa pine may be found in association with Rocky Mountain juniper with a grass understory. The transition is complete at about 2,800 m, where finer-grained soils of the grasslands give way to coarser, better-drained soils preferred by montane zone trees. The most characteristic tree is the ponderosa pine. Mountain mahogany, kinnikinnick, wax currant, and wild rose are present in the lower portion; in the upper zone, ponderosa pine is joined by Douglas fir as a codominant tree, along with aspen, limber pine, and lodgepole pine. Fauna include black bear, elk, mule deer, mountain lions, porcupines, and Abert's squirrels. Steller's jays, hummingbirds, black-billed magpies, and western tanagers are birds found in the montane zone.

Rivers and creeks that cross the montane surface ensure the growth of riparian vegetation, especially Colorado blue spruce, narrowleaf cottonwood, alder, and willow. Birds include belted kingfishers and Americana dippers, and red-winged blackbirds are found where cattails are present (Sullivan 1992).

The subalpine vegetation zone extends from about 2,800 m to treeline (about 3,400 m) and is characteristic of portions of the Hogback. Several conifers are important constituents of the subalpine zone. The more common include Engelmann spruce and subalpine fir with an understory shrub list of myrtle blueberry, whortleberry, and Colorado currant. Stands of lodgepole pine are particularly located in areas that have burned. They survive fire well and thus have been called "fire pine." On exposed areas with coarse, rocky soils, limber and bristlecone pines grow with thick, stocky, and often twisted trunks. Aspens also grow in the subalpine zone, particularly in moist areas. The lower reaches of the subalpine zone, near treeline, are characterized by so-called krummholz growth, a German term for "twisted wood" or "elfin timber," where the spruces, firs, and pines may be stunted and deformed by the high winds at this elevation.

Vegetation in the alpine tundra zone is characterized by low, deep-rooted, cushionlike plants. These plants have adapted to a harsh environment, with long, cold, windy winters and a short, cool, growing season with intense thunderstorms. Common plants include willows, sedges, alpine avens, American bistort, clover, arctic gentian, king's crown, loenigia, and yellow stonecrop. Bighorn sheep, yellow-bellied marmots, pikas, and white-tailed ptarmigans are present year-round in the tundra. Mountain goats are commonly seen, but they are not ancient, having been introduced in the 1940s.

## Plant and Animal Resources

At the Massey Draw site in the Hogback subregion, the "bone levels" at the site indicate intensive butchering and hide processing, while the "camp levels" indicate tool manufacture and other activities. Bison were the main faunal resource: more than 85 percent of the faunal remains were bison, with jackrabbit, black-tailed prairie dog, and pocket gopher also used. Bison remains consist of both bulls and cows; the bulls were the focus of processing, which took place primarily in the spring. There is no evidence for reduction of the bison through bone grease (marrow) extraction; instead, remains were apparently stripped for meat.

The bison at Dutch Creek show that some bones were butchered, mostly upper and lower limb bones. This suggests that the bison were killed and initially processed elsewhere and brought to the site as more easily transportable pieces. This pattern is analogous to that at Massey Draw, and may mean that Dutch Creek is also a spring bison procurement site (see Box 2F).

> Box 2F. Food Resources
>
> The archaeological record provides several means of learning about prehistoric use of animal and plant resources for food. Direct evidence includes actual plant and animal remains; indirect evidence consists primarily of processing tools. Analysis of animal bones may yield information on species hunted and their proportional contribution to the prehistoric diet, along with butchering techniques, seasonality, and resource area exploitation.
>
> Sometimes the presence of a certain animal bone may indicate only that the animal was present at the site, not necessarily eaten (particularly rodents such as mice and rats). Plant food use is documented through the recovery of seeds and plant parts (termed macrobotanical remains), which allow identification of species as well as seasonality.
>
> Faunal remains often are recovered from living areas and hearths as whole or partial bones and may be burned or unburned. Macrobotanical remains are usually recovered by a process known as flotation, in which the contents of a hearth are dumped into a water matrix in which the plant parts (the light fraction) float. They are scooped out with a mesh strainer and dried before being identified. The remains at the bottom of the flotation tank (the heavy fraction) are also analyzed. The plant parts preserved depend not only on their individual characteristics (hardness, softness, density, brittleness, etc.), but also on the manner in which they were deposited (charred by fire, quickly covered by sediments, or gradually obscured by dust over many years) (Apple and York 1993).
>
> Tools that give indirect clues to subsistence activities include grinding stones, mortars, and pestles, often indicating preparation of plant seeds and materials through pounding and grinding. Projectile points and cutting, and scraping tools suggest hunting and processing of animal meat and hides. Occasionally direct evidence of the material processed can be found as residues on grindstones and pots.
>
> Usually the tools are washed to obtain microscopic pollen preserved from processing a particular plant. Organic residue analysis, a relatively new technique, is sometimes performed on lithic and ceramic artifacts as well. Through biochemical and immunological analyses, these residues, present in the form of plant pollen and animal blood, are identifiable to at least the family level of classification. Human bones can also be analyzed to discover the prehistoric diet, but this has been done rarely in Greater Denver.

Alder and pine were the primary fuels for fire at Dutch Creek, while goosefoot (a chenopod) and pigweed (an amaranth), or sunflower, sage, mint, and rose were used for food or medicine. (It is hard to tell amaranths and chenopods apart when they have been ground, so they are often referred to together as cheno-ams.) Also in the Hogback subregion, the Dutch Creek site is located near the streamside vegetation zone as well as grasslands, each of which has many trees, shrubs, forbs, and grasses (Anderson et al. 1994: Table 3). Plant remains from Dutch Creek did not yield quite such a diversity. However, cheno-ams with small but abundant seeds that ripen in late summer and fall were processed.

In the Streams subregion, the plant assemblage at the Rock Creek site includes grasses, pigweed, milkvetch, goosefoot, prickly pear, purslane, bulrush, dropseed, and cocklebur. No domesticated species were recovered from site excavations; however, many of the plants at the site are adapted to habitats created by human disturbance (Gleichman, Gleichman, and Karhu 1995). Abandoned sites are examples of such habitats (giving archaeologists clues to finding sites through observing the ground cover) and plants that are pioneers in colonizing these habitats have been termed "camp followers." The site excavators note that these plants generally have economic uses (Gleichman, Gleichman, and Karhu 1995:130), and suggest that this indicates long-term and intensive plant interaction resulting in alteration of the plant's adaptation—a symbiotic relationship. Interestingly, they propose this factor as one of the reasons the same sites were repeatedly used through time, a relatively common archaeological phenomenon.

Faunal remains at Rock Creek from the Archaic and Ceramic components indicate that small mammals (prairie dog, mice, vole, pocket gopher) were probably eaten, because some burned prairie dog and bird bones were found. Large mammals, such as deer, bison and elk, were more commonly eaten. Cut marks on the bones of these species demonstrate butchering patterns. At this site remains from the Archaic period indicate more dependence on small mammals and birds, perhaps because of micro-environmental fluctuations affecting availability of the larger animals. Bones from the Archaic and Ceramic periods are burned, and their condition suggests that they were crushed. It is postulated that they were boiled or baked for marrow extraction. Large numbers of metates at the site also suggest intensive seed grinding, which in conjunction with the heavily processed faunal bone may indicate stresses on the available food sources (Box 2G).

> Box 2G. Bone Processing
>
> From the Yarmony site just west of the Greater Denver study area near Eagle, Colorado, Ron Rood (1991) has interpreted the bone processing activity as pounding the bone to increase its surface area and boiling fragments to render grease (fat). Therefore, a faunal collection indicating marrow extraction may include the middle sections of long bones, a few articulator ends, and many small bone fragments, all of which may be charred or burned (Tucker, Tate, and Mutaw 1992).

Culturally modified bison bone in an arroyo wall indicate that the Senac Dam site, in the Plains subregion, was a bison processing locus, though not a kill site. Bison were processed for meat removal, marrow extraction, and probably hide working. Evidence from the site points to a local environment that was rather mild, possibly warmer than during the preceding era. Other animals include pronghorn, deer, fox, raccoon, badger, bighorn sheep, rabbit, prairie dog, dove, grouse, and turtle (O'Neil and Tate 1986). One site area focused on antelope and deer, supplemented by prairie dog. Bones at the site indicate that antelope and deer were butchered elsewhere and parts brought into camp, where they were stripped for meat and broken for marrow. Younger animals were probably brought in whole, in order to strip the softer skins for clothing. Prairie dogs seem to have been consumed whole, as they were found near the hearths.

Cheno-ams were important at Senac Dam. Other charred seed included grass, ball cactus, and fragrant bedstraw, among others. At this site, changes are noted in plant use over time. For example, earlier occupations have more charred seeds than later ones. The main fuel is juniper charcoal, with some unidentified shrub, probably sage, second in frequency. Juniper was probably carried to the site; it occurs as isolated stands in the area. The occupants seem to have purposely chosen it over pine for its hot-burning qualities, which may have been necessary for firing ceramics, an activity evident at one feature (O'Neil et al. 1988). At a nearby site pine was the primary fuel, perhaps because there were more pine trees during the period of that site's occupation. Pine stands are still present today.

At Monaghan Camp, another site in the Plains subregion, cheno-ams again were primarily used for food, while saltbush is identified as the major fuel. Significantly, alum root (typically used for medicinal purposes) was found at the site. This plant presently grows at higher elevations in moist, rocky areas, and its presence at Monaghan Camp indicates collection in the nearby mountains. Bone at the site is primarily prairie dog, but the assemblage also includes badgers and rabbits.

In the Black Forest subregion, Franktown Cave had an unusual amount of normally perishable materials. Environmental indicators in the collection include coprolites, bone, shell, macroflora, soil, charcoal, corn kernels and corncobs. Floral material collected include cactus, yucca, cane, legume pods, grasses, cattail, juniper, pine, willow, aspen, cottonwood, and chokecherry. Parts of maize plants included cobs, kernels, and cornstalks. Bones identified included bison, beaver, elk, deer, porcupine, turkey, weasel, pack rat, prairie dog, cotton rat, and rabbit.

*Seasonal Rounds*

The concept of a seasonal round, or a pattern in which mobile or semisedentary groups exploit areas within a certain region seasonally, is commonly used to explain the lifeways of prehistoric peoples. William B. Butler has argued (1986, 1988) that the Front Range generally should be seen as an area continually and extensively exploited by hunter-gatherer groups whose primary affiliation was from the plains. In some cases the Hogback Valley was the western edge of the area being exploited, but during most periods the western edge extended up into the mountains in a seasonal cycle using the plains in winter, mountains in spring and summer, and transitional zones in spring and fall. S. J. Bender and Gary Wright (1988) suggest, on the other hand, that the seasonal round encompassed the mountains, transitional zones, and plains, and that distinctive exploitation of the plains proper did not occur until the introduction of the horse. They believe that this broad spectrum occurred both before and after the Altithermal period.

Others claim that the Front Range has always been included in part of a seasonal round that included groups with primary affiliations with the plains, mountains, and transitional zones. Kevin Black (1991) argues for the continuous use of mountain and plains environments regardless of climatic shifts. He believes that the mountains represent year-round exploitation by nomadic to semisedentary groups, with long-term continuity in these patterns of exploitation. Finally, he proposes that these groups have a separate archaeological identity from the adjacent lowland patterns (indicating a separate cultural affiliation from plains groups), which began as early as the Paleoindian period. Mountain groups had winter base camps in valleys, such as the Hogback Valley, on both the eastern and western slopes of the Rockies. Plains groups came into the area separately, using summer camps in high altitude locations.

James Benedict's model of "seasonal transhumance" (1992a) traces distinctive rock types from high altitude sites in the Front Range to quarry sources at lower elevations. This implies that people used rocks from the Front Range as they went into the high Rockies, where they could only live in the summer. For prehistoric groups hunting large mammals such as elk and bighorn sheep, he proposes two systems, both with winter base camps in the Hogback subregion. In the "up-down system," Benedict suggests that during late summer and fall Early Archaic hunter-gatherer groups traveled up as high as the Continental Divide to hunt elk and bighorn sheep communally. They lived in winter base camps in the Hogback. During the Ceramic period a "rotary system" took over as a counterclockwise grand circuit, with hunter-gatherer groups traveling up to 400 kilometers over the course of a year. They moved north along the flanks of the Front Range during spring, crossed into North and Middle Parks, and by late August or early September went to the Continental Divide for communal game drives. In the winter they descended to their base camps in the Hogback.

Jane Anderson and her colleagues (1994) postulate that in the Hogback region prehistoric groups used discrete areas as focal points for obtaining resources, rather than for specific site locations. Massey Draw and Dutch Creek may thus represent "one of a series of similar [resource] accumulations produced by the long-term results of short-term, intermittent episodes of Archaic land use" (Anderson et al. 1994:247). They characterize this series as a "resource procurement landscape" along the Hogback, of which Massey Draw and Dutch Creek were just two locations. Differences in resource predictability, they note, result in variability in the basic patterns of annual settlement and subsistence, such as those that are schematically outlined at these two sites. As in the Hogback site of Massey Draw, the use of the site by Archaic peoples during the early part of the year seems to be calculated on resource availability.

Recent evidence from the Rock Creek site generally supports portions of Benedict's model, at least for the Early Ceramic period (Gleichman, Gleichman, and Karhu 1995). However, at Magic Mountain, where excavations were recently resumed after a thirty-year hiatus, the grand circuit theory for the Ceramic period is difficult to address. No exclusive relationship has been established between the Hogback subregion site of Magic Mountain and high altitude sites farther west. As Stephen Kalasz and his colleagues note, the concept necessitates the identification and excavation of a full range of site types from similar time periods in mountain, foothill, and plains contexts (Kalasz et al. 1996). The Magic Mountain occupants may represent a mobile foraging strategy, with longer periods of habitation indicated by the presence of structures. Kalasz concludes that at Magic Mountain a more localized eastern plains/foothills adaptation is indicated based on ceramic types, which are more related to the eastern plains than to one farther west.

## The Archaeological Evidence

Paleoenvironmental data for the Paleoindian period are virtually nonexistent from sites in Greater Denver. However, recent geomorphological investigations at the Lamb Spring site, located on Willow Creek at the juncture of the Hogback and Streams subregions, promise to contribute greatly to the understanding of this early period of human occupation of the study area. During 1997, a series of soil cores were extracted from numerous localities across the site, focusing on the area of the spring itself. Soil analysis will provide clues to past environments and will also be used to evaluate earlier theories that the site was utilized by humans before the commonly accepted beginning of the Paleoindian period at about 12,000 years ago.

More archaeological evidence is available for the Archaic through Ceramic periods, in terms of paleoenvironmental reconstructions. Interestingly, two scenarios are coming to light relating to the nature and magnitude of paleoenvironmental changes in the basin. Some changes from warmer and dryer conditions to cooler and wetter are noted in each subregion, but paleoclimatic changes appear to be less extreme in the Streams, Plains, and Black Forest subregions, whereas the Hogback subregion exhibits well-documented changes that resulted in significant variations in available resources. This variation in degree of change is probably related to the elevational ranges in the Hogback subregion as compared with the more homogeneous elevations found in the other three subregions. This pattern can be further investigated only through the excavation of more sites in the various subregions.

Scott (1963) used the basic principle that alluviation along the drainages in the basin has occurred in the middle of each warm and dry climatic period. Along permanent streams, he identified terraces that point to repeated erosional and depositional events linked to certain combinations of temperature and precipitation. He thus identified climatic cycles of ever-decreasing duration in the Chatfield Reservoir area (in the Streams subregion) that would have influenced the human beings inhabiting the area. His episodes include periods of dry and warm conditions occurring at 8800 B.C. (Broadway alluvium), 3780–3450 B.C. (pre–Piney Creek alluvium), around 900 B.C. (Piney Creek alluvium), and A.D. 650–850 (post–Piney Creek alluvium). These climatic episodes surely had some effect on the local flora and fauna (Nelson 1979a), as the foothill vegetation zones shifted downward during wet cycles and the plains grasslands moved upward during the warm, dry periods identified by Scott (1963). Still, because of the dramatic impact of elevation on climate (Hansen et al. 1978), changes in the Chatfield Reservoir area with its relatively homogeneous elevation were probably relatively slight. Data from Rock Creek in the Steams subregion on the extreme northern boundary of the study area support this observation. Food remnants recovered from the excavation of several hearths do not vary much between the Early Archaic and Ceramic periods, indicating continuity in resource availability and a relatively stable ambient vegetal environment (Gleichman, Gleichman, and Karhu 1996). Changes in density and diversity probably occurred following subtle changes in climate, but these are hard to identify in the archaeological record of Greater Denver.

During most of the occupation the Senac Dam site, located in the Plains subregion (Late Archaic through Ceramic), the environment fluctuated, but generally was warmer and drier than during the preceding 3,000 years. More sage and composites (of unknown species) were present between A.D. 245 and 875, and less pine and grass. At about 875, climate at the site was moister and cooler, with more pine, juniper, and grass. By 950, approximately the end of the Early Ceramic occupation, a dryer climate caused erosion. Altogether, indications are that during the time the lower depositional unit at the site was laid down, 1050 B.C.–A.D. 235, the local climate was cooler and moister than today. Warmer and dryer conditions prevailed between 875 and 1055, followed by a cooler, moister interval (1550–1850). Changes in resources at Senac Dam are more a matter of relatively small-scale quantitative variation then of large-scale disappearances of plant and animal species from the archaeological record.

Pollen recovered from archaeological contexts at Bayou Gulch, a campsite located on the northern edge of the Palmer Divide on the edge of the Black Forest subregion where it meets the Streams, has been compared to the modern pollen rain. It indicates that similar plant species were present, at least during the Early Ceramic period and today (Short and Stravers 1981). Kevin Gilmore (1991) has used pedologic (soils) data from the site to trace local changes in the climate that did occur during the prehistoric through protohistoric periods represented at the site. His studies are offered as a model of the paleoclimatic changes that affected the Palmer Divide area east onto the plains. Specifically, Gilmore correlated a series of thin aeolian deposits at the site with episodes of aeolian activity from northeastern Colorado, the Rocky Mountain Basins, and the Nebraska Sand Hills. Episodes such as these, when compared to regional models of paleoclimatic fluctuation, are often useful in recreating a sequence of local conditions and fluctuations.

Another model was developed by James Benedict (1973, 1979, 1981, 1985), based on a wide range of data including ages of glacial features and events and local archaeological sites, using radiocarbon, lichenometric, and rock weathering rind dating methods. Benedict's model is recognized as having good potential for reflecting climatic changes in the Rocky Mountain region and the areas adjacent to the Front Range, such as Greater Denver. In sum, Benedict and Bryan Olson present evidence for a two-drought model for the Altithermal, the first from 5000 to 4500 B.C. and the second from 4000 to 3500 B.C., with the intervening 500 years reflecting conditions similar to modern ones (Benedict 1979; Benedict and Olson 1978).

The collection of aeolian deposits on the southeast side of major drainages along the Front Range and into the Greater Denver study area indicates that a prevailing wind from the northwest carried sand from Cherry Creek to its current position south and east of the creek. Aeolian deposition indicates that vegetation was sparse, allowing sediment to be transported by wind, a condition linked with times of decreased moisture such as droughts (Chorley et al. 1984). Based on patterns of aeolian deposition at Bayou Gulch, Gilmore does not observe two distinct periods of drought during the Altithermal, but instead notes that conditions before approximately 5000 years ago were more favorable for aeolian processes and thus reflected a steady drought. A period of landform stability and soil development is then noted, indicating an increase in moisture, which correlates with such periods in Benedict's and other models. A return to a dryer climate is indicated between 1400 B.C. and A.D. 300 at Bayou Gulch, again correlating with Benedict's model as well as with evidence for renewed dune formation in northeastern Colorado and the Nebraska Sand Hills—drought indicators. Another period of landform stability, soil development, and presumably increased moisture is noted between A.D. 300 and 950. Between 950 and 1400 there was another period of aeolian deposition and drought, not as widely reflected in the region as others. Between 1400 and 1850 there was more stability, followed by drought.

Gilmore's (1991) comparison of the episodes evident at Bayou Gulch indicates some congruencies with these regional patterns, yet also shows deviations, which are believed to represent local climatic fluctuations that are on a scale small enough as to not be represented in the regional sequence. This may be due to the fact that Benedict's models focus on the foothills and mountain areas, areas of relatively variable elevation, rather than this portion of the Black Forest which has fewer changes in elevation.

As mentioned above, a different pattern is noted at sites excavated from the Hogback subregion, where paleoclimatic fluctuations are relatively well documented and appear to have significantly affected local resource availability. At the Massey Draw site, one pollen column was taken from near the creek bank and bone bed (Column 2) at the site, while another was taken farther up the hill in the camp area (Column 3). The pollen record indicates that changes in the vegetation community at this site have been "dramatic" (Anderson et al. 1994:A-3). Records before about 4440 B.C., during the Early Archaic, are similar with very large cheno-am frequencies. Sage and arboreal pollen are also high; grass is lower. The pine population appears reduced at the site, possibly as a result of upward treeline movement in the foothills associated with the warmer and drier conditions of the Altithermal. Following the interval ending at 4150 B.C., local changes in vegetation are relatively rapid. Cheno-am frequencies drop, sage and rabbitbrush apparently replace saltbush altogether. Grasses and pine increase in number. These changes indicate a significantly cooler, intermediate environment. However, significant changes in lifestyle in association with these changes are not evident in the archaeological record (Anderson et al. 1994).

At the Dutch Creek site, about three miles north of Massey Draw, excavations of deeply stratified deposits have yielded information on long-term change (Jepson and Hand 1994). The Late Archaic (post-Altithermal) is the focus of studies at this site. They indicate that human populations in the Plains margin area (our Hogback subregion) enjoyed a significant increase in subsistence diversification over previous inhabitants, while bison were no longer a reliable, readily available food resource. As Jepson and Hand (1994) explain, this was probably most evident in the Hogback and Palmer Divide (our Black Forest) subregions as a result of unusually large numbers and varieties of plant and animal species. This is true because the transition zone between grassland and montane forest vegetation communities contains a wide array of faunal species that were accessible to the prehistoric inhabitants of Dutch Creek within a short distance from the site. Other information gleaned from the Dutch Creek site indicates reduced effective moisture during the Altithermal, when conditions would have resulted in less vegetation cover within the drainage basin and an increase in sediment yield, and a later reduction in moisture and plant cover and increased sediment yield correlating with the Triple Lakes-Audubon interglacial. Radiocarbon dates indicate that sediment at Dutch Creek was aggrading rapidly during this interglacial period, a condition that was occurring less at nearby Massey Draw.

A site located farther into the mountainous portions of the Hogback subregion near the far western edge of the Greater Denver study area, Dancing Pants shelter, also indicates changes in resource exploitation and paleoenvironment. At the site, the Pikes Peak Granite forms a natural shelter that was inhabited by several groups of prehistoric people over an extended time period. As is often the case with sheltered sites, the granite itself weathered through the years, depositing rocks and sediment on top of the archaeological remains inside and just outside of the front opening of the shelter. It is for this reason that rockshelter sites often yield deep, stratified deposits that chronicle the lifeways of prehistoric inhabitants, as well as changes in the environment through time (Liestman and Kranzush 1987).

Dancing Pants shelter is located along the South Platte River. Excavations at the site and a radiocarbon date from the valley floor below the site indicate that the South Platte River was close to its present level by thirty-five to thirty thousand years ago, significantly before the first human occupants (Wallace and Friedman 1985). For the past five thousand years Dancing Pants shelter was intermittently occupied. According to Richard Madole (1978), the times of most frequent occupation correspond with times of expanded cirque glaciers and snowfields in the higher elevations, including the Triple Lakes and Audubon glacial advances (Benedict 1973, 1981, 1985).

Human use seems to correlate with slightly wetter and generally cooler climates. In this region, a body of data supports the theory that changes in human activities correlate with minor fluctuations in Holocene climate. In the Hogback subregion, these shifts tend to be migrations to higher or lower elevations depending on the direction of climate change. In general, during cooler and wetter times the lower elevations were more favorable, as they received more precipitation and runoff, while the higher elevations were largely inhospitable being covered by glaciers. During warmer and dryer regimes, the lower elevations would have been less attractive and groups likely selected higher elevation settings to take advantage of the cooler temperatures afforded (Madole 1978).

Madole (1978) states that these climatic oscillations during the Holocene affected a broad region. However, he notes that different environments responded in different ways, mostly dependent on elevation. For example, when the glaciers and snowfields were forming high in the mountains, lakes and marshes were accumulating in the Plains and Streams subregions. During these times, areas of sand dunes stabilized and were revegetated, grassland expanded into areas previously covered with sagebrush, and forests expanded into former grasslands. During nonglacial times, drying of the climate resulted in desiccation of lakes and marshes, caused the retreat of forests, and the expansion of grasslands once again.

The discovery of gold in the bed of the South Platte River near present-day Denver in 1858 was the first image the rest of America shared of the area that would become the Mile High City. Gold here occurs in two forms—relatively pure, native gold, which may occur as ornate crystals, shiny yellow flakes, or rounded nuggets, and gold embedded in ore minerals in combination with other elements. The type discovered in the South Platte was native gold, found in stream gravels known as placer deposits. It was obtained by digging the sands and gravels of river bottoms, where the gold would have settled. The miners' goal was finding the lodes from which the native gold of the streambeds came. Silver also was found just west of Denver, while lead and zinc, located farther up in the mountains, were also mined (Chronic 1980). Soon after the onset of the Gold Rush, the area began to be visited by journalists and others. Boosters, who were promoting Colorado for a variety of reasons, explicitly promoted environmental variables, such as climate, mineral waters, and the scenery of the mountains, as resources in themselves. The presence of dinosaur fossils in the Hogback, as previously discussed, was widely publicized as early as the 1870s to interested parties in the east. This information brought scientific expeditions to investigate the area and exploit this resource.

The rivers that became the site of the city of Denver also were represented as a valuable resource in the historic period. When W. H. Larimer arrived in 1858, he noted that the South Platte was heavily wooded and that Cherry Creek also bore timber at its head (even today, it has a heavy tree cover). He speaks of cutting timber to make a cabin, and going up Cherry Creek, cutting pines three feet in diameter to get wood for clapboarding and the door. Horace Greeley in 1859 also refers to a fine belt of cottonwood trees along the rivers, immense—three to four feet in diameter. These trees were roughly hewn and formed the walls of nearly every edifice in Denver and Auraria. They were plastered with mud on the outside. The ceilings too used cottonwood split saplings (Bark 1978).

The remaining trees in later years were used for manufacture of wooden bushel baskets. D. W. Working, who lived at Four Mile House, in 1928 recorded selling 60 cottonwood trees for $1.50 each to Mr. Simon from a basket factory. The rich soils of the bottomland were described by Larimer in 1871 as "peculiarly productive, without artificial supplies of moisture," and supporting dense vegetation including a variety of nutritious grasses, flowering plants, shrubberries, and cottonwood forest (Archives of Four Mile Historical Park).

Actual and perceived environmental conditions on the plains were not always consistent. From the first publicized explorations of the western Great Plains in the early 1800s to the drought conditions that prevailed in the 1930s, reports combining western Great Plains environmental reality and myth reached populations in the eastern United States. Both the "myth of the desert" and the "myth of the garden" could be found in early reports and influenced who migrated westward and for what reason (Baltensperger 1979; Emmons 1971; Lawson 1976; Lewis 1965a,b, 1966, 1979; Morris 1926; Parker 1964; Smith 1950). Many early settlers sought to transplant their eastern lifestyles to their new homes in the West. It was these efforts to maintain lifestyle continuity, while concomitantly making the necessary adaptive adjustments, that influenced many aspects of life on the plains during the nineteenth and early twentieth centuries.

Several of the earliest western Great Plains explorers from the United States had less than favorable assessments of the area's potential. In 1810 Zebulon Pike wrote that "in time it may become as celebrated as the sandy desert of Africa," and Stephen H.

Long concluded in 1822 that the land was "almost wholly unfit for cultivation and, of course, uninhabitable by a people depending on agriculture for subsistence" (Bark 1978:14). The western boundary of this "desert" (Lawson 1976:4–5) encompasses present-day Greater Denver. This rich and varied environment was the setting for both prehistoric and historic populations.

CHAPTER 3

## Prehistoric Sites

If we could create a time machine that showed moments of time at any place in the prehistoric past, what might appear on the screen? Let us focus on the confluence of the South Platte River and Cherry Creek. At the beginning of our story, Paleoindians might pass by in groups, wearing leather clothing. Some of them follow herds of mammoth or bison to replenish their supply of meat, hides, bones, and sinew. A few millennia later, Archaic people might have rested under the trees, talking and laughing, with full baskets of plums beside them and a couple of rabbits caught in their nearby snares. The rabbits would provide savory rabbit-on-a-stick for dinner, as well as fur for clothing trim and a soft blanket for warmth in the coming winter. Perhaps as they rested they played a game tossing engraved stones. Later still, we might see Early Ceramic peoples trekking to a funeral at the village of relatives a few miles north on the South Platte, having followed the Cherry Creek valley for twenty miles or so. Men, women, and children wear beads of eagle bone and have painted their faces with red and yellow pigments in a base of bone grease. One person is marked as a shaman by her blue-green stone amulet and bangles made of freshwater shells that rattle as she walks. Children skip ahead, for the young are especially eager for the feasting and ceremonies that are part of funerals.

These snapshots of the past are imaginary, of course, but they are based on Greater Denver archaeology as it has been pieced together from the relics of prehistoric peoples—what is left of their houses and villages, their food, their technology, and even their bodies. The quality and quantity of evidence of prehistoric peoples in Greater Denver has been increasing rapidly in recent years. Spectacular finds are few, but discards and scraps are the stuff of archaeology. Bone splinters and stone chips may not have much intrinsic appeal to most people, but they are important in interpreting the lives of prehistoric groups. Remnants of ancient meals can be extracted from stone tools or soil samples if the site is excavated carefully enough and the traces of plants and animals are properly interpreted. This kind of research requires a team of people with many different skills, as a number of recently excavated sites in Greater Denver attest.

The ways of life of prehistoric people can be partly reconstructed through the traces they have left, but it is important to be mindful also of the gaps in our knowledge. It is tempting to overemphasize the technological, ecological, and economic aspects of these early inhabitants, because those are the facets easiest to interpret from material remains. But it would be a mistake to suppose that the lives of prehistoric people were simple, or even that their material culture was as impoverished as it appears to be when we have little left but stones, bones, traces of plants and fires, and a very few shelters. It is likely that their lives were rich with ceremonies, stories, art, and music, not to mention relationships with people, spirits, and their environment.

It is more difficult to learn about a society's ways of organizing itself and to penetrate its members' belief systems than to understand their methods of obtaining food, making and using tools, and adapting to their environment. Nevertheless, some aspects of society and ideology can be inferred from the artifacts, features, ecofacts, and their relationships to each other. Both ethnographic analogy (comparing objects found in sites to those of living groups that have been studied) and the direct historical approach (using data from known or likely descendants of the site occupants) may lead down productive trails. But we must beware of ethnocentric assumptions deriving from the present that can creep unnoticed into our perceptions of the past. The ancient inhabitants of the region that became Denver were people without writing, metals, or cities, but they had as much brainpower as we have today, and it is important to give them credit for using their minds and their environment wisely according to their own ways of organizing and their own perceptions of the world.

Archaeological reports are careful not to go beyond their concrete evidence. This chapter tries to put some flesh on the archaeological bones by sketching as much as we can about what people's lives might have been like. This is a process not of "inventing facts," but of stretching inferences from the data to their limits, accompanied with notes about how firmly a particular interpretation may be established and what other evidence would shed more light on it. Our narrative is chronological—creating a sequential story from the disconnected archaeological remains.

Such a narrative can be difficult to construct, however, even for individual sites. A site may represent continuous, intermittent, or seasonal occupations by related groups over a considerable time span, or multiple occupations separated by centuries. Radiocarbon dates are vital, but they are never precise, and not every feature in every site is dated. Rodents digging burrows, water, and other agents including later human occupants may mix items from different time periods.

Other perspectives are also essential in looking at prehistoric sites. One is thematic: what people ate (subsistence), how they lived (technology), where they obtained raw materials (trade or travel). Another is regional, considering differences in land use. For example, Figures 3.1 and 3.2 show the differences in clustering of campsites (more evenly spaced) and lithic sites (more clustered) for all periods in the Greater Denver area. The clustering may indicate two kinds of sites: stone quarries (where blanks were produced for later toolmaking and chips were left behind) and animal quarry viewing points (where the hunting party may have chipped tools to while away the time as they watched for game). These perspectives will be noted throughout this chapter as they shed light on the lives of prehistoric peoples.

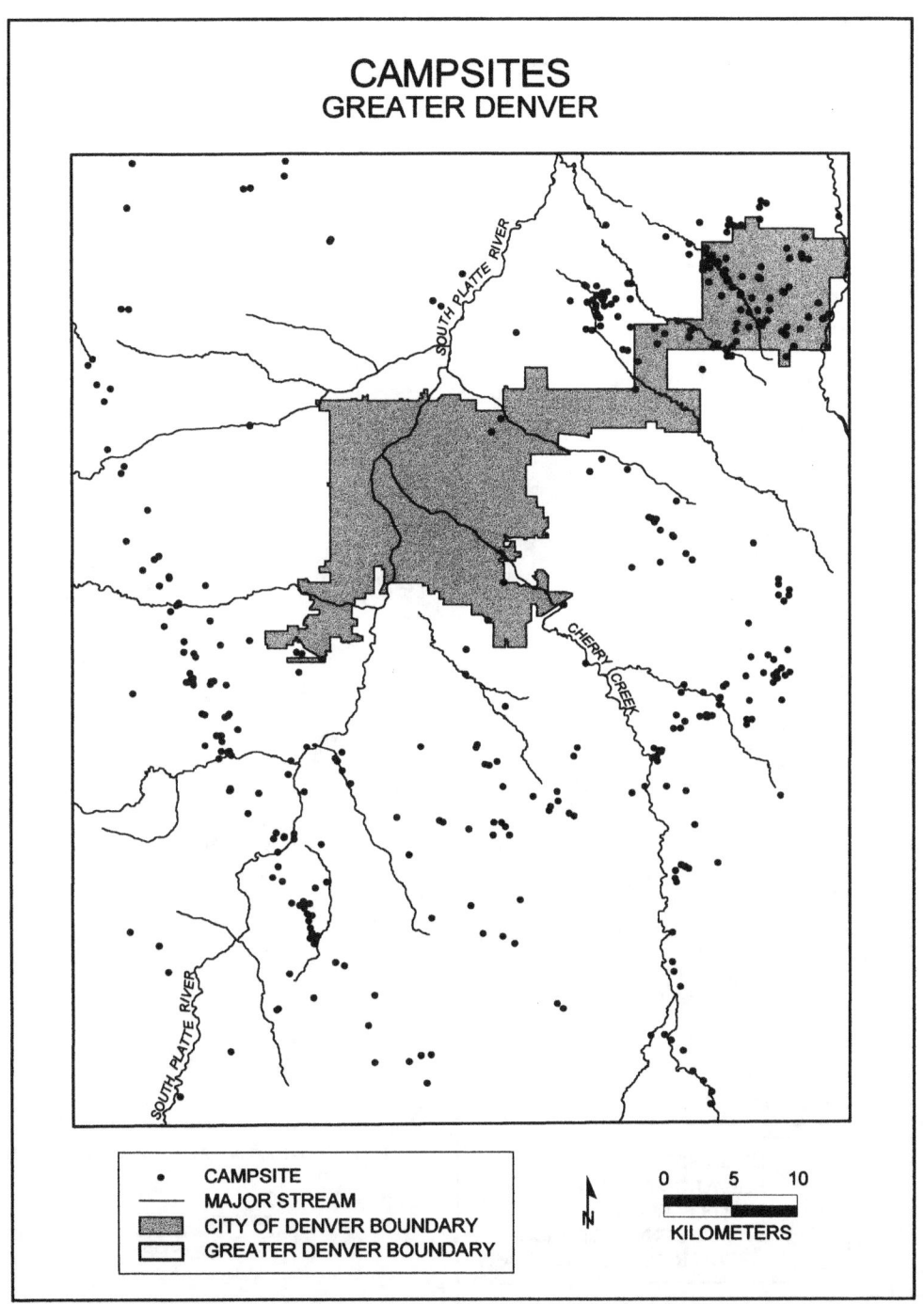

Figure 3.1. Campsites of all periods. Francine Patterson.

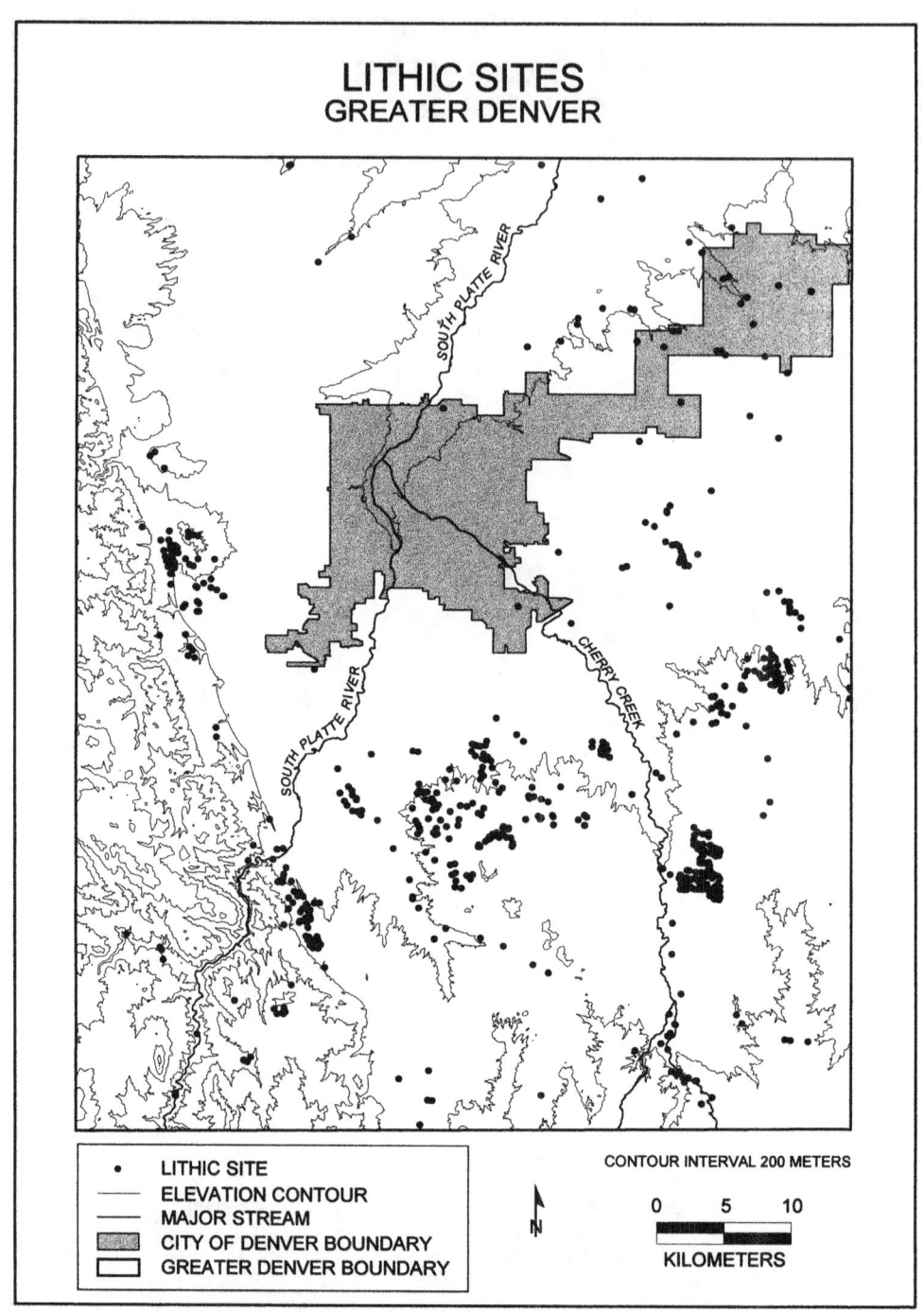

Figure 3.2. Lithic sites of all periods. Francine Patterson.

## REGIONS, TIMES, AND THEMES

Prehistoric time periods in the Denver Basin are conventionally divided into Paleoindian, Archaic, and Ceramic, each with subdivisions. The subdivisions designate varied lifeways, including different adaptations to local environments. In a general way, each period is recognizable by its developments in stone tool technology, especially the use of stone tips for spears, darts, or arrows, which archaeologists call projectile points (see Box 3A, Fig. 3.3).

> Box 3A. STONE TOOL TECHNOLOGY
>
> The pointed stones affixed to various types of projectiles vary in length through time (Fig. 3.3). Paleoindian projectile points are the longest (H, I, J). Among these, the earliest types, called Clovis and Folsom, are very elegant. Fine retouch flaking makes undulations across the face of the point. They are finished "fluting" with a thinning flake removed lengthwise from each side of the point. At Lindenmeier and elsewhere they were attached to foreshafts made of bone and hafted by means of inserting the stone point into a split in the end of the shaft, and gluing and/or wrapping with sinew or cord. Considering the thickness of mammoth and bison hide, various devices might have been used to halt or slow down the animals so that they could be given the coup de grace with a spear or several spears at once. Game drives made of stone piles, which funneled a bison herd toward a cliff to cripple or kill the animals as they tumbled over, are known elsewhere in the Rocky Mountains, although none have been reported in the Greater Denver study area.
>
> Late Paleoindian and Archaic peoples used a device known as an atlatl, which had the effect of lengthening the throwing arm for greater force and accuracy. A modern society devoted to the atlatl, including throwing contests, shows that the technology works well. Projectile points became shorter (E, F, G). So far as we now know, the bow and arrow arrived with the Early Ceramic people. Arrows had shorter and lighter shafts, and projectile points accordingly became both shorter and thinner (A, B). Very tiny points were made by Middle Ceramic and contact period groups, sometimes with two side notches and one notch in the base.
>
> Knives are tools used for cutting. They are thin and sharp on one edge only. Scrapers are thick stone tools with steep, rounded working edges. In the Franktown Cave collection most tools have a large flake skillfully removed from the upper face of the tool, making them comfortable to hold; these have been called "thumb-rests." Borers and drills have long thin pointed ends, and spokeshaves or notches have a semicircular notch made in the edge of the tool. Projectile points are always flaked on both sides ("bifacial"), and they are usually symmetrical. Although some knives are asymmetrical, some symmetrical bifacial tools may have been hafted knives. Only careful attention to edge wear can discriminate between points and knives in these cases. Reworking broken points can make them appear to be different "types," and broken projectile points may have been reused for their points or sharp edges, or reworked into cutting tools.
>
> The emphasis archaeologists place on stone tools derives from the fact that such tools comprise the most abundant artifact category in most ancient sites. We now know that stone tools are not necessarily all related to hunting (Gero 1991), and that we must question whether men only were hunters (Brumbach

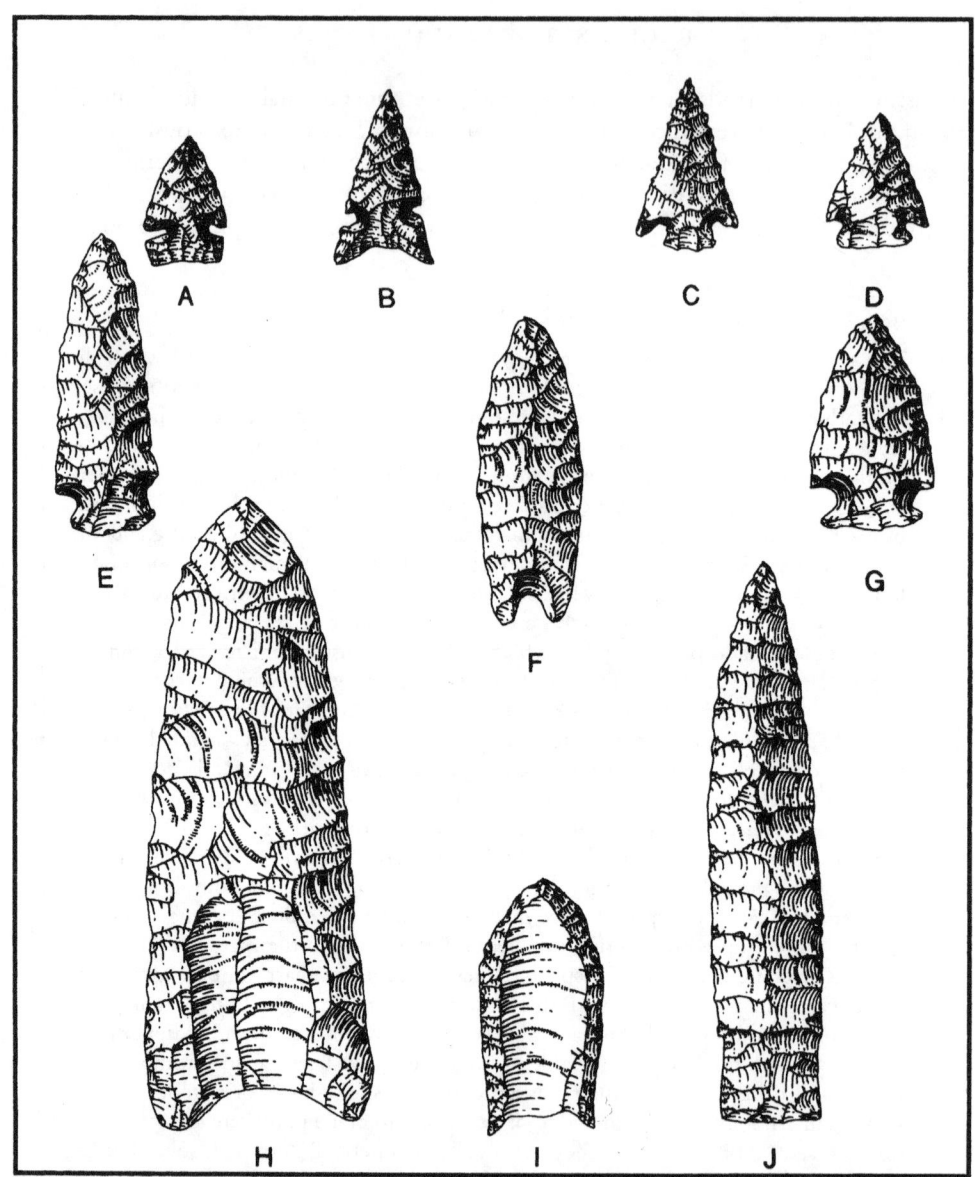

Figure 3.3. Projectile point styles, Greater Denver area. (A) Middle Ceramic, Plains side-notched; (B) Middle Ceramic, Desert side-notched; (C) Early Ceramic, Magic Mountain corner-notched; (D) Early Ceramic, Bayou Gulch corner-notched; (E) Early Archaic, Mountain Albion corner-notched; (F) Middle Archaic, McKean lanceolate; (G) Late Archaic, Pelican Lake corner-notched; (H) Paleoindian, Clovis period; (I) Folsom; (J) Plano period, Eden (Cody complex).

> and Jarvenpa 1997; Wadley 1997). Furthermore, ethnographic analogy suggests that trapping was probably an important method of obtaining animals (Kehoe 1990). It seems likely with these new studies that hunting has been overemphasized in the typical view of the past.
>
> This is not to say that hunting did not exist. The questions are rather about how people defined hunting, who participated, and in what way. We also would like to know about food preferences—which animals were considered tastiest, and which may have been taboo to different groups. Some of the animals hunted in this region changed through time, not only as a result of the extinction of large Pleistocene animals but perhaps due to differing cultural attitudes. Changes in food processing and cooking are evident in the archaeological remains, reflected in the sizes, shapes, and number of grinding stones. Bones reflect cooking practices as well as butchering, and the cutting up of meat from small animals has been neglected as well (Gifford-Gonzalez 1993). We are beginning to have a less skewed and more inclusive understanding of prehistoric peoples (Nelson 1997), but much more work is needed.

This chapter describes how the regions we have designated Hogback, Black Forest, Streams, and Plains vary in the resources available, particularly due to elevation, water, rockshelters, caves, and locally available raw material for tools. The Hogback subdivision provides water, food, and shelter for humans and animals along the Front Range. The Black Forest is higher than the Streams and Plains regions and catches more moisture. Therefore more trees grow, especially pines, as well as shrubs that offer a range of edible nuts and fruits. Taller trees and underbrush make the area attractive to deer and other forest animals. Natural shelter was available in the form of caves and overhangs, used by the early inhabitants to escape the elements—summer downpours, often with hail, and winter blizzards. The major streams of Greater Denver, the South Platte River and Cherry Creek, joining together in the area that became downtown Denver, offered riverine environments. These permanent streams had attractions that differed from the smaller and intermittent streams farther east. Fish and shellfish could be exploited, along with the herbs that grow in the environment of grassy riverbanks. The High Plains may appear to be relatively featureless, rolling hills with intermittent streams, but they were inhabited nonetheless. Trees and shrubs grew along the drainages, providing firewood and food and attracting animals. Variations in elevation and aspect seem to be most significant for site placement, with the tops of hills and south-facing slopes often preferred. Thus each subdivision had its own attractions and possibilities, and together they demonstrate the variety of plant, animal, and human adaptations that even a relatively small area like Greater Denver could support. The variety of habitats may partly explain why the city of Denver has continued to grow and thrive. The various regions are appreciated by current residents, with each community in the subregions having a distinct flavor, based on its elevation, views, native flora, and characteristic rock formations.

## Overview of Chronology

The humans who left evidence of their presence in Greater Denver arrived at least as early as 12,000 B.C., but the traces left by these first inhabitants are indistinct. The first people are known as Paleoindians, meaning simply ancient Indians, since there is no way for us to know what they called themselves, or even whether they had descendants in any known later group. The Archaic adaptation began about 5500 B.C., with a new emphasis on grinding stones. When pottery is added to the material culture inventory, groups are labeled Ceramic. This nomenclature for prehistoric groups in Colorado in general follows that used throughout much of North America, so it can be considered as a convenient shorthand for broad changes, rather than as a description of local adaptations (Stone 1999).

Paleoindian groups are identified by the style of their projectile points, which are often named for their place of first discovery. Standard divisions of Paleoindian are pre-Clovis (before 11,500 B.C.), Clovis (11,500–9500), identified by fluted points associated with mammoth, Folsom (9500–8500), when the major game animal was a large form now extinct, and Plano (8500–5500), associated with modern bison hunting and evidence of a more diversified subsistence base (Eighmy 1984). In fact, horses, as well as relatives of the camel, are represented in the Late Pleistocene bone piles that have been excavated, but there is little evidence that horses were hunted by early humans before becoming extinct in Colorado (although they were hunted at the same time and earlier in Europe). Several point types are grouped into the Plano time period. These include Agate Basin, Alberta, Eden, and the Cody Complex, to name those that are found in Greater Denver. Paleoindian groups thus changed their characteristic projectile points through time, continuing until 5500 B.C., when most of the very large game animals disappeared.

In Greater Denver traces of Paleoindians are found in occasional projectile points, a few stone tools associated with mammoth, and possible bone tools associated with mammoth bones (Stanford 1979). However, some large Paleoindian sites are close enough to Denver that it seems reasonable to assume that Paleoindians must have roamed this area, even if no campsites have been recognized so far. It was reported to one of us (well after the fact) that Paleoindian projectile points had been found when digging a basement for a building at Fitzsimmons Army Hospital in the 1960s, but at that time there was no mechanism for reporting such sites, or laws to require that they were properly excavated. This site, along with uncounted others, was lost to science.
Little is known of Paleoindian lifeways, although their skill as hunters and as stone knappers is much admired (Wormington 1957). Paleoindian projectile points have been found at various sites, often only a single example at a site. It is possible that these represent "curated" points—points that later people found and kept as talismans or charms.

The succeeding people are called Archaic, a term that implies both a time period and a way of life. These groups lived during a warmer and drier period (see Chapter 2) and made smaller stone points to be hafted to darts instead of spears. The presence of grinding technology and plant remains attests to the use of many plants that could be ground and eaten or used as medicine. Some evidence of dwellings and shelters is beginning to be found. Thus the Archaic peoples in the Denver Basin are better known than their predecessors. Sites dated by radiocarbon assay and evidence of changes in point styles allow archaeologists to divide the Archaic into three stages, designated as Early (5500–3000 B.C.), Middle (3000–1000), and Late (1000–1). During the Archaic time period the Hogback zone was well utilized. Whether this region was more thickly populated, or whether the sites were used only seasonally, is not yet clear, but many sites suggest seasonal occupation (Johnson et al. 1997).

The addition of pottery containers marks a change in lifeways, although archaeologists are not in complete agreement about what that change entailed locally (Scott 1993). This stage is called Ceramic and is likewise divided into three substages. Since the first pottery is similar to that known from the eastern woodlands, it is often known as Plains Woodland, an odd self-contradictory term that many archaeologists would like to discontinue, although it is deeply embedded in the literature and would be difficult to root out. Early Ceramic is an alternative name that is not much better, but it avoids the juxtaposition of plains and woodland, as well as the implication that the pottery, and perhaps the people, arrived across the plains from the eastern United States. Perhaps they did, in gradual steps—some "Plains Woodland" sites show specific associations with sites in Kansas (e.g., Hazeltine Heights), and the growing of maize was part of their culture—but the nomenclature should not prejudge the question.

Early Ceramic pots have a simple, wide-mouthed, conical shape. They are undecorated except for cord marking covering the exterior, much like pottery found throughout North America (Jennings 1968) and over much of East Asia (Nelson 1993). Too much should not be made of such resemblances. The shape is relatively easy to construct and can have a wide variety of uses, from storage to cooking to serving food. Early Ceramic pottery has two kinds of exterior treatment, one with deep cord marks and the other with the markings smoothed or occasionally obliterated. Based on a single site, Franktown Cave, this change is presumed to be chronological (Withers 1954), but more recent excavations cast some doubt on this, as the two types seem to coincide at Rock Creek.

The succeeding ceramic stage is called Middle Ceramic. The most common type of pottery is traditionally known as Upper Republican, after sites along a river of that name in Nebraska with headwaters in eastern Colorado. In Greater Denver, this pottery is uncommon, and its presence may represent only an occasional visiting group from farther east and north. Nevertheless, when the pottery is found it is a useful time marker for the period A.D. 1000–1500. The appropriateness of the term "Upper Republican" has been questioned. Because the pottery seems to be made in Greater Denver of local, not imported clays, it may have been made by the same people who made the previous pottery, who simply modified their pot shapes and exterior surfaces (Brunswig et al. 1995). Another possible explanation is that temporary visitors were in Greater Denver long enough to require new pots without becoming permanent residents. In terms of chronology, Middle Ceramic pottery coincides with groups living in earth lodges and practicing agriculture in Nebraska and Kansas, and perhaps suggests some kind of interaction between the descendants of Woodland pottery makers and people to the east. But some suggestions of contact with the peoples of the Four Corners region are also present (e.g., sandals at Franktown Cave). Thus the question of who made the pots and where they came from are unresolved. One site (Graeber Cave) with Middle Ceramic dates has clear Shoshonean affiliation. Shoshonean occupation of the mountains at this time might have discouraged horticulture in Greater Denver, for it would have made food stores vulnerable to raiding.

Pottery designated Late Ceramic is called Dismal River, again after sites in Nebraska. These are contact period sites, dated to A.D. 1500–1700 and will be discussed in the following chapter. Most sites in the plains from this time period are thought to represent Apache groups, although the Cheyenne and Arapaho groups were using the Denver region when first recorded by Euro-American explorers in the early nineteenth century. Other pottery falling into the Late Ceramic period is classified as Ute or Shoshonean, with undecorated exteriors and flat bases. Late Ceramic pottery is rare in the Denver Basin, but somewhat more common than Middle Ceramic.

## Paleoindian Sites

### A Paleoindian Recipe

*After killing a bison, cut up the carcass with a heavy, sharp stone knife and bring the hump with the tender meat near the cooking fire. With a smaller knife, cut bite-sized pieces and sharpen the ends of several thin but sturdy branches. Skewer the meat on the sticks and lay them across two piles of stones built on either side of the fire. Pieces of wild garlic or onion may be threaded on the sticks between the meat chunks. Chokecherries sweetened with honey make a tasty side dish, served in wooden bowls.*

The Paleoindian period (12,900–5500 B.C.), as noted above, is not well represented in Greater Denver (Fig. 3.4). Occasional projectile points of late Paleoindian types have been found in every division of this region, and bones of extinct animals such as horse, camel, extinct species of bison, and mammoth are not uncommon, but no site has been found in Greater Denver with stone points clearly associated with these animals.

The large Folsom site of Lindenmeier, with hundreds of projectile points, is about 100 miles to the north, and the Folsom type site is less than 200 miles to the south. The trail between the two would have followed the foothills, so it is reasonable to suppose that Paleoindians roamed the Denver area, hunting and trapping large animals and gathering berries, fruits, nuts, and other wild edibles of the foothills and high plains. Large animals were dispatched with dart points mounted on bone foreshafts (Cotter 1935a,b; Wilmsen and Roberts 1978). It is likely that a variety of snares and traps were also used, although hard evidence is lacking because the cords, ropes, and nets would have been made of perishable materials.

Several possible explanations for the scarcity of Paleoindian sites in Greater Denver can be considered. The least likely explanation is that the Paleoindians had little imperishable trash such as stone and bone. Surely like other peoples, they would have strewn the landscape with their discards. It is more conceivable that sites existed, but that they have not been recognized because it is not yet possible to discriminate the lithic debitage of other periods from that of the Paleoindians. Some surface evidence has been picked up and carried away. Finely flaked projectile points are one of the few elements of the assemblage that can be assigned with certainty to Paleoindians. These nicely crafted artifacts have been attractive to other humans who have passed through the area, and therefore the points tend to be removed soon after they become visible on the surface. The few that are found in later site assemblages may be such "curated"

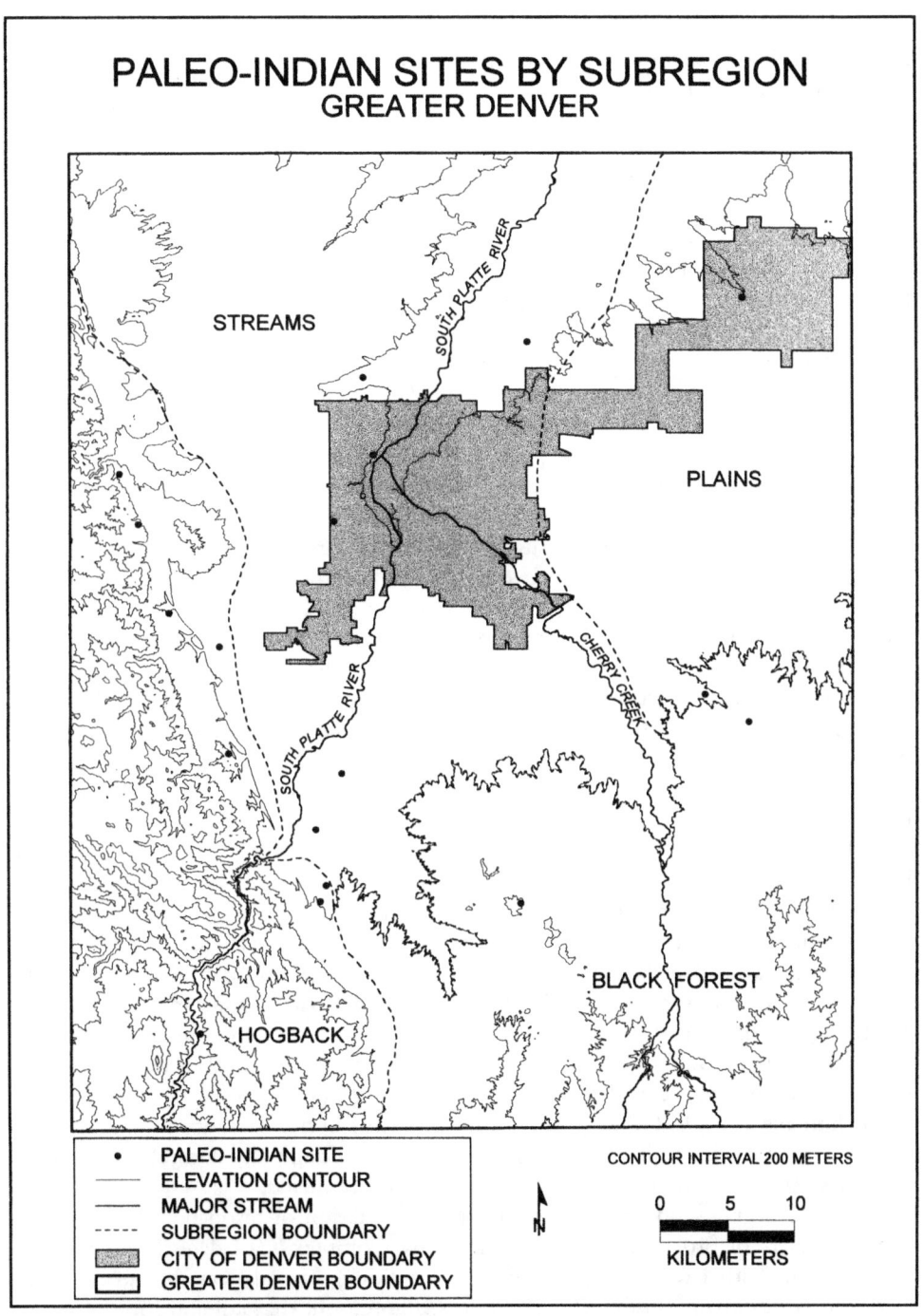

Figure 3.4. Distribution of Paleoindian sites by subregion. Francine Patterson.

points—that is, treasured by later prehistoric groups but lost again or deliberately redeposited. And it is clear from many collections made by avocational archaeologists that perhaps hundreds of Paleoindian points have been found in Greater Denver, although the precise provenience may have been lost. But while surface collecting undoubtedly has occurred, the most likely explanation of the lack of base camps is that most sites are deeply buried and are exposed only with human or natural removal of the upper soils. Both the sites of Blackwater Draw in New Mexico and Lindenmeier in northern Colorado came to light because of arroyo cutting into earlier deposits (Malde 1964). The Lamb Spring site, the only major site in Greater Denver where Paleoindian deposits have been excavated, is another deep site which was exposed only by relatively recent human activity.

Lamb Spring is a large archaeological site with extensive Pleistocene faunal remains, situated not far from the South Platte River as it emerges from the mountains. In the Late Pleistocene this spring attracted many animals, some of whose bones are found at the site. When geologists probed the site they recorded bones of mammoth, horse, camel, bison, and mountain sheep. Retouched stone flakes were found, but unfortunately they were not diagnostic of any specific time period, although they did demonstrate the work of humans at the site. Nevertheless, many of the animals whose bones are represented are known to have become extinct in the Holocene period, so there was every reason to assign the lowest levels of this site to the Paleoindian period. Lamb Spring was subsequently excavated by the Smithsonian Institution, under the direction of Waldo Wedel in 1961 and 1962 and Dennis Stanford for several seasons in the 1980s (Stanford, Wedel, and Scott 1981; Rancier, Haynes, and Stanford 1981; Fisher 1992).

Eight distinct geological strata were identified by Glenn Scott in the first probe of the site. The lowest unit, the underlying bedrock, is the Dawson Arkose, a conglomerate that forms bluffs in the Black Forest region (see Chapter 2). A jumble of bones was found in Unit 1, a blue-green silty clay just above bedrock, from which a bone collagen date of 13,140 ±1,000 years before the present (about 11,000 B.C.) was obtained. This date and Unit 1 were correlated with the Broadway alluvium of Late Pleistocene age, indicating that this layer is on the early side of the Clovis time period. Remains of about twenty-four mammoths were found at the bottom of this level, along with bones of two horses, at least eight camels, and two members of the dog family. Some of the bones were C14 dated to 11,884–11,592 B.C., again confirming the early dates. Recent coring around the site is designed to produce more refined environmental data, but it has not yet been published. Although no stone tools were found in this layer, some bones appear to have been deliberately flaked, and flakes of animal bone could have served humans as tools. Other possible indications of human activity include piles of long bones, which are unlikely to have been created through any natural agency. They could have been stacked together after the meat was removed.

Unit 2, a gray sandy clay, contained a concentration of bison bones, along with seven complete or broken points from the Cody Complex. C14 dates from this level are consistent with late Cody times. Boggy conditions in and near the spring could have aided in capturing bison. The excavators pointed out that tail and foot bones are missing, although other small and fragile bones were present. A possible explanation for the lack of these bones is that they were removed along with the hides and taken elsewhere, where the hides were processed into clothing and perhaps tents. Although bone tools such as needles and awls have rarely been preserved in Greater Denver sites, Paleoindian ancestors surely needed tailored clothing to cross the Bering land bridge, and the missing hides may be one indication of clothing here. In the Lindenmeir Folsom site, north of Fort Collins, bone needles confirm tailored clothing, and a fragment of tanned leather was found in the lowest layer of the Magic Mountain site.

Other possible evidence for early Paleoindian occupations of Greater Denver was recorded in the 1950s by Charles and Alice Hunt (Hunt 1953). The Hunts noted pieces of worked bone and charcoal eroding from Wisconsin Glacial deposits in several places along the South Platte River northeast of downtown Denver. They also recorded a split bone in the banks of Sand Creek, a piece of worked bone associated with a stone core and a scraper, and similar cut bone fragments in two sites six and eight miles east of the South Platte River in Adams County, in the area that became Denver International Airport. Except for the airport sites, these reports were not followed with further investigations, but in the light of other manifestations of possible bone tools in Colorado, they seem acceptable as Paleoindian. The Swallow site in the Hogback subregion is reported to have a possible Paleoindian level, but these findings have not been published yet. It is suggested that the Folsom point reported at Swallow may be out of context (Johnson et al. 1997:135). The nearby Crescent site has a C14 date in the Plano range, and contains a Cody knife (Stone and Mendoza 1994). Bayou Gulch has four point fragments that may represent the Plano stage. No Paleoindian burials have been found in Greater Denver, but at least one has been found in Colorado. It is an adult male flexed on the left side. Grave goods include nine stone tools, four elk teeth, and two cut mammal ribs.

Isolated Paleoindian finds are recorded in every subregion. Several Paleoindian stone projectile points have been found associated with later deposits. In the Black Forest subregion, four point fragments of Plano style were uncovered at Bayou Gulch (Gilmore 1991). A possible Plano point was found in the Senac Dam survey (Tate and Friedman 1986:33), an Alberta point was found near Parker, and an Eden point appeared in a survey of Daniels Park. In the Denver Airport survey a lithic scatter included an Eden projectile point along with a scraper and four flakes of petrified wood (Tate 1989). The site of LoDaisKa also contained a single projectile point that was attributed to the Paleoindian stage (Irwin and Irwin 1959).

> Box 3B. Nonedible Resources: Stone, Minerals, and Shell
>
> The commonest use of stone by prehistoric peoples was for making tools, followed by use as building material. Different textures and hardness of stone were needed for different purposes, and a wide variety of raw materials was available near Denver to fill those needs. Particularly notable is the local availability of petrified wood, which weathers out of the Dawson Arkose. It can be found in profusion along the Cherry Creek valley, as well as in places near the Hogback, for example on Green Mountain. Petrified wood is a good source of cryptocrystalline stone, which flakes easily and makes excellent drills and projectile points. Sandstone for metates and granites and other hard stone for manos are found in many places. The Dawson

Arkose also contains chunks of rhyolite, a stone useful for making scrapers. Known quarries of some flakable stone types are in Roxborough Park and Daniels Park, where vein quartzite and amphibolite can be obtained. Each of these quarries has a scatter of tools and debitage. Another quarry site in Roxborough was a source of quartzite, and yet another produced jasper, petrified wood, opal, and quartzite.

Some stone may come from distant sources. Amazonite is a turquoise-colored stone. It is not quarried locally, although small worked pieces were found in several sites such as Bradford House III, the Aurora burial, and Franktown Cave. Catlinite pipe fragments have been discovered at Roxborough Park and Franktown Cave, suggesting trade networks as far away as Minnesota. A steatite pipe at Bayou Gulch indicates another possibly distant source. White Knife flint from Nevada was found in one instance. Obsidian flakes and projectile points are reported, for example at most sites in the Hogback as well as Bayou Gulch, and the Moffitt site. No obsidian quarries exist in Greater Denver. Although this black, glassy stone can be obtained in various places in the Rocky Mountains, the only study intended to locate a specific source identified a place in New Mexico (Johnson et al. 1997:146).

Thermal alteration was accomplished by placing chunks of rock in a hot fire or burying them in sand under a fire. Experiments by Helen Pustmueller and Janet Clawson at the University of Denver showed that heat treatment of only 400°F changes silicified wood from mustard yellow to a dark red. Heat also produces a glassy surface, but when the material is overheated it turns grainy and circular spalls flake off the surface—a process called pot-lidding. A perhaps accidentally overheated projectile point is in the Franktown Cave collection, dark red in color and with a definite round flake popped off its surface (see Box 2C).

Ocher in different colors has been noted at several sites. At LoDaisKa four lumps of red ocher and three of yellow were recorded, as well as eleven "pigment stones." Green pigment was noted at Hazeltine Heights, and pink coloring is found on manos at Franktown Cave. Both black graphite and white talc have been found at Hogback sites and identified as pigments. Bradford House II had two lumps of ocher.

Shells were used for a variety of purposes, including tools and ornaments. Unio, clam, mussel, and Olivella shells are mentioned in various reports. Mussel shells were reported at three sites near the Chatfield Reservoir, two on Plum Creek and one on Deer Creek. Shells recorded as "freshwater clams" were found at Franktown Cave and in Hogback sites. Unio shells and their relatives are found in fresh water, but Olivella must have been traded over long distance, for they grow in shallow salt water such as the Gulf of Mexico or the Gulf of California. Thus Olivella shell is another indicator of long-distance trade among prehistoric American groups. Olivella shells so far have only been found in Early Ceramic burials, not in living sites. Perhaps they had some meaning associated with death.

## Archaic Period (5500–1 B.C.)

*An Archaic Recipe*

*Gather a basket of ripe seeds from the pigweed (amaranth) plant, and another basket of ripe seeds from goosefoot (chenopod). Grind the seeds separately on a flat stone, using an oval stream cobble. Mix the ground flour together in a skin bag, and pour on water to cover.*

*Let stand overnight. In the morning, heat small pebbles in a hot fire and add them to the skin bag one by one until the mixture thickens. Let it cool a bit, then remove the pebbles. For more flavor, chunks of prairie dog meat or bone grease can be added. Serve still warm in bowls made of hollowed-out tree knots.*

People of the Archaic period lived in shelters, buried their dead, and extensively used grinding stones and pestles to pulverize seeds and nuts into flour, implying new ways of cooking. The Archaic stage is divided into Early, Middle and Late periods recognized by changes in projectile point types. Archaic points are shorter and relatively wider than those of Paleoindians, and are provided with stems for hafting, having bilateral notching along the lower sides or edges (Box 3A). These devices are called side-notches or corner-notches depending on their placement. Sinew was probably wrapped through the notches to bind the point to the shaft.

Archaic sites in the Denver region include large sites with hearths, pits, and grinding stones, implying that they were campsites of some duration. Similar sites are also found in Nebraska (Wedel 1961). Archaic burials are individual and not in cemeteries. The largest group of individuals buried near each other in Greater Denver is three, at the Swallow site. One implication of this kind of burial is that bodies were disposed of expeditiously. Little ceremony is apparent, and the burials are often cramped with the heads weighted down with heavy stones, often used grinding slabs. Archaic dwellings and shelters are also known, allowing a great deal more to be inferred about the lifeways of the people who lived during this stretch of time than is known about the Paleoindian people in Greater Denver.

The distribution map of Archaic sites (Fig. 3.5) indicates that all subregions of Greater Denver were occupied in Archaic times. Our map does not distinguish among Early, Middle, and Late Archaic, because too few sites in the database are specified in this way. Still, an overall sense of the distribution of Archaic sites is useful. The map shows that the Archaic period is particularly well represented in the Hogback region, which seems to have been more thickly populated than elsewhere.

Archaic lifeways may have been a response to a changing climate. The Archaic period began during a time of increased average temperatures and dryness. It is regionally called the Altithermal, though a similarly warm period is known as the Climatic Optimum in Europe, where dryness was not a factor. Higher temperatures during this period have been also documented in East Asia; thus warmer temperature was a global phenomenon, but precipitation consequences differed between and even within particular localities. Local response to climate warming might have involved a movement of plant and animal resources toward and into the wetter mountains (Benedict 1985, Stone and Mendoza 1994). Temperature and precipitation fluctuated within the Altithermal (see Chapter 2). Judging from the animal bones associated with human activities, the kinds of animals that were obtained reflect a greater diversification of food habits. The change in projectile point size implies a basic change in hunting technology. Small and medium-sized animals such as deer and rabbit appear more commonly in Archaic assemblages.

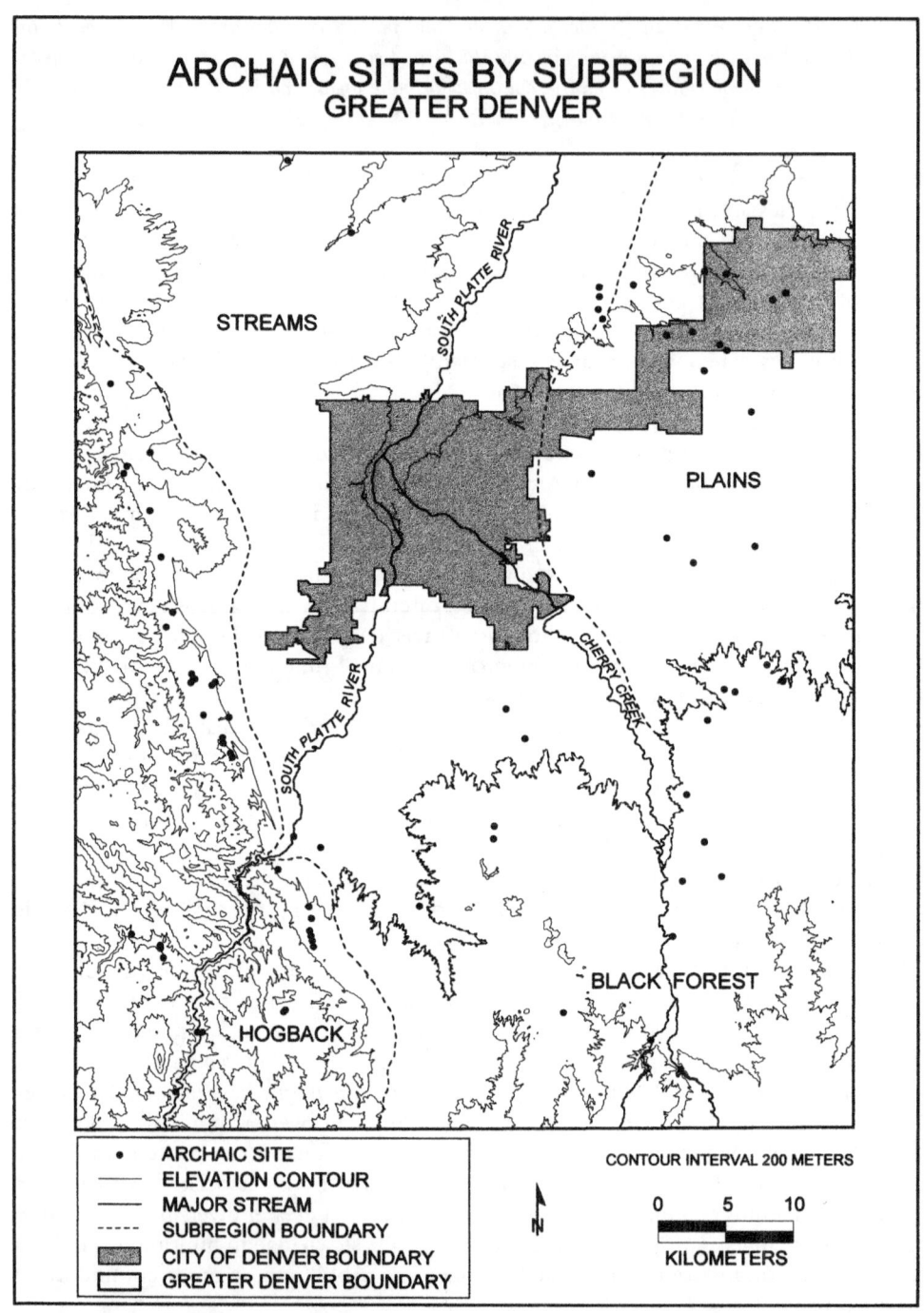

Figure 3.5. Distribution of Archaic sites by subregion. Francine Patterson.

Box 3C. Surveys

Surveys have been extremely important for locating archaeological sites in Greater Denver. Many parts of the United States became known archaeologically as a result of the River Basin Surveys based at the Smithsonian Institution. In Colorado the River Basin Surveys began as early as 1949, but much of the work took place in the 1960s and '70s, as dams began to be built. These surveys were useful for understanding the regional distribution of sites through time. Along Plum Creek (Nelson 1979a) the sites appear to be mostly Archaic, because many grinding stones were found but little pottery. In contrast, the survey of Cherry Creek Reservoir produced mostly sites with pottery (University of Denver site cards). The larger number of sites on Plum Creek than on the South Platte River may indicate a preference for the smaller stream, or it may mean that sites on the larger river disappeared under repeated episodes of alluviation and erosion.

Several areas of more recent surveys have expanded our knowledge exponentially, especially in the Plains subregion, where systematic study only began in the 1980s. For example, in the Arapaho Motorized State Recreation Area survey (Abernathy 1982), 600 acres were surveyed. Discoveries included twelve prehistoric sites and four isolated finds. All sites were lithic scatters, but even they extend our understanding of land usage. Nearby the Senac Dam survey (renamed Aurora Dam) (Tate and Friedman 1986; Tate1987; O'Neil and Tate 1987; O'Neil et al. 1988) covered 1,455 acres, recording thirty-five prehistoric sites and eight isolated finds. Of these, eight were campsites with hearths, fire-cracked rock or charcoal lenses, and ground stone. Six camps are on ridges or hilltops and two on terraces of Senac Creek. The site density is one site per thirty-five acres. Two sites were tested, one proving to be a short-term camp and the other a longer occupation. Most dates fall between A.D. 300 and 1000, within the Early Ceramic period. Faunal analysis shows the use of bison, bighorn sheep, pronghorn, deer, fox, raccoon, badger, rabbit, prairie dog, dove, grouse, and turtle. Seasonality studies indicate that the site was occupied mostly in the spring.

The cultural resource inventory of Roxborough Park covered an area of about 750 acres. One of the most interesting finds of the Roxborough survey is the large size of the sites—a number of them cover several acres, and some are stratified multicomponent campsites. For example, an Archaic to Woodland campsite covered 2,700 square meters and another Archaic site was at least 11,000 square meters. The site density was 40 sites in 750 acres. Quarries for locally used stone raw materials were another important find (Tate 1979). The density of sites along Parker Road was astounding. Overall, more than one site per mile was located; in the five miles or so north of Franktown, a site was found about every half mile (Miller and Fiero 1977).

In the Betts Ranch survey, it was similarly discovered that most campsites were near Cherry Creek (Tate, Mutaw, and Friedman 1989). Many quarry sites with multiple loci were located in several surveys. These groups of quarries are found where silicified wood erodes from the Dawson Arkose (Mutaw and Tate 1990; Joyner 1988; Shields 1993). The Highlands Ranch survey also identified stone quarries (Burney et al. 1979). Other surveys for transportation, such as those for the new international airport (Chandler, Reed, and Horn 1989; Chandler 1989), the C-470 surveys (Graham 1996; Jepson 1990; Joyner 1988) and the Centennial Airport studies, allow a sense of just how dense prehistoric sites must be in unexplored parts of Greater Denver.

## Early Archaic, 5500–3000 B.C.

Lifeways changed noticeably with the shift from Paleoindian to Archaic. As noted above, a pattern of global warming began during the period designated Early Archaic; the local consequence was considerable desiccation on the High Plains. As a result, even in the Hogback region, which probably was the most agreeable to human habitation, Early Archaic sites are few. For the Archaic in general, ground stone is found in abundance, suggesting more intensive use of plant foods, especially nuts and seeds. Possibly new ways to make food more lasting and more portable (for example by drying) were also invented. Furthermore, seeds and nuts are storable and might have been cached when abundance exceeded need. Some storage pits have been found at Archaic sites.

Another Archaic invention is the pithouse. Pithouses are known to have been used in Rocky Mountain sites, for example at the Yarmony site along the Colorado River, which dates between 5500 and 5000 B.C. (Metcalf and Black 1991). Similar pithouses have not been found in Greater Denver during the Early Archaic period, but this lack may be due to the fact that other shelter was available in rock overhangs and shelters in the Hogback and the Black Forest. Why construct a shelter when nature had provided a choice of shelters? The knowledge of how to make houses in open sites was certainly available, and materials for their construction were at hand. The scarcity of recognizable Early Archaic sites is notable.

Characteristic Early Archaic projectile points are found in several sites. The local sequences of the Archaic are based on a deeply stratified site in the Hogback called Magic Mountain. At Magic Mountain, Early Archaic points were found in Unit 7, undated but older than about 4000 B.C., the oldest date from the stratum above it. The Rock Creek site also contained well dated Early Archaic pits and hearths. An early Archaic projectile point was found in situ at a lower level of the Bayou Gulch site (Gilmore 1991:66) in the Black Forest subregion. It is impossible to identify Early Archaic sites without projectile points or radiocarbon dates, so it is unknown how dense such sites really were. However, what is known suggests that sites were sparse but widespread.

### Hogback Early Archaic

Hogback sites have defined the Early Archaic period. In particular, the Magic Mountain complex from the site of that name continues to be a reference point. The projectile points are large corner-notched and side-notched points.

Magic Mountain is an unusual site for this region because it is not within a rockshelter but beside one of the water gaps in the Hogback. The Early Archaic manifestation in Zone F, the lowest level excavated, includes prismatic blades with modifications to form specific tools, especially end scrapers (Fig. 3.6). Microliths were also fashioned into scrapers, perforators, and knives. Many grinding stones were found, including base stones with deep basins indicating a pounding motion instead of the later flatter base stones used with a back and forth movement of the upper stone. In addition, there were large tools such as choppers of several types. The Early Archaic living area appears to have been small, perhaps 30 meters long by 10 meters wide, stretching along the stream.

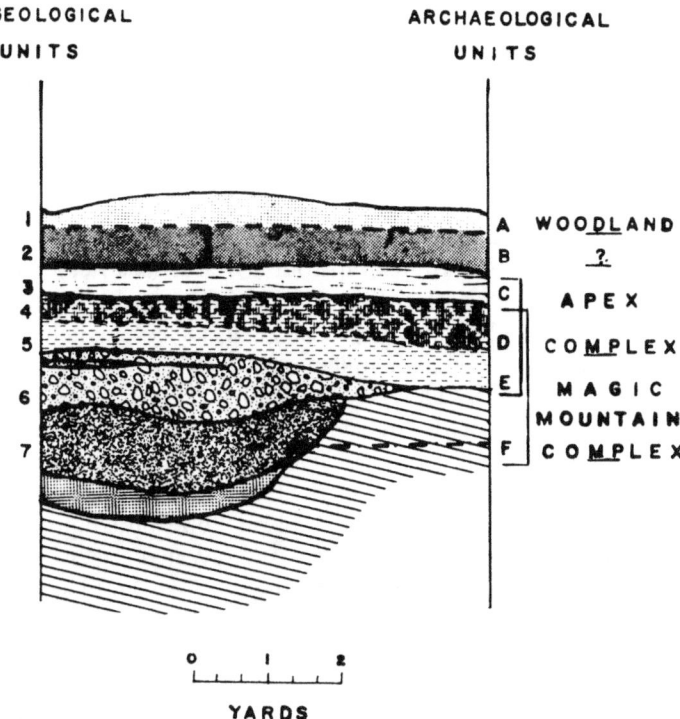

Figure 3.6. Magic Mountain archaeological and geological levels. From Cynthia C. Irwin-Williams and Henry T. Irwin, "Excavations at Magic Mountain: A Diachronic Study of Plains-Southwest Relations," *Denver Museum of Natural History Proceedings* 12 (1966); reproduced by permission.

An outcrop of the Fountain Formation, which was covered up by later deposits, may have provided some shade during parts of the day. This may explain why almost all the grinding stones were found within two meters of it. Two stone-lined hearths were at the edge of the rock as well.

The large number of projectile points and scrapers has been interpreted as indicating dependence on hunting and the use of skins (Irwin-Williams and Irwin 1966:182). However, the grinding stones suggest plant usage as well—perhaps nuts pounded in the deep basins.

Zone F also produced two pieces of engraved bone. One is roundish and flat, with diagonal lines in two directions. The other is probably made on a rib fragment with incised horizontal lines. These may be evidence of Archaic games. An unusual pattern of preservation allowed some perishable artifacts to survive. These include seven pieces of wood, of which two are definitely worked. One resembles a dart shaft that was found at the nearby site of LoDaisKa. A fragment of leather confirms the fact that the tanning process was known and used.

Bradford House III is an example of an Early Archaic occupation of a rockshelter. It occupies an area of 25 by 5 meters. Among the 1400 artifacts cataloged, evidence of Early Archaic included the characteristic Magic Mountain (MM3) projectile points. A storage cist was surrounded by a curved stone wall, with three layers of rock. No artifacts were found within the cist fill, but it belongs to the Archaic layers, and was deeper than some MM3 projectile points. Massey Draw has an Early Archaic hearth as well as a rock concentration or possible alignment.

At the Crescent rockshelter, Early Archaic projectile points were found (Stone and Mendoza 1994). C14 determination from a hearth in a deep backhoe trench in front of the shelter, as well as a hearth from the shelter itself, produced dates around 4200 B.C. (Ford 1983). Other sites with Early Archaic levels include Dancing Pants shelter with dates back to the sixth millennium B.C., LoDaisKa level D (Irwin and Irwin 1959, 1961), and the Swallow site, which has dates beginning about 4200 B.C. The Helmer Ranch site has Early Archaic projectile points as well, and a date of 3792 B.C. Cherry Gulch and Falcon's Nest also have Early Archaic projectile points.

The Massey Draw site was located by the Colorado Department of Transportation, anticipating the construction of C-470. A bison bone protruding from a road cut called attention to the site. On excavation the site revealed two activity areas, a campsite and a bison processing area, occupied during the Early and Late Archaic. Based on the age of the young bison, the site seems to have been used during the spring season. Only some carcass segments were transported to the site, implying that killing and butchering took place elsewhere. This appears to have been the "kitchen" area. Final processing at the site indicated the use of bones for marrow (Anderson et al. 1994, Jepson 1994).

The Massey Draw site throws some light on plant resources in the Early Archaic. Around 5000 B.C., during the Altithermal, more weedy seed species such as chenopods and amaranths (goosefoot and pigweed) were found, and less artimesia (sage) and trees. Some chenopods were identified on a mano, showing that the seeds were ground and presumably used for food. Since there are no archaeologically visible containers, we must assume the seeds were ground and cooked in baskets or leather containers by the stone-boiling method. Other plant remains, including rose hips, sunflowers, and others, were probably used for food or medicine.

*Black Forest Early Archaic*

The major site in the Black Forest region with indications of Early Archaic settlement is Bayou Gulch. At this site a corner-notched Early Archaic point lay on top of the Altithermal soil (Gilmore 1991). Several projectile points resembling MM3 types were found at Franktown Cave in the lowest levels, so this may indicate another Early Archaic occupation not far away. Cherry Creek Canyon rockshelter has a few indicators as well. It is hard to understand why this region would not have been more frequented, since its extra altitude allows trees to grow, giving more shelter to deer and other game. Perhaps it is represented among the numerous lithic scatters, most of which lack diagnostic artifacts.

*Plains Early Archaic*

The important site of Monaghan Camp was unearthed courtesy of Denver International Airport. Because the site was located between concourses A and B, after it was excavated it had to be bulldozed for construction of the concourses. The area was well known to local collectors, who have been surface-collecting the region for at least half a century, especially as tools and pottery appeared on the surface after plowing.

The site occupied the top of a low knoll. Excavations covering almost 50 square meters unearthed numerous hearths, some lined with stone slabs. Occupations from the Middle and Late as well as Early Archaic appear to be represented. Small and medium-sized mammal bones were found, but they were too fragmentary for specific identification. Perhaps this is the earliest evidence of processing bones for marrow and bone grease. Chenopod and amaranth seeds were collected and ground into flour, and resources from the foothills and mountains were collected. Traces of allium, a plant that grows in the mountains and is used for medicine rather than food, are found in this plains site, indicating that people ranged widely from their dwellings to obtain the various resources they needed (Tucker 1990). Some Early Archaic concentrations of fire-cracked rock and ground stone represent the Early Archaic at Peste Negra, on the Rocky Mountain Arsenal (Clark 1997).

*Streams Early Archaic*

At the Rock Creek site an Early Archaic layer is reported in the fifth millennium B.C. For the most part, Early Archaic sites on the banks of the larger streams are probably covered in alluvium from numerous floods and will be found only accidentally.

---

Box 3D. STRUCTURES

Various kinds of structures have been found in Greater Denver, most of them dating to the Early Ceramic period, but it is important in this regard to note that structures are known in Colorado and nearby states dating back to the Archaic period. There are various indications of structures not only at Hell Gap, in southeastern Wyoming (Irwin-Williams et al. 1973), but even in the high Rocky Mountains of Colorado, for example, at Windy Gap and the Yarmony site.

Structures are found in a variety of forms, made with different materials. These include pithouses at Box Elder-Tate Hamlet (Tate et al. 1989) and possibly Bayou Gulch (Gilmore 1991); stone walls one to three courses high at Magic Mountain (Kalasz et al. 1995), as well as in Roxborough Park and at Hall-Woodland Cave (Nelson 1967); lean-tos in Ken-Caryl Ranch (Adkins 1993) and at Dancing Pants shelter (Wallace and Friedman 1985); and stone circles in Rocky Flats and several sites in the Kassler Quad (University of Denver site cards). Jackson Creek has a suggestion of structures in charred logs associated with cobbles and stone rings associated with an Early Ceramic occupation (Wynn, Huber, and McDonald 1985). The George W. Lindsay Ranch site features two squarish stone enclosures from a Woodland occupation, identified as such by 144 small corner-notched projectile points, seven ovoid bifaces, and 27 cord-marked sherds. The structures are 1.3 meters apart, each roughly 4 meters on a side. Structure A contained a hearth;

> structure B had three hearths and a storage pit, 8 inches deep and 14 inches across in diameter. In addition to projectile points, other tools included scrapers, knives, polished stones, a ground stone fragment, and utilized flakes (Nelson 1971). A site near the South Platte that has since disappeared was recorded as having "some twenty-five prehistoric house foundations" in 1955 and was still noted in 1976 as containing "15 tipi rings" (University of Denver site cards). Some sites are gone forever, but excavation techniques have improved over the years. As more excavations are conducted in Greater Denver, the time periods, density, and distribution of habitation structures will become better understood.

## Middle Archaic (3000–1000 B.C.)

By the Middle Archaic, people were occupying the Black Forest and Plains and Streams subregions. The droughts were in the past, and more water was available away from the foothills, greening these regions at least seasonally and improving the habitat for the people and the plants and animals they depended on for food. The bones of many present faunal species are found in sites, including mammals such as deer, antelope, bison, and bobcat, a variety of smaller mammals including prairie dog and rabbit, as well as birds, turtles, and freshwater clams. Artifacts diagnostic of the Middle Archaic include several varieties of large projectile points with indented bases, belonging to the McKean complex. A wide diversity of tools, including knives, scrapers, spokeshaves, and drills made by chipping stone, and grinding stones including both handstones (manos) and shaped grinding slabs (metates), reflect varied activities. Although there has been no evidence in Greater Denver, we should be mindful that perishable artifacts have been found elsewhere. For example, Mummy Cave contained coiled basketry, plant fiber, cordage, netting, leather trimming, and grinding stones (Husted 1978).

> **Box 3E. Dogs**
>
> There is no definite evidence of the existence of domesticated dogs, but it is likely that dogs had already been domesticated in Siberia and accompanied Paleoindians across the Bering Strait. Stone circles have been reported from Middle Archaic sites north of Colorado (Frison 1978). If the small stone circles imply the use of tents, these may indicate the use of dogs to pull the tents on a device called a travois (Kehoe 1960; Powell 1990). Other evidence of the dog family is equally elusive, but slim data are present in every time period except Paleoindian (Wood 1998:4). A canid bone was found at Lamb Spring, but this could belong to a wolf or other undomesticated animal of the dog family. Bayou Gulch had a bead made from canine metapodial in the Middle Archaic, about 1700 B.C. At Bradford House III, a pendant made from a canine tooth was found from the Early Ceramic. None of these are necessarily from domesticated animals. Dog bones were present at Box Elder-Tate Hamlet (Tucker, Tate, and Mutaw 1992) as well as at Hall-Woodland cave (Nelson 1967). Most interestingly, blood residue analysis on stone tools at Rock Creek shows that dogs were butchered (Gleichman, Gleichman, and Karhu 1995). This could indicate either that domesticated dogs were used for food or that wild canids were skinned for their pelts.

## Hogback Middle Archaic

At Magic Mountain the Apex Complex is the name given to artifacts from Middle to Late Archaic times. In Zone D, the most unusual artifact was a stone engraved with an anthropomorphic stick figure. Besides changes in projectile points, Zone D is characterized by an increase in side scrapers and a decline in end scrapers. Also notable are the addition of choppers and leaf-shaped bifaces (probably knives). The implications of these tool changes are not well understood. A change in scraper shape could relate to different sizes of hides, whereas choppers and knives are likely to be food preparation equipment. Perhaps a shift to smaller game explains both differences. Atlatl weights were found in this level. An artifact that may have been a pendant or possibly a plummet was also present.

Middle Archaic is defined at Bradford House III by McKean points and an atlatl weight. The features excavated included 21 hearths, a storage cist, and a human burial. The Archaic hearths contained up to 90 cobbles and were mostly found along the drip line, an arrangement often noted in rockshelters, perhaps because it is the best placement to keep the fires sheltered from rain or snow yet allow the maximum amount of smoke to escape.

Falcon's Nest contained an important Middle Archaic component, dated around 2000 B.C. The site is in a sandstone outcrop on the western side of the Hogback. This large (20 x 20 m) south-facing shelter produced about 5000 cataloged artifacts, including pottery, knives, scrapers, bone beads, and small corner-notched projectile points. Three burials were found: an adult male, an adult female, and an infant buried with the woman. Other features included 52 hearths. The majority of the animal bones are from deer (Adkins and Kurtz 1993; Adkins 1976; Rathbun 1977). Frank Adkins and Carolyn Kurtz (1993) quote a member of the Colorado Archaeological Society as reporting "intense McKean" activity in Waterton Canyon before industrial activities destroyed the sites. This is borne out by University of Denver site cards, which record both Archaic and Ceramic sites quite densely in this area.

Cherry Gulch is a mostly Archaic open site near Red Rocks Park. A series of projectile points give good indication of the ages of the strata. In approximately the middle of the site (by depth) was a layer of fire-cracked rock, called the "fire rock midden," which is described as "much like a cobbled floor" (Nelson 1981:5). In the light of subsequent finds at other sites, it is conceivable that the concentration actually does represent a stone floor, made of previously used cobbles. It was specifically noted that no charcoal was present, although the rocks were blackened. Manos, scrapers, and probable knives were found throughout the deposits.

Crescent rockshelter, near Deer Creek, is a shelter four meters in depth, with a midden (trash heap) sloping down hill from the shelter. It was excavated by the Colorado Archaeological Society and the University of Denver in the 1980s, and in the 1990s by field schools from Metropolitan State and the University of Colorado at Denver. During the first year of the Archaeological Society-University of Denver excavation, a sampling strategy was designed, and all artifacts and ecofacts were plotted. One of the goals of this three-dimensional plotting was to identify living floors. Results showed that living floors could be recognized that sloped slightly downward toward the front of the cave (Ford 1983; Nelson, Plooster, and Ford 1987) (Fig. 3.7). In subsequent excavations a burial was found outside the shelter. Hearths, ash, and burned rock were the major features encountered. Resource procurement at the site through time was found to change little from Archaic to Early Ceramic times (Mendoza 1993, Stone and Mendoza 1994).

The Olson site is a small, shallow rockshelter with an area of approximately 100 square feet. It has southeast exposure and is located just south of Colorow Cave (see Chapter 4). Levels 6 through 9 appear to be the result of Archaic occupations. This is further supported by the fact of more ground stone implements in the lower levels. Pieces of unworked bone and bone tools are scattered relatively evenly throughout all nine levels, suggesting that preservation is relatively good. The site collection includes mostly chipped stone debitage. Excavation also showed that two major rockfalls occurred since the site was first occupied. Based on the number of artifacts found in each level, Levels 9 through 6 show increasingly intense occupation of the site up to the Early Ceramic boundary (Olson 1973; Goetz 1996).

Hogback sites that have evidence of middle Archaic include Dutch Creek, which contains an unlined basin designated as a hearth, and LoDaisKa, where the third level included projectile points related to the McKean complex.

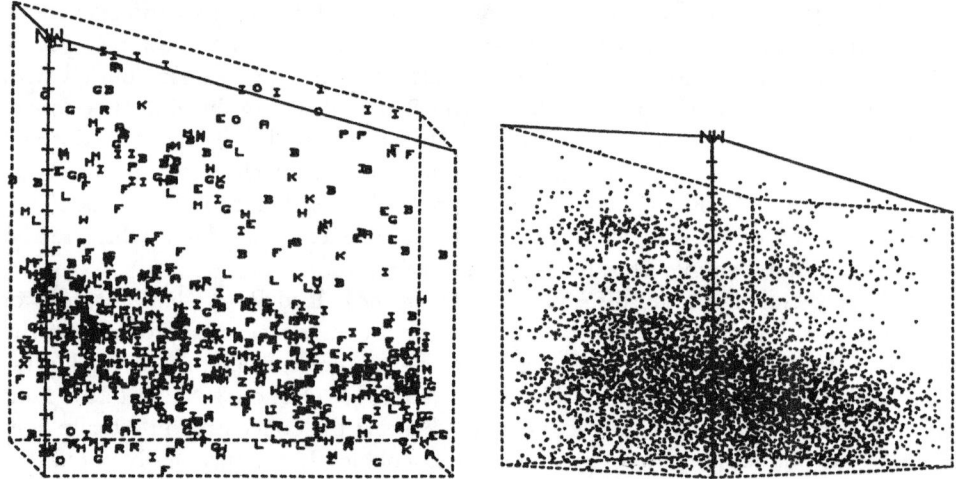

Figure 3.7. Living floors identified in Crescent rockshelter, grid square D-9, where prehistoric surfaces have nearly the same slope as the present surface (upper line). Ticks along the northwest corner are at 10-cm intervals. Left, artifacts (azimuth 275°, elevation 5°); at least two levels can be distinguished, with greater density of material at the lower level. Right, bone pieces, with locations known to within a 50x50x10-cm space (azimuth 310°, elevation 3°) and specific points assigned with a random number generator; four separate layers can be perceived. From Sarah Milledge Nelson, Myron Plooster, and David L. Ford, "An Interactive Computer Graphic Technique for Identifying Occupation Surfaces in Deep Archaeological Sites," *Journal of Field Archaeology* 14 (1987); reproduced by permission.

Dancing Pants shelter is the only site in the foothills that falls within the region we designated as Greater Denver. We include it under the Hogback region as the nearest approximation. It was occupied from the sixth millennium B.C. to the fourteenth century A.D., with some gaps. An interesting feature of this rockshelter is that rocks were added to natural boulders to make a wall, and upright granite slabs with rocks placed between a dry laid stone structure were found in the rear of the shelter, possibly for storage. The slab-lined floor was similar to stone cists for seed storage found at LoDaisKa. In addition, post impressions in two features suggest that a lean-to was constructed over the front of the shelter. Most hearths were in this area, just under the drip line as in several of the Hogback shelters. Macroflora found in the rear of the shelter near a paved area included ground nut, cheno-ams, high-spine compositas, opuntia cactus, and other plants. A mano wash showed evidence that chenopods and amaranths were ground, presumably for food. Pollen of pine, goosefoot, pigweed, groundnut, buckwheat, potato/tomato, sunflower, cactus, kinnikinnick, and raspberry was found in the soil samples. Less common plants represented were mint, legumes, rose, spiderwort, and grass. These findings are consistent with current flora now found near the site. Among the faunal remains, mule deer is the most common. Elk and mountain sheep were also present in smaller numbers. Many small animals were represented, including rabbits, rodents, and several birds, some with bright colored feathers that were probably used for ornamenting clothing or baskets. The most common stone was identified as jasper from the Trout Creek area in Chaffee County in the Rockies, where many campsites are found. Other rock types were linked to probable sources in the Denver region (Wallace and Friedman 1985; Liestman and Kranzush 1987).

*Black Forest Middle Archaic*

As for Early Archaic times, little in the Greater Denver region is reported as Middle Archaic. However, Bayou Gulch Feature 14 has dates close to 1700 B.C., and points resembling the McKean Complex. Archaic occupations are found in Stratum 2a (Fig. 3.8). They include a wide variety of mano types and a bone bead made from a canid metapodial (Gilmore 1991). A survey of Castlewood Canyon Sate Park also turned up a McKean point (Eddy et al. 1981).

*Plains Middle Archaic*

Box Elder-Tate Hamlet is a large campsite discovered in the spring of 1989 during the survey for Denver International Airport. The site covers 29,000 square meters and is located on the north slope of a low ridge south of Second Creek (Tate et al. 1989). While it is best known for its Early and Middle Ceramic pithouses, one of the hearths was dated to the Middle Archaic and another in close proximity is assumed to be contemporaneous. Neither of the Middle Archaic hearths contained plant materials, only animal remains, while the other hearths contained both (Tucker, Tate, and Mutaw 1992). Monaghan Camp likewise has evidence of Middle Archaic settlement. Other evidence was found in Arapahoe County along the E-420 right of way (Graham 1996).

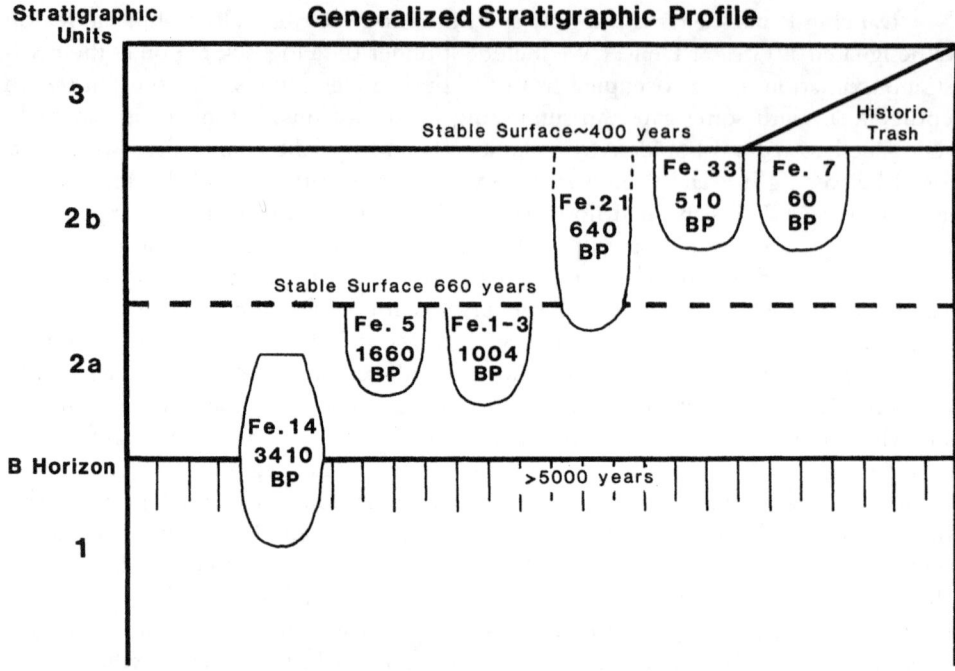

Figure 3.8. Generalized profile of the sediments at the Bayou Gulch site. From Kevin P. Gilmore, "Bayou Gulch: Geoarchaeology of a Multicomponent Site in Central Colorado" (master's thesis, University of Colorado); reproduced by permission.

*Streams Middle Archaic*

Rock Creek has Middle Archaic dates in the vicinity of 1400–1500 B.C.; as with all stages of the Archaic, few sites are found in the Streams subregion. Middle Archaic projectile points, however, have been found by collectors.

### Late Archaic (1000–0 B.C.)

Late Archaic levels are often found in multicomponent sites. They are characterized by a wider variety of game species in the site, presumably indicating a more varied diet. Increase in plant use is implied by an increase in ground and pecked stone tools. Large corner-notched projectile points, large side-notched points, and triangular expanding stem points are diagnostic of the Late Archaic. More intensive use of the Black Forest subregion is particularly evident in a larger number of sites, which include more campsites than lithic scatters. It is notable that virtually all Late Archaic sites also have an Early Ceramic component. Perhaps the fact that the same locations were utilized indicates continuity between the groups, in spite of the additions of pottery and maize with the groups we designate as Early Ceramic. Or perhaps the overlap in C14 dates indicates peaceful coexistence between people with Early Ceramic and Late Archaic lifeways.

## Hogback Late Archaic

The evidence for Late Archaic sites in the Hogback is found at intermittent sites along the water gaps. In the Dutch Creek site, seven hearths could be dated, of which one, a rock-filled hearth, was from the Late Archaic. Faunal material included bison, deer, pronghorn, elk, cottontails, jackrabbit, marmot, and rodent (Gilmore 1989).

A relatively shallow site was discovered eroding from the banks of Van Bibber Creek, which cuts through the Dakota sandstone. The excavated areas were divided into three levels, designated Zones A, B, and C. The deepest layer, Zone C, was only 20–35 inches below ground surface. Many large bones had been split but not burned, indicating marrow extraction. Six projectile points, three end scrapers, and two pieces of ground stone were found, perhaps part of a grinding slab and hand stone. A radiocarbon date of 190 B.C. was obtained. Zone B had two areas of rock piles consisting of manos and metate fragments, mostly fire blackened. These may be the contents of roasting pits that reused ground stone artifacts. Corner-notched projectile points, a single bone bead, three knives, and two scrapers were found, as well as a flesher made from a deer or elk long bone. A great many grinding stones, including both manos and metates, were uncovered. Dates fall in the Late Archaic and Early Ceramic age ranges (Nelson 1969). At Massey Draw around 500 B.C. large quantities of artimesia pollen are found, possibly brought in on larger sticks that were used for fuel or to erect a shelter (Cummings 1994). The Swallow site had Late Archaic projectile points at a depth of about one meter. Hearths are basin-shaped and lined with stones.

Late Archaic burials are found in the Hogback. At Magic Mountain, three burials were found, each under a stone cairn, including some grinding slabs. Some simple grave goods were present (Irwin-Williams and Irwin 1966: 195–96). Two burials were unearthed in the interior of the shelter (Colorado Archaeological Society 1986). Bradford House III had a Late Archaic flexed burial, in a pit with the head at the bottom and two metates placed over the skull. The date is around 500 B.C., roughly contemporaneous with Massey Draw.

## Black Forest Late Archaic

In the Black Forest subregion, Late Archaic projectile points are found in the Early Ceramic time period. At Bayou Gulch, a Late Archaic type with large corner notches was possibly associated with Feature 5, dated at A.D. 310, quite late for Archaic but consistent with the fact that Late Archaic projectile points are often found mixed with the lowest Early Ceramic levels. Franktown Cave has a lower hearth with Late Archaic style projectile points, but it calibrates to A.D. 229–390, falling within the Early Ceramic range. Other Late Archaic projectile points were found at Cherry Creek Canyon (Thompson 1956).

## Plains and Streams Late Archaic

In the Plains, Monaghan Camp, Box Elder-Tate Hamlet, and the Moffitt site all had evidence of Late Archaic occupation. The Moffitt site, like those in the Black Forest, contained

Late Archaic projectile point styles associated with the Early Ceramic stage (Tucker 1994; Tate 1991). The considerable overlap of these stages needs better documentation and consideration of whether they represent two groups of people simultaneously, different activities, or other causes. Late Archaic is not commonly found in the Streams subregion.

## CERAMIC SITES
### Early Ceramic, A.D. 1–1000

*An Early Ceramic Recipe*

*Grind maize on a grinding stone until it becomes a fine, even flour. Add water and shape into balls about the size of a fist. Flatten each ball by patting in both hands until the dough becomes a thin round. Heat a flat stone and grease it with bison fat. Cook very quickly on the stone. Fold the resulting "tortilla" in half and fill with chunks of deer meat that have been boiled in a pot. Garnish with wild greens cooked in another pot. May be eaten with the fingers.*

The Ceramic period is marked by the addition of pottery (see Box 3F), as well as a shift to smaller projectile points, which is thought to indicate use of the bow and arrow. Maize (corn) is found in several sites, raising questions about where and how it was grown. The people who made the pottery lived in medium-sized settlements. The Hogback area contains the largest number of sites with Woodland pottery, but the other subdivisions also have a substantial number of sites (Fig. 3.9).

Although, as we have seen, Archaic burials are known, many more burials are found in the Early Ceramic period. They tend to be in cemeteries. That is, individuals were buried in an area that was set aside for the dead, rather than in the midden or singly. Two such cemeteries are at Hazeltine Heights and Magic Mountain; both were partly destroyed before they could be properly excavated. Burial grounds imply more permanence in settlement than individual burials do, as well as claims to land.

Investing time in making dwellings also implies some permanence. Dry-laid masonry structures have been found, although only at a few sites. The walls are only two or three stones high and probably served as the base of a dwelling with a superstructure of hide.

### Hogback Early Ceramic

At Magic Mountain the Early Ceramic occupation includes cord-marked pottery, small corner-notched projectile points, grinding slabs with shallow basins, and flat slabs. "Charm stones," smooth polished pebbles, were found in this level as well. Whereas the earlier excavation was divided into two Ceramic zones, A and B, the most recent excavators believe that A and B should be considered as one unit based on the features excavated. One of the most interesting discoveries in the new excavations is the presence of architectural elements. These include the Lower Feature 11 and Upper Feature 9 structures, which include a floor and a low wall. Both features are constructed from cobbles and boulders immediately available in the stream debris. Feature 9 has a tamped

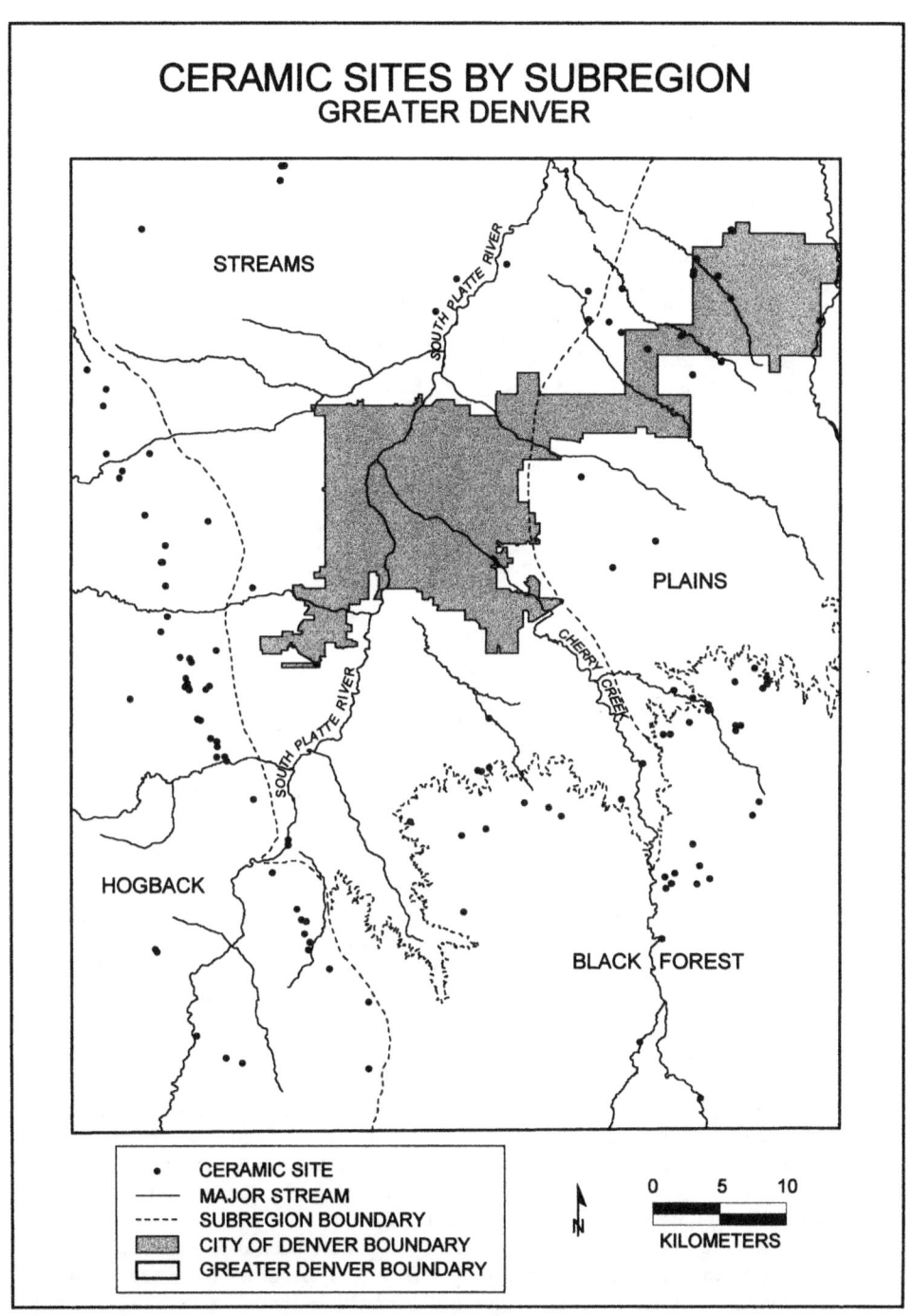

Figure 3.9. Distribution of Ceramic period sites by subregion. Francine Patterson.

Figure 3.10. Structures at Magic Mountain. Photograph by Harold S. Nelson.

sandstone floor (Fig. 3.10). The two features have very similar C14 dates, and roughly the same boundaries, which may be evidence for reuse of the site. The artifact distribution is different, however, between the upper and lower features. There is dense lithic and faunal debris outside Feature 11, which is interpreted as a midden, not an activity area. Concentration B in Feature 9, on the other hand, has a high percentage of formal tools. The artifacts are distributed more inside than outside, suggesting a work area with prepared floor rather than a dwelling (Kalasz et al. 1996).

> Box 3F. Plains Woodland Ceramics
>
> The Woodland ceramics discovered in Greater Denver so far are exclusively wide-mouthed pots with pointed bases, paddled all over the exterior with cord marking. Several nearly complete pots have been found, some in contexts that suggest they were sunk in the ground and presumably used for storage. A nearly whole pot, known as the Lilian Mee vessel, was found east of Parker Road (Ellwood 1983). The pot was said to come from a pit, but later excavation was disappointing (Joyner 1989). It is 22.5 cm high and has the conical base of Woodland pottery, but with a slightly incurving rim. The exterior appears to be brushed rather than cord-marked. A C14 date obtained from the pit in which the pot was recovered is about A.D. 600 (Kalasz et al. 1996), which fits well within the known Woodland range.
>
> Another almost complete pot was found in the Rocky Mountain Arsenal. It is similar to the Mee vessel. The reconstructed Franktown Cave pot is missing all parts of its conical bottom, suggesting that it might have been deliberately broken to be set in the ground, like the Mee pot (Fig. 3.11). Another half vessel from Rainbow Creek in the Hogback region is illustrated here, with the accompanying artifacts (Fig. 3.12).

Figure 3.11. Nearly complete Woodland jar from Franktown Cave. Photograph on file at the University of Denver.

Figure 3.12. Partial Woodland pot and other artifacts from Rainbow Creek. Photograph on file at the University of Denver.

> The transition from Early to Middle Ceramic pottery is not well understood. Ann Johnson studied the ceramics collected in the Denver International Airport survey, and divided them into two types, one typical of Plains Woodland, and the other which she assigned to the Smoky Hill tradition from Kansas (Tate et al. 1989). The latter is now regarded as more likely to be Upper Republican (Marcia Tate, personal communication). Priscilla Ellwood (1983, 1987) found differences in the Bayou Gulch ceramics, but they were coexistent in most of the layers, so they cannot be used as time markers. One type is coarse, and may be for cooking and storage, while the other is made with finer clay. On this type the cord marks are more distinct than on the other. The Rock Creek site demonstrates continuity between the earlier deeply cord-marked and later smoothed or brushed types. Ellwood has studied all the reconstructed Woodland pots. She finds that the pottery seems to be made from local clay and tempers.
>
> In his surveys in the 1920s, E. B. Renaud noted that Woodland pottery sites cluster in the region we have called Greater Denver. Even with considerable additional work, this pattern continues to hold. Whether the Early Ceramic sites represent a group that became detached from its eastern counterparts, or whether it was an offshoot that maintained connections with groups farther east, it is significantly different from any western pottery and stands out as intrusive.

At Bradford House III, about 200 sherds of cord-marked Early Ceramic pottery and small corner-notched points were found in the upper levels, along with polished bone awls, two bone beads, a bone gaming piece, and a canine tooth pendant. Macroflora from the site included acorns, pits from wild plants such as chokecherries, and squash seeds (Medina 1974, 1975). No wild squash is found in the area, so unless they are a contamination from historic times, as Linda Scott Cummings and Thomas E. Montoux (1997) believe, they are so far unique. If the squash seeds are prehistoric, further reassessment of Early Ceramic cultivation is required.

At Willowbrook, Early Ceramic hearths consisted of unlined pits, one of which had a radiocarbon date of about A.D. 700. Flaked stone artifacts included 23 projectile points, scrapers, bifaces, drills, manos, a pestle, and an ax. A bone awl and cord-marked ceramics were also found (Leach 1966). Only five sherds (all cord-marked) were found in the upper levels of Cherry Gulch, indicating a small Early Ceramic occupation. Crescent also has series of dates in Early Ceramic, although, only eight cord-marked sherds were found, among more than 10,000 animal bones and 5,000 lithics. This suggests several hypotheses. Perhaps little pottery was used at the site. Perhaps people were unusually careful about breakage. Broken pottery might have been reused. Or the sherd discard area of the site has not been found.

Van Bibber Creek sherds are found in Zone A, including cord-marked, surface-roughened, and plain varieties. This layer was very close to the surface. It included both corner-notched and side-notched projectile points, along with cutting tools, scrapers, a drill, an atlatl weight, a complete metate, and four manos.

The uppermost layer at LoDaisKa contained ceramics and corncobs. The excavators believed that the pottery was related to Fremont sites farther west, but subsequent research has thrown some doubt on this conclusion. The second stratum was called

Plains Woodland, with cord-marked potsherds and corner-notched projectile points. Maize was also found in this level (Irwin and Irwin 1959).

The Swallow site is beneath a small overhang in a sandstone bluff. The shelter was used intermittently over a long period, between 4200 B.C. and A.D. 1200. A lean-to structure, possibly of Early Ceramic age, extended the sheltered area. The Early Ceramic occupation has many hearths ringed by large cobbles. Parts of a bison leg were recovered, but most of the bones were from deer. This preponderance of deer bone indicates a more specialized diet than in the Archaic. Bone beads and bone awls were also found (Colorado Archaeological Society 1986). In the upper layers of Falcon's Nest, bone beads and small corner-notched points were present.

Hall Woodland Cave is a small shelter four meters wide and seven meters deep, in an outcrop of the Idaho Springs Formation just west of Golden. Rocks piled up outside the shelter may be prehistoric. Early Ceramic corner-notched projectile points were the commonest type, although one trinotched point was found. Cord-marked pottery confirms that this assemblage largely represents an Early Ceramic occupation. Other artifacts include ground stone manos and metates, hammerstones, gravers, scrapers, and knives. A rod with a groove around one end was made of metamorphic rock, for which there is no known nearby source; its shape has no counterpart in Greater Denver. The fragmented bones imply marrow extraction. About 75 percent of the identifiable bones are from mule deer. Also present were cottontail rabbit, meadow mouse, dog, elk, and bison. This site is thought to be a winter occupation area, since the angle of the sun in winter would illuminate most of the cave (Nelson 1967).

Many other Early Ceramic sites have been recorded but not excavated. One, the Jarre Creek site, appears to have been a large hilltop settlement, with tepee rings. It also had "much" pottery, side-notched points, grinding stones, and a chopper. Another was buried in Piney Creek alluvium. Some cord-marked pottery and many corner-notched points were observed, as well as a great deal of bone, including bone awls. Rainbow Creek is another excavated but unpublished site in the Hogback subregion (University of Denver files).

*Black Forest Early Ceramic*

The Bayou Gulch site is a large open site near Cherry Creek. In spite of the fact that many artifacts had been removed by local collectors, a dense surface scatter of artifacts was recorded over an area of more than 20,000 square meters (Miller and Fiero 1977). No comprehensive report was ever published, although C14 dates (Butler 1981), a pollen report (Short and Stravers 1981), and a study of the pottery (Ellwood 1987) provide some details. Stratigraphy and stone tools from this excavation were studied by Kevin Gilmore (1991).

Small corner-notched projectile point types that are usually associated with Early Ceramic are the most numerous. Sixteen drills were found in the upper levels, suggesting that beads and other ornaments were being manufactured. End scrapers accounted for more than half of the unifacial tools, 62 in all. Gilmore points out that at Magic Mountain end scrapers were also more frequent in the Early Ceramic level.

The number of potsherds recovered at the site (510) represents a large collection for the Denver area but a small percentage of the overall assemblage. Thus pottery use (cooking and storage) occurred less often than other activities in this locality. Features included 32 hearths.

The Ceramic occupation seems to have been more permanent than those of the Archaic period. Gilmore believes that there was greater effective moisture in A.D. 310–950 and that the climate may have deteriorated after that, making the site less suitable for agriculture. However, since maize pollen was found in nine soil samples, this seems likely to have been a place where maize was cultivated during the Early Ceramic period. Chenopods and amaranths were moderately well represented, as were grasses (Short and Stravers 1981), adding variety to the diet.

An unusual pit, about one meter in diameter, was lined with about 6 cm of clay in a thick rim around the top 15 cm. Fire-cracked rocks were found in the basin, but no charcoal, although there were three chipped stones and one potsherd. A posthole beside the pit suggests some sort of associated structure. Two hypotheses about the basin and posthole are that the hearth was for meat smoking and the post supported a rack on which to hang strips of meat, or that the hearth was inside a sweat lodge. The latter seems more likely, since the rocks appear to have been heated elsewhere. The trench profiles from this excavation show from five to nine strata. The materials were never published, although a short report is on file with Historic Franktown (West 1991), and materials and maps are curated with that group as well.

Franktown Cave is an unusually large natural shelter with a rich archaeological assemblage. As the only site in Greater Denver with perishable artifacts, it may be the most important prehistoric site in Greater Denver. The cave is on private property near the base of a rimrock cliff about 70 meters above Willow Creek (a tributary of Cherry Creek) and 20 meters or so below the canyon rim. The interior dimensions of the rock overhang are 40 meters long and 20 meters front to back. Excavations were carried out in 1942 by Hugh Capps (who had received his MA from the University of Denver in 1941), in 1949 and 1952 by Arnold Withers and in 1956–57 by Gerold Thompson, a graduate student at the University of Denver. A short expedition to clean and check the profiles and to verify the previous maps took place in 1975 under the direction of Sarah Nelson. The backdirt was probed at the same time and found to contain small objects such as cord and flakes, implying that previous excavations had not been screened. However, screens appear in photographs from the 1949 excavation. Thus the top of the backdirt pile may have been left by pothunters, who left additional evidence of their activities from time to time.

None of these excavations have ever been published, although several master's theses from the University of Denver have used the collection (Pustmueller 1977; Plessinger 1985; Sayres 1984). An undergraduate honors paper by Sarah Studenmund (1976) examined the pottery, the grinding stones were studied by Darby Stapp (1977), Charles Manz (1976) examined the formal stone tools, and the perishable artifacts were described by Judy Radspinner (1977). A description of the basketry by James Adovasio in 1972 is also on file. Most of a large Woodland jar was reconstructed from a group of sherds by unrecorded students, perhaps in the 1960s. Thompson made a list of identified faunal material. Sarah Nelson studied the distribution of the artifacts with a computer program written by Myron Plooster. Thus, although the site is unpublished, a great deal of time has been lavished on its study.

At least three occupations are represented at Franktown Cave. Two C14 dates were obtained on charcoal from hearths. One date is from the lower hearth with Late Archaic style projectile points, which calibrates to A.D. 229–390, falling within the Early Ceramic range. The other date is associated with Early Ceramic projectile points but calibrates to 1039–1228, which is Middle Ceramic in time range. The long storage of these samples in paper bags may have contributed to making both dates somewhat more recent than they should be.

The organic material was mostly in the top 20 cm of the deposits; however, one layer noted as "organic matted material, pipe and shirt" was at a depth of 100–110 cm, under a layer of charcoal and ash. Other organic fill is marked "probably rodent action" on the 1956 map. The juxtaposition of moccasins and sandals is particularly interesting. It marks an intersection of southwestern and plains lifeways in an unusually graphic way.

Floral material collected includes cactus, yucca, cane, legume pods, grasses, cattail, juniper, pine, willow, aspen, cottonwood, and chokecherry. Several parts of maize plants include cobs and kernels (Fig. 3.13a). Artifacts made of wood include part of a bow, arrow shafts, heddles, awls, stakes, digging sticks, and fire drills (Fig. 3.13b). Unidentified pieces of worked wood include flat pieces with shallow cutmarks, rods with squared ends or notches and a point, and flat-sided objects. Fiber cordage is all 2-ply with a Z-twist. String made of "grassy fibers" is also present, as well as wooden pieces with cottony fibers adhering. Fibers were tied in several different knots, including reef, granny, and square knots (Fig. 3.13c). Pine needles bundled together, possibly as tinder for fires, and a coiled vine are also among the collection (Radspinner 1977).

Fur coils and large and small pieces of hide were present, including a piece that had been trimmed off with the stake holes remaining. Fibers were mostly found in Grid Square B3, including knotted and packaged yucca leaves and 2-ply cordage. Leather cords were also found, and a piece of hide that was the waste end from stretching. A wooden stake was found nearby (Fig. 3.13d). One possible turkey feather was collected. The sandals are plaited, using whole yucca leaves (Fig. 3.13e). The moccasin type was identified as pre-horse because of its soft sole, and of a style that comes from the East or Midwest, according to notes left by Richard Conn. The side is sewn to the sole (Fig. 3.13f). The basketry consists of rod and bundle technique, which according to James Adovasio was a standard technique used by Mogollon and Anasazi after A.D. 500, although it is known much earlier. Another five fragments of basketry were made with bundles (Fig. 3.13g). They represent trays or steep-sided bowls, using a technique known in the trans-Pecos area of Texas and New Mexico. Thus there is a suggestion of connections with the southwest as well as the plains and farther east (Adovasio 1999). A circular object resembling a "dream catcher," or perhaps a hoop for the hoop and pole game, is another important artifact (Fig. 3.13h).

Thompson's study of the bones identified the following species: bison, beaver, elk, deer, porcupine, turkey, weasel, pack rat, prairie dog, cotton rat, and rabbit. Many of the identifiable bones were parts of skulls, jaws, and teeth. More than half the bones, including

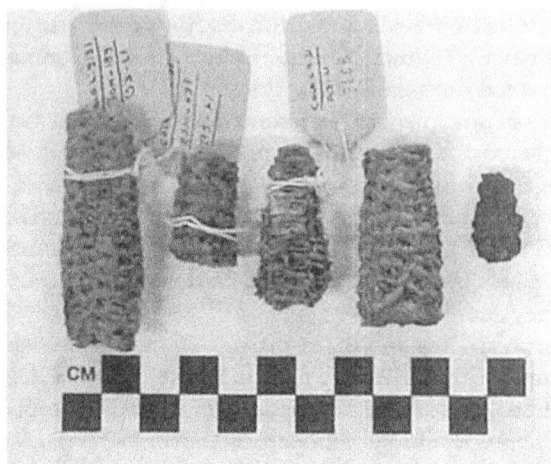

Figure 3.13. Franktown Cave materials. (a) Maize cobs. Photograph by Kevin Gilmore.

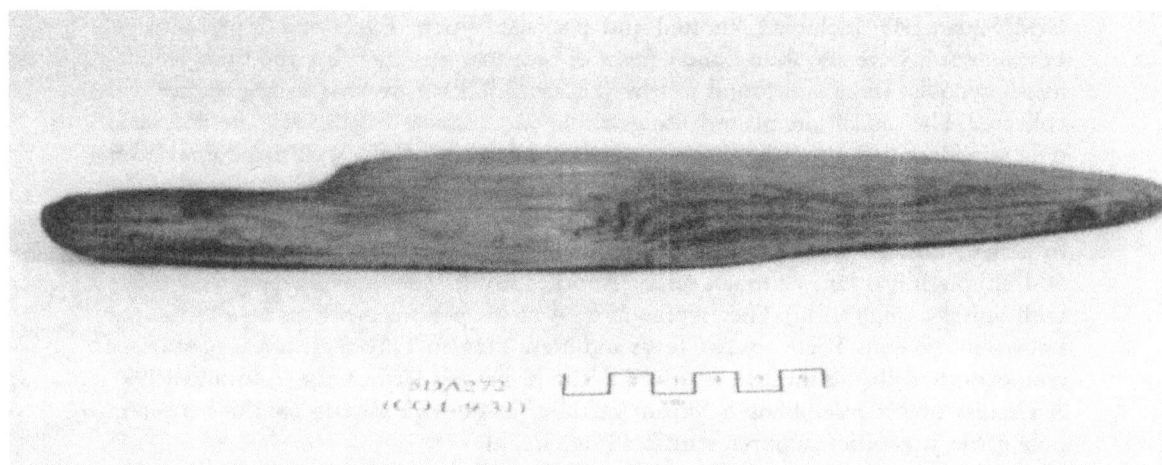

Figure 3.13b. Wooden artifact. Photograph on file at the University of Denver.

Figure 3.13c. Fiber bundle. Photograph by Kevin Gilmore.

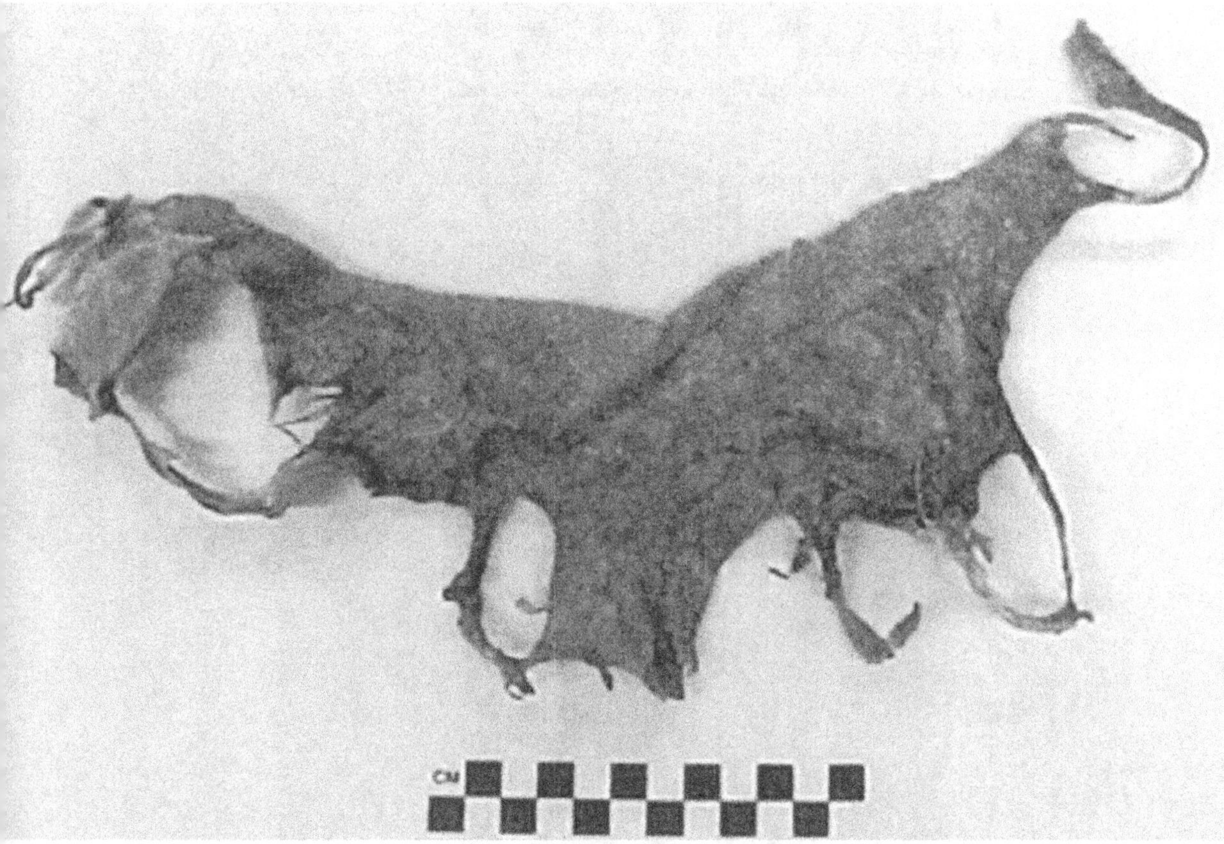

Figure 3.13d. Deer hide with stake holes and wooden stake, showing manner of stretching and drying hides. Photograph on file at the University of Denver.

Figure 3.13e. Yucca sandal. Photograph by Kevin Gilmore.

Figure 3.13f. Moccasin. Photograph on file at the University of Denver.

Figure 3.13g. Rod and bundle basketry. Photograph by Kevin Gilmore.

Figure 3.13h. Object made of bent twig and string. Photograph by Kevin Gilmore.

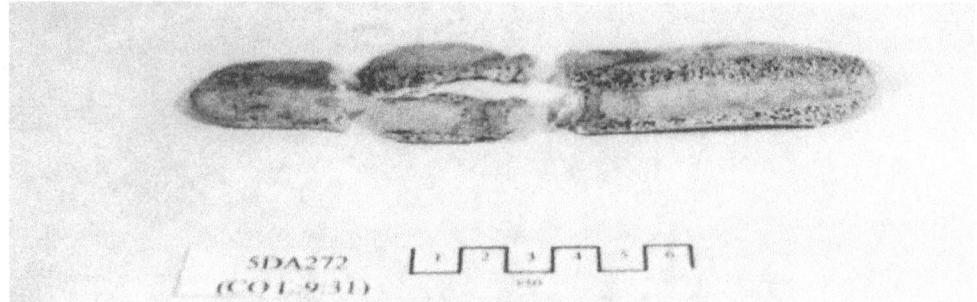

Figure 3.13i. Broken spatulate object made of bone. Photograph on file at the University of Denver.

most of the 88 identified bison bones, were found in square B5. Unworked bones were mostly found in this square, while burned bones were found only in B4 and B3. Bone artifacts include three beads, six awls, and nine tools with unknown usage, one of which is spatulate in shape (Fig. 3.13i).

Distributional analysis shows that grinding slabs and projectile points are clustered in different parts of the site, especially in the top two levels. An unusual artifact is a rectangular stone with a longitudinal groove. Others like it were found at Bayou Gulch (Miller and Fiero 1977) and Magic Mountain (Irwin-Williams and Irwin 1966).

Another excavated rockshelter along Cherry Creek is called Cherry Creek Canyon Cave. Most of the artifacts were in the upper meter. One hearth had large pieces of charcoal and some charred bone. Oddly enough, sherds were present from the upper layer down to almost two meters. Analysis of the sherds shows that some of the vessels were conical, but others were hemispherical bowls. Several other rockshelters in this region had some evidence of prehistoric inhabitants. Both hand stones and base stones were present. One had been used to grind paint, and still has traces of red pigment. Projectile points associated with the pottery are small and corner-notched, while those from lower levels are described as "late lithic complex" (Thompson 1956).

*Plains Early Ceramic*

Pithouses in Greater Denver are important new discoveries. At Box Elder–Tate Hamlet the northernmost pithouse measured about 2.5 meters in diameter and was 85 cm deep. This semipermanent structure was dated to the Early Ceramic. It was partially subterranean, and originally roofed with an entrance facing southeast. The interior contained several hearths and a storage pit. The hearths were found to include animal bone fragments and plant parts. Upon analysis, it was learned that saltbush was the most common fuel, but rabbitbrush, wild plum/chokecherry, and cottonwood/willow were also burned. The pithouse eventually burned up and was abandoned during the Early/Middle Ceramic transition period. The second pithouse is more or less contemporaneous with the first. It is slightly smaller, considerably shallower, and with fewer features, including three postholes along the northwest arc and three hearths. This pithouse did not burn but was simply abandoned. Thirteen hearths are spread around the pithouses, mostly dating to the Early and Middle Ceramic. At the north end of the site, in the area where most of the surface artifacts were found, a single Early Ceramic hearth was found. Plant remains included charred saltbush and goosefoot seeds, with fragments of rice grass, wild rose, and, less frequent, an unidentified root or tuber. Faunal bone included deer or pronghorn, birds, a canid, prairie dog, and cottontail (Tucker, Tate, and Mutaw 1992).

At a large campsite in the Rocky Mountain Arsenal, 142 sherds of a Woodland vessel were collected in 1983 from what was described as a "fire pit." The wide-mouthed pot is 26.3 cm high with a mouth diameter of 20 cm (Clark et al. 1993). This suggests that a habitation site was once present to the northwest of Denver International Airport as well.

The Senac site is a large open campsite located in rolling grasslands on lands that were part of a World War II bombing range. The site covers 5.25 acres and straddles Senac Creek at the location of a small spring. Excavations north of the creek revealed numerous hearths and hundreds of artifacts and bones. Data from the site suggest that the occupants used the site seasonally for hunting and gathering, mainly in spring and fall, from A.D. 245 to 1055, during the Early Ceramic period. There was evidence for numerous activities, including stone and bone tool manufacture, hide and fiber processing, food processing, and possibly ceramic manufacture. However, camp activities seemed to have focused on faunal processing (Tate and Friedman 1986; O'Neil and Tate 1987).

Animal bones were identified as bison, pronghorn, deer, fox, raccoon, badger, bighorn sheep, rabbit, prairie dog, dove, grouse, and turtle. Pronghorn antelope, deer, and prairie dog were used most frequently. It is inferred that pronghorn and deer were butchered before being brought to the site, because only the limbs were present. The bones were broken for marrow (see Box 3G). Prairie dogs had been brought whole and their heads removed. They may have been roasted without further processing and consumed near the fires. Plant remains found in the hearth were dominated by plants of the pigweed family (Chenopodium), which were probably used in soups and stews. Other plants included grass seeds, ball cactus, and unidentified fruits and berries (O'Neil et al. 1988).

Several Woodland potsherds demonstrate that the site is Early Ceramic. Manos and metate fragments were also found, in small quantities. An abundance of flaked lithic tools and debitage was found at the site, including contemporaneous projectile points from dated contexts, some of which were used with atlatls and darts and others used with bows and arrows. There was also a considerable variety of worked bone, including awls and perforators, a bone wrench/shaft straightener, and fiber processors. The latter included a yucca comb, such as is often found in sites in the Southwest, used to separate yucca fibers to make cordage. Decorative bone beads were also present (O'Neil et al. 1988). The nearby survey of the Buckley Air National Guard Base turned up a number of lithic scatters and possible camps. Preferred locations were on hilltops or ridge tops facing south or southeast.

In the Aurora burial two individuals were buried together, a child of about five in the upper part of the pit, and an adult male, about thirty-five to forty, below. The adult was flexed, placed on his right side. The child's incomplete bones suggest a bundle burial. Radiocarbon dates are not consistent, but they indicate that both burials are from the Early Ceramic period. Burial goods include four flakes, a broken gneiss atlatl weight, and a broken ground and polished amazonite pendant. The latter two are definitely associated with the adult. It is notable that the adult's teeth had extreme dental abrasion, shovel-shaped incisors, and no caries (Guthrie 1983). The shape of the incisors indicates a relationship to East Asian populations. This burial appears to be an exception to the rule that Early Ceramic burials took place in cemeteries. No other burials are known nearby, nor is there any evidence of a habitation site.

The Van Ness site was mostly Early Ceramic. Five hearths were all unlined but filled with cobbles. Flotation samples from hearths showed that the inhabitants were eating cheno-ams, cactus fruits, pine nuts, and a member of the bean family. The sunflower is also represented. Animal bones had been fragmented into small pieces, but a few pronghorn antelope could be identified (Kalasz et al. 1996).

> Box 3G. Bone Processing
>
> The highly nutritious marrow in the middle of bones is eaten as a special treat by many people. Meat bones can be split open lengthwise after the meat is eaten, and the marrow can be simply chewed out. Bone grease is made by boiling the bones in water. Often the process is made more efficient by chopping the bones into small pieces first, because the containers for boiling are relatively small. Because grease is an important element in the human diet, this form of processing became common as soon as suitable containers were available. Archaeologists find that the purpose of chopping animal bones into small pieces was to obtain the marrow and bone grease. Bones could also be fashioned into tools, as we see from sites with good preservation of bones. Awls, needles, gaming pieces, and hoes were commonly made of bone.

*Streams Early Ceramic*

A cemetery at Hazeltine Heights on the east side of the South Platte River was discovered in the early 1960s when a backhoe trench excavating house foundations cut through a prehistoric cemetery. Seven burials were excavated there by students from the University of Colorado. Some indications of a village were nearby. Surface finds included fire-cracked rocks, side-notched projectile points (probably Early Ceramic), and five manos of various shapes. The upper layer had been mixed with historic artifacts by plowing. Excavated materials include a wide flat object made of granite worked on both sides, scrapers, and ground stones.

The burials were judged to be roughly contemporaneous, but three of them are clearly sequential because later pits intrude into earlier ones. The burials had been greatly disturbed by the backhoe, but those that remained entirely or partly articulated were flexed. A woman about thirty years old wore beads made of Olivella shells. Extreme tooth wear was noted in this skull, although only one tooth was missing. One corner-notched biface was associated with burial 3 or 4, and green pigment of undetermined origin was found with burial 4. A juvenile was accompanied by beads. About 70 beads were found altogether and seem to have formed part of a necklace with a matching anklet. Some were made from bird and mammal bone with traces of red pigment; some were made of Olivella shell. Five pendants of various shapes were made of Unio shell. Some of the beads are engraved with incised lines. Burial 7 was a juvenile of about seven years. This child also had ornaments, including possible eagle bone beads painted with red pigment, beads made from small mammal bones, and an ovoid pendant of Unio shell that had been placed in the mouth. Fragments from other burials rescued from the back dirt included at least two infants and several adults. A radiocarbon date that falls in the eighth or ninth century was obtained from the burial. Skeletal analysis showed relationships with people living in what is now Kansas rather than Nebraska (Buckles et al. 1963), but this is not surprising, given the date.

The Cherry Creek Reservoir survey found several areas indicative of Early Ceramic occupation, either sherds or projectile points or both. Manos and metates and fire-cracked rock were also found at some of these sites, suggesting village settlements.

### Middle Ceramic (A.D. 1000–1500)

Middle Ceramic is not well represented in Greater Denver if it is to be defined by the presence of "Upper Republican" or "Smoky Hill" pottery (Fig. 3.14). The center of the Upper Republican Complex is in Nebraska, where the dwellings are one-room wattle-and-daub houses with four posts. Maize, beans, and squash were grown (see Box

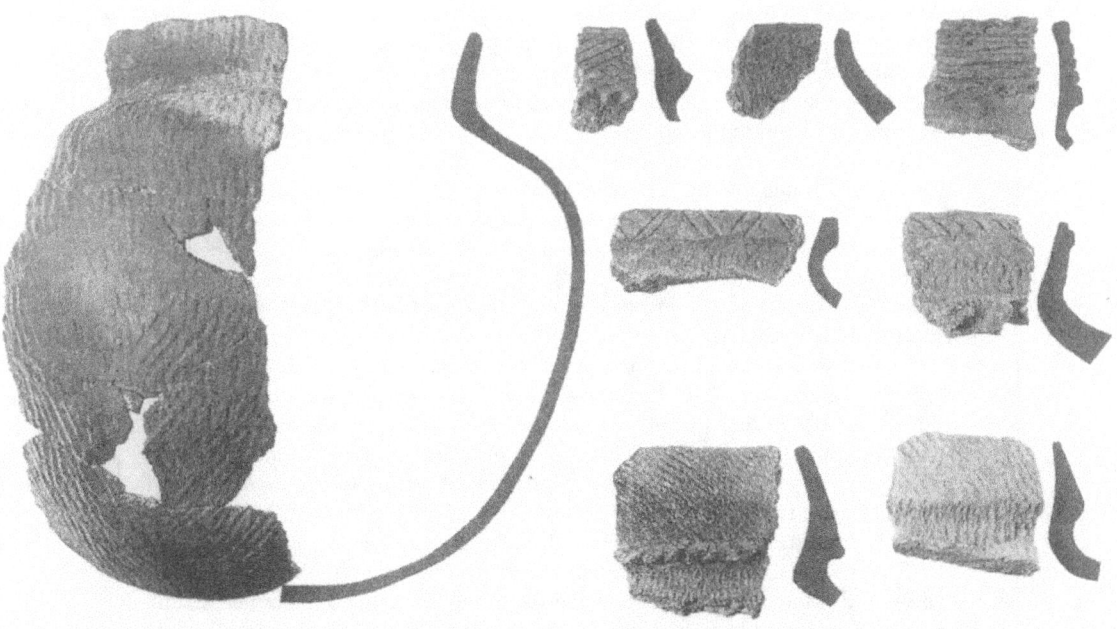

Figure 3.14. Middle Ceramic pottery. Photograph on file at the University of Denver.

3H). The village architecture in northeastern Colorado is probably related to those sites. Evidence grows thinner in the Denver region; for some reason it was a less suitable environment for those groups. As has already been noted, Box Elder-Tate Hamlet contained pithouses and hearths dating to both Early and Middle Ceramic times. The upper date at Franktown Cave also falls within the Middle Ceramic period, and a few rim sherds are from collared vessels. It is possible that some of the Middle Ceramic in the Denver Basin represents the last of the Early Ceramic people, rather than an intrusive group of people from Nebraska or Kansas.

Rock Creek produced dates that would suggest Middle Ceramic, but the excavators found little difference in the pottery by C14 dates. A study of the potsherds demonstrates that at least ten different vessels are represented, including both Early and Middle Ceramic types. The micaceous clays used to form the pottery are available locally (Gleichman, Gleichman, and Karhu 1995). The Swallow site is likewise only 100 meters from a source of micaceous clays (Adkins and Irish 1994). Some of the sites in the Cherry Creek Reservoir appear to have Upper Republican affiliations; at least the sherds did not come from typical Woodland cord-marked pottery. Smooth pottery with a pinkish exterior is found at these sites, but they are undated and could be Late Ceramic.

> Box 3H. Cultigens
>
> The presence of maize at several sites has been suggested as reflecting imports, but the preponderance of the evidence leans toward the local growing of the maize plant. Certainly soils and water were adequate for the task, and grinding stones suggest specific maize flour production. The clinching evidence comes from Franktown Cave, where other parts of the plant were preserved as well as cobs and kernels. Furthermore, the worn teeth of Early Ceramic burials indicate a change in diet. Although seeds were ground in the Archaic, the extra grinding required by maize causes more grit from the grinding slabs to get into food, wearing down molars.
>
> It should not be surprising that maize was grown in Greater Denver. It was extensively cultivated in the eastern United States at the same time and before (Johnson and Johnson 1998:203). In the west and southwest, maize is even earlier. The Irwins believed that maize was grown at the LoDaisKa site in the Middle to Late Archaic (Irwin and Irwin 1961:114). They note that it resembles a form of maize called chapalote and is very similar to maize found in Bat Cave, New Mexico during the Archaic period.
>
> Some examples of maize finds are popcorn and dent corn from LoDaisKa and small cobs and kernels at Franktown Cave. Corn kernels were also found at one of the Chatfield sites on the east side of Plum Creek, which was extensively trenched by Tom Bridge in 1975. This last site included scrapers, fragments of projectile points, utilized flakes, debitage, and a piece of yellow ocher, in addition to two corn kernels. The materials were shallow, only 25-30 cm below the surface, but the corn appears to be well associated with the artifacts (Nelson 1979a).
>
> At Bayou Gulch maize pollen was extracted from two samples from stratum 2b and was also scraped from three metates and one mano from the same stratum. Another suggestion of local farming is a digging tool made from the right scapula of a bison, which has scratch marks consistent with soil cultivation and other striations suggesting hafting material. The associated date was about A.D. 950. Kevin

> Gilmore (1991) also argues that, since there were fewer types of manos, this could mean more dependence on one plant—maize. Thus the accumulating evidence points to the local growing of a corn crop and considerable residential stability. Radiocarbon dates on stored maize in western Colorado have dates of A.D. 400 and 820 (Wenger 1956), so similar dates in eastern Colorado should not be surprising. For examples of other discoveries of maize outside Greater Denver, see Gilmore (1999:236-40).
>
> What is not clear is how maize was cooked, since comales, the flat cooking surfaces used for cooking tortillas in Mesoamerica, seem to be absent. Perhaps some of the thin flat "grinding stones" found in various sites, and called "palettes" at Magic Mountain and LoDaisKa, fulfilled this function. Similar slabs were found at Franktown Cave, significantly not associated with manos. It also seems likely that some form of soft cooking (wrapped in corn husks or leaves, for example), must have used the ubiquitous wide-mouthed pots.
>
> Squash seeds were found in some abundance at Bradford House III. They may be a contaminant from historic times, but other evidence should be looked for. Indications of beans were found at the Van Ness site (Kalasz et al. 1996) and at Franktown Cave. More evidence will have to be found before the trilogy of corns, beans, and squash can be accepted as the Ceramic period subsistence base.

Thus there was definitely some presence of Upper Republican peoples in this region (Fig. 3.15), but the scarcity of the sites suggests that the Nebraska villages were the permanent sites, and that the local sites represent expeditions rather than settlements. The reason for declining settlements in Greater Denver may be cultural as well as environmental. A larger Shoshonean settlement in the mountains might well have discouraged farmers in the foothills.

Figure 3.15. Upper Republican rim sherd from Franktown Cave. Photograph on file at the University of Denver.

### Hogback Middle Ceramic

Unlike all other prehistoric periods, very little evidence of Middle Ceramic is found in the Hogback region. One rim sherd at Willowbrook has a row of fingernail markings on the interior of the lip, affiliating it with the Middle Ceramic. The Crescent site has Middle Ceramic in its top layers, and a trinotched point was found at Hall Woodland Cave. At Van Bibber Creek, a few sherds might mark a short Middle Ceramic visit. Glenn Scott (University of Denver site card) notes one site as "Upper Republican" but does not indicate what artifacts were present. The presence of people during this time period was ephemeral.

### Black Forest Middle Ceramic

Likewise there is little evidence of Middle Ceramic occupation in the Black Forest. A basin feature (F37) was uncovered on the last day of the Highway Department excavation at Bayou Gulch, and therefore was never fully exposed, but it was estimated to be 4 meters in diameter. Such a large feature implies a dwelling, but this seems inconsistent with the low frequency of potsherds. A steatite pipe was found in association with the floor of this feature, raising the possibility of ceremonial use. These may be Middle Ceramic manifestations, along with scanty evidence at Franktown Cave, including two sherds from globular rimmed jars and small side-notched projectile points.

At the Cherry Creek Canyon site, two sherds with fine temper and thick walls may be evidence of Middle Ceramic. They have partly obliterated cord markings on the outside, and the inside is very smooth (Thompson 1956).

### Plains Middle Ceramic

The Moffitt site is located on a hilltop, with ceramics, chipped stone including Early Ceramic projectile points, ground stone, and hearths (Tucker 1994; Tate 1991). The artifact scatter is large, covering more than twenty acres, but with a distinct cluster. One feature with charcoal and fire-cracked rock was dated in the thirteenth century, which falls within the Middle Ceramic period, corroborated by three sherds from an Upper Republican vessel with a rounded base.

Pollen was predominately from grasses, and burned grass seeds were found in fire pits. Other pollens include sagebrush, ragweed, pigweed, wild buckwheat, juniper, and pine. These are wind-blown pollens, so they do not necessarily relate to the diet, but they do describe the flora available to the occupants of the site. Pieces of charcoal came from brushy plants such as willow and saltbush, as well as the cottonwood tree, which, although it grows quite tall, drops branches in high winds or heavy snows, making it easily collectible for fuel. Ground stone artifacts show that at least some of their food was processed by grinding with an upper rounded stone on a base stone. Macroflora included both starchy tubers and seeds: goosefoot, pigweed, flat sedge and nutgrass. These were probably plant foods.

Many animal bones were found in small pieces, making them difficult to identify, but suggesting marrow processing. About 60 percent of the bones could be identified as coming from medium-size mammals, such as deer.

Three projectile points were styles associated with the Ceramic stage, one of which is usually classed as Late Archaic. A single obsidian flake was found at the site, but most of the tools were made of local materials, especially silicified wood and quartzite.

At the Senac site a large rimsherd, believed to be Upper Republican, postdates the Early Ceramic occupation (Tate, personal communication).

*Streams Middle Ceramic*

The Rock Creek site, excavated by Peter Gleichman and others in 1990–93, provided a wealth of information from carefully controlled excavations and detailed analyses (Gleichman, Gleichman, and Karhu 1995). Excavations unearthed 30 pits, mostly firepits, and 3,477 artifacts. Both animal bones and microflora were intensively studied and blood residue analysis was performed. A series of radiocarbon dates show that at this site the Ceramic Period occupation, with mixed Woodland and Upper Republican types, ranged from the ninth to the twelfth centuries, spanning the time period of the supposed transition from Early to Middle Ceramic. It is noteworthy that there was no evidence of a cultural change during this time period. The artifacts implied varied activities, and collection of food and raw materials seems to have ranged from the mountains to the plains. It is particularly interesting that no domesticated plants were recovered, although the nine kinds of plants that were found are considered economic plants, and they are species that grow best in ground disturbed by humans. Chenopods (goosefoot) and grasses were the most commonly found. The manos and metates show that these plants were ground before consumption. Blood residue analysis on stone tools showed that the blood of bison, rabbit, deer, and dog had adhered to some of the tools. A clay-lined pit, 56 cm in diameter, is smaller than the one at Bayou Gulch, but seems to be otherwise similar. Eleven pieces of fire-cracked rock were found in the fill. This site seems to confirm the idea that people of Middle Ceramic times did not have permanent homes in Greater Denver, but came to the area to gather and hunt. The dog, however, might have been their own domesticated animal.

---

Box 31. Medicinal Plants

There are many uses for plants, from food and medicine to raw materials for clothing, utensils, tools, and shelter. Plants were also used for fuel and for bedding. Thus, although we cannot know exactly how the plants found in archaeological sites were used on a given occasion, we can reason by analogy with Native Americans who are known to have used these plants. At the very least it is possible to say for what purpose they might have been brought into the site. For example, goosefoot, which is found in many sites, has many uses. Both the seeds and the leaves were eaten—the leaves were usually boiled, while the seeds were parched and ground. Poultices made of the leaves were used for burns. The whole plant could be boiled to make a tea that was used to treat diarrhea (Cummings and Montoux 1997). Amaranth seeds and leaves were similarly used. Chenopods are full of vitamin C, while amaranth is a good source of iron. The amaranth can be used to reduce swelling or ease toothache. A brew of the leaves was variously used for dysentery, ulcers, diarrhea, mouth sores, and throat ailments, as well as to stop external bleeding.

Another plant commonly represented in Greater Denver sites is alder. It was probably used as fuel; in addition the leaves were applied to wounds to control bleeding. Cactus pads could also be peeled and used to dress wounds, and the pads could also be steeped for a medicine for the lungs, or the juice applied to warts (Cummings and Montoux 1997). The saltbush plant could add flavor to foods or be applied to the skin to ease insect stings. A particular variety of this plant was used as an emetic or for stomach pain. The dried and powdered leaves could be sniffed to aid the nose, and the root when ground up was good for toothaches.

The inner bark of pine could be used for larger bandages, and pine pitch could be used as a salve for sores. The pitch could also be used to draw out splinters. A tea made of the needles was used for coughs and colds, and a tea from the buds was a laxative. Even aromatherapy is not new—pine needles could be heated and the fumes sniffed for back pain. Mountain mahogany could be used to treat stomach ailments, and was also given in a tea to new mothers.

• • •

Newer information about prehistoric inhabitants of Greater Denver has shown that there is more of a Paleoindian presence than was previously thought. It also appears that the Archaic peoples, or some of them, were more settled. The overlap of Late Archaic projectile points with Early Ceramic potsherds and dating suggests a merger or coexistence of peoples. Obsidian, possibly from the Rocky Mountains, turns up in sites in the eastern United States, although which group did the traveling is hard to say. Distant trade is in fact evident in several raw materials, and points to widespread trade routes, in pipe stone, shells, and colored stone.

It is interesting that little pottery is actually found, relative to other artifacts, in Early Ceramic sites. The pottery itself suggests eastern rather than southwestern connections, which would suggest that the source of maize and other cultigens is eastern also. The meeting of east and west may be a story told by the sandals and mocassin that coexist at Franktown Cave. The rarity of Middle Ceramic sites makes one wonder if there were already rival groups in the mountains, ready to raid the stores of maize. Certainly there seems to be continuity between Early and Middle Ceramic.

Although there is much we cannot know, one thing we can be sure of is that the groups included men and women, children and adults. What meanings, if any, may have been attached to age and sex are not so easy to assess, nor do we know whether particular tasks were assigned accordingly. It is difficult to know about leadership and the ways society was organized, but these are important questions to consider to avoid reading the present into the past (Nelson 1997).

Little remains of the ceremonies of these ancient people except the occasional burial, but we can be sure they held ceremonies. Only a few bone beads and stone pendants have been found, perhaps because ornaments were made for the most part of perishable materials. "Paint stones" have been reported from several sites, and grinding stones with traces of pink pigment have been found. Ocher in various colors has been noted at several sites. Were these pigments applied to human skin, clothing, basketry, houses, all of these, or something else? We may not have the answer to this question, but we know that they did add color to their lives.

The wealth of known prehistoric sites in Greater Denver is impressive, and no doubt many other sites lie deeply buried. Together, the sites we know about reveal many things about prehistoric lifeways in this area, about change through time and adaptations to new conditions. Future excavations will no doubt broaden our understanding of the ten millennia before either the historic Native American tribes whose names we know or Euro-Americans appeared in Greater Denver.

CHAPTER 4

## Contact, Conflict, and Coexistence

Greater Denver as a frontier is particularly evident during the contact period, when groups of Native Americans intermingled with mountain men, gold seekers, and settlers. Native American peoples were on the move along with other peoples; several groups of Native Americans occupied or passed through the Greater Denver area either successively or simultaneously.

The distribution of language groups of Native Americans demonstrates that peoples have migrated sometimes quite far from their relatives. Population movement was not new to North America with the explorations and settlement of Europeans. What was new was wholesale replacement: as Europeans arrived in North America from all directions, the previous inhabitants of the continent were squeezed into less and less space. Since most of the pressure was from the east, some eastern Native American groups moved westward, sometimes dislocating other groups who moved yet farther west. But for those arriving from the east the mountains made a barrier, especially in Colorado. Not an impassable barrier to be sure, but one that required different skills and adaptations. Humans had at least to pause when faced with the mountains rising abruptly above the plains.

Although various groups of Native Americans who had been agricultural became nomadic on the plains, large agricultural village sites still existed, especially in the northern plains. Some of them were visited by the Lewis and Clark expedition. The first Euro-Americans to arrive in Greater Denver were explorers, followed by exploiters. This chapter outlines what we will call a "contact" period between the Native American populations who called this region home and the various Euro-American groups who entered the area and decided it suited them, too (Fig. 4.1). We include the history of interaction among the groups—which, although mutually helpful at first, became discordant, disruptive, and at times deadly.

The period is not easily defined; there are variations in the preferred terminology, and terms are sometimes used interchangeably. It is known elsewhere as "Protohistoric," "Late Ceramic," or "Late Prehistoric." Since our focus is on archaeological sites, we would like to be able, with the aid of ethnography and ethnohistory, to associate sites with particular known groups such as Apache or Ute. Unfortunately, sites in this time frame are difficult to differentiate. It was a time of great change and conflict, and many new categories of material culture were shared among the Euro-Americans

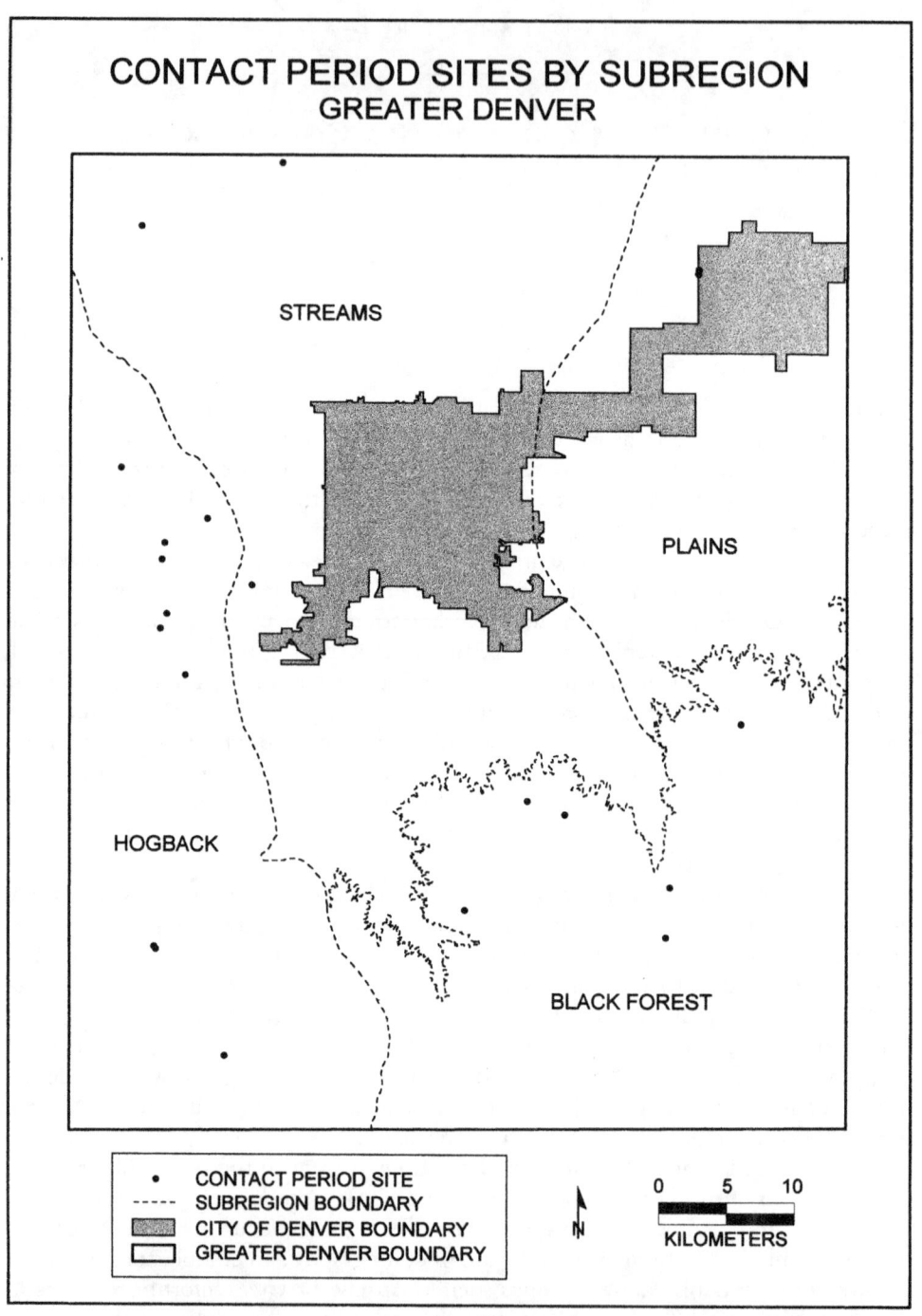

Figure 4.1. Distribution of Contact period sites by subregion. Francine Patterson.

and the local tribes. In a Native American contact period site we might expect to find metal projectile points, European weapons or bullets (the acquisition of the gun was a significant turning point in Native American history), glass beads, or other items of trade. We might find evidence of the use of horses (another important change) along with evidence of continued hunter/gatherer/horticulturalist patterns, or stone circles that once held down hides or brush structures.

Of the many lithic scatters, stone circle locations, and campsites located in this area, few contain material remains that can be associated definitively with this time period. Virtually none can be affiliated with a specific group of people, even if the time period is known. Archaeologists in Colorado have widely acknowledged the difficulty of compiling information about this period, because in Greater Denver it is documented only minimally with archaeological evidence. In 1980 Bill Butler asked, "What happens in Colorado from about A.D. 1300 to A.D. 1800? Where in the archaeological record are the Cheyenne, Arapaho, Ute and Comanche?" The questions, unfortunately, are still valid.

For the most part, we have to rely on ethnographic and ethnohistoric accounts of the Native Americans who were in the Denver area at the time of European contact. Furthermore, sometimes these accounts are from regions outside Greater Denver, such as southeastern Colorado near the Purgatoire River and even as far south as what is now New Mexico. Direct observations in the immediate area are less common.

Nevertheless, the outlines of the events and patterns that occurred in the larger geographic region can be used to make generalizations that are applicable to Greater Denver. The discussion that follows will have a broad base in the *region* surrounding Denver. It is an important framework. The sociopolitical history of Denver—the pieces that came together to form the character of this community—began in a larger context.

The first Europeans seen by Native Americans in this region were in Coronado's 1540 expedition, which went into New Mexico and across the southern plains to Quivera, a location in south-central Kansas. Coronado's journey did not bring him near the Denver area, nor did it provide any direct accounts of groups this far north, but it did provide the first accounts of the inhabitants of the southern plains, and the contact and trade that ensued would reverberate far and wide. Eventually, the introduction of the horse, the gun, and new networks of trade would mark a period of upheaval and transformation.

During this time, and through the 1600s, the Apache dominated the plains area, and the Utes were firmly established to the west in the mountains, on occasion making forays onto the plains. In 1683 Apaches were reported as far east and south as the Colorado River in Texas (Hackett 1931 as cited in Buckles 1968). Fray Pasados, a Spanish historian who lived in New Mexico in the 1650s and 1660s, wrote that the Ute and Apache shared the lands between the San Juan River and the Great Salt Lake. The Apache were recorded on the plains of eastern Colorado as early as the 1640s or 1660s during a Spanish expedition in search of some rebellious Taos Indians who had taken refuge among the Apache north of the Arkansas River (Buckles 1968). Knowing that these groups occupied the area and documenting their presence with archaeological evidence are, however, two different things.

## Dismal River

The Dismal River is located in southwestern Nebraska. Archaeologists have coined the term "Dismal River Aspect" to describe a protohistoric culture now believed to be associated with the Apache of the historic period (Gunnerson 1968, 1987). The connection is made in a campsite in Kansas with clear Dismal River attributes. A historic map from a 1700s Spanish expedition identified an Apache camp in that location, thus a strong link is made (Cassells 1983). However, archaeologists rarely have the good fortune of discovering a reliable historic document that positively connects artifacts in the ground with a moment in time or a specific group. More often we can only make broad associations and informed assumptions based on types of artifacts and sites.

> Box 4A. Dismal River Ceramics
>
> Pottery can be formed in a variety of ways. The pinching method may remind you of your first ashtray or an item produced in kindergarten: a ball of clay is literally pinched into shape. Coiling involves building up the walls in layers of clay "rope" and then smoothing the walls out. The basic vessel form may have been formed by lump modeling or coiling, followed by use of a grooved (or thong wrapped) paddle and an anvil (perhaps a smoothed stone or piece of wood). In the paddle and anvil method, a wide, flat instrument (paddle) was used to form the outside of the pot while a smooth stone or similar tool (anvil) was held opposite it on the inside wall. Decoration was uncommon, but occasionally can be found in the form of parallel lines incised or impressed across the lip of the vessel, for example.
>
> Temper is required to reduce cracking during the firing process. It is often fine sand or grit, though surface collections from eastern Colorado sites often include sherds with a greater concentration of mica temper (Gunnerson 1968:177). After the vessel is formed, it must be dried completely before it is fired, or it is likely to crack. Ceramics will react to a variety of firing conditions. If, for example, there was less oxygen or the temperature of the fire was low, then carbon would not burn out of the clay, resulting in a black core. Lack of oxygen can also be taken to an extreme so that it (oxygen) is "reduced" in the clay itself, creating an overall grey-black appearance.
>
> Some micaceous pottery was made on the plains. "In spite of the evidence for contacts between the Dismal River people and the southwest, it seems unlikely that these Plains Apache took up pottery making as a result of Pueblo influence. Their fundamental approach was non-Pueblo in that they used a paddle and anvil in shaping and thinning. Furthermore, marks on Dismal River vessels show clearly that the type of paddle used (grooved or thong wrapped) was like that employed by such Plains village tribes as the Mandan, Hidatsa, Arikara, Pawnee, or Witchita" (Gunnerson 1968:179).
>
> Box 4B. Dismal River Stone Tools
>
> Most Dismal River cutting tools are crudely made. There are few well-made knives; more often than not, sharp flakes are used without significant alteration. Snub-nosed end scrapers are quite common and technically unrefined except on the scraping edge itself. One of the diagnostic stone tools for Dismal River is a combination end scraper with a carefully chipped graver point. Another diagnostic

> tool is a drill that is essentially cigar-shaped, one to four "handles" or knobs, on the sides that could have made rotating the tool easier (Gunnerson 1968).

## Apache

The Apache dominated the plains during the 1500s and 1600s. Their language belongs to the Athapaskan language group. Linguists have traced the genealogical relationships between different languages. English, for example, is a part of the Germanic branch of the Indo-European language family. These linguistic paths can often be linked with the migratory paths of different groups. In the case of the Apache, their Athapaskan relatives from the northwest may have come into Colorado (and continued southward) via the plains or an intermontane route. Either way, their presence in what is now Colorado is only thinly documented by archaeology.

Fortunately, for the contact period and later there are other sources of information, such as documentary accounts. The collaborative work of James H. Gunnerson and Delores A. Gunnerson on the ethnohistory of the High Plains (1988) provides an overall description of early accounts of the Plains Apache by sixteenth- and seventeenth-century Spanish explorers. For example, Fray Alonso de Benevides, a Franciscan monk in 1630s "New Mexico," described a "huge Apache nation" on the plains east of the Rio Grande. His description included the following:

> With these hides they trade through all the land and gain their living. And it is the general dress as well among Indians and Spaniard, who use it as well for service as bags, tents, cuirasses, shoes [*calcado*], and everything that is needed.... When these Indians go to trade and traffic, the entire rancherias go, with their wives and children, who live in tents made of these skins of buffalo [*sibola*], very thin and tanned; and the tents they carry loaded up on pack-trains [*requas*] of dogs, harnessed up with their little pack-saddles, and the dogs are medium sized. And they are accustomed to take five hundred dogs in one pack-train, one in front of the other, and the people carry their merchandise [thus] loaded, which they barter for cotton cloth and for other things which they lack. (quoted in Gunnerson and Gunnerson 1988:3)

Accounts such as this are invaluable, but firsthand observations are rare and not always accurate. It is necessary to keep in mind the political and cultural biases the observer might have had (examples follow later in the chapter), and to realize that broad spans of time and distance separate many of the early accounts. Benevides was writing about a group of people living a great distance from present-day Denver. So, while it is perfectly reasonable to assume continuity and similarity, it still pays to approach the archaeological manifestations of these various historic groups (and their protohistoric counterparts) with an objective eye. Gunnerson and Gunnerson caution:

> In considering the ethnohistory of the high plains, one must keep the time dimension clearly in mind. The earliest eyewitness accounts are about two hundred

years earlier in the southern two-thirds of the area than in the northern third. Also, many tribes known in the mid 1800s, when the entire Central High Plains had emerged into history, had arrived there at different times, and some of the groups that were in the area in early historic times had already been forced out. It is something of a paradox that we have documentary information for groups in the area in the 1500s and early 1600s for whom we have been unable to identify archaeological sites. Furthermore, with the influx of trade goods, very few camp sites within the area dating from the last half of the 1700s and the 1800s have been identified as to tribe. It will probably never be possible to define archaeological assemblages with enough precision to identify as to tribe most sites in the Central High Plains after A.D. 1750. (1988:53)

Then what would a Dismal River or historic Apache site look like? What can we say about the known archaeological assemblages of the Plains Apache? Here are a few examples.

Excavations in 1948 by the University of Nebraska at the White Cat Village site in south-central Nebraska near the Kansas state line resulted in the description of the distinctive Dismal River house style. Archaeologists identified the classic five base, or center post, pattern in dwelling construction.

> Most of the excavated structures have shown a pattern of five vertical posts 5 to 20 inches in diameter, set 1.0 to 1.5 feet deep, forming a circle 12 to 15 feet in diameter. In each case the diameter of the house was about twice that of the circle of center posts. The house floors were slightly below ground level. In the center of the house was a fireplace at or slightly above floor level, but whether the raised hearths had been intentionally prepared or represented an accumulation of ashes and dirt has not been determined. The walls of Dismal River houses apparently consisted of small poles about two inches in diameter, set shallowly in the ground and leaned against stringers connected to the tops of the five center posts. It is probable that the walls and roofs of the structures were at least partially covered with earth, for burned clay has been found in some of the house excavations. (Gunnerson 1968:172–73)

Nevertheless, some conclusions can be drawn, from this and many other tenuously affiliated sites. Gunnerson argues that it can be safely assumed

> that the Dismal River Aspect represents part of the lineal descendants of the nomadic bison hunters observed on the High Plains by Spaniards as early as 1540–1541. The transition of these people from a nomadic way of life to a semisedentary, semihorticultural existence affords a fascinating instance of culture change in which the beginning and end can be documented historically. However, if we are to understand the cultural processes that were involved and the part played in the transition by other ethnic groups, we must find datable Dismal River sites earlier than any yet known, and also sites that can be proved ancestral to Dismal River. (1968:185)

Meanwhile, let us turn our attention to some of the other groups present in the study area during this period. Two probable Apache sites in Colorado are the Hatch site, in the northeast (see J. Wood 1967), and Cedar Point Village, near Limon (W. R. Wood 1971). At the Cedar Point Village site, seven pithouses were discovered. Plain pottery without decoration and projectile points that were unnotched or side-notched triangular shapes were associated with these dwellings. These allow the site to be classified as Dismal River.

Although the unnotched and side-notched triangular projectile points found at the Cedar Point Village site near Limon are typical of chipped stone points found at Dismal River sites, it is the pottery at Cedar Point Village that most reliably indicates its affiliation. Even this evidence is considered tenuous (Eighmy 1984:148). Other archaeologists (e.g., Cassells 1983; W. R. Wood 1971) agree that, however logical it would seem to associate sites such as this with the Plains Apache, a great deal more study needs to be conducted.

At the Hatch site, archaeologists recovered charcoal from a hearth that dated the site to the 1800s. The tepee rings at this site are some of the many that might be attributable to the Apache in Colorado. The same association is suggested at the Carrizo Ranch tepee ring sites, though they are not called Dismal River (Cassells 1983). In fact, according to Robert Brunswig's 1995 synthesis of Apachean ceramic data (Brunswig et al. 1995), in the archaeological database of the entire state only eight sites are officially listed as having Dismal River components. Clearly, we are missing some clues. A thorough search of other literature and archaeological collections produced almost 70 sites, but this number is still much smaller than the actual number of Apache campsites that must have existed.

Furthermore, most current Dismal River attributions are tenuous at best. In many cases there simply is insufficient information to draw conclusions. For example, the only Dismal River affiliation listed in the database for the study area is an unnamed site recorded by the University of Denver. The site recorder did not provide any discussion of his rationale for this determination. From the information on the site card it is not possible to retrace the logic or to assess the site on any other level. The data available are insufficient to provide any insight.

## Ute

Generally speaking, the Ute were located in the area that extended from the Colorado Front Range on the east to Utah's Oquirrh Mountains on the west (Jorgensen 1972:29). Their language belongs to the Shoshonean linguistic stock, related to Aztec and Hopi, which ranged from California to Colorado and Wyoming. While the Ute traditionally held areas west of the Front Range (Jorgensen 1972; Schroeder 1965; Stewart 1966), they ranged well onto the plains for bison hunting (Nickens 1988). Their use of the area seemed to depend in part on the somewhat transitory nature of political alliances. In the 1500s and 1600s they were allied with the Apache and ranged as far south as the Texas panhandle. From about 1700 to 1750 the Ute and Comanche, also Shoshonean, were allies and were frequently reported together, raiding and hunting on the High Plains.

In 1706, Juan de Ulibarri journeyed from Santa Fe to west-central Kansas, through Apache territory. He recorded, for the first time, that Comanches and Utes were attacking Apache groups. By the time Antonio Valverde visited them a dozen years later, the Apaches had been decimated by the raids. The Utes remained allied with the Comanches until the mid-1700s, after which the Ute joined forces with the Spanish to eliminate the Comanches.

This was the beginning of a period of profound change for North American indigenous populations. Population shifts, territorial battles, economic pressures, and disruptions in traditional patterns of social organization were characteristic of the times. All these changes were direct or indirect results of Euro-American contact and were intimately tied to two phenomena of Euro-American origin: the fur trade and the introduction of the horse (Weber 1980:16, 1990). Both phenomena are key elements in post-contact Native American culture change. They are singled out here to exemplify the type and extent of changes wrought by the Euro-Americans. Although the beaver fur trade began in the Northeast and Great Lakes area, it set into motion processes that eventually reached the plains and the Southwest. The introduction of the horse, on the other hand, came from the opposite direction—the Southwest—and in a relatively short time horses were found throughout the tribes of the plains and plateau regions. New forms of economic exchange that accompanied Euro-American goods resulted in a shift affecting Native American groups and the Hispanic population in the Southwest. These groups, having been interdependent but self-sufficient units, became subordinate members of the international trade community (Weber 1980:16; 1990).

About the same time that the beaver pelt-gun trade network moved in from the northeast, an equally momentous catalyst for cultural change was spreading from the southwest. The Ute practiced a hunting and gathering lifestyle, but they became embroiled in the workings of the Spanish empire and some members of the tribe were enslaved. When the Spanish retreated southward after the Pueblo Revolt of 1680, the Ute headed north, returning to their homeland and taking many Spanish horses with them. Through the Ute, horses spread throughout the Rocky Mountain region (Pettit 1990).

With the adoption of the horse, the hunting and gathering adaptation to the Plains environment changed profoundly (Fig. 4.2). Small, scattered groups coalesced into large, powerful tribes with an annual cycle, geared increasingly to the requirements of the horse herds, no longer solely to the availability of resources for human consumption. As with guns in the east, the acquisition of horses created wealth and power differences both within and among tribes. Mounted groups expanded their territory at the expense of unmounted groups, and plains social organization was almost completely restructured and reorganized. Not only were groups within the plains region changing locations, expanding, and contracting, but new groups were drawn to the plains as well. The Comanche moved from the Wyoming area to dominate the southern plains, while the Lakota (Sioux) thrust westward onto the northern plains. The Ute retained their home base in the mountains but added a plains hunting season to their yearly rounds and a

Figure 4.2. Ute encampment near Denver, 1874. Courtesy of the Colorado Historical Society.

plains aspect to their material culture. With the meeting of the horse and gun frontiers in Montana, the classic "Plains horse culture" was formed (Weber 1980, 1990).

The later trade in buffalo hides on the plains was in many ways an extension of the previous beaver trade. Although individual fur traders and companies like the American Fur Company had carved out territory in the region, the trade depended on the cooperation of the Ute and Comanche, without whom trading was impossible and against whom trespassing was deadly. The Native Americans' quest for guns and other trade goods provided incentive for participation in the fur trade. Iron pots to cook in, metal knives that did not require the frequent upkeep of their stone counterparts, trade cloth, glass beads, and other decorative or functional items were incorporated into the material culture of the various tribes. However, their involvement in the fur trade was not simply a matter of choice, nor driven solely by a desire for Euro-American goods. Once guns were available to any group, they became a matter of necessity and survival, since groups without access to firearms were at the mercy of those who had them. This differential access to power and trade goods was exploited by Euro-Americans and

Native Americans alike. Continued access to trade goods was predicated upon access to beaver or bison. A domino effect of population pressure and cultural conflict was created when tribes moved west from their own traditional territories into that of others, searching for new beaver lands (Weber 1990).

Some site types archaeologists might expect to be associated with the Ute include sheltered camps, wickiups, scarred or peeled trees, open camps, and open lithic scatters. Ute-affiliated sites are somewhat more common than others in the study area, but they are still not widespread.

Greater Denver has four recorded sheltered camps from the Late Ceramic period, all with a Ute affiliation—one in the Black Forest subregion and three in the Hogback subregion.

### Cherokee Mountain Rockshelter

The Cherokee Mountain rockshelter overlooks Plum Creek from a bluff of sandstone (Nelson and Stewart 1973). This shelter is on the southwest face of a mesa and lies just below another shelter recorded during the survey of Cherokee Ranch, twenty miles south of Denver. The upper shelter contained a fire hearth and a few burned bones, as well as a few scattered flakes, but Charles Nelson and Bruce Stewart were more concerned with the lower shelter. This area revealed three intermixed levels containing artifacts from the Late Prehistoric period and a few sherds and projectile points that suggested Shoshonean occupation. Other artifacts included end scrapers, knives, a drill, hammerstones, a shaft smoother, manos and metates, and bone awls. Based on the presence of small side-notched points, the authors date the site to about A.D. 1250 to 1590. They note also that

> There is a high degree of consistency in the projectile points from all three levels. This consistency argues for occupation of the site either by closely related groups near one another in time, or successive occupations by a single group. The first alternative is quite possible: in the late prehistoric period, most groups on the Plains seem to have used side-notched points, including the Upper Republican, Antelope Creek Focus, Franktown Focus, and late Shoshonean groups of eastern Colorado. (Nelson and Stuart 1973)

The pottery sherds provide the most distinctive identifiers for cultural affiliation of the shelter's inhabitants. The authors report (citing Mulloy 1958 and Annand 1967) "Brushed and fingernail indented sherds have been related to Shoshonean groups [including the prehistoric Ute] although the diagnostic sherds from flat bottoms are lacking."

### Graeber Cave

Graeber Cave is located in a mountain cliff, with a southern exposure, at the mouth of North Turkey Creek. It was probably occupied on a seasonal basis. About one hundred sherds of micaceous clay ceramics were recovered. Bone fragments and stone tools indicate hunting as a major activity. A ceramic vessel identified as Shoshone Intermountain ware (finger-pressed, flat bottomed) is considered especially significant as it represents one of the few partially reconstructable vessels of its kind in Colorado (Nelson 1966). However, a corner-notched point in association with the pottery confuses the issue (Liestman and Kranzush 1987). The radiocarbon dates for this site fall within the Middle Ceramic period (1291–1407 and 1282–1399). One of these dates comes from a piece of punctuated pottery. This site dates to a period earlier than the standard consensus of Shoshonean occupation, perhaps substantiating the theory that Middle Ceramic people in the other subregions avoided the area because of Shoshonean groups, as suggested in Chapter 3.

*Colorow Cave*

Colorow was a chief of a northern band of Utes (Fig. 4.3). His band spent each summer in the Roaring Fork Valley between Glenwood Springs and Aspen. Chief Colorow gained infamy as a part of the violent uprising against Indian agent Nathan Meeker in

Figure 4.3. Chief Colorow of the Utes. Courtesy of the Colorado Historical Society.

1879, saying, of the stake driven through Meeker's mouth, that it was necessary "to stop his infernal lying." He was a common sight in many Colorado frontier towns, including Denver, obtaining something of a legendary status (Marsh 1982). He is reported to have used this cave as a temporary shelter, along with others of his band, numerous times throughout the late 1800s. Today the cave is used as a party venue and dance floor (Colorado Archaeological Society 1986).

*Possible Ute Pottery*

Arapaho County was the location of an unusual find. A small globular pot, with fingernail indentations and an outflaring rim with a handle of twisted clay, is stylistically Ute, but its thermoluminescence date is in the sixteenth century. The date may be wrong, but it is possible that Utes utilized the plains this early (Kalasz et al. 1996).

*Wickiups*

A wickiup has been defined as "a conical timbered structure, constructed of gathered or cut poles arranged together to form a cone with the pole butts resting on the ground surface or pushed slightly into the ground" (Scott 1988). Wickiup sites are associated with Ute occupation because they are found in traditional Ute territory and have been dated to the historic Ute occupation period. They were, however, constructed by many societies and therefore are not necessarily diagnostic traits for Ute archaeology. Nevertheless, the probability is high that many of the wickiup sites near Greater Denver were associated with a Ute occupation.

Wickiups vary in size from 1 m to over 6 m in diameter. The interior may have a single hearth or none, for the hearth was just as likely to be outside. Generally, they contained unprepared dirt or juniper bark floors. Most activity areas were located outside the structure. Wickiup remains are infrequent in Colorado. Douglas Scott (1988) identified only 61 recorded sites in 13 Colorado counties.

*Scarred Trees*

Culturally scarred trees are those that are stripped of their bark from approximately 30 cm above the ground to 2 m or more. After the bark was peeled from the tree, it was used as a food source, raw material for various objects, building material, and for medicinal purposes (Martorano 1988). Usually the scar is oval or rectangular in shape with one or more points at either end; often the lower scar edge is horizontal with the upper end coming to a point. Often these trees are located outside a campsite. No specific side of the tree was preferred for the procurement of the bark. The evidence that ties peeled trees to the Ute is based on dendrochronology, historic accounts in books, government records and documents, and interviews with local informants.

Most culturally scarred trees in Colorado are found near or west of the Continental Divide. According to Martorano (1988), ponderosa pines are the only species identified as culturally peeled; they grow at elevations of approximately 1,676–3,048 meters in this state. There are no known scarred trees sites in Greater Denver; however, Black (1992:99), during his survey of Dinosaur Ridge in Jefferson County, mentions that "one possible scarred tree was located on the crest of the hogback." Greater survey coverage of the area will possibly reveal more scarred trees.

### Open Camps

Greater Denver has seven recorded Late Ceramic open camps, one of which has been associated with a Ute occupation. There are also six open lithic sites, three of which are considered to be Ute.

A site at the Inspiration Tree Picnic Area and Horse Trail is located on the east slope of the hogback, overlooking the valley of Rooney Gulch. An intermittent stream approximately 200 meters away is the nearest water source. Ute Chief Colorow is known to have visited the adjacent "Ute Council Tree," also known as the "Chief Colorow Council Tree" or the "Inspiration Tree." The tree is a large ponderosa pine around which the chief and his band were said to have held council meetings in the 1860s and 1870s.

### Comanche

The Comanche, like the Ute, were of Shoshonean linguistic stock. They were first recorded in 1705 when the Spanish reported them trading in Taos. In the next year Ulibarri reported that the Comanche and allied Ute were about to attack that community. At that time their homeland was thought to be in the valleys around the headwaters of the Arkansas River. Comanche may have been an offshoot of the closely related Shoshone peoples in western Wyoming, southern Idaho, and northern Utah. From this region the Comanche are believed to have spread in two directions: east onto the plains and to the southeast. The Comanche, initially a mountain-based hunting and gathering people, later became highly mobile plains bison hunters and raiders (Hyde 1959:64–65; Kenner 1969:28; Shimkin 1940:40; Wedel 1959:75–76; Weber 1990). While documentary evidence of the Comanche in Greater Denver is thin, numerous accounts of them in the general region exist.

By 1706 the Comanche were raiding in southeastern Colorado from a base that included Greater Denver. Ulibarri reported Penxaye Apache in the area between the present-day towns of Pueblo and Trinidad retreating from expected attacks by Comanche and Ute. During the following years, attacks by combined Ute and Comanche groups ranged along the Spanish frontier in western Arizona, northern New Mexico, and southern Colorado. "The High Plains from the upper Colorado River of Texas northward to the Platte in Nebraska, and the Colorado Piedmont fronting the Rockies, were firmly in the hands of the Comanche" (Wedel 1959:76).

Spanish attempts to "civilize" some Comanche bands included the construction in 1787 of a fixed village on the Arkansas River near present-day Pueblo, Colorado, in hopes that the Comanche would take up horticulture and stock raising. The Comanche abandoned the settlement after only a year, perhaps because of the death of a headman's favored wife—the Comanche were not comfortable remaining where someone had died—and a general distaste for the confinement of a settled life (Moorhead 1968:161–63; Weber 1990).

Comanche hostilities in the ensuing years decreased. There were reports of struggles with the Osage to the east, and by the late 1700s the weakened Comanche were seeking peace (Gunnerson and Gunnerson 1988). Pressures from the north and the east, from the encroaching Arapaho and Cheyenne, forced them south of the Arkansas River by the early nineteenth century. The Comanche continued their southern and southeastern expansion during the latter half of the eighteenth century. The dissolution of the still formidable Apache barrier east of Pecos by voluntary removal allowed the Colorado Comanche to expand unchecked south and southeast. Until 1758 their winter camps stood on the Arkansas, but by 1761 they had extended southeast to the Canadian River of the Texas Panhandle (Weber 1990).

## Comancheros and Ciboleros

The lives of the Hispanic settlers in the region have been discussed only recently in the history and ethnohistory of the southern High Plains (Kenner 1969). Archaeologically, even less attention has been paid to this group. However, these individuals played an important part in the plains economy prior to the arrival of the Euro-Americans in the 1820s, and continued through the American occupation into the 1870s. They are considered in this section, as they represent an important element in the ethnohistory of the region (Carrillo 1990).

Plains Comanche, Apache, and Ute had a well-established pattern of trade with Pueblo Indians from various villages in northern New Mexico by the beginning of the eighteenth century. The Hispano traders of New Mexico soon joined this network. The New Mexican traders offered, among other items, beads, trinkets, and a wide variety of ironware ranging from knives and axes to bridle bits and cooking utensils. In return, the tribes bartered "buffalo hides, meat, tallow, and captives" (Anderson 1985:44–45; Kenner 1969:37, 40; Stoffle et al. 1984:58; Carrillo 1990).

Despite this active trading, tensions remained high among the groups. Attacks and raids by the tribes resulted in reprisals by the government forces of New Mexico. In August of 1779 Governor Juan Bautista Anza, with the aid of 800 soldiers, settlers, Pueblos, Ute, and Jicarillas, defeated the Comanche chieftain Green Horn (Cuerno Verde), near the base of Greenhorn Mountain, near present-day Pueblo, Colorado. Peace negotiations were concluded between de Anza and Ecueracapa, a Comanche chieftain, at Pecos in 1786. Peaceful relations lasted at least fifty years, and even longer in some locations. This brought about changes in the region, the most significant being the expansion of the New Mexican frontier (Anderson 1985:45; Athearn 1985:18; Friedman 1985:32–33; Kenner 1969:50–63; Stoffle et al. 1984:51–54).

One of the major changes that resulted from the peace treaty was the emergence of the *comancheros*. The term, which is not found in Spanish documents, first appeared in print in *Commerce of the Prairies* by Josiah Gregg in 1844. Because of its detailed descriptions of the Santa Fe Trail and New Mexico, the book was read extensively by many army officers who served in New Mexico in the 1840s and 1850s. When New Mexican traders were met on the plains they were labeled comancheros. They consisted primarily of two groups: the "indigent and rude classes of the frontier villages" (Gregg [1844]1954:257) and the Pueblo Indians who had traded with Plains Indians centuries prior to the arrival of the Spaniards.

About this time trade also was occurring between the comancheros and other tribes inhabiting what is now Colorado. Hides and pelts were traded with the Kiowa on the Arkansas River, with the Pawnee along the Platte River, and with the Arapaho, who by now were located between the South Platte and Arkansas Rivers. Although the Arkansas River Valley served as the center of trade of buffalo hides, New Mexican traders were operating as far east as the Kansas River (in present-day northeastern Kansas). The confluence of the Purgatoire and Arkansas Rivers served as a regular rendezvous area between Plains Native Americans and New Mexican traders.

The comancheros carried trade goods that were greatly desired by the Plains Native Americans, including bread, flour, and cornmeal, as well as sugar, dried pumpkins, onions, tobacco, barley meal, and other dried foods. Manufactured items such as hardware and cloth were rarely traded during the nineteenth century because they were difficult for the comancheros to obtain for themselves (Kenner 1969:84–86).

Using homemade ox carts, the comancheros ranged over a vast region and were quite adept at traversing the subtly featured landscape of the plains. They were reported as far north as the South Platte River in 1811, and as late as 1849 in the vicinity of the Wichita Mountains in Oklahoma and the Davis Mountains in Texas. Other reports indicate that, in addition to the expeditions out to the Comanche and Kiowa, bartering took place with the Sioux, Cheyenne, Arapaho, Crow, Ute, and Shoshone. The principal trade months were August and September, and most trips lasted only a few weeks (Kenner 1969:82–88).

Another important group that came into prominence at the same time as the comancheros was the New Mexican buffalo hunters or *ciboleros*. This name derived from the Spanish name for bison, *cibolo*. The new pattern of New Mexican-Plains Native American relationships that evolved after the 1786 treaty stimulated organized bison hunts on the plains, although the Pueblos had hunted bison sporadically in New Mexico before the arrival of the Spanish. While the Spaniards and the Pueblos probably obtained most of their buffalo meat and hides through barter, buffalo hunting is mentioned in seventeenth-century documents. For example, a great bison hunt occurred in Texas in 1683, when an estimated 8,000 buffalo were killed (Kenner 1969:98–100). As Gregg ([1844]1954) observed, the weaponry, clothing, and other characteristics of the ciboleros closely resembled that of Native Americans of the High Plains.

Two major political changes—the shift from Spanish to Mexican control and subsequent shift from Mexican to American control—did not greatly affect the activities of the comancheros and ciboleros. However, events occurred over a relatively short period of time which effectively ended their activities. After the Civil War ended, and Euro-American migration westward began in earnest, the Plains Indians were subjugated and placed on reservations. Bison were nearly exterminated by Euro-American buffalo hunters to satisfy the fashion demands for buffalo robes by easterners and Europeans. The demise of the ciboleros is closely linked with the demise of the Native American occupation in Colorado. A traditional way of life which had endured for centuries thus came to an end (Kenner 1969:112-14).

Many of the former Hispanic buffalo hunters and traders turned to herding sheep for their livelihood. It is suspected that these individuals and their descendants left their mark in the region (Kenner 1969). What we see of their presence in the archaeological record may include the remnants of old sheep camps or artifacts such as chipped stone or glass tools.

Although many prehistoric archaeologists consider stone tools unique to Native Americans, there are enough references to the practice of Hispanic flint knapping and stone tool use to make this view questionable. For example, lithic and chipped glass tools are an integral part of some ceremonies of the Penitentes, a religious sect active in New Mexico and Colorado (Carrillo 1996).

In two unnamed sites noted on University of Denver site cards, for example, artifacts of worked glass have been found. One contained four pieces of chipped glass that had been flaked on one side in a manner that resembled scraper-like tools. At the other, there were also four pieces of flaked glass in addition to two pieces of chipped stone. These two sites also contain early historic trash such as farms and ranch equipment, plate fragments, and children's toys. The recorders of the sites list a cultural affiliation of "Native American/Hispanic," but acknowledge the difficulty of pinning it down (Burney and Mehls 1987). Hispanic lithic technology appears to be one of expediency. Certainly it was much less formal than that of the local Native Americans. Thus we expect a Hispanic lithic toolkit to be characterized by few formal tools, a high percentage of utilized flakes, and a few small finishing flakes.

## Cheyenne

Today the Cheyenne reside on two separate reservations, one in Montana, the other in Oklahoma. They are an Algonquian-speaking group, like the Arapaho. The first historic records of the Cheyenne place them in the vicinity of Lake Superior. Near the end of the seventeenth century they migrated westward to the Red River, which forms the boundary between Minnesota and the Dakotas. There they are known to have lived in sedentary villages, practicing agriculture much like their neighbors the Mandans and Arikaras. It was from these groups that the Cheyenne learned to make pottery. Grinnell (1962) likens their subsistence to that of the Pawnees. The Cheyenne planted and cultivated corn in the spring and then left to hunt buffalo on foot. They would return in the fall to harvest their crops and settle down for the winter. Sometime in the mid- to late 1700s, the horse was introduced to Cheyenne territory.

Like that of many of their neighbors, the Cheyenne way of life was revolutionized by their use of this animal. Hunting bison was much easier and safer on horseback, and as a result the Cheyenne focused a greater share of their time and energy on hunting. As they followed the herds onto the plains, their territory changed. Although they lived

Figure 4.4. Arapaho and Cheyenne encampment near Denver, 1861. Courtesy of the Colorado Historical Society.

near the Black Hills, by the early 1800s they had begun to winter in the plains along the South Platte and the Arkansas (Hoig 1989) (Fig. 4.4).

Despite changes wrought by traders, soldiers, and emigrants, the Cheyenne were still full participants in the plains horse-buffalo tradition through the mid-1800s. This lifestyle was shared by a number of groups who roamed the Great Plains—the Arapaho, Sioux, Comanche, Pawnee, Gros Vente and others. This nomadic lifeway depended on two essential elements: the horse and the buffalo. The horse allowed groups of various geographical origin to inhabit the plains permanently. The buffalo, virtually a sea of animals, were their main prey.

Bison provided the backbone of Cheyenne subsistence. The meat was eaten fresh or dried for later use, often in the form of pemmican, a mixture of berries and meat and fat. The bones were used for tools, the internal organs for carrying bags. In fact, the Cheyenne word for water container is related to their word for heart, the organ used for that purpose (Grinnell 1962). Buffalo robes were used both as blankets and as cushions, processed buffalo hides were also used to make clothing, footwear, bags and—most important—tepees. The hides were also traded.

Groups were organized into bands or camps, made up of one or more kindreds. The kindreds consisted of the parental pair, their daughters with their husbands and children, and perhaps other relatives (Hoebel 1960). This matrilocal pattern may have its origins in their time as gardeners and their association with matrilineal groups like the Mandan and the Hidatsa.

Within the family itself there were differentiations. The Cheyenne pattern divided labor based on gender. Men were the hunters and took care of the horses, conducted raids, and defended the village. Women were the tailors, the architects, and the cooks. Because of their familiarity with the botanical stores of the plains, women also gathered and processed a number of medicinal herbs. Both sexes practiced the healing arts, but medicine women were especially important during birthing; they processed the root of *Balsamorrhiza sagittata* for easy delivery, and made a milk medicine from bark that was taken before breast-feeding (Grinnell 1962).

The typical dwelling was the tepee, made of tanned buffalo hide drawn over poles, which was ubiquitous among the Plains tribes. As Grinnell (1962) points out, during the summer little protection from the cold was needed, but hail and thunderstorms are not uncommon on the plains in the summer and the temperature cools at night. During the rest of the year wind and snow intermittently are forces to be contended with. The tepee, with its fire burning in the center, served as a warm and portable shelter.

The tepees were constructed by women, who owned them. A single woman would tan the skins and collect the sinew to sew them together, but groups would be called in to assist with the final construction of the lodge. When it was completed, only the woman who owned it was able to pass in and out until it had been dedicated (Grinnell 1962).

---

Box 4C. Women's Roles and Status in Cheyenne Life

Lewis Garrard observed the moving of a Cheyenne camp:

> After a ride of two hours, we stopped, and the chiefs fastening their horses, collected in circles, to smoke the pipe and talk, letting their squaws unpack the animals, pitch the lodges, build fires, arrange the robes. . . . I was provoked, nay angry to see the lazy, overgrown men, do nothing to help their wives; and, when the young women pulled off their bracelets and finery, to chop wood, the cup of my wrath was full to overflowing. (Garrard [1850]1955:55–56)

Garrard was not alone when he denounced the workload of Plains Indian women. To many Euro-Americans, the hard physical labor performed by plains women was abominable (Hoig 1989). Middle to upper class white women worked hard, but their role was to be "the light of the home," as a Victorian magazine called it (Green 1983). Undeniably, Cheyenne women worked hard, but they also possessed great influence. George Bird Grinnell called women "the rulers of the camp. . . . If the sentiment of the women of the camp clearly points to a certain course as desirable, the men are quite sure to act as the women wish" (1962:128–29). Their influence was felt in matters such as camp movement, the decision to go to war, and tribal councils.

The respect garnered by Cheyenne women is evident in courtship and marriage. Women could reject a suitor or even elope, although these were not common occurrences. Polygyny was practiced by some men, but care was taken in choosing a second wife in order to avoid conflict. Usually the second wife was related to the first, often a sister. The concern was that a disgruntled first wife was likely to leave. Divorce, initiated by either party, occurred in the case of incompatible marriages. A widow controlled her remarriage, often stipulating that her new husband help support and care for her children (Berthrong 1963). Despite (or perhaps in part due to) the flexibility of marriage patterns, Cheyenne marriages were often very happy. Husbands and wives were partners and tended to bear deep, lifelong affection one for another. Grinnell eloquently writes of such marriages, "I have seen many examples of such attachment, seldom expressed in words, but shown in the daily conduct of life, where in all his occupations the man's favorite companion was the wife he had courted as a girl and by whose side he had made his struggle for success and now at last had grown old" (1962:128).

In addition to constructing tepees, women tanned hides for other tasks, especially for the manufacture of clothing. The woman's toolkit for tanning hides consisted of a scraper (either metal or stone), a flesher made of an elkhorn with a stone or steel blade in the end, the proximal end of a buffalo humerus (for scraping hides), and a softening rope or buffalo shoulder blade with a hole for softening the tanned hide. Fleshers were often family heirlooms passed from mother to daughter (Grinnell 1962).

Every woman also owned a sewing kit that included awls of catfish spine, thorns, or sharpened bone; thread of either sinew or twisted milkweed bark; and items for use as decoration such as porcupine quills, dried black grass, and fine roots. These were all kept together in a leather bag worn at the waist. Women took great pride in their skill as seamstresses and quillers. In fact, talented women belonged to quilling societies. Like members of the men's war societies, on ceremonial occasions these women were asked to count coup. For the warriors coup meant those taken in battle, for quillers it meant the number of robes they had decorated (Grinnell 1962).

Other important women's tools included those used to procure and prepare food. Each woman had her own digging stick, which was usually made of wood with a knob to hold onto and a point at the end. The digging stick was given to women by the Great Medicine Spirit and it had sacred aspects. It was one of the pieces of ritual paraphernalia used in the Sun Dance (Hoebel 1960). Stone hammers were also an important part of women's equipment. Large hammers were used to break up firewood and large bones and to drive tent stakes. Smaller hammers were used to crush up bone in order to extract marrow. The smallest resembled mortars and pestles and were used primarily for grinding up chokecherries for pemmican, and processing herbs. (Grinnell 1962)

*Arapaho and Cheyenne Archaeology*

Raised to a fever pitch by the 1845 annexing of Texas and fueled by the philosophy of Manifest Destiny, expansionism roared through North America. In the summer of 1846, a group of Cheyenne trading at Bent's Fort witnessed the end of an era. The

Army of the West was preparing to invade Mexico. Seventeen hundred troops under General Kearny's charge filled the Arkansas valley. The sight prompted a number of Cheyenne to remark that they had no idea there were "so many people in the white men's tribe" (Lavender 1954:276). Kearny's troops marched on to Santa Fe, taking the capital without bloodshed. Ironically, Kearny's task was made easier by the hope in New Mexico that the U.S. government would do a better job of protecting them from Indian raids than the Mexican government had.

The Army of the West had seemed a flood of white faces when they arrived, but two things happened in 1848 that assured they were only the first trickle. Within two weeks of each other the Treaty of Guadalupe Hidalgo was signed and gold was discovered at Sutter's Mill in California. The increasing emigrant and army trains either slaughtered buffalo or scared them away. The always-scarce firewood supply was depleted along every travel corridor. Worst of all, many travelers took to shooting Indians on sight. Cheyenne troubles mounted with introduced diseases; it has been estimated that in 1849 approximately half the Southern Cheyenne were wiped out by cholera (Lavender 1954). Conflicts and struggles continued to escalate.

Although the army had established Fort Laramie and Fort Kearny along the Platte, troops were not enough to keep the peace. A treaty, it was argued, would be much cheaper for the government than a war on the Plains. Indian Superintendent D. D. Mitchell proposed that the tribes be assigned to specific areas marked by geographic boundaries such as rivers and mountains. They were to travel only within their own regions and would be held responsible for any skirmishes that might occur on their land (Berthrong 1963). The Treaty of Fort Laramie, signed in 1851, recognized the aboriginal possession of the area between the North Platte and the Arkansas by the Cheyenne and Arapaho. The western boundary was made up of the Rocky Mountains, and the eastern edge contained about the western third of Kansas. This included, of course, the land that was to become Greater Denver. Because the passes through the Colorado mountains were so difficult, the main travel routes avoided this area, going either north or south. Fur traders recorded many encounters with Arapaho and Cheyenne groups in the nineteenth century. In 1859, traders recorded an Arapaho village near the present city of Castle Rock (quoted in Eddy et al. 1981).

The 1851 treaty served its purpose for a number of years. But the discovery of gold at the confluence of Cherry Creek and the South Platte in 1858 brought a new wave of immigrants into the heart of Cheyenne and Arapaho territory. Mostly in anticipation of problems to come, agents began negotiations in 1860 that led to the signing of the Fort Wise Treaty of 1861. This treaty exchanged the traditional Cheyenne hunting land between the Platte and Arkansas Rivers for a smaller reservation extending from Sand Creek to the Huerfano Creek along the Arkansas River (Royce 1899).

When the Cheyenne were still sedentary, they made pottery. Other cooking and eating dishes included bowls made from turtle shells or the knots of box elder trees and spoons made from the horns of mountain sheep or buffalo (Grinnell 1962). As the tribe became more nomadic and trade increased on the Missouri, pottery-making disappeared (Berthrong 1963). Metal kettles and tin cups were popular trade items. They were, among other things, much less breakable than the pottery.

One of the distinguishing marks of historic Plains Indian sites is the metal projectile point. In fact, a site in the Comanche National Grasslands has been assigned a Cheyenne affiliation based on the presence of a metal point. Grinnell (1962) claims that, after the introduction of metal, stone tools were abandoned as everyday items, although they took on ritual power. However, he goes on to state that "the Cheyennes, like the Blackfeet and the Pawnees, say that wounds made by the old stone arrow points were more likely to be fatal than those made by the arrowpoints of later time" (Grinnell 1962:183). This statement seems to indicate that in order for them to have known the difference, stone points were still present, or at least talked about. Other trade goods are sometimes found in sites or on surveys, including glass beads that were found in a site along Cherry Creek (Miller and Fiero 1977).

## Arapaho

The Arapaho were closely related to the Cheyenne (Kroeber 1902). Gunnerson and Gunnerson (1988:ix–x) note the numerous gatherings that took place among various tribes in locations in and around the study area. These included Cherry Creek, Fort St. Vrain, and Fort Lupton, where an intertribal Sun Dance was held in August 1843. Francis Parkman (1945:255) tells of sighting an abandoned Arapaho camp on the South Platte in 1847. He estimated 300 hearths, as well as sweat lodges. Other meeting places included the hot springs (named "fontaine qui bouille" or "bouit") on Fountain Creek, near Pueblo. "These are said to have been considered sacred by various Indian tribes, and the area around them was neutral ground" (Gunnerson and Gunnerson 1988:x). Inhabitants of the plains and Front Range foothills frequently left arrowpoints and other items of material culture as offerings to the spirits/water monsters believed to reside in the springs.

An interesting account that resulted from the increased contact between the Euro-Americans and the area's previous inhabitants was written by Augusta Hauck, whose father was a homesteader along Boulder Creek in the late 1880s. It is a tale of an Arapaho hunt that took place in the fall of 1862. Jean Matthews Kindig (1987) evaluates the story as a reliable source of information about the Arapaho. Although it has flaws, she concludes, it can in large part be substantiated by other historical documentation and should be considered important resource. Below are some excerpts from the Hauck manuscript:

> To the squaws and larger children fell the work of dressing the game that had been killed in the round-up. The first step was to skin the carcasses, next, the meat was cut into pieces, so as to hurry the drying process. These thin slices were then hung on improvised racks, made of the branches of large willows and cottonwoods. These were built tight to keep the "jerked" meat out of the reach of their dogs. The tops of the protruding tepee poles were also hung with the thin slices of flesh.
>
> Scattered between the trees, tepees, and racks of the drying meat could be seen many small groups of squaws, usually two or three in number, bending over

taughtly [sic] stretched hides, scraping, graining, or braining, in the order that the tanning process called for. Some were carefully watching the skins suspended over the smokepits. While others were shrinking the buffalo skins over hot embers, to thicken them for moccasin soles and shield surfaces. Tanning of the skins was a particular work and fell to the squaws, and great pride was taken in this art, to see who could turn out the finest fur robes, buckskin and rawhide. The curing of intestines for containers in which to keep beads, seeds, and small arrows, was an art in itself. Here and there were groups holding the strong tendons, while some of the squaws with sharp flint knives were splitting the sinews into threadlike fibers, later to be used in the sewing of leather garments, moccasins and beadwork. (Kindig 1987:19)

The hides used for tepees were often held down on the outside by stones or sometimes sod pieces (Brasser 1982). When the tepees were taken down these anchors were left behind. Remaining circles, of course, would indicate the presence of a formerly occupied area. These remnants of past activity are often called "tepee rings," though "stone circles" is sometimes preferred because stones were also used to anchor brush structures (Brasser 1982) or for other purposes (Keyser 1979). It has been suggested that snow was sometimes used to anchor tepees during the winter months. Later wooden or bone pegs were frequently used, as they could be easily carried from location to location (Powell 1990).

Though the Cheyenne and Arapaho used tepees, so did many other groups, and none of the known Late Ceramic tepee ring sites in Greater Denver have been given a specific ethnic or tribal association. Part of the problem in assigning stone circle sites to any particular group of people is that there are usually very few associated remains found with them (Smith, McNees, and Reust 1995; Mulloy 1960). Also notable is the fact that none of the stone circle sites tentatively assigned to the Late Ceramic period here are located within the Plains subregion; all of them are in the Hogback subregion. For example, a site in Jefferson County, on the top of a terrace overlooking the South Platte, contains 15 stone circles, as well as projectile points, scrapers, knives, manos, and metate fragments. It was first recorded in 1954 by the University of Denver and revisited by that same institution in 1967. The first recorder noted that there were fire pit features associated with the stone circles, but no mention was made of those features by the second recorder. Based on the presence of rock rings this site is assigned a Late Ceramic affiliation, but we cannot say who used the site. Indeed, its proximity to other Ute sites and Ute territory might tempt one to make the assumption that the site is Ute.

## Native Americans and Euro-Americans

Other descriptions of Native Americans in and around Denver written during the latter half of the nineteenth century were with few exceptions unsympathetic and derogatory. Tales of travel and adventure in the untamed west were quite popular. One of the more colorful narratives to emerge from this period of westward expansion was that of Horace Greeley, who wrote *An Overland Journey from New York to San Francisco*, *in the Summer of 1859.* From Denver, on June 16, 1859, Greeley penned this chapter in his saga, a good portion of which bears repeating here, since it reflects Denver itself and appears to be indicative of the popular thought at the time.

> "LO! THE POOR INDIAN!"
>
> Some two or three hundred lodges of Arapahoes are encamped in and about this log city [Denver], calculating that the presence of the whites will afford some protection to their wives and children against a Ute onslaught.... An equal or larger body of Utes are camped in the mountains some forty or fifty miles west [in the Hogback region], and the Arapaho warriors recently returned in triumph from a war party, on which they managed to steal about a hundred horses from the Utes.... They are going out again in a day or two, and have been for some days practising secret incantation and public observances with reference thereto.... But the Indians are children. Their arts, wars, treaties, alliances, habitations, crafts, properties, commerce, comforts, all belong to the very lowest and rudest ages of human existence.... To the prosaic observer, the average Indian of the woods and prairies is a being who does little credit to human nature—a slave of appetite and sloth, never emancipated from the tyranny of one animal passion save by more ravenous demands of another.... Squalid and conceited, proud and worthless, lazy and lousy, they will strut out or drink out their miserable existence, and at length afford the world a sensible relief by dying out of it. (Greeley 1964 [1860])

Astonishingly ethnocentric as these comments seem reading them today, such tirades were commonplace at the time. Article after article and book after book were no less harsh. The extent to which the people of Denver completely dismissed the idea of a Cooperesque nobility among the Indians cannot be underestimated. Indeed, it was the overall consensus that savagery and filth were the preeminent characteristics of the region's native inhabitants. According to Ward Churchill, "The overwhelming preponderance of writing concerning the American Indian during U.S. expansion was designed to create an image allowing conquest: 'for the Indians own good,' to effect 'betterment' and 'progress.' Perhaps to assuage the guilt of what amounted to cultural genocide, the writers and readers of such literature convinced themselves that the 'savage' would be better off shedding their 'heathen' ways for 'civilization'" (1992:35). Lawrence Michael Kennedy (1967), in a thesis entitled "The Colorado Press and the Red Men: Local Opinions About Indian Affairs, 1859–1870," documents more than a decade of popular wisdom on the subject. Early newspapers, particularly the *Rocky Mountain News*, regularly vilified Denver's neighboring tribes. On July 9, 1859, the *News* reported that three miners camped in the nearby mountains had been ambushed by Ute scoundrels. One of the men escaped unharmed, but the two others were shot and scalped. Later the "North American Thugs," as the Ute were called, attacked another group of seven, killing them all. "Blood calls for blood," they editorialized, claiming that dozens of others had fallen victim to the "blood-thirsty savages." If the government did not adequately punish the brutal perpetrators, the paper suggested,

Figure 4.5. Tepees in encampment in the South Platte Valley, 1874. Courtesy of the Colorado Historical Society.

the people ought to take matters into their own hands (Kennedy 1967:25). In January 1862 the *News* printed "An Illustrated History: Colorado Territory," the accompanying text of which described the Indians as "a wretched, ignorant, squalid race! Void of all feeling attributed to them; treacherous, crafty and indolent," and predicted that they would "vanish before the strides of civilization" (Kennedy 1967:38).

Despite this and many other scathing editorials, the *News* at other times called for moderation in dealing with the Indian presence. Not only did they acknowledge that all Denver was "squatting" on land still held in treaty by Native Americans (Fig. 4.5), there was a general sentiment that some of the Euro-American population brought trouble on themselves by harassing the tribes and providing them with liquor that exacerbated the problem. More significantly, the paper's editors had a Denver-centric point of view. Should the Denver population continue to provoke the Native American populations residing near them, the effect could be a disastrous Indian war. The overarching concern, it seems, was the damage it might do to Denver's image as a wonderful place to live. A key role, in fact, of the area's papers was to promote immigration from the East. The *News* commented, "At this critical juncture in its development, Colorado Territory must have peace and a level-headed approach to Indian Affairs" (Kennedy 1967:36).

The concern Denver seemed to be manifesting about its "Big City" image is exemplified in concerns about a Ute "scalp dance." In 1871 a special Ute Agency was established in Denver as a post for those Utes not removed to White River Reservation. Agent James B. Thompson wrote a report to his commissioner in Washington, D.C., concerning the attempts by U. M. Curtis (an agency interpreter) to profit from the exhibition of a scalp dance "under canvas" in the city. Mr. Curtis had arranged with the Ute for a show of "war attire," parades, and the dance, for which he had sold tickets. After much disagreement, conferences with the mayor and other officials, and no small amount of confrontation, Curtis's "reply was that the Mayor and myself [Thompson] might go to hell, that the show would go on and he would like to see any man or men prevent it." Thompson successfully stopped the event (Covington 1953).

Despite the agent's efforts, however, the very next year a scalp dance was held. Chauncey Thomas wrote down the account of his mother, who was a spectator:

> Mother said there were about a thousand white people there, watching the proceedings . . . She remembers that old Colorow was within about twenty feet of the carriage, and that he was really wrought up. . . . She says that they had a rope circle, perhaps seventy-five to one hundred feet in diameter, the Indians standing outside of it, each holding the rope with both hands, waving it up and down, hopping up and down themselves, grunting, and sometimes yelling, but not circling; perhaps about two hundred of them male and female, but no children holding the rope. . . . Inside this rope circle there were three very old squaws, dirty, repulsive old hags, each holding aloft a long pole, and on the tip of each pole was a fresh scalp, stretched to about the size of a dinner plate, and these old women were crow-hopping in characteristic fashion around inside the rope circle, chanting gutterally. (Covington 1953: 123)

The *Rocky Mountain News* reported in July 1874 that "The Utes, with the pious Piah at their head, held a scalp dance last evening, near Sloan Lake, over three bloody Cheyenne topknots, which dangled from three poles. The barbarous scene was witnessed by a crowd of at least five hundred people. . . . It was disgusting to notice, among the spectators, lots of ladies, prominent in church and society circles, straining for a sight of the reeking scalps, which they scanned as eagerly as if they had been new bonnets" (Covington 1953:123–24).

Such accounts—filtered of the blatant racism and sexism—possess value in their potential to shape our knowledge of prehistory and history, if we subscribe to a direct ethnological/historical approach. At least they provide an opportunity to sample the opinions of the times; at best they provide insight into a transitional period in the lives of both Native and Euro-Americans. Certainly the lines between the contact period and fully historic periods are blurred (Fig. 4.6). Some contact was immediately destructive. In other circumstances, traditional lifeways persisted for decades after outside influences began to filter in. Building a more thorough understanding of this period will certainly increase our knowledge of prehistory.

Figure 4.6. Utes posing in downtown Denver, 1882. Courtesy of the Colorado Historical Society.

Recorded contact period sites in Greater Denver are few (22) and fail to provide extensive information about the period in this area. The majority of the sites in Greater Denver provide insufficient data to determine cultural affiliation. We have already discussed the few sites that have been assigned to a particular time period or group of people, and what we know about the remaining sites is even less. Nevertheless, archaeologists look for broad patterns in scattered data, and the accumulated information ultimately gives rise to useful generalizations. Some general observations from the data available include the following.

- The contact period is represented in all four subregions, though it is most predominant in the Hogback, where 11 sites have been recorded. The other three regions are more sparsely represented: the Black Forest contains six sites, the Streams has three, and only two have been recorded in the Plains.
- Open camps and open lithic site types are most prevalent in all subregions except the Streams.
- Open architectural sites appear in the Black Forest, Streams, and the Hogback, but none are recorded for the Plains.

- Sheltered sites, as might be expected based on physiographic characteristics, are found on the Hogback, which contains three, and the Black Forest, which has one.
- Twelve sites have only a Late Ceramic occupation.
- Ten sites begin with an earlier occupation, but Late Ceramic is the final (latest) component.
- Two sites have a historic as well as a prehistoric component.

The Ute occupation of the Front Range is perhaps better documented than that of other tribes; use of the area by Plains Indian tribes is virtually invisible in the archaeological record. No tepee ring sites (stone circles), commonly associated with plains nomadism, have been recorded in the Plains subregion, and the Dismal River (Apachean) site is tenuously ascribed.

Our knowledge of this period remains imperfect. Scholars disagree on the precise dating and terminology; the temporal lines are not clearly drawn. Where a time period begins and ends is difficult to determine. The subsequent historic conflict and coexistence between Native American inhabitants and Euro-Americans stretched out over decades. The Denver area, we should remember, was influenced by European expansion much later than areas south of the study area. Still, the broad patterns of history that are illustrated in regionwide accounts of cultural interaction can and do inform our understanding of the Denver area.

CHAPTER 5

# Historic Archaeology

In the late 1850s prospectors found gold in the Platte River and Cherry Creek. Their activities set in motion a dynamic that would permanently change social, political, and economic relationships in the area. Soon merchants, bankers, hotel operators, ranchers, farmers, and a host of others heard the call of the Rocky Mountain West. Skirmishes over land development, battles for political power, and struggles to secure a railroad connection followed in short order. Denver was on the way to urbanization.

We have already seen the consequences for Native Americans, who had increasingly restricted access to the Denver region as more settlers came from the east. This chapter will explore the processes and effects of urbanization for these early settlers. Our focus is on the subregion we have designated Streams, which contains the bulk of Denver's urban core.

"Urban" is a term that implies a set of conditions very different from "rural" or "suburban." These conditions include greater population density, an ethnically diverse population, concentrated resources (e.g., labor, capital), integration into national and international transportation systems and markets, and centralized administrative control as reflected by the construction of public buildings and spaces.

> Box 5A. Ralston, a Frontier Cemetery
>
> The Ralston Cemetery, near North Table Mountain on the northwestern periphery of the study area, provides us with an example of Denver area material culture prior to urbanization. Other cemeteries in the Denver area, notably Mt. Olivet, a Catholic cemetery very near Ralston, reflect the hallmarks of urbanization—standardization, control of public spaces, and an ethnically diverse population. Ralston is a frontier cemetery because it reflects none of those characteristics. The cemetery makes use of a natural feature, a hill (Fig. 5.1). The graves ring the hill, with no particular pattern (Fig. 5.2). The headstones generally face east, which is typical of a Christian cemetery, but they vary as much as 14 degrees in their orientation.
>
> The original fence line of the cemetery is clearly demarcated by an area of native shortgrass prairie vegetation, including yucca, prickly pear, primrose, sand sage, beeweed, and lupine (Fig. 5.3). Where there are no monuments, the grave sites are marked by stone outlines or bunches of irises. Ralston is, above all, organic. It was not laid out by an authority who sold plots and platted out the city of the dead. It grew by accretion, one burial site at a time. Ralston's earliest remaining headstones date to 1869, two years before the introduction of the railroad and the standardization of Denver public spaces.

Figure 5.1. Ralston Cemetery, Arvada. From Bonnie J. Clark, ed., Archaeological Investigations and Cultural Resources Management Plan for the Archaeological Resources of the Rocky Mountain Arsenal, 1997; reproduced by permission.

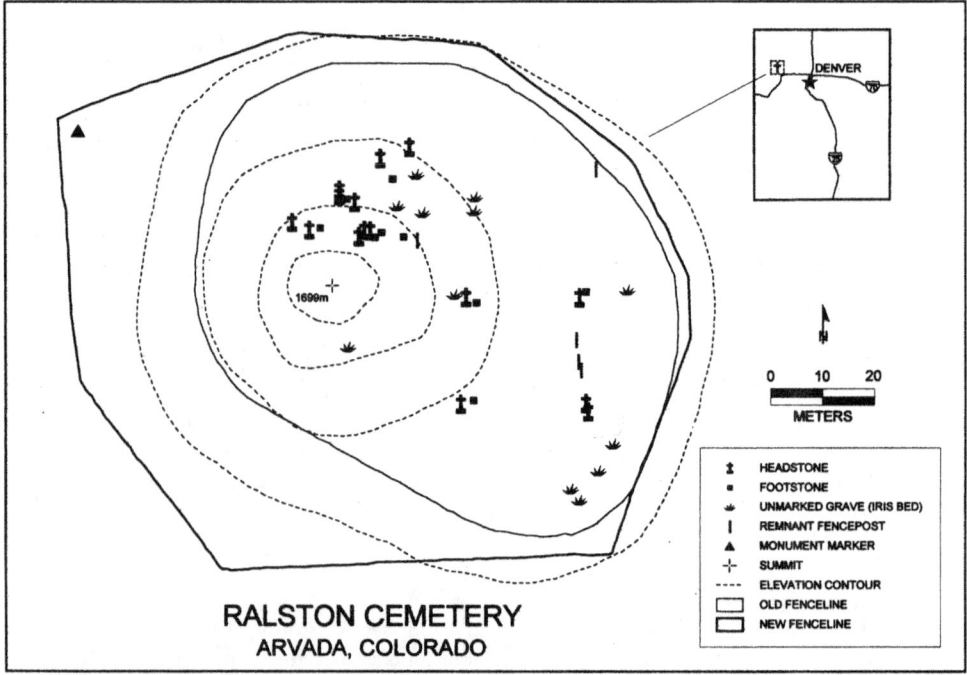

Figure 5.2. Map of Ralston Cemetery. Francine Patterson.

Figure 5.3. Vegetation at Ralston Cemetery. From Bonnie J. Clark, ed., Archaeological Investigations and Cultural Resources Management Plan for the Archaeological Resources of the Rocky Mountain Arsenal, 1997; reproduced by permission.

The participants in this urban development brought with them behavior patterns learned elsewhere. Different ways of conducting life such as constructing houses, preparing food, conducting business, and dumping refuse had to be adapted to a frontier environment. The nature and results of these behaviors can be explored in archaeological contexts. In this chapter we use the urban archaeological record to discuss the lives of early Denverites caught up in a maelstrom of changes that transformed Denver from a tent city to a thriving metropolis within a period of less than fifty years. The common hurdles and challenges that faced people of diverse ethnic backgrounds in urban Denver, as well as the coping strategies used by particular groups for achieving their ends, are of interest.

At the same time, Denver did not become a carbon copy of an eastern town. What made Denver different from other examples of urbanization in the West and elsewhere? There are few models for Denver's urban growth, but Gunther Barth's (1988) formulation of the "instant city"—a city that grows up out of wilderness in less than a generation—is one. The archaeological research reported in this chapter will allow us to evaluate this model and refine and amend it. As tends to happen in inquiries such as this, we will raise more questions and research directions than provide answers.

Our approach in this chapter is to bring together archival and archaeological data that can illuminate Denver's urbanization. The written record necessarily reflects the social, political, economic, and religious values of a time and place filtered through the perspective of the predominant worldview. The archaeological record can supply a corrective by disclosing the actual locations where events transpired and participants interacted. The two records when used together produce a particularly powerful hybrid framework for making sense of historical realities, one with broad scope and appeal.

There have been 480 sites with historic archaeological remains recorded in the Denver Basin (Fig. 5.4). Thus we cannot deal with every archaeological project and site relevant to urbanizing Denver. We focus on three projects that speak to different aspects of the urban story and allow glimpses of life in a variety of social contexts. The Tremont House Hotel gives us insight into life at the urban core, the Mile Houses into the lives and circumstances of those traveling to and from Denver, and the Rocky Mountain Arsenal into life at the urban periphery (Fig. 5.5).

## Historical Background

The history of Denver has been well covered in several books (Dorsett 1977; Leonard and Noel 1990) and articles. In this section we recount Denver's history with an eye toward changes in its material culture and built environment, which are of particular interest to archaeologists.

Denver had modest beginnings in 1858, with the founding of Auraria and Denver on opposite sides of Cherry Creek. The earliest structures were crude cottonwood log shacks, chinked with mud, with log chimneys plastered with heavy adobe, dirt floors, and no glass windows (Fig. 5.6). These structures reflected the transient lifeways of the early inhabitants who came to find gold. But permanence came quickly—Thomas Warren opened the first Denver brickyard in 1859. At that time the streets of Denver

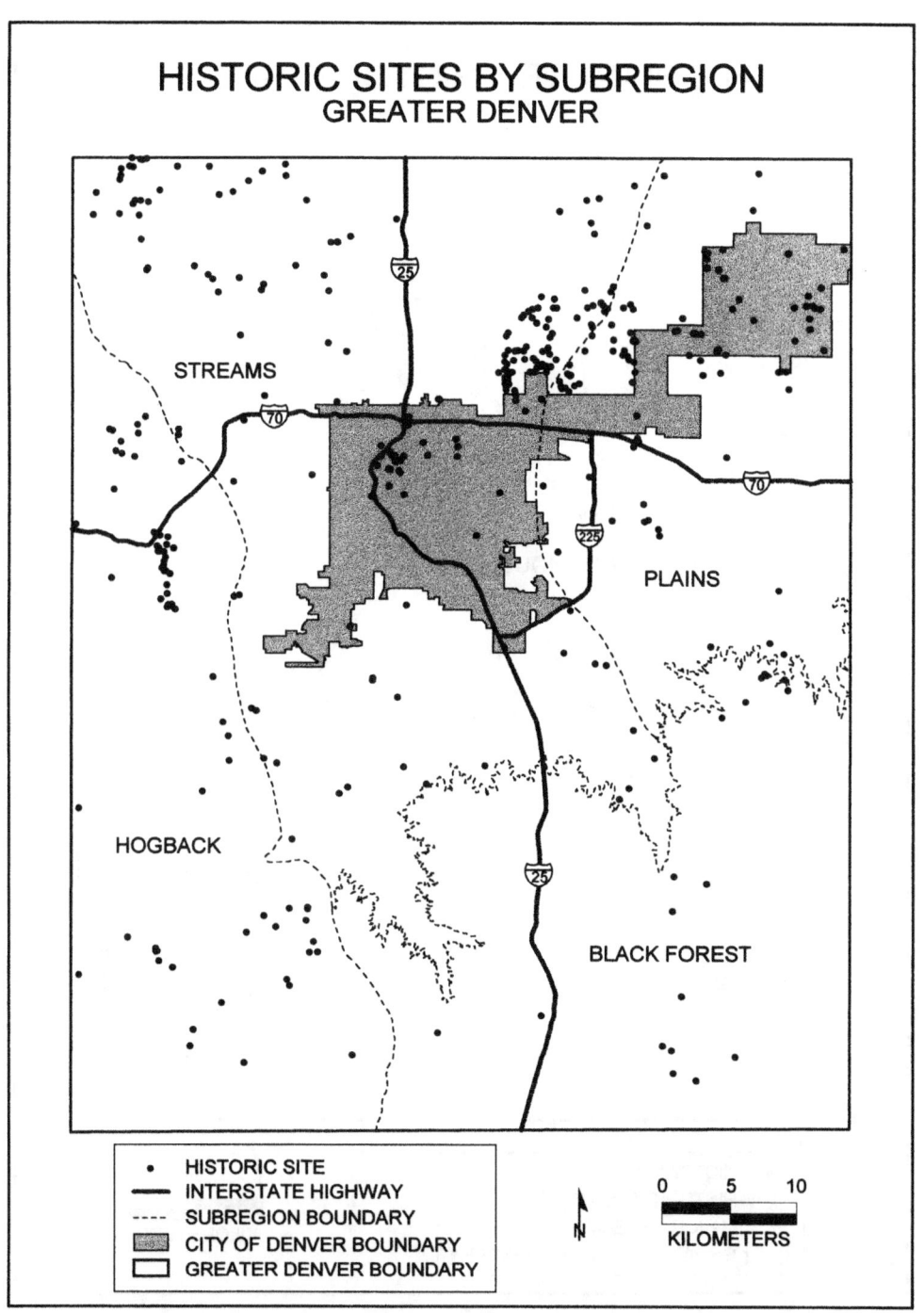

Figure 5.4. Distribution of historic sites by subregion. Francine Patterson.

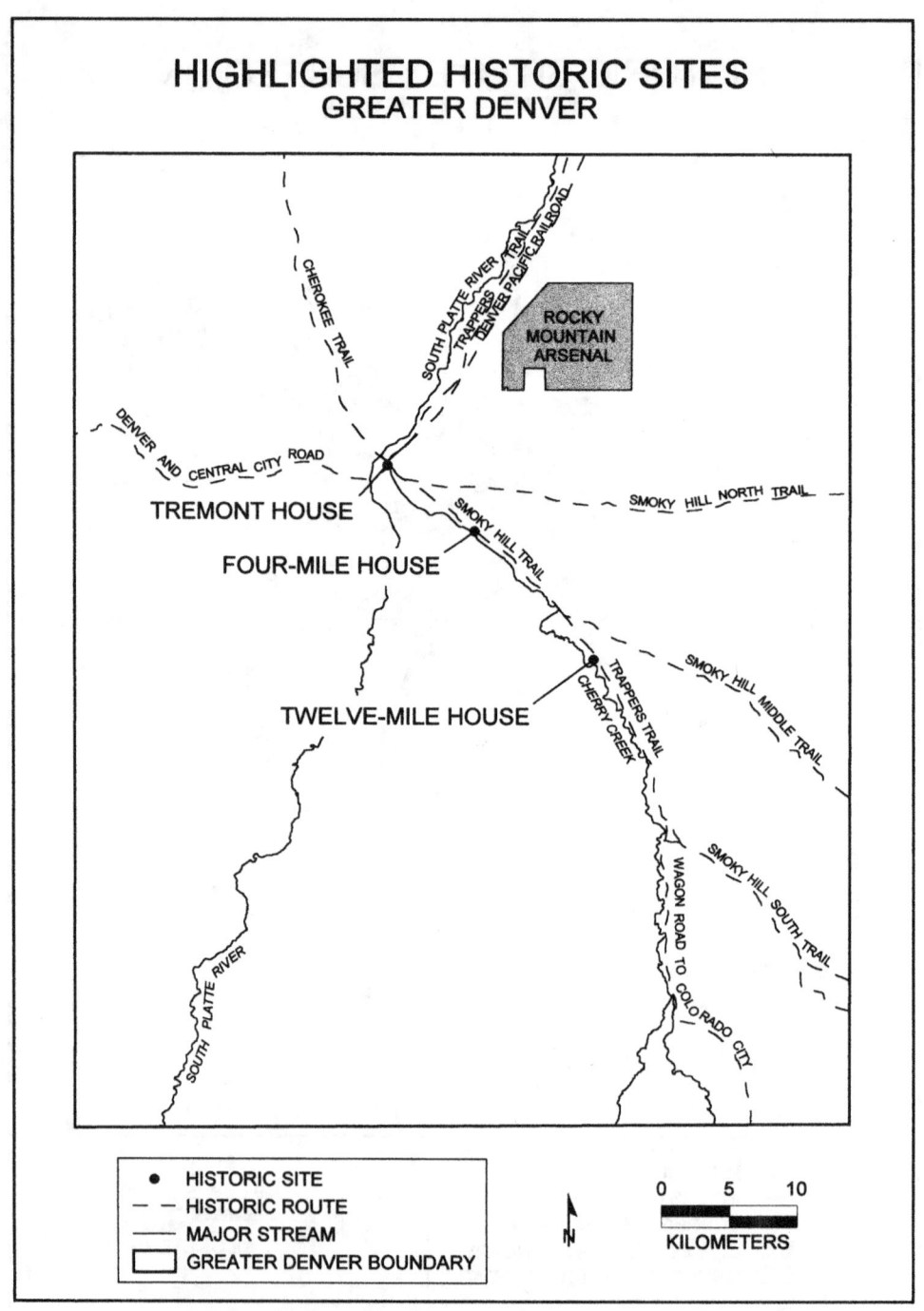

Figure 5.5. Historic sites discussed in this volume. Francine Patterson.

Figure 5.6. House at the corner of Wynkoop and 12th Streets, Denver, erected by A. H. Baker, the first house after the commencement of the official survey, November 1, 1858. Illustrates the earliest house type in Denver. Courtesy of the Colorado Historical Society.

and Auraria were ungraded and without lawns, flowers, or trees. Sidewalks consisted of dirt trails along the edge of the road. Water was carried in by barrels from the creek or obtained from private wells.

The spring of 1859 brought an increase in population, and new buildings sprang up in the two little towns. The influx of miners and visitors created a need for housing and services. By the time the *Rocky Mountain News* published its first issue in April 1859, Auraria consisted of 150 homes, three stores, two hotels, one bakery, one print shop, two saloons, two meat markets, a blacksmith, a carpenter, a tinsmith, and a tailor (Fig. 5.7).

Compared to the great cities of the East, the two towns were crude, dirty, disorganized, expensive, and culturally deprived. However, despite the primitive appearance of the two settlements, numerous trappings of civilization had already arisen. Billiards, chess, and debating clubs, a circulating library, newsstands, horse racing, poetry readings, and religious services were available to early residents of Denver and Auraria.

By 1860 the two towns were engaged in fierce competition. Denver City had grown faster than Auraria and had more hotels, saloons, and businesses. This was in part a result of the Denver City Company's success, through political maneuvering, in bringing the Leavenworth and Pikes Peak Stage Company to its side of the creek.

DENVER CITY AND AURARIA.

Figure 5.7. Sketch of early Denver and Auraria. Courtesy of the Colorado Historical Society.

Auraria was more residential, but managed to support a small business district. The rivalry was settled only when the two towns were united under one name, Denver, on April 15, 1860. Auraria became known as West Denver.

As the years progressed, log homes increasingly gave way to frame and brick structures, with wooden floors, glass windows, and shingle roofs. Numerous two-story business blocks were constructed in both parts of town, and more businesses opened. It was definitely not "respectable" in one way, however, as one out of every three buildings contained a saloon.

The gold in Denver's rivers was inconsequential, but the mountains proved to be full of metals. During the period between 1860 and 1870, over $27 million worth of gold came out of the mountains. Denver was becoming a regional business and cultural center, although it remained a town largely supported by transients. In 1860 the population was still under 5,000. It was estimated that during the 1860s between 100,000 and 150,000 unattached men passed through Denver on their way to the gold fields and mining camps. Businesses that served this population were thriving. The *Rocky Mountain News,* in an article dated September 6, 1860, indicated that "The Broadwell, the Platte, the Tremont, the Vasquez, and the Jefferson Hotels, are all doing a good business for this dull season" (*Rocky Mountain News* 1860:3).

Figure 5.8. The David Bruce Powers wagon train from Leavenworth, Kansas, circled in the 1500 block of Market Street, Denver, January 20, 1868. Courtesy of the Colorado Historical Society.

By 1870 the permanent population had added only ten individuals. Transients no doubt brought revenue and stimulated business in Denver, but this type of population did not lead to permanent economic growth. The miners came into town to spend their newfound riches on gambling, liquor, prostitutes, and room and board. But because they did not own property they could not be taxed and they had no vested interest in the community. Streets remained ungraded and treacherous in bad weather. There was no system to obtain public water from the river. Tallow candles were the only form of lighting.

Transportation was the key to growth and development in Denver (Fig. 5.8). Before the arrival of the railroad, the only means of transportation were stagecoach and freight wagon. The first stage line opened for business in 1859. By 1860, there were three competing lines, bringing closer contact with the rest of the country. But stages moved slowly and it took a great deal of time for information and news to reach the isolated community.

Supplies, especially construction materials and food items, were hard to get and often very expensive. Glass and nails remained expensive throughout the decade. Brick was an inexpensive building material because it could be made onsite in Denver. Milled lumber became cheaper and more readily available after the Excelsior Mill opened in 1861.

Until the mid-1860s, the availability of perishable food items such as fruits and vegetables was irregular and the quality questionable. By the summer of 1859 local gardens provided fresh produce, although prices were high. Adequate growing seasons in 1861 and 1862 made vegetables readily available, but a drought in 1863 ruined most of the crops and raised prices again. The year 1864 saw an improvement in produce quality, but crops were once again lost in 1865, this time to grasshoppers. Around this time, the Highline Canal was built to carry water into town. A portion of the water was made available to residents for lawns and trees, in an effort to beautify the desertlike community and make it seem more like an eastern town.

In addition to the produce grown locally, Denver was fed by the wheat fields of Kansas and the vegetable crops of the fertile land north of the city, especially potatoes. Some items were shipped from the Missouri Valley, New Mexico, and even across the Rockies from Utah, but prices were high and shipments irregular. Flour, sugar, cornmeal, potatoes, lard, bacon, and beef were plentiful, although quality and price varied. Butter and cheese were also readily available. Wild game, such as venison, rabbit, turkey, and prairie hens, were common food items until they became scarce in the immediate area because the effects of development on wild habitats. After about 1865, settlers turned to domestically raised cattle and hogs. The arrival of the railroad in 1870 finally tied the region into the nation's transportation and communication network. As a result, mail service improved and yard goods, building supplies, fashions, periodicals, and books became more readily available. By 1872 the previously relatively stable population had doubled.

More typically urban developments occurred, including street grading and the installation of gas in 1871, water pipes in 1872, and electricity in 1880. The city began to "assume metropolitan airs":

> Distinct commercial and residential sections emerged with a central business district around Blake, Larimer, Market, and Fifteenth Street, and a stylish residential area southeast from Fourteenth and Arapaho, where John Evans's house set the pattern for merchants, promoters, and land speculators. Following a serious fire in April 1863, the city rebuilt in an improved style. In the business area, two- and three-story brick structures replaced wooden frame houses after the municipality forbade construction with wood downtown. Residential areas blossomed with two-story houses in Victorian styles, while the completion of an irrigation ditch in 1865 made possible the planting of trees and lawns. The whole effect delighted visitors, who found this "square, proud, prompt little place" an oasis of architectural quality in the dreary West. (Abbott et al. 1982:67)

During the period 1870 to 1900, over $224 million worth of gold and $541 million worth of silver were removed from the mining districts in Colorado. This immense wealth spurred population, building, and business booms in Denver, which quickly became the hub of Colorado's rail network. Boosterism, made easier by improved communication with the eastern cities, attracted new businesses, entrepreneurs, and investors and led to an economic boom. The increase in out-of-state investors resulted in more information about Colorado Territory and Denver being spread back to the east, and people flocked to Denver. Mining speculation was relatively minor, with the majority of investment capital going into transportation, real estate, banking, utilities, and manufacturing.

The arrival of the Denver and Rio Grande Railroad in 1871 (Athearn 1962) and the construction of other railroads through the Platte Valley in the 1880s changed the early character of the South Platte area. By the late 1880s, this area had developed into an important wholesale and warehousing market. By the turn of the century, most of Denver's wealthy had left the older neighborhoods along the South Platte and moved "uptown" toward the state capitol, where they built large mansions. At the same time, major industries such as the Anheuser-Busch and Blatz Breweries opened up new facilities on Wazee Street adjacent to the railroad yards. Many small businesses and industries, including hotels and boardinghouses, livery stables, foundries, and blacksmith and repair shops sprang up to service the railroad lines. Coal yards and stonecutting works represented industries that located adjacent to or within the railroad yards north of Wazee (Carrillo 1987:6).

By the turn of the twentieth century, factories, warehouses, railroad yards, and aging housing lined the banks of the South Platte River. The poor moved into the old neighborhoods. In the one-half-mile-square area between Colfax Avenue, Speer Boulevard, and the South Platte River nearly 8,000 people—one-quarter of them immigrants—inhabited the crowded boardinghouses, small frame homes, and old hotels in 1890. Eastern European Jews began to settle in the area in the 1880s after the German and Irish populations moved uptown. By the early twentieth century, this area was predominately Jewish.

The late nineteenth century also witnessed the emergence of a commercial section on Blake Street east of 13th Street known as Chinatown. The main part of this district consisted of a series of common-wall brick buildings on the north side of Blake. This block represented the third Chinatown district in Denver. The first had been located on 16th Street between Wazee and Blake, and the second on 20th and 21st Streets between Market and Blake. This latter district eventually relocated between Market and Larimer Streets and gained notoriety as the vice-filled "hop alley." Denver's Chinese population grew gradually until the turn of the century, when 3,000 inhabitants were counted (Fig. 5.9). Over the next two decades, the Chinese districts were repeatedly pillaged and many of the occupants were forced to leave the city. As a result of the constant intimidation of the Asian community, the Chinese population dwindled to about 160 by 1930 (Rudolph 1964; Carrillo, Johnson, and Van Ness 1987; Hermsen 1990; Carrillo 1991).

A recent archaeological project provided an opportunity to explore the Chinese occupation of Denver. The 20th Street viaduct replacement involved the disturbance of a lot on the corner of 20th Street and Market. This was the location of dwellings

Figure 5.9. Masonic lodge in Denver's Chinatown. Courtesy of the Denver Public Library.

identified on maps as "Chinese Quarters," as well as a Chinese laundry and Chinese drugstore. It was also the location of a bordello once operated by a Denver madam named Mattie Silk, called the House of a Thousand Mirrors. The site was excavated before the construction of the viaduct (Kalasz et al. 1994). With great expectations a series of trenches were excavated through the area. The foundations of several buildings were located, as well as a scattering of artifacts, but no in situ deposits were located—no cellars full of artifacts, no privies, just a few courses of brick from Mattie Silk's foundation and some random bottles. In fact, not a single artifact conclusively linked to the Chinese occupation of the area was located. The archaeological slate of this site has, for all intents and purposes, been wiped clean.

At the turn of the century the so-called power elite who ran the city had made improvements (such as street paving) to their own neighborhoods and the business district, but left the rest of the city to fend for itself. When Mayor Robert Speer took office in 1904, he began the "City Beautiful" movement, waged a war on poverty, and expanded many of the services to include the poor neighborhoods. To improve the appearance of the community as well as modernize the city, many older brick structures were torn down and replaced by larger, more elaborate commercial buildings. West Denver, however, remained a lower class neighborhood full of small, rundown brick and frame houses.

The low lying area of West Denver, bordered by Cherry Creek on the east and the South Platte River on the west, was a frequent victim of flooding. Major floods in Cherry Creek occurred in 1864, 1876, 1885, and 1912 (Fig. 5.10). Each time West Denver was devastated by raging flood waters, and each time it was rebuilt. The July 1912 flood swept many of the small frame and brick homes off their foundations. Of those that remained more than 75 buildings were determined to be unsafe and ordered demolished by the city building inspector.

Between 1900 and 1910, the population of Denver increased nearly 60 percent because of a large influx of immigrants. By 1920 the growth rate had slowed but continued. The population of Denver in 1920 was 256,491, about evenly split between men and women, in contrast to the 1860 population of 4,749, 76 percent of whom were men.

The early 1900s marked a period of railroad consolidation in the Platte Valley during which the principal lines came under the control of the Denver and Rio Grande and the Colorado and Southern Railroads. These two companies subsequently expanded their railroad facilities. The railroad expansion encouraged further industrial development in the area. Wazee Street became a solid warehouse district early in the twentieth century, and additional warehouses went up west of the 14th Street viaduct, replacing the stone yards originally located there. Several of the latter buildings were connected to additions located under the viaduct, evidently built after its completion in 1898. The streets south of Wazee were characterized by similar warehouse and manufacturing expansion on a smaller scale (Carrillo, Johnson, and Van Ness 1987).

The residential elements in this increasingly industrialized area were gradually pushed further west. By the 1940s, factories and warehouses had displaced virtually all the earlier residences east of 11th Street. In 1944 the 1300 blocks of Wazee and Blake

Figure 5.10. Flooding in Cherry Creek, 1912, view southwest from Larimer Street and Cherry Creek. Courtesy of the Colorado Historical Society.

were demolished to accommodate expansion of the Wazee Market, a wholesale produce market that eventually extended from 9th to 13th Streets between Wazee and Walnut. In the early 1970s, many of the remaining historic buildings in the area were demolished to allow the construction of the Auraria Higher Education Center. At the same time, the extensive late nineteenth-/early twentieth-century railroad complexes of the Platte Valley yards began to disappear. With air and freeway transportation drawing business away from the railroads, rail related buildings were abandoned and often demolished (Carrillo, Johnson, and Van Ness 1987).

The construction, use, abandonment, demolition, and replacement of structures is in the nature of urban growth. Obviously, this cycle has major impacts on the archaeological record available for study in urban areas. As we have seen, it can even obliterate the material remains of so colorful an establishment as Mattie Silk's. Below we briefly summarize some of the work that has been done to tap this record for insights about the development of urban Denver.

## Urban Archaeology in Denver

A history of urban archaeology in Denver is necessarily brief, because the practice of archaeology does not have a long history in the city. Susan Collins (1993) has summarized this history, and what follows draws on her summary.

The first documented historic archaeology project in the city was conducted in 1971. This project involved the excavation of a brick-lined shaft on the grounds of the Forney Museum, in the South Platte Valley. The investigators, David Gillio and Douglas Scott, demonstrated that future scientific historical studies could provide a wealth of information about the earliest periods of the city's existence.

In the mid-1970s important work was undertaken at two sites we discuss in greater detail below. This includes the work by Douglas Scott and E. Charles Adams at the Molly Brown House (Scott and Adams 1973), and a series of excavations by different investigators and institutions at the Four Mile House (see Nissley 1979). In the late 1970s the first historical archaeological project to be performed in compliance with the National Historic Preservation Act of 1966 was conducted in lower downtown Denver, or LoDo (Patterson 1977a, b, 1979; Patterson and Garcia 1977; Collins 1979). This work accompanied the construction of a new storm sewer system in the area.

Razing the Auraria neighborhood in the 1970s for construction of the campus that is now home to the University of Colorado at Denver, Community College of Denver, and Metropolitan State College stimulated other archaeological work. The first excavations at Auraria were performed in 1981 in the area of the Tivoli Brewery. Subsequent excavations were undertaken in the general area by Dr. Jonathan Kent of Metropolitan State College. Excavations at the site of the First German Presbyterian Church revealed late 1870s and early 1880s artifacts. Excavations conducted at the site of the Hungarian Flour Mill, located between 7th and 9th Streets and Wazee Street, produced secondary trash deposits dating to the early 1900s (J. Kent, personal communication 1989). Other excavations on campus were conducted occasionally.

The realignment of Speer Boulevard in 1987 gave archaeologists an important opportunity for large-scale archaeological investigation of Denver's history. This work—at the site of the Tremont House Hotel—was supported by the Colorado Department of Transportation in compliance with the National Historic Preservation Act. Collins (1993:xx) notes that archaeological work at the Tremont House "excited the imagination of numerous volunteers, site visitors, the press, and local officials." She also points out that the Tremont project "was the first extensive historical archaeology project to combine professional coordination, governmental support, media attention, and public participation" in the Greater Denver area. Because of the Tremont House's significance, it is fitting that we start our substantive inquiry into Denver urbanization with that site.

## LIFE IN THE URBAN CORE: TREMONT HOUSE HOTEL

The Tremont House Hotel was Denver's premier lodging, dining, and entertainment establishment during the 1860s and early 1870s (Fig. 5.11). Archival research indicates that it was in operation continuously between 1859 and 1912, when it was flooded and razed.

The site was investigated by archaeologists in conjunction with the 1987 Speer viaduct replacement project (Carrillo 1989; Carrillo and Jepson 1995). This project entailed substantial construction and realignment along a portion of Speer Boulevard, a major northwest-southeast traffic artery that spans the South Platte and connects Interstate 25 to downtown Denver. Remains of the Tremont House were located south of Cherry Creek in the city's lower downtown area approximately half a mile (0.8 km) southeast of Cherry Creek's confluence with the South Platte River. The remains of the hotel were located beneath a parking lot that had been paved in the 1970s (Fig. 5.12). The hotel remains were determined to lie almost entirely within the disturbance zone of the viaduct replacement project. As mandated by state and federal historic preservation laws, research was conducted before the start of road construction to retrieve scientific information from the site prior to its destruction.

Figure 5.11. The Tremont House Hotel, c. 1870. From Richard F. Carrillo, Sarah J. Pearce, Stephen Kalasz, and Daniel A. Jepson, *The Tremont House (5DV2954): Historical Archaeological Investigations of an Early Hotel in Denver, Colorado* (Denver: Colorado Department of Transportation, 1993); reproduced by permission.

Figure 5.12. A brick foundation wall of the Tremont House, exposed during 1987 excavations. From Richard F. Carrillo, Sarah J. Pearce, Stephen Kalasz, and Daniel A. Jepson, *The Tremont House (5DV2954): Historical Archaeological Investigations of an Early Hotel in Denver, Colorado* (Denver: Colorado Department of Transportation, 1993); reproduced by permission.

On the basis of initial cultural resource investigations for the project (including survey and limited testing), the site was assessed as eligible for nomination to the National Register of Historic Places. It was determined to have potential to contribute data to a variety of research themes, including but not limited to the composition and evolution of western architectural styles and construction techniques throughout the latter half of the nineteenth century, economic practices and change (e.g., food and markets) in an early urban community, degree of integration into national and global markets, and cultural/behavioral variability as reflected in artifact density and variety. In short, the Tremont House provided an opportunity to study Denver's historical development in response to changing environmental and economic conditions over some fifty years.

## A Brief Archival History of the Tremont House

Most of the archival information about the hotel was obtained from newspaper articles. These provide a rich source of information, but sometimes the information is inaccurate or misleading, as revealed by the archaeology conducted at the hotel.

Hotels were plentiful in early Denver because of the transient nature of the population. The construction of hotels, inexpensive boardinghouses, and temporary apartments was an important aspect of Denver real estate. Built in the late fall of 1859 and originally called the Temperance Hotel, the first Tremont House was a two-story wood frame building with a side gable roof behind a clapboard sided facade, facing east on B Street (later known as Front Street and 13th Street) (Fig. 5.13). Its dimensions were 40 feet by 50 feet.

In June 1860 the first owner, Mrs. Maggard, built a two-story frame addition, 22 feet by 80 feet, on the north side, cross-sectioning the original gabled roof and forming an L-shaped structure. The windows were six over six, double hung sash windows with slightly pedimented window surrounds, reminiscent of the Greek Revival style. The main entrance featured four-paned sidelights on either side of the wood frame door. A second story door opened onto a balcony with a turned balustrade supported by decorative brackets. The cornice was simple, overhanging and supported by paired decorative brackets. The two chimneys were brick, and a flagpole extended above the center of the facade.

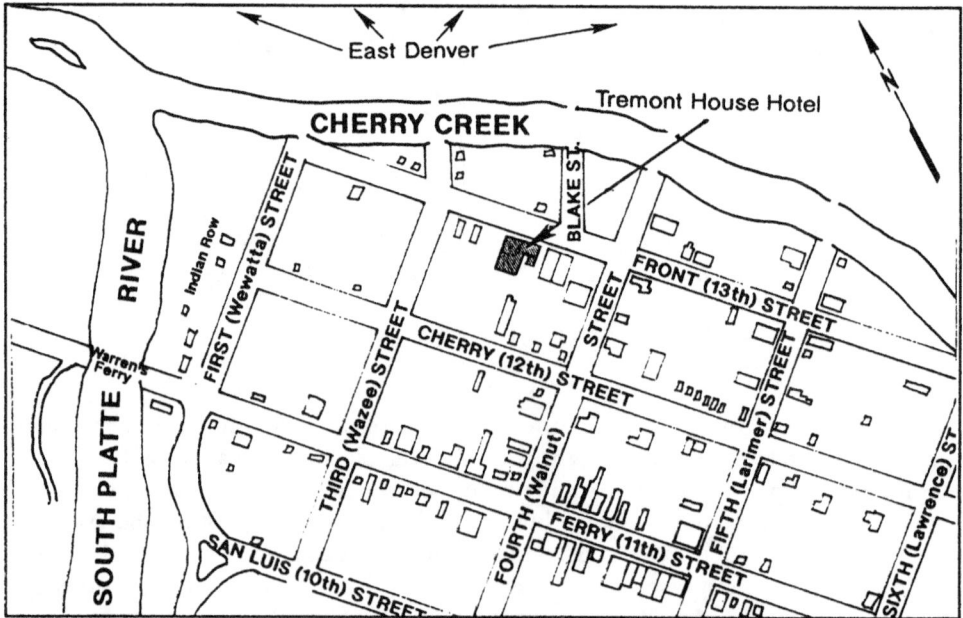

Figure 5.13. Denver and Auraria (West Denver) in 1860, showing the location of the Tremont House. From Richard F. Carrillo, Sarah J. Pearce, Stephen Kalasz, and Daniel A. Jepson, *The Tremont House (5DV2954): Historical Archaeological Investigations of an Early Hotel in Denver, Colorado* (Denver: Colorado Department of Transportation, 1993); reproduced by permission.

The *Rocky Mountains News* in its August 27, 1860, issue reported that:

The Subscribers, Proprietors of the above House (formerly known as the Temperance House) having completely renovated and refined it in modern style, would solicit the patronage of their friends and the public generally. Having added a Bar, well stocked with the choicest beverages of the Eastern Market, and all the comfort of a first-class hotel. We mean that the Tremont shall rank second to none. (*Rocky Mountain News* 1860:1)

The origin of the name may derive from an earlier log cabin owned and operated by David Taylor of Boston as the Tremont Hotel. Sharing the block with the Tremont House in 1860 were two hotels, the Missouri House and Star Hotel, William Dunn's grocery store, an undertaking parlor, a gun shop, several law offices, livery stables, and a lumber yard (Fig. 5.14). All were false front, wood frame buildings.

The Tremont House was at its finest during the early 1860s. Nelson Sargent and his wife turned the hotel and its food into the best in Denver. The hotel survived both

Figure 5.14. An 1860s photograph of West Denver, showing the Tremont House (left) and other buildings. From Richard F. Carrillo, Sarah J. Pearce, Stephen Kalasz, and Daniel A. Jepson, *The Tremont House (5DV2954): Historical Archaeological Investigations of an Early Hotel in Denver, Colorado* (Denver: Colorado Department of Transportation, 1993); reproduced by permission.

the 1863 fire that destroyed much of East Denver's commercial district, and the 1864 flood that caused severe damage in low lying West Denver. Photographs of the flood show the hotel surrounded by flood waters, and advertisements mention cleaning and renovating the interior, but apparently there was no permanent structural damage.

Ownership turned over rapidly. Sometime before December 21, 1865, after owning the hotel for more than five years, Sargent sold it to Charles F. Parkhurst, who was listed as the owner in 1865 and 1866 (*Rocky Mountain News* 1865:4). By July 24, 1866, "Messrs. Parkhurst and Shepard" sold their interest in the Tremont to David W. Powers, who had come to Colorado in 1863 from Boston. The hotel was once again renovated, repainted, papered, and cleaned. The refurbished hotel offered "Tucker's Celebrated Spring Mattresses" as well as the best food in town. Both mountains and plains supplied fresh game to the table: venison and elk along with rabbit, turkey, and prairie hens. Locally raised cattle and hogs substituted when wild game became sparse nearby.

In May 1867 Powers sold the hotel to W. Q. Brown, who enlarged it by 25 new rooms. Business was obviously good, and in July Brown took on a partner named Brastow. Nelson Sargent regained control of the hotel in 1869. Mr. McCarty became the next proprietor in 1870 and remodeled the hotel several times during his ownership.

Sometime between 1865 and the early 1870s, the frame structure was replaced by a three-story brick building. It featured a sloping flat roof, a plain bracketed cornice, shaped lintels and shutters on upper story windows, arched windows and entrance with keystones on one side of the ground floor, and a typical nineteenth-century commercial storefront with clerestories, kickplates, and a recessed entrance on the other side. A colonnaded porch supported a second floor balustraded balcony. The dimensions of this building are unknown. A photograph dated 1865 shows the frame structure, and dated 1871 shows the three-story brick building. The transformation is not well documented, however. The frame building was not refaced with brick because the roof shape changed from gable to flat, but no mention is made that the building had been torn down and a new one built, and there was no significant gap between articles and advertisements that might indicate total reconstruction of the building. In fact, the hotel continued to advertise in the newspaper, so one can only assume the hotel was open for business. Newspaper articles frequently referred to remodeling, improvements, and renovations to the building without listing specific details. It is possible that the building was replaced in 1867, but the newspaper chose to report only the addition of 25 rooms, not total reconstruction. The change remains a mystery. A possible explanation is that the 1871 photograph was incorrectly dated. The *Rocky Mountain News* reported in 1872 that the new owner, McCarty, had renovated the building inside and out such that it was no longer recognizable to old-timers. The newspaper said "it looked like a new building." A mistake of one year on the date of a historic photograph is not impossible and could be the answer to this question.

On June 13, 1871 the Tremont Hotel was considered one of the best hotels in Colorado, and was highly recommended to the traveling public. In 1874 another addition included a baggage room (12 ft by 20 ft), a reading room (18 ft by 18 ft), and a washroom (12 ft by 20 ft). It is presumed that the baggage room and washrooms were added to the rear of the hotel. The reading room may have been part of an existing section of the building.

McCarty sold the hotel in 1875 to W. C. Rippey, although McCarty remained in charge as host (*Rocky Mountain News* 1875:4). Rippey owned the hotel through the mid-1870s, during which time the building survived another major flood, on July 25, 1875. Once again, the low lying areas of West Denver were inundated, but damage was less severe than in the 1864 flood and most buildings suffered only minor damage.

The next major change to the building occurred between 1874 and 1887. The building appears on the 1887 Sanborn Insurance map as a two-story, L-shaped structure (Fig. 5.15). This is verified by a sketch of the hotel in the 1890 article on the history of Auraria in the *Rocky Mountain News*. In 1878 the Tremont House was sold to Frank Kenry. An unsubstantiated report states that the third floor was removed and the building stuccoed about this time. The 1887 Sanborn map indicates that the two-story brick

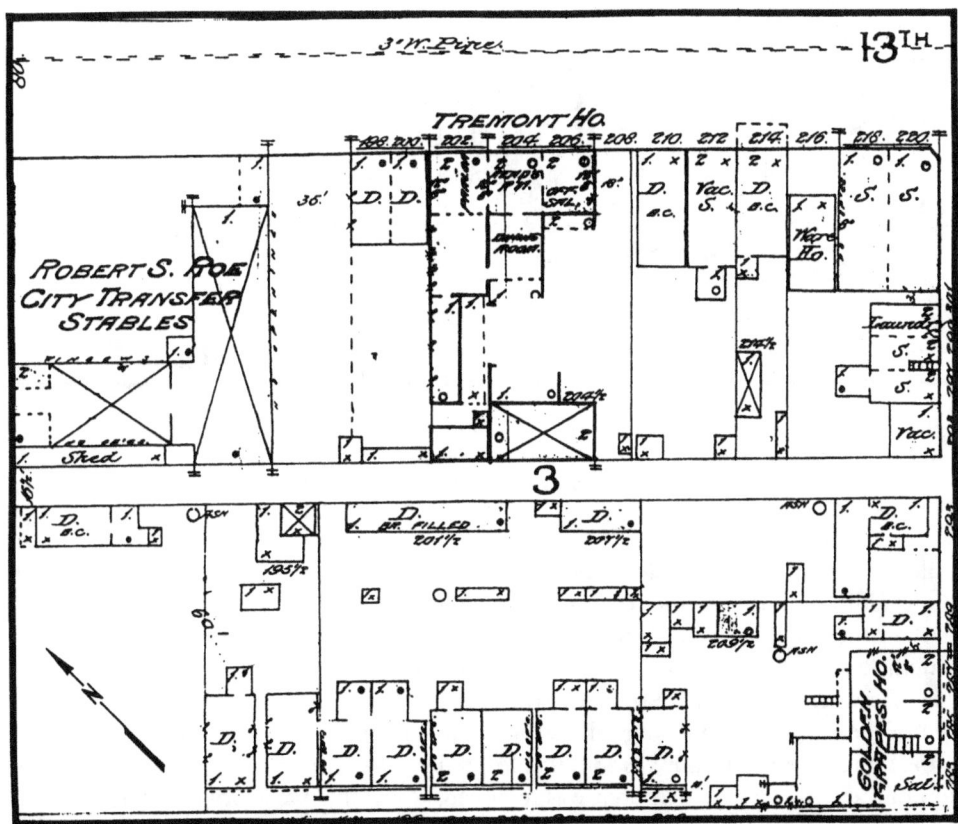

Figure 5.15. Sanborn Fire Insurance map of the Tremont House, 1887. From Richard F. Carrillo, and Daniel A. Jepson, *Exploring the Colorado Frontier: A Study in Historical Archaeology at the Tremont House Hotel, Lower Downtown Denver* (Denver: Colorado Department of Transportation, 1995); reproduced by permission.

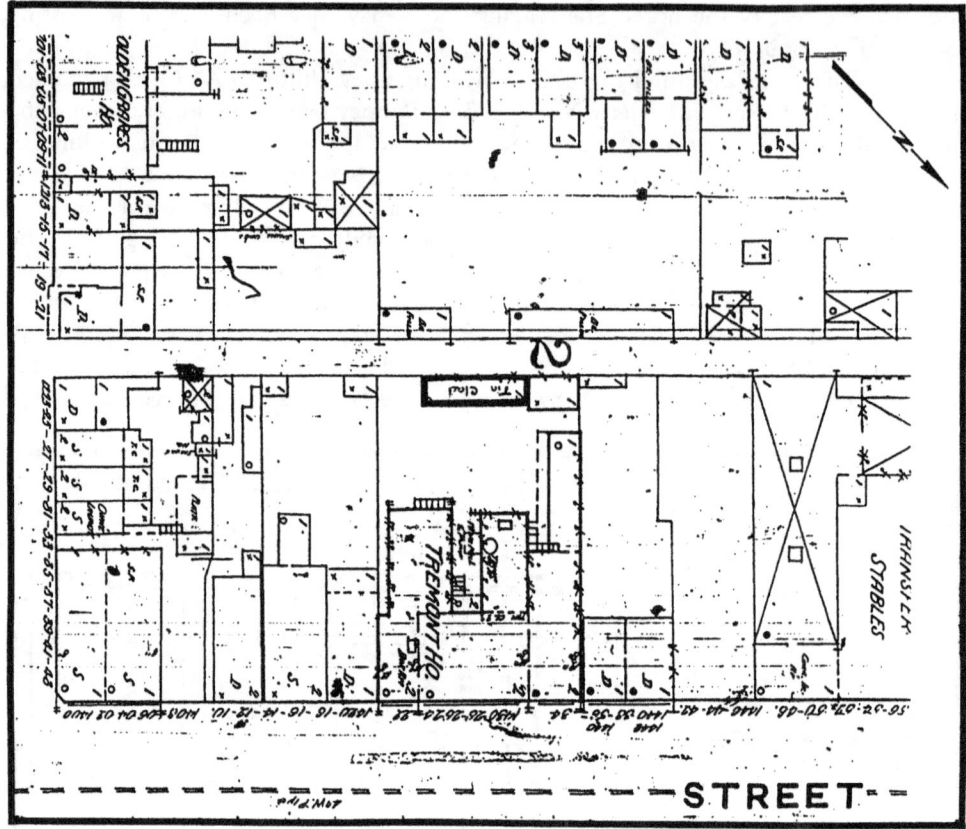

Figure 5.16. Sanborn Fire Insurance map, 1890, showing renovations to the Tremont House. From Richard F. Carrillo and Daniel A. Jepson, *Exploring the Colorado Frontier: A Study in Historical Archaeology at the Tremont House Hotel, Lower Downtown Denver* (Denver: Colorado Department of Transportation, 1995); reproduced by permission.

building had a one-story frame addition on the rear with a frame porch, a one-story frame addition to the dining room in the rear, and a two-story frame porch on the rear of the office/saloon area. Outbuildings consisted of a frame shed, a two-story brick structure, possibly a barn, and a one-story brick shed.

Between 1887 and 1890, a two-story brick addition was constructed on the south side of the rear of the building. The saloon remained in the front of this section, and a frame staircase, possibly a fire escape, was located on the rear of the new addition. A portion of the two-story frame porch was removed, as was the two-story brick outbuilding. A tin shed was built in its place. A frame pump shed was also added to the rear (Fig. 5.16). No changes were made to the exterior of the building between 1890 and 1903.

As the years went on, the *Rocky Mountain News* reported less and less about the first-class quality of the hotel. The change in population in West Denver was beginning to take a toll on the grand old hotel, and by 1880 the Tremont House had lost its standing as one of Denver's premier hotels. Newer, bigger, and fancier hotels were being built in East Denver, taking away the customers of the smaller hotels in West Denver. The Windsor Hotel at 18th and Larimer opened in 1880, followed by the Albany in 1885, the Metropole in 1891, and the Brown Palace in 1892. Newspaper coverage shifted to these new centers of social life. West Denver was being taken over by warehouses and railroad yards. Affluent residents moved uptown towards the State Capitol (built between 1890 and 1894), leaving the West Denver neighborhoods to immigrants and various ethnic groups. Frequent floods took a toll on the West Denver area, occurring again in 1878 and 1912. West Denver never fully recovered from the 1864 flood, when many businesses relocated to higher ground leaving little new development on the west side of Cherry Creek until the warehouse building boom of the 1890s.

In 1890 the *Rocky Mountain News* published a story about the history of Auraria and West Denver, describing the Tremont House as one of the great hotels where "scenes were pretty lively at times, and not a few of the schemes which have since done much for the advancement of the city were incubated within the walls." Nelson Sargent was credited with bringing the hotel to its finest hour, but in 1890, the newspaper reported that "he has lost status in recent years and 20 years have passed since [the Tremont] lost rank."

The year 1912 marked the last appearance of the Tremont House in the Denver city directories. It was serving mainly as a boardinghouse, with a saloon still operating on the first floor. On the afternoon of July 14, 1912, flood waters from an afternoon downpour raged down Cherry Creek, inundating the West Denver area with water several feet deep. The area hardest hit was bounded by 10th Street, Curtis Street, Cherry Creek and the Platte River. Many frame and insubstantial brick buildings were torn off their foundations, leaving thousands homeless. Even more substantial buildings were heavily damaged. The *Denver Republican* reported that two days after the flood the Tremont Bar had mud and sand piled as high as the bar, and that by 6 p.m., after a crew had worked all that day, there was still at least two feet of mud left.

The damage was so severe that the day after the flood the building inspector condemned between 50 and 75 buildings on either side of Cherry Creek and the Platte River. On July 21, 1912, a headline in the *Denver Post* announced "Old Turner Hall and the Tremont Ordered Wrecked." The owners were ordered to begin tearing them down within five days or the fire department would do so.

No substantial buildings were built on this lot after the Tremont House Hotel was demolished in 1912. The final Sanborn map, dated 1929, shows a frame shed standing in the rear of the lot on which the hotel stood. Later maps show that the lot was used only as a junkyard and storage area by the American Forge Works.

## Results of Archaeological Research

Archaeological work at the Tremont House Hotel produced a diverse assortment of new information that provided fresh insights into a variety of historical and archaeological topics. It not only contributed new understandings of urbanization, but also corrected some of the historical accounts of early urban lifeways.

*Architecture*

The Tremont House was constructed of a variety of materials (stone, brick, milled lumber, etc.), and it is evident that considerable architectural changes occurred at the hotel throughout its existence. Excavation revealed the original structure foundation as well as substructures and features of two building additions. This work also revealed some inconsistencies in historical accounts. The historical documents suggest that the original wood frame structure (identified below as structure 1) was razed and subsequently rebuilt entirely with brick in the late 1860s or early 1870s. However, no archaeological evidence was recovered to support this hypothesis. If this were the case, more uniformity would be expected in the extant structure foundations. Instead, the archaeology revealed that the evolution of the hotel involved additions to the north (structure 2) and south (structure 3) of the original structure. The enlarged brick hotel of the 1870s encompassed all or most of the wooden structure, but did not displace it entirely.

The separate sections of the hotel were designated as structures 1, 2, and 3 (Fig. 5.17). Each structure was different in architecture and contents. Structure 1 consisted of an extensive L-shaped brick foundation. It is believed to have been the original hotel building, as its shape and dimensions conform most closely with the documented descriptions of the original structure. The cellar had a wood-plank floor. A brick fireplace was located along the north wall, and a coal chute with attached plank-lined coal storage bin was situated on the west end. A large quantity of food-related refuse found within the chute and bin (bottles, dishware, bones) indicated abandonment of these features during the 1870s and their subsequent usage as trash dumps. The fireplace in the cellar is an oddity for a storage area and suggests that the space may have been used as living quarters, possibly by a maintenance person. The discovery of a clock in the cellar was also curious, but perhaps indicates the degree to which people of the day were concerned with time management, a typically Victorian concern (Leone and Shackel 1987). The cellar had a rear entry that was added to the original structure, perhaps during a later renovation when this area was no longer used for coal storage and distribution.

Structure 2 was built next. Located immediately north of, and attached to, structure 1, it had a rectangular rhyolite stone and brick foundation and a brick-floored cellar. This cellar, like the plank cellar in structure 1, had a rear entrance at its west end. However, intact artifacts recovered from this cellar indicate that, unlike its structure 1 plank counterpart, it was in use until the 1912 flood filled it with sand (Fig. 5.18). The commonly accepted model of stone as the initial building material in this period would suggest that the structure 2 foundation belonged to the original Temperance Hotel, but the foundation outline and historical descriptions of the hotel indicate that a different sequence occurred, involving the use of brick prior to or at the same time as stone. The artifacts from structures 1 and 2 also indicate that structure 2 was actually the first substantial addition to the hotel. It appears that brick and stone were being used contemporaneously in early architecture—a piece of evidence that lends support to Barth's characterization of Denver as an "instant city."

Structure 3 was a rectangular brick foundation located south of structure 1, the last addition to the hotel, built between 1887 and 1890. Although the Sanborn map

Figure 5.17. Excavation pits at the Tremont House site, near the end of the excavation project, looking west. From Richard F. Carrillo and Daniel A. Jepson, *Exploring the Colorado Frontier: A Study in Historical Archaeology at the Tremont House Hotel, Lower Downtown Denver* (Denver: Colorado Department of Transportation, 1995); reproduced by permission.

Figure 5.18. Artifacts in flood deposits on the Tremont House cellar floor, including intact bottles and ceramic containers. From Richard F. Carrillo and Daniel A. Jepson, *Exploring the Colorado Frontier: A Study in Historical Archaeology at the Tremont House Hotel, Lower Downtown Denver* (Denver: Colorado Department of Transportation, 1995); reproduced by permission.

shows it as connected to structure 1, archaeological excavation revealed the two structures to be unattached. This structure had no cellar and apparently did not share foundation elements with the other structures. Oddly, many artifacts from this area were found to date from earlier time periods. The area was probably vacant prior to 1887 and offered a convenient spot for dumping trash produced during preceding decades.

*Artifacts*

Well over 26,000 artifacts were recovered during the Tremont House excavations, including some of the earliest historic settlement period material ever recovered in the Denver area. The list of artifact types is impressive, covering a broad array of items one would expect to find in the refuse of a hotel. This includes glassware, crockery, dishes, silverware, furnishings, fragments of clothing, writing accessories, clocks, toothbrushes, and numerous other items (Fig. 5.19a–d). Many pieces were retrieved intact, but, surprisingly, the majority of the items are fragmentary, and in some cases unidentifiable.

Although some of the artifacts recovered from the Tremont House excavations can be used as "diagnostic" horizon markers, none can be definitively assigned to a single historical period. Approximately 2,100 objects were found to be reliable time indicators, and these were particularly valuable in establishing the types/quantity of items in use in a given period. Laboratory analysis of these artifacts indicated three distinct intervals. Artifacts with beginning manufacturing dates between 1855 and 1859 were the most prevalent, comprising nearly 40 percent of all diagnostic materials. There were lesser peaks in 1875–84 and 1895–99. The high percentage of early artifacts can be attributed primarily to changing patterns of dumping as the hotel evolved. During the hotel's early period, for example, it appears that vacant lots adjacent to the site area—particularly to the north, west, and south of the original structure—were used for dumping refuse. An abandoned coal chute within the hotel, dating to the 1860s and early 1870s, was apparently also used to dispose of 1850s–60s manufactured artifacts. The hotel's rapid growth during the 1870s led to the use of these former dumping areas for additional construction. This competition for space evidently made it necessary to dispose of most post-1870s trash offsite. Much of the later (post-1870s) material recovered at the site was found in cellar 1 of structure 2 and in fact represents items left in place after the 1912 flood and subsequent razing of the hotel.

Artifacts recovered from the Tremont House excavations include some produced in Colorado, particularly Denver, during specific time periods (Figure 5.20a). These were found in association with larger quantities of other diagnostic artifacts were produced in various parts of the United States and Europe. This combination of materials places the Tremont House within a series of local, regional, national, and international economic market systems that exhibited varying changes through time.

Other artifacts were identified according to their function, where possible, and included goods such as hair combs, keys, beads, and gambling dice (Fig. 5.20b). A few undeniable ethnically marked artifacts were also recovered, including thick ceramic containers with what appear to be remnants of Chinese lettering (a section of Denver's Chinatown was at one time located in the block across the street from the hotel, on

Figure 5.19. Artifacts recovered during the Tremont House excavations. From Richard F. Carrillo, Sarah J. Pearce, Stephen Kalasz, and Daniel A. Jepson, *The Tremont House (5DV2954): Historical Archaeological Investigations of an Early Hotel in Denver, Colorado* (Denver: Colorado Department of Transportation, 1993); reproduced by permission. (a) Ironstone sugar bowl, pitchers, and teacup.

Figure 5.19b. Ironstone bowls.

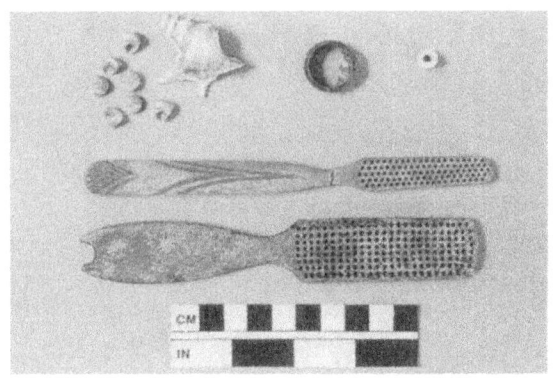

Figure 5.19c. Assorted decorative and utilitarian objects.

Figure 5.19d. Pipe stems and bowls.

Figure 5.20. Tremont house artifacts. From Richard F. Carrillo, Sarah J. Pearce, Stephen Kalasz, and Daniel A. Jepson, *The Tremont House (5DV2954): Historical Archaeological Investigations of an Early Hotel in Denver, Colorado* (Denver: Colorado Department of Transportation, 1993); reproduced by permission. (a) Earthenware crocks from local merchants.

Figure 5.20b. Celluloid and bone dice and celluloid guitar pick.

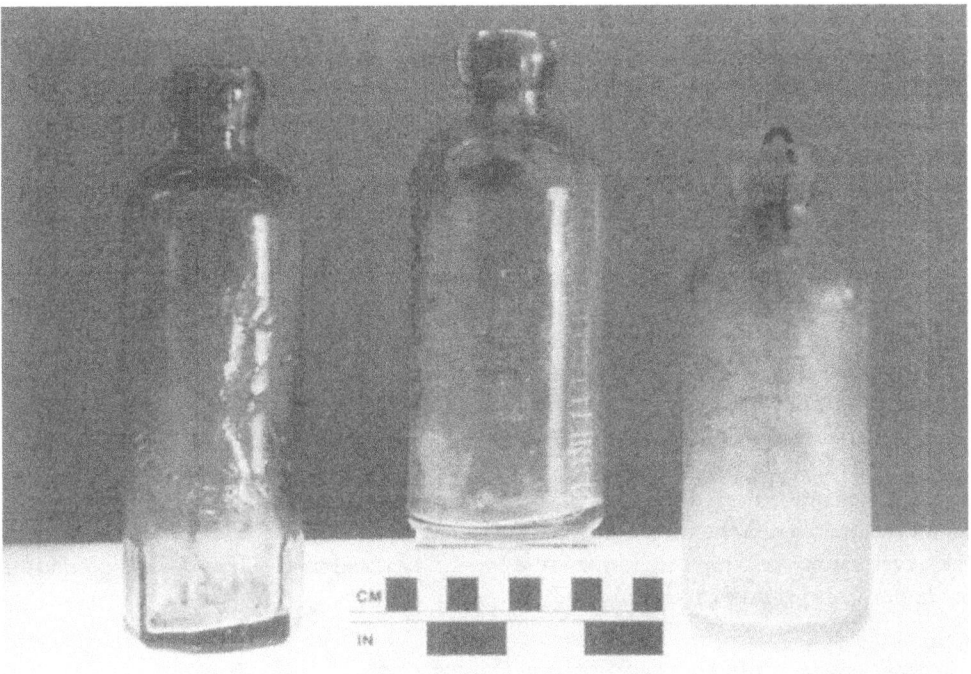

Figure 5.20c. Locally manufactured seltzer or mineral water bottles.

the corner of Blake and 13th Streets). Many glass products have embossed writing that verifies their function and age (Fig. 5.20c). A substantial quantity and assortment of china and tableware (including porcelain and earthenware) were used for food service. Maker's marks imprinted on these items identified manufacturer and approximate dates of production and use. Nearly 20 different ceramic manufacturers from England and the United States, which collectively created pottery between 1839 and 1910, were represented in the Tremont collection. Other pottery included assorted redwares, consisting of a variety of unglazed flowerpots.

## Food Remains

In addition to commercial and domestic goods, nearly 4,000 bones representing thirty different varieties of fish, birds, and mammals were recovered. Most of them were undoubtedly served in the hotel restaurant, but animals such as rat, dog, and coyote are not believed to have been food sources (although one rat bone showed evidence of having been cooked!). As expected, cattle were the most common domesticated mammal and chicken the most common fowl. Domestic animals comprised nearly 90 percent of the total remains, but wild game was obviously important and a fairly frequent contribution to the Tremont menu, especially during the hotel's first decade. Pig was the principal domestic species during the earlier period, while cattle became predominant during the later years of hotel operation. This shift is likely attributable to the large-scale cattle drives from Texas after the Civil War and to the regional development of the cattle industry on Colorado's eastern ranges.

Sheep were not present in significant numbers. This is surprising, as sheep were available from New Mexico in the early 1860s and from southeastern Colorado by the mid-1860s. It may reflect cultural preference by the Tremont House clientele rather than product availability. Recent work conducted at Boggsville Historic Site tends to reflect a similar pattern, which is considered at Boggsville to be related to ethnic preferences (Carrillo, Johnson, and Van Ness 1997).

Wild and domestic species apparently played equally important roles. The wild animal remains revealed some interesting patterns. Fish, bison, and greater prairie chicken constituted the major groups recovered from earlier contexts. Through time, however, rabbits became the dominant species. This trend may reflect over-exploitation of larger game animals and birds.

## Inferences and Conclusions

Archaeological fieldwork recovered a large sample of the hotel's material goods, thereby providing a detailed picture of day-to-day activities and expanded knowledge of the early phases of Denver urbanization. Archaeological research has confirmed the historic record of the hotel's significance in the development of Denver. It has also served to clarify and even correct facets of the documentary record about both the hotel and early Denver.

Perhaps the most important processes illuminated by the Tremont House record are related to marketing and the movement of goods. Given the isolation of the High Plains, the lack of a substantial industrial base, and the high cost of goods shipped by wagon from points east, early urbanites were compelled to purchase expensive imported manufactured goods. Rural areas often did not have access to many of these imported items (as reflected in archaeological contexts from such sites [Carrillo, Zier, and Barnes 1991]), but the Tremont House archaeological record confirms the extensive availability of goods manufactured on the eastern seaboard and in Europe. This is an excellent indication that the animal-powered transportation system functioned to provide Denver with an array of imported goods regardless of cost.

The Tremont House was initially a first-class hotel, and it is therefore not surprising that a high proportion of the early artifacts were expensive imports rather than more utilitarian pieces. The hotel was advertised as providing all the luxuries guests could require, and we must assume that the proprietors went to great lengths to obtain superior commodities. A pattern involving the extensive use of manufactured artifacts, known as conspicuous consumption and equated with the Victorian era, was evidenced at the Tremont House. It appears that even during the 1860s–early 1870s period, when Denver was dependent on animal-powered transportation for manufactured items and other products, the economic climate encouraged the import of such items. The demand for all types of products was great, and regardless of cost, Denver was being adequately supplied. The presence of European items (ceramics, wine, perfume) and other imported fare (oysters) suggests that, although Denver's population remained stable during this period, the transient mining population provided adequate economic incentive to escalate procurement of luxury items, regardless of cost.

The growth, status, and popularity of the Tremont House throughout the early and mid-1860s is fairly well documented in the historical record. This is corroborated archaeologically by architectural remains, which indicate that most of the major structural additions to the hotel were made within its first 15 years of existence. Beginning in the 1870s, the hotel's popularity began to wane. Many factors contributed to its eventual demise, not least its location in an area prone to flooding, but increased competition and changes in the character of the West Denver neighborhood toward the railroad were also important. Archaeological evidence for this pattern is convincing. For example, a wide array of pitchers, decanters, and cruets were recovered during the excavations. Those with identifiable manufacture dates between 1850 and approximately 1875—probably in use during the hotel's earliest period—were uniformly sturdy, finely hand-etched, often handblown, and of excellent quality. Conversely, those produced after about 1880, when the character and reputation of the Tremont was fading, tended to be undecorated and machine-made, with screw tops and inferior decoration. Other artifacts, such as ceramic dishware, showed a similar progression, from generally superior to common and nondescript. An architectural addition in late 1880s was flimsy and second-rate. Yet, reduced as it was to a second-rate boardinghouse in its last years, there is no solid archaeological evidence to suggest that the hotel was used for illicit activities such as prostitution or gambling.

As noted earlier, the findings of historical archaeology may conflict with historical documents. By perusing only newspaper accounts, the primary source of information for the 1880s, one might assume that the hotel closed during this period. In reality, the neighborhood surrounding the hotel (Auraria) became home to a burgeoning warehouse district inspired by the railroad. This district was inhabited by a large and diverse immigrant population who tended not to be mentioned in newspaper articles; nor were product advertisements directed at them. The archaeological indications disprove any suggestion of the hotel's demise and instead reveal that the Tremont House was a functioning business until 1912.

The Tremont House artifact database represents an initial baseline for future urban historical archaeological studies in Denver. Although the population densities in Denver changed considerably, especially after 1870, further data are required from comparable sources in order to identify the specific variables that may be responsible for these changes. This need notwithstanding, the information derived from the Tremont House will serve as a benchmark for comparison with archaeological patterning observed at other historic sites, both in Denver proper as well as in urban environments subject to similar stages of historical development.

## Aboveground Archaeology:
## Politics, Planning, and Denver City Streets

Denver in its early days was a place where urban met frontier. The following example of "aboveground archaeology" illustrates how the processes of creating an urban environment in Denver led to some interesting frontier patterns of settlement and discontinuity. The Denver city street plan—unusual in its use of two differently aligned grid systems—is useful for illustrating these processes and patterns. The two grids served distinct sections of the population and contributed uniquely to the development and character of the community.

### Denver City Grid(s): Background

When founded in 1858, the town of Auraria used a grid with streets running roughly parallel to Cherry Creek. Cross streets ran perpendicular to the creek. The town of Denver associated its grid with the Platte River. According to Bonnie Clark (1994:4), the Denver alignment was chosen primarily based on engineering logic: because the streets approached the river at right angles, bridges could be shorter and more structurally sound. This plan, however logical, departed somewhat from standard town grids of the time in that it was not oriented to the cardinal directions. The U.S. National Land System (also known as the Public Land Survey System, or PLSS), which was established to expedite the sale of huge parcels of raw land to hungry and willing immigrants (Kunstler 1993), squarely divides the majority of the country. The system consists of thirty-five survey zones, each based on a system of grid coordinates (these separate zones are designed to adjust for measurement error and earth curvature). Each grid begins with an east-west "baseline" and a north-south "principal meridian." Townships (six miles square) are divided into sections (each one mile square), which are further divided into parcels for homesteading (usually 160 acres, a quarter-section). This national grid was considered quite rational and democratic, demonstrating fairness and equality in its organization. It was easy to regulate and maintain and provided a straightforward method for identifying land ownership and location.

The result of this system of land division, according to Mark Monmonier (1995:114), "was an 'authored landscape' in which the survey grid had a marked effect on settlement patterns and the shapes of counties and smaller political units. In the typical Midwestern county, roads commonly follow section lines, the rural population is dispersed rather than clustered, and the landscape has a pronounced checkerboard appearance." According to Dell Upton (1992:54), the grid affected more than patterns of settlement; it "created order and unity by organizing the otherwise chaotic juxtaposition of individual selves." Grids were presumed by nineteenth-century planners and architects to guide citizens down the straight and narrow path, so to speak. The order, organization, and separation imposed by the gridded layout fostered an urban ideal. Every location was provided equal access, and natural inequalities of topography were eliminated. The grid was perceived as neutral and nonhierarchical. The key to the success of this layout, however, was wrapped up in its transparency. The order must be seen as natural and must virtually go unnoticed. In Denver, the street layout failed to remain transparent.

In 1860 Denver and Auraria consolidated, and the new Denver began its quest for political power. Prominent citizens of the community were civic- and business-minded enough to do their part in this endeavor. After all, the Rocky Mountain West was a literal and figurative gold mine, as many businesses stood to make big profits as suppliers to the intrepid prospectors and others settling the region. One such savvy entrepreneur was Henry C. Brown, who owned a plot of land in what is now the core of downtown Denver. In 1867 Colorado's Territorial Congress decided it was time to select the site of the future state's capital. Colorado City, Golden, Canon City, Pueblo, and Denver all competed for the honor. Site selection would depend in part on the donation of a suitable plot of land. Brown came forward and donated his land for Denver's cause.

City ordinances required that any land to be annexed to the city must first be platted. Brown had previously platted his land, but not in accordance with the original city plan, which, as you will recall, ran in alignment with the Platte River. Brown's holdings included a bluff that ran north-south. It was his opinion that anything but a north-south alignment of streets in his addition to the city would mar the beauty and value of the land (Clark 1994:6). Despite pressure from the city to alter his layout, Brown got his way. Furthermore, not only did the north-south alignment remain in what was to become the site of the state capitol, other land developers followed Brown's new grid orientation. Eleven of thirteen new additions to the city of Denver before 1868 abandoned the old city layout for the new.

Interpreting the Grid

Among the first things that comes to mind when analyzing Denver's city grids are the odd intersections where the two systems converge (Fig. 5.21). The junctures may not appear particularly strange or disorienting on paper, but they can create trepidation, if not alarm in real life. Particularly in heavy traffic, there is the momentary panic of not knowing which lane to be in to proceed in the direction you *think* is the way you need to go, and when there is no hope of switching lanes to correct a split-second mistake in judgment because you are surrounded by dozens of cars with drivers who, for some reason, appear to know exactly what they are doing and where they are going. It is certainly possible that in the 1870s the slower pace of carriage or pedestrian traffic may have offset the confusion at the intersections. Nevertheless, the disjunctive juncture, if you will, of the two systems would have had a negative effect. Remember that grids were consciously designed to organize, separate, and order a city, and were believed to have that same effect on the people within the city. They did so, however, in a way that was transparent and felt "natural." A glaring disruption in the ease and flow of the system would undermine its ability to create orderly citizens. Considered in this manner, we suggest that the urban processes of land development and capitalist expansion in Denver resulted in a frontier pattern of disunity and conflict.

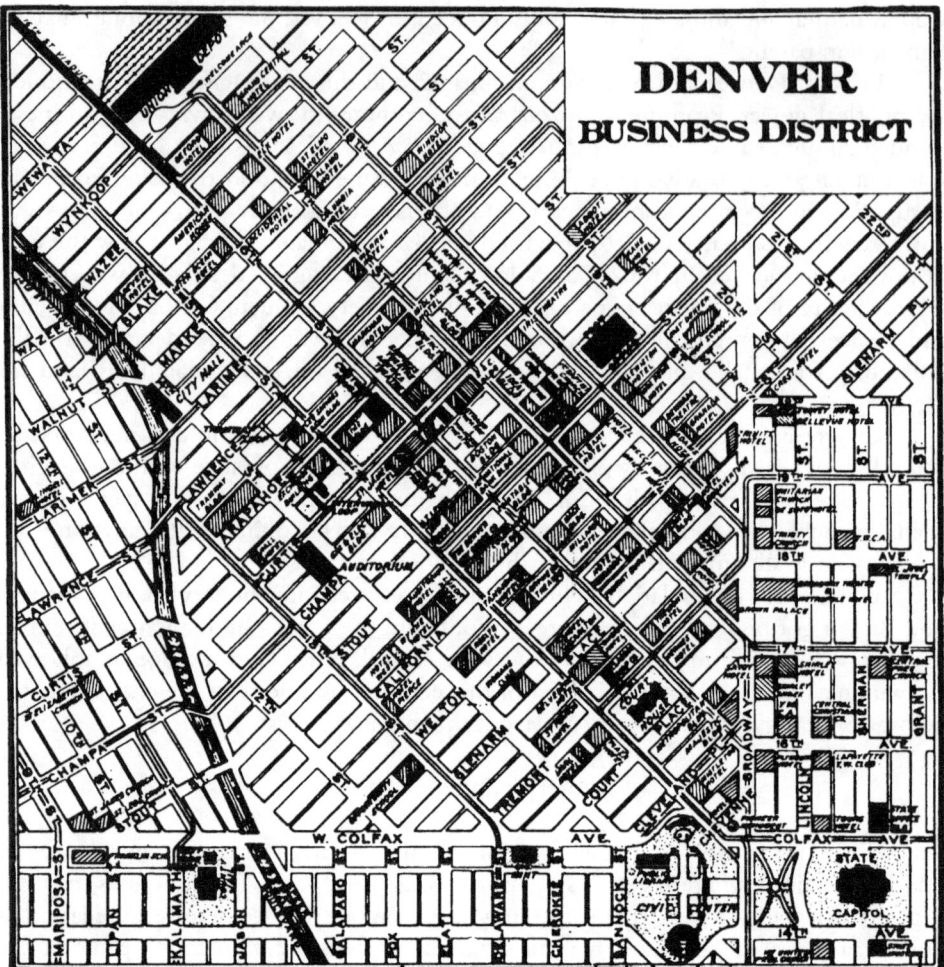

Figure 5.21. Denver business district, 1925. Courtesy of the Denver Public Library.

To further explore this possibility, let us return to the history of the grid's development, where the context of the times sheds more light on the city's new alignment. As mentioned earlier, the new grid was established as part of a battle to win the capitol for Denver. At the same time, the city was embroiled in other crucial contests. In the 1860s railroad companies were making do-or-die decisions for hundreds of communities throughout the country as they expanded their networks of tracks. One bend in a railway's course, away from a particular town, could close down that community in no time. Conversely, becoming a stop on a major rail route could make the difference for dozens of commercial enterprises. The *Rocky Mountain News* was hopeful that the proposed Pacific Railroad would come through Denver when it wrote that it "must pass through the South Platte gold fields, and this, our consolidated city at the eastern foot of the Rocky Mountains, will be a point which cannot be dodged" (Abbot, Leonard, and McComb 1982:81). The news that the Pacific Railroad would take its transcontinental route through Cheyenne, Wyoming (100 miles to the north) sent many nervous businessmen and other citizens packing. Some persevered, however, and between 1867 and 1870 plans were made by Denver promoters to build their own line to connect with Cheyenne. Numerous political skirmishes and a few financial mishaps later, the Denver Pacific Railroad was opened. The next several years saw a number of other railroads connect with Denver, but the late 1860s was touch and go. An 1868 map promoting the future Denver Pacific is a telling document (Fig. 5.22). The typeface for "Denver Pacific Railway" is large and prominent, giving a feeling of certainty and reality, though at that time the project was nowhere near real or certain. The map also

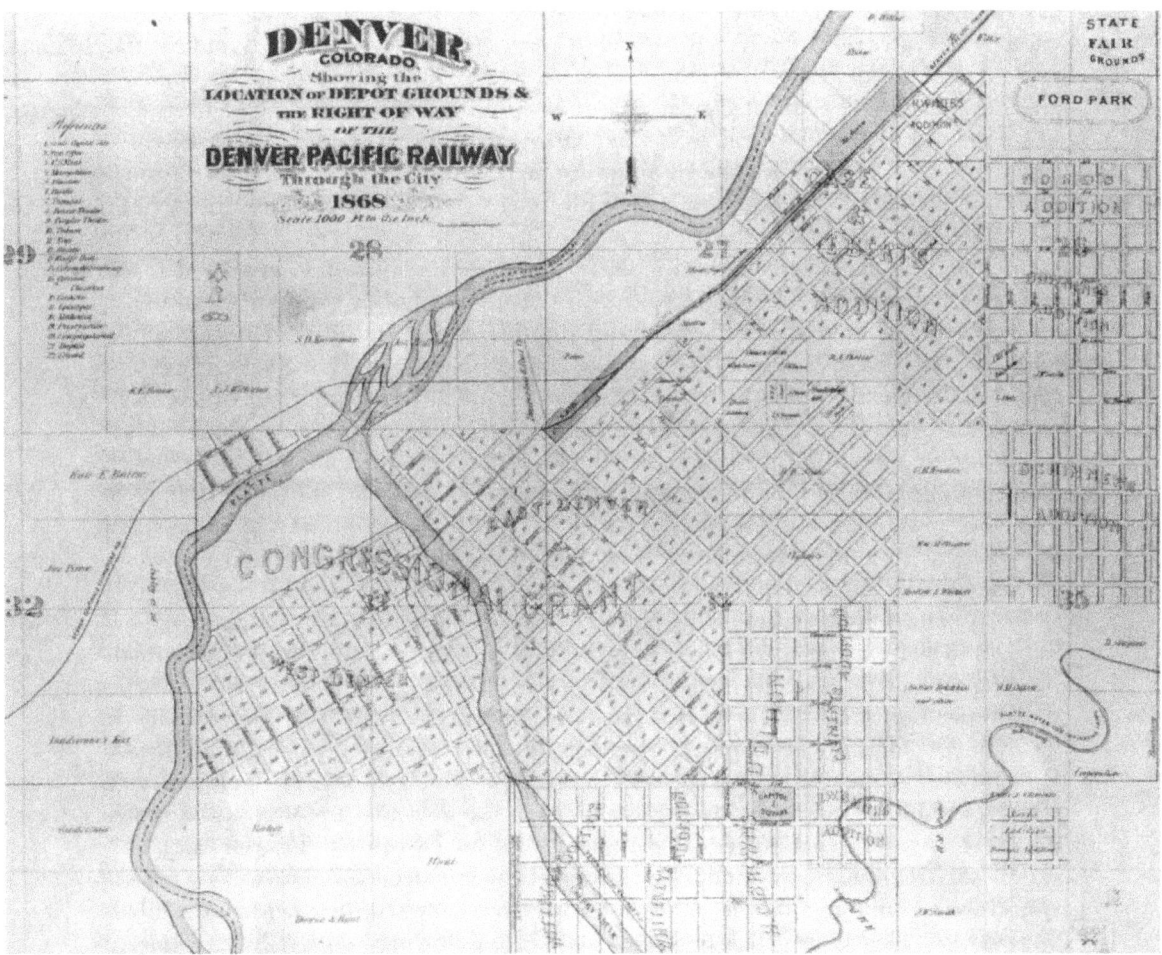

Figure 5.22. An 1886 map promoting the Denver Pacific Railway. Courtesy of the Denver Public Library.

highlights the state capitol site, churches, newspapers, and other features of a thriving, sophisticated metropolis. This is a map of a future Denver its promoters *hoped* it would be, an example of the way maps do not merely reflect space but can create it (Leone and Silberman 1995). Maps make statements; they emphasize certain features and downplay others, depending on the biases of the mapmaker. They are created through culturally determined behavior and they are "powerful tools of persuasion [that have] . . . a remarkable effect of our view of the world" (Monmonier 1995:1).

Now let us return to the grids. Within the context of the railroad struggle and the boosterism that accompanied it, the city grid takes on a different tenor. The 1868 map touting the many features of Denver is also the first one that includes the additions to the city oriented on the cardinal direction grid. The proponents of Denver were involved in a desperate attempt to save their city from becoming just one more mining town that had outlived its heyday. Denver needed to change from a rough and tumble western village to a center of commerce. It needed to convince people with money and prestige that it was a place where they would want to settle. The 1868 map placed emphasis precisely on those aspects of Denver that implied civilization at its highest form. The spaces created by the new grid were not aligned with natural features, but represented a conquering of nature, order rising from disorder. Thus the spaces of the north-south grid can be seen as another of the civilized features of the new Denver (Clark 1994:8).

The map and the enthusiastic promotion of Denver were successful. Many wealthy and influential people did settle in the city. Moreover, in a trend that is not particularly surprising, they chose to live in the new additions of town, oriented on the new cardinal direction grid. Again, urban processes created frontier patterns. City boosters and planners fostered the impression of a "New City," a bustling, important center of commerce and culture; the new grid alignment underscores this vision. The result is that "prominent" (affluent, influential) citizens flock to the new Denver, marginalizing the sections of town on the old grid pattern and the people who live there. The core of power and influence resides within the new layout and the periphery of middle or lower classes is relegated to the outskirts. At the same time, the railroad and the capitalist machine continue to the peripheralize the non-Anglo/non-Protestant communities through the distribution and expansion of Victorian ideals.

Spatially, these ideas are borne out with great clarity. The shifting emphasis of land use within the two grids reflected New Town Victorian preoccupations with morality, religion, and humanistic self-cultivation. In the new grid, schools and churches were twice as prevalent as hotels and theaters (Jones and Forrest 1985). In Old Town, the ratio of educational/religious structures to entertainment was 1 to 10. Lower Downtown, on the old grid, experienced a shift in the 1870s from booming retail stores to wholesale markets. Many businesses left the area for "uptown as the growing streetcar system encouraged development" (Lower Downtown District n.d.). This exodus was followed by a period of severe depression and decline in Lower Downtown. Construction came to a halt, less and less activity was centered there, and by the 1950s "LoDo" was "Skid Row." This process was reversed following its 1973 designation as a historic district and subsequent interest in preservation and urban renewal. As a result, the LoDo area has recently seen a significant upswing.

Just as business centers on the old grid failed to thrive, neighborhoods in that system were ignored by the Anglo-dominated upper classes of the city. West Colfax—at one time known as "No Man's Land"—was settled by Eastern European Jewish immigrants in the late nineteenth and early twentieth centuries. "Attracted by others with similar language, cultural and religious backgrounds, the immigrants made 'No Man's Land' into Denver's version of a European neighborhood" (West Colfax Neighborhood Plan 1987). Likewise, the Five Points neighborhood became home to a marginalized group. Platted in 1868, but in accordance with the old grid, Five Points was populated mostly by African Americans. During the 1920s through the 1940s, the neighborhood experienced a peak of business success. Many thriving businesses were black-owned, and the neighborhood was a mecca for jazz musicians and fans. "The focal point of the neighborhood was the Rossonian Hotel and Lounge [which featured] such famous entertainers as Louis Armstrong, Duke Ellington, Ella Fitzgerald and Denver's own George Morrison" (Five Points Business Association 1994). From the mid-1950s, Five Points began to experience a serious decline. Income levels were exceptionally low and crime rates exceptionally high. Today Five Points residents are engaged in a number of efforts to reclaim their community and, in fact, property values have gone up, thanks to a number of revitalization projects.

This analysis of the Denver city grid emphasizes the urban processes of political power play, economic manipulation, and city planning, all based on a carefully constructed model of order and organization. It demonstrates how those processes created patterns of street/city development and land use which reflect the frontier character of the city of Denver. It is another example of how our built environment/material culture is imbued with meaning.

### GETTING TO DENVER: THE MILE HOUSES

Today most people arrive in Denver through Denver International Airport or via I-25 or I-70. Planes, trains, and automobiles convey vacationers and new settlers rather easily. But Denver has not always been so easy to reach. In the beginning the two main arteries that accessed Denver skirted the Rocky Mountains. The California-Oregon or Overland Trail ran along the North Platte through Wyoming; the Santa Fe Trail ran to the south, along the Arkansas River. To get to Denver early travelers generally followed one of these main trails, then turned north or south. These two major arteries were connected by the Cherokee Trail, named for a group of Cherokee Indians and whites who traveled from Oklahoma to California along this route in 1850, headed for California gold. The whites considered traveling with Cherokees desirable because they were on friendly terms with most Plains Indians. The trail tied together a number of routes utilized by the Native Americans of the region. In Colorado the Cherokee Trail ran from La Junta (where the Santa Fe Trail turned south) west to Pueblo. From there it followed Fountain Creek along the foothills. From Fountain to Franktown it followed a path later known as Jimmy Camp Road, and then ran along Cherry Creek to its confluence with the South Platte (Fig. 5.23). Parts of the Cherokee Trail are still visible.

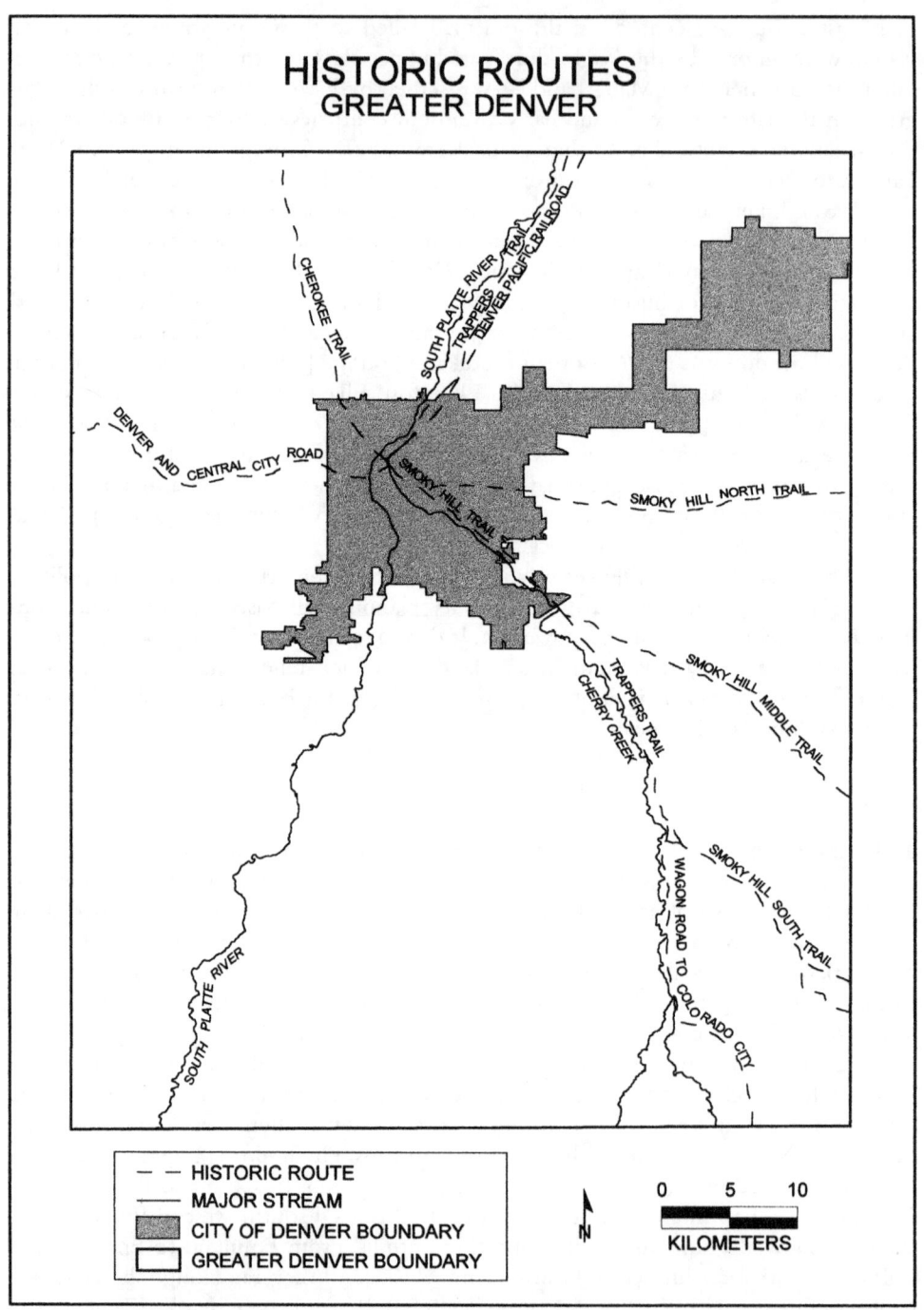

Figure 5.23. Historic trails in Greater Denver. Francine Patterson.

The Cherokee was not the only trail that followed Cherry Creek. Starting with the 1859 gold rush, a number of freight and stage companies ran lines directly from the Kansas City-Fort Leavenworth area to Denver. Called the Smoky Hill Trail, it had a number of variants (Lee and Raynesford 1980; Long 1943). After following the Smoky Hill River through Kansas to Kit Carson and Limon, the trail divided into three branches, Smoky Hill South, Starvation Trail (or middle Smoky Hill), and Smoky Hill North (Fig. 5.24).

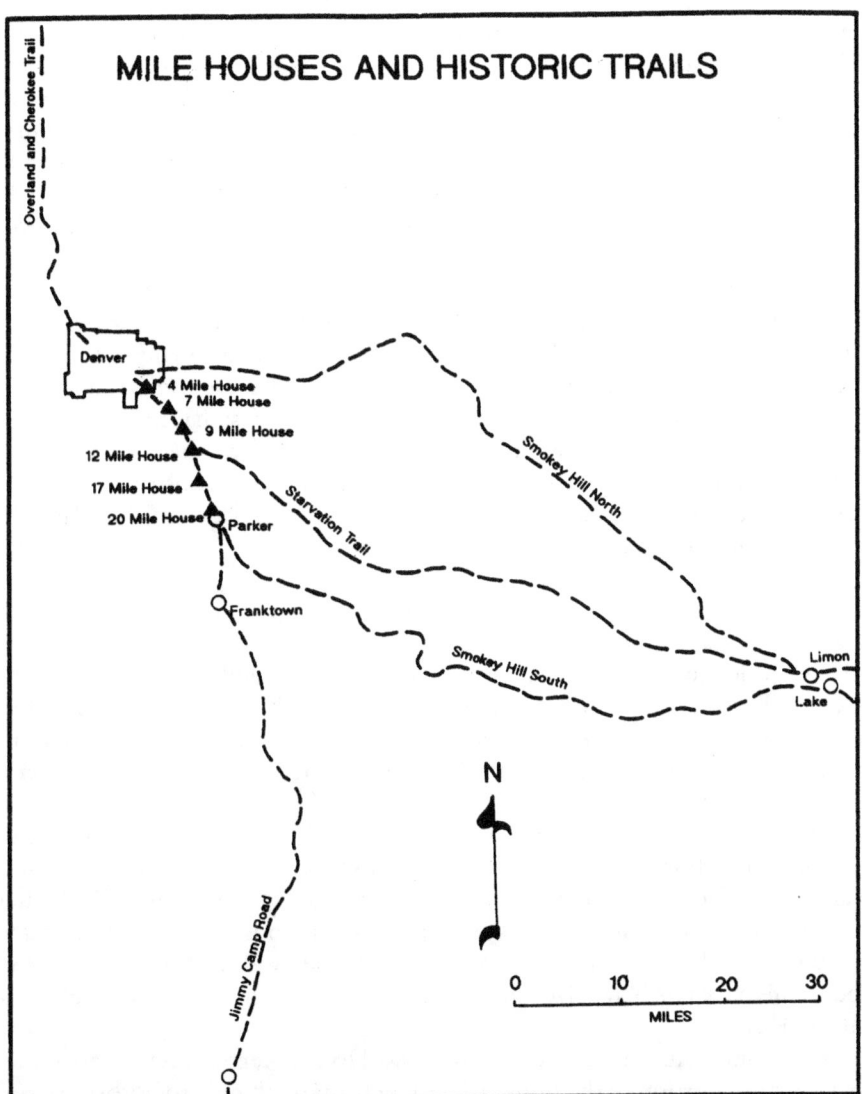

Figure 5.24. Mile houses and historic trails of the Denver area. From Marcia J. Tate, The Cherry Creek Mile Houses; reproduced by permission.

Much of the stage travel to Denver used the Smoky Hill North route, but in 1859–60 the Leavenworth and Pikes Peak Stage and in 1864–66 the Butterfield Overland Despatch used the Cherry Creek route into Denver. Most travelers were associated with the Denver to Santa Fe stage and freight or were local travelers, such as those who used the Denver and Colorado Express between Denver and Colorado City (Peters 1976). The arrival of the railroad in 1870 slowed travel on the trail, and the original Cherokee/Smoky Hill Trail was abandoned, replaced by a county road that ran along the ridges, farther from the creek (Peters 1980).

From 1859 through 1865 a number of inns were built along Cherry Creek, named for their distance from the junction of the Cherokee Trail and the "Cut-off Trail" from the Overland Trail, located at approximately 14th and Grant about a mile from what was then Denver (Peters 1976). The inns served many different purposes: stage stops, taverns, stores, and hotels. Each house was independently owned and provided a different set of services. The needs of travelers of the trail differed as well. Those who were coming with freight traveled slowly and needed to stop often to rest their horses. The stage travelers stopped less often. Many accounts put them at Twenty Mile House (located in Parker, currently an attached garage for a private residence) for the night, stopping at Four Mile House only to freshen up before heading into town (*Rocky Mountain News* 1956). Individual sojourners trickled in at their own pace.

The Mile Houses were the earliest historic sites in the Denver Basin to be excavated. To date only Four Mile House and Twelve Mile House have been subjected to archaeological investigation. The fragmentary nature of the archaeological data at the Mile Houses compromises their utility in detailed historical reconstruction. But a few archaeological observations suggest new insights into the history of the Mile Houses and by extension the urbanization of Denver.

## Twelve Mile House

The Twelve Mile House served as a stage station, hotel, bar, and post office. The original house at Twelve Mile was a one-story, three-room log cabin, probably built by Earnest Spact. John Melvin acquired the property in 1865 (Harvey 1935). Three years later he built a two-story, ten-room frame addition to the original house (Fig. 5.25), specifically with trade along the trail in mind.

A variety of activities occurred at Twelve Mile House. The stage stopped daily to leave mail, change horses, and drop off weary passengers. Local Ute Indians visited to trade and to get food. When the railroad came through, Mrs. Melvin, with the help of a black woman from Running Creek, fed the 80-man construction crews. As a result of the railroad, trade on the trail slowed and life at the Twelve Mile House was transformed to life on a ranch. Mr. Melvin died in 1900 and the property was sold in 1906 to Peter Kerker.

Shortly after purchasing the Twelve Mile House, Kerker decided to move the newer, two-story portion of the house to his ranch, one-half mile southeast of its original location. The house was lowered onto a foundation, its top story removed, and a new hip roof installed. The modified Twelve Mile House was moved in the late 1940s

Figure 5.25. The Twelve Mile House about 1900. Courtesy of the Denver Public Library.

to the town of Watkins to be used as a store. The top of the house caught fire in 1970. Afterward the house was renovated; a new red brick veneer was added and a low gabled roof completed the renewal.

The original three-room log structure purchased by the Melvins was apparently moved about 100 feet west. It was used as a barn for a time and then abandoned. It eventually fell apart and probably burned (Tate 1984).

### Archaeology of the Twelve Mile House

Currently the Twelve Mile House site is located two miles south of the Cherry Creek Reservoir. The reservoir was constructed by the U.S. Army Corps of Engineers as part of the effort to reduce flooding in the Denver area. The Corps, along with the State Historical Society, was interested in identifying the site of Twelve Mile House and assessing its archaeological potential (Tate 1979). This was not an easy task given that the researchers had no original structures to help them locate the site. The results of that work were reported by Marcia Tate and her colleagues (Tate et al. 1979) and are summarized here.

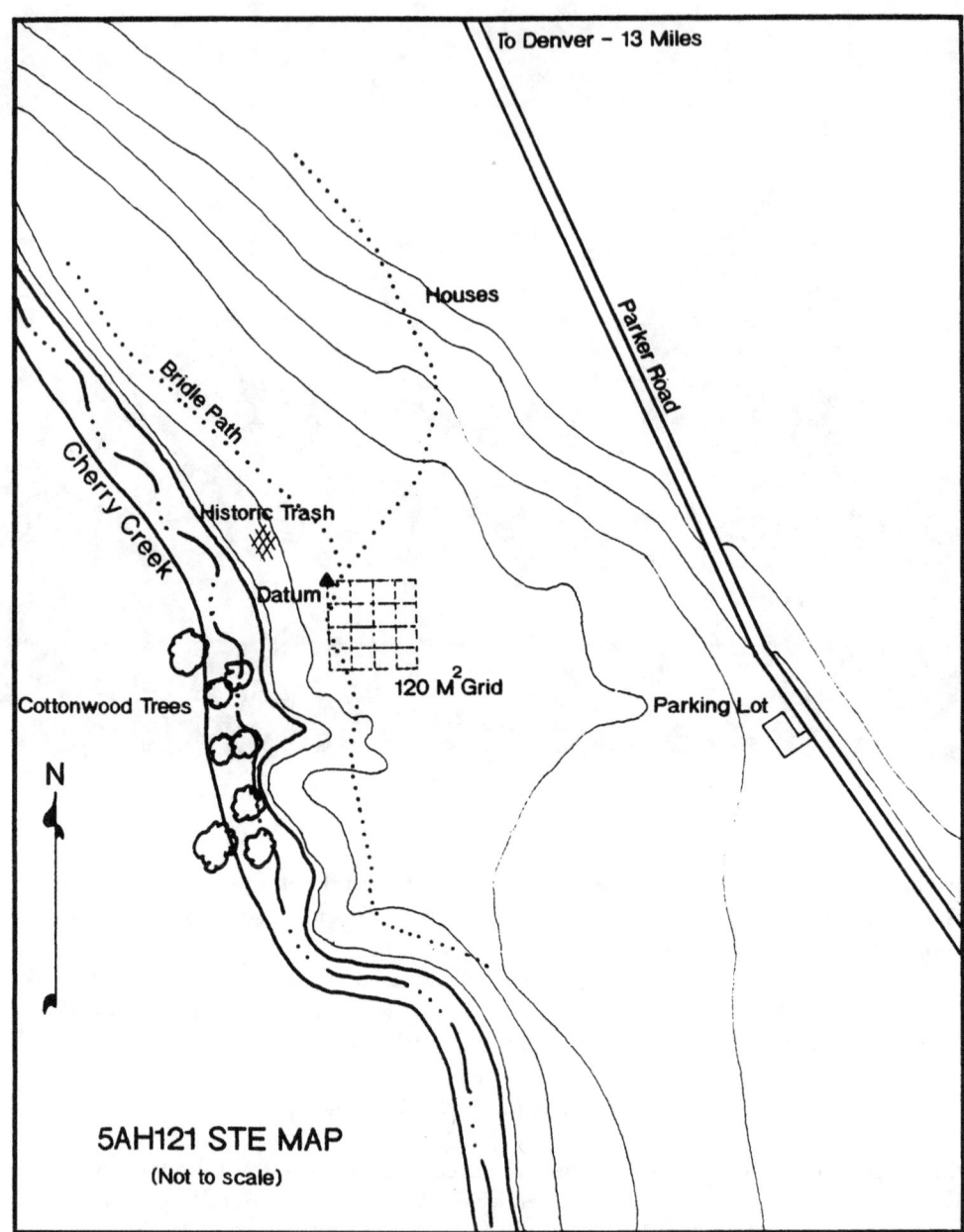

Figure 5.26. Survey map of the Twelve Mile House. From Marcia J. Tate, The Cherry Creek Mile Houses; reproduced by permission.

The phase 1 survey revealed cultural materials scattered over an area 120 meters square with no discernible features (Fig. 5.26). Researchers established a grid over the area which divided it into 5-m-square units. A random sample of eight units was selected for excavation to give an idea of site stratigraphy and the extent of buried materials, and in the hope that some foundations might be uncovered.

Phase 1 testing did not positively locate the Twelve Mile House. It indicated that materials on the site were mixed, with older and newer items coming from the same deposits. It did, however, reveal the presence of artifacts from between 1860 and 1900, thus relating to the trail-era occupation of the area.

Phase 2 testing used systematic reconnaissance of the area with metal detectors. Surface and subsurface items were identified and recorded. The reconnaissance identified an area in the center of the grid with a higher concentration of domestic artifacts (nails and ceramics) as opposed to ranching and agricultural artifacts (barbed wire, horseshoe nails). Mechanical trenching was then one in the area of domestic artifacts. The trenching and metal detector survey identified five possible features, including the original cellar, a chimney foundation, and three privies. The feature identified as the cellar consisted of deposits of cultural materials in an irregularly shaped area 10 m by 7.5 m located from approximately .8 m to 1.8 m below the present ground surface.

A number of artifacts were recovered. Domestic artifacts included silverware, ceramics, bottles, a shoe, a watch case, and stove and lamp parts. Agricultural material include horseshoes, wagon parts, an ax, and wire. The majority of artifacts were structural, including nails, rock, and latches. Three temporally diagnostic artifacts were recovered, two from the area identified as a cellar, the third from the backyard. The cellar contained a once-clear soda bottle turned purple by solarization (often called sun-colored amethyst) labeled "Standard Bottling Company, Denver Colorado." It dates between 1888 and 1890. Also from the cellar came a brown ceramic jug from Gross and Printz, dating from 1890 to 1899. From the yard area came a metal label with an inscription reading "Dr. L. H. Wood, 17th and Lawrence." Dr. Wood practiced at that address from 1886 to 1890.

The archaeology of the Twelve Mile House did not reveal any structural foundations. Cabin houses frequently did not have foundations, but the lack of one for a two story-frame structure is more surprising. It could have been destroyed when the house was moved. The chimney foundation and possible cellar, in combination with the artifactual evidence, indicates that this was a dwelling in use around the 1890s. It is tempting to say that the lack of a foundation and the later date of the artifacts implies a structure other than the Twelve Mile House. However, the researchers were thorough in their investigation of the region. Although no early diagnostic artifacts were located, they are probably deposited in buried trash dumps, with only later artifacts actually found on the surface. Given that the property was sold in 1906, the lumping of artifact dates around the 1890s represents items discarded in the last years the site was occupied. There is good reason to believe that this is indeed the location of the Twelve Mile House.

## The Four Mile House

Four Mile House Historic Park is located along the north bank of Cherry Creek. Once relatively distant from Denver, it is now surrounded by once suburban, now urban growth (Fig. 5.27). The site currently incorporates about twelve acres, including the original Four Mile House and grounds and several reconstructed buildings (Fig. 5.28). It is operated as a historic park with house tours, children's activities, and occasional living history events.

Figure 5.27. The Four Mile House location, 1980. Photograph courtesy of Four Mile House Historical Park.

Figure 5.28. Four Mile Historic Park, looking northeast. Photograph courtesy of Four Mile House Historical Park.

The first Four Mile House was a log house constructed in the summer or early fall of 1859 by Samuel Brantner and his brother Jonas. The next year the Brantners transferred the property to Mary Cawker, a widow or divorcée who lived there with her two children. It was Mary Cawker who first used the house as a stage station. One of the primary functions of the Four Mile stage station was to allow travelers to spruce up before entering Denver (*Rocky Mountain News* 1956). The occupants of the stage would come in and tidy up, and often the driver would trade out the horses for a fresh team to take them the last four miles into town (Peters 1976). During the Cawker years the Four Mile House also served as a tavern, a store, and a place to stay. Some people camped out; others slept in the house itself. Although not a formal hotel, the house had a large second-story room that was used for overnight guests as well as frequent square dances. Cawker built a large corral and stables with rock from a quarry located on her property near what is now Leetsdale Street. She used these to board horses and mules, some of them for the local pony express (not to be confused with the more famous regional organization). Sometimes freight carriers would establish camp at the

Four Mile House, going into town to unload their goods and coming back to spend the night (Peters 1980).

In the wake of the 1864 Cherry Creek flood, the creek bed moved almost a quarter of a mile north. Mary Cawker, discouraged by the flood, sold the Four Mile House to Levi and Millie Booth. The Booths continued to operate it as a stage stop and tavern. During this time the Butterfield Overland Despatch used it as a stage station. A passenger on the last Butterfield stage wrote of the Four Mile: "At last, four miles from the town [Denver], we reached a neat little tavern, beside which grew some cottonwoods. Here were two or three ranches in the process of establishment. The water from the wells was very sweet and cold" (Taylor 1867).

After the demise of the Butterfield line (after just nine months of operation), the Four Mile House became primarily a ranch and farm. The Booths purchased adjoining tracts of land and eventually expanded into a ranch of over 600 acres. Even before the railroad arrived taking with it the trail traffic, the Bee House was constructed to house hired hands. The Bee House is so named because Millie Booth later utilized it as the center of her honey making endeavors. In addition to her apiary, Millie was involved in butter making and poultry raising. The Booths excavated a cellar under the original Four Mile House for keeping milk and cream cool. Millie also supervised the work of turning ten acres of apples into cider (Working 1975).

Ella Grace Booth, one of Millie's and Levi's daughters, married Daniel W. Working, a fellow farmer. After their wedding in 1892, they built a house west of the Bee House. Their children provided researchers at the site with oral history about the activities at the site and the location of various structures. Levi Booth died in 1912 and Millie in 1926, leaving the ranch to the Workings. In 1945 the site was sold out of the family.

When the Four Mile House site was acquired by the city of Denver, only one original structure stood, the Four Mile House itself. The building consists of three portions: the original 1859 log structure, an 1883 brick addition, and a frame addition. The frame addition was actually part of a different structure whose original construction date is unknown. It was moved in 1883 and added to the house at the same time as the brick addition. Ella Grace Booth Working remembered her father covering the log portion of the house in clapboard (Fig. 5.29).

The original portion of the house is made of hand-hewn logs which the Booth daughter remembers being covered in clapboard just as soon as there was a lumberyard nearby (RMN Sept. 16, 1956). The 1883 brick addition stands in striking juxtaposition to the original log house. The factory-made brick is set off by intricate porch columns (Fig. 5.30). Inside the house the difference is also evident. The living room is filled with matched furniture the Booths purchased from a catalogue and had shipped in on the railroad (Fig. 5.31). The evolution of Denver architecture, tied to changing modes of transportation, is built into the house. The frontier era is characterized by handcrafted structures utilizing indigenous materials. After the railroad arrived, factory-made goods and materials were readily available and fairly inexpensive.

Figure 5.29. The Four Mile House with clapboard siding covering the original walls. Photograph courtesy of Four Mile House Historical Park.

Figure 5.30. The Four Mile House with its brick addition. Photograph courtesy of Four Mile House Historical Park.

Figure 5.31. Reconstructed living room of the Four Mile House, as part of the museum. Courtesy of Four Mile House Historical Park.

*Archaeology of the Four Mile House*

Four Mile Historic Park is the most extensively excavated historic period site in the Denver Basin. It has been the object of seven archaeological investigations over a fifteen-year period from 1976 to 1991 (Fig. 5.32). Although there are no current investigations at the site, it probably has not seen its last. Thus far a wide range of techniques have been used, including mechanical trenching, hand trenching, excavation of 1-by-1-meter units, magnetometer, probing with a metal rod, and simple recording of artifacts picked up after a disturbance. In what follows we summarize the most important work at the site.

In 1976 work was performed by students and faculty from the University of Colorado at Boulder with assistance from the Office of the State Archaeologist of Colorado. At the time of this initial investigation, the only standing structure was the Four Mile House itself. But photographs and other archival information indicated that at least two other main structures, the Bee House and the Working House, had stood on the site at one time. In addition to locating the two demolished structures, the 1976 investigations attempted to locate outbuildings seen in historic photographs, the Smoky Hill/Cherokee Trail as it passed through the site, and evidence of past agricultural activities.

The archaeological remains at the Four Mile House site have been subjected to many of the impacts that make sites difficult to find and interpret. The Cherry Creek flood of 1933 is primarily responsible for eliminating evidence of buildings to the south of the Four Mile House. Then in the 1970s the site was "cleaned up" and surface artifacts—metal, wood, concrete, glass, and tin cans—were hauled away. In addition, high spots on the landscape were graded down and depressions were filled in with dirt. The combination of these activities has made surface identification of many features difficult if not impossible. Nevertheless, a few miscellaneous outbuildings were located, including a root cellar or tool shed, the pump house, and a possible cowshed or barn. Two areas suspected to be the location of privies were identified as well. Other features known to have existed—the chicken house, icehouse, and corral—were not located.

The next step was the excavation of 17 test trenches in areas suspected to contain structural features (Fig. 5.33). The excavations did not expose any additional foundations. A trench was dug near the Working House, but at least part of the foundation was already visible. However, surface evidence of the Bee House was found during trenching. Between the Four Mile House and the Working House foundation was a small stand of spruce trees. At the base of those trees are two perpendicular lines of square cement pylons reinforced with metal rods. The cement blocks were spaced about 50 cm apart. It was suggested that these pylons were part of the foundation of the Bee House.

A number of nonstructural features were located during the trenching of the site. Most of these consisted of trash concentrations or dumps, many dating to relatively recent periods. However, one trench exposed a number of artifacts that appeared to date between 1850 and 1900. Artifacts included numerous fragments of medicine and utility bottles. A telephone pole insulator, a fragment of a glass lamp, and some fragments of unmarked ironstone pottery were also located.

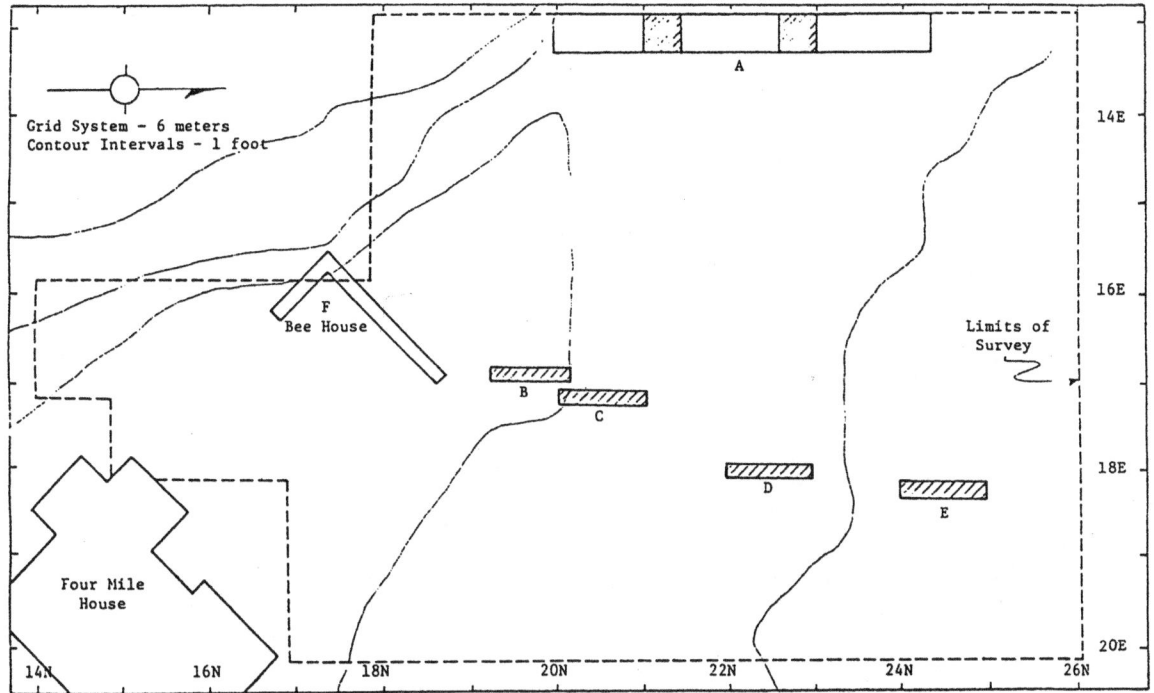

Figure 5.32. The archaeological investigations at the Four Mile House. From Claudia Nissley, Progress Report #1, Four Mile House; reproduced by permission.

In 1978 Colorado State University, under the direction of Elizabeth Morris, held an archaeological field school at the Four Mile House. The 1978 investigations followed up on those conducted in 1976. The Colorado State University team trenched in the area inferred to be the location of the Smoky Hill/Cherokee Trail. They also excavated in the area of a well near the Four Mile House and investigated two possible privies identified by Claudia Nissley (1976).

The artifacts recovered by the field school team included a wide array of domestic artifacts—ceramics, a thimble, part of a clock, a celluloid hairpin, beads, and garter belt snaps. In addition three stone flakes, Native American artifacts, were recovered. A piece of flaked glass was also recovered. The artifacts, many of them mixed in with ash, indicate that the area was a trash dump used by the residents of the Four Mile site from about the 1880s through the 1890s.

The search for the well began with photographs that indicated it was located directly east of the cellar door. The well was located; it was lined with red, pressed brick and measured 70 cm across. Stone and fragments of deteriorating wood indicate that at one time a wooden structure with a stone platform or foundation was positioned

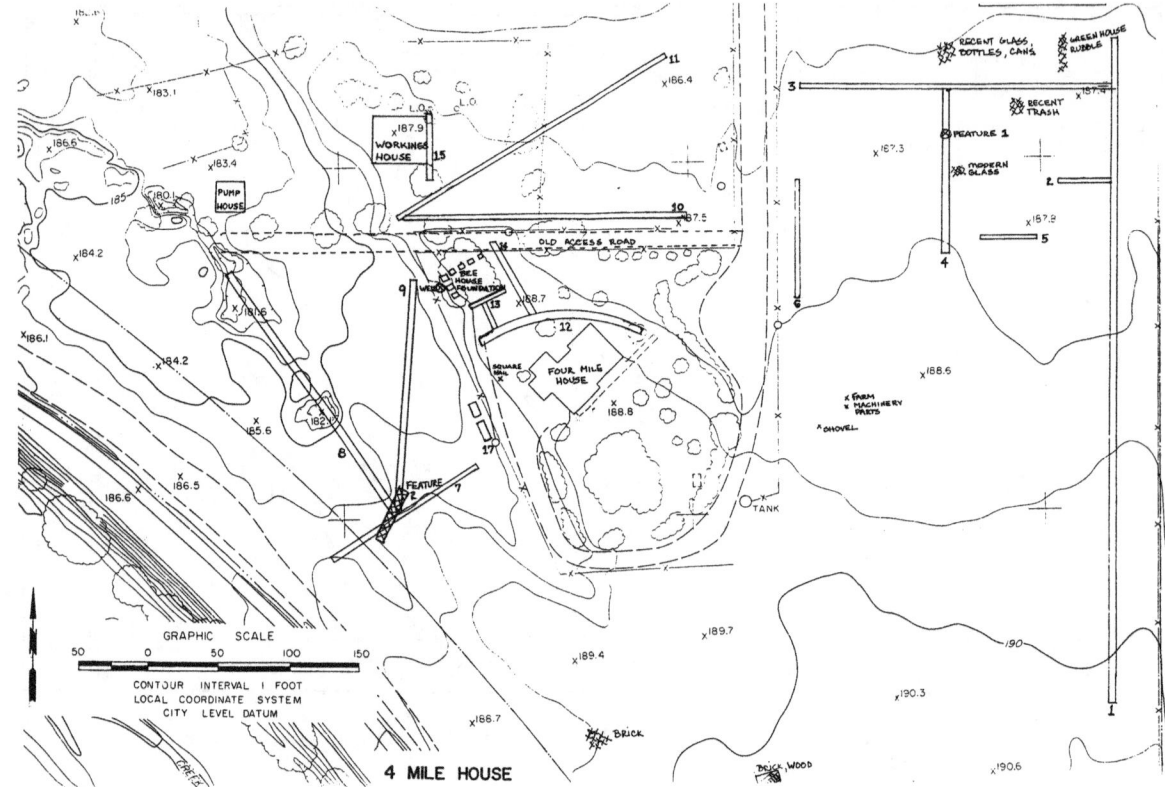

Figure 5.33. Test trenches at the Four Mile House. From Claudia Nissley, Progress Report #1, Four Mile House; reproduced by permission.

over the well. Later photographs show a steel pump over the well. The pipe that fed the pump was still in place. The excavation of this feature led to an accurate reconstruction of the well house, as well as exposing the original well.

Another trench was opened in an attempt to locate the Smoky Hill Trail. It was hoped that the trench would cut across the trail and expose it in cross section in the profile of the trench. At the southern end of the trench were found irregular stones averaging about 15 cm in diameter. That end of the trench was expanded, revealing a narrow path leading directly to the front step of the Four Mile House. The path consisted of a layer of pea-sized gravel formed in an arc over and mixed in with the larger stones. Dan Mayo (1978) quotes Bette Peters as asserting that caretakers of the Mile Houses were required to maintain a stretch of the road. The layer of pea gravel is narrowest and highest near the house and widens and gently slopes as it extends northeast, presumably to the Smoky Hill/Cherokee Trail.

Sealed features such as outhouses, or privies (a more genteel term archaeologists prefer, perhaps because it makes them feel better about digging in them), are critical to the historical archaeology of sites. Such feature fill may often be linked to specific, datable deposition events. In contrast, artifacts in the general site area, often called sheet trash, have low archaeological integrity. The Four Mile House was constructed prior to the advent of indoor plumbing. Thus at least one privy would have been necessary. There is also specific documentation regarding the outhouse there. In cities, outhouses were often lined in stone and were periodically cleaned out (Geismar 1993). But in more rural areas, or where there was room for it, the outhouse was merely moved to an adjacent location. Earl Working, a Booth grandson, remembers the outhouse being moved about ten feet west around the turn of the century. The Four Mile House privy was fairly elaborate, with a frame building complete with a window and three seats, one specifically designed for a child's shorter legs.

Searching the area described by Earl Working, Nissley (1976) identified two potential privies based on surface evidence and probing with a metal rod, which indicated soft soil (as opposed to the harder, more consolidated soil on the rest of the site). The 1978 field school excavated a trench (23) in one of those possible privy areas. The trench revealed layers of trash, brick, and ash. The excavation was then expanded horizontally to find evidence of an underlying feature. Bricks were eventually located on all four sides, revealing a nearly square privy measuring just over 1.5 m on each side. Excavation through the top 155 cm of fill revealed trash dating from the late 1940s and 1950s, including a newspaper dated 1951. At 155 cm, however, the fill became noticeably darker, a good indication of organic materials such as those expected in a privy. Further strengthening the inference of this feature's use as a privy was the recovery of a number of small seeds, including tomato, cherry, squash, and watermelon. Artifacts were mostly recovered from the edges of the privy. They included ceramics with a flow-blue pattern, a number of matchsticks, and several bottles.

It appears that this was the turn-of-the-century privy remembered by Earl Working. The pressed brick used in the construction seems to be of the type used for the foundation of the 1883 addition to the Four Mile House. The artifacts themselves date between 1910 and 1920. There were probably smaller artifacts deposited throughout the privy's history. Typically artifacts that one wants to hide are conveniently disposed of in a privy. The larger (and thus datable) artifacts were not deposited in the privy until after it had seen a decade or so of use. They were then deposited either as trash disposal or to aid in percolation. The 1940s and '50s artifacts were probably dumped to fill up the privy space after it had been abandoned.

Investigations at the Four Mile House took a different turn in 1979. As part of the University of Denver field school under the direction of Sarah Nelson, Mark Guthrie conducted a proton magnetometer survey of the site (Guthrie 1979). Proton magnetometers are a type of remote sensing, a method of gaining information about buried material without actually excavating. The technique works by measuring anomalies in the soil (soft spots, foundation remnants, etc.). Generally large anomalies are interpreted as buried features, whereas smaller anomalies can be caused by phenomena uninteresting to archaeologists, such as decaying tree trunks, recent tin cans, or modern water lines.

The proton magnetometer survey was carried out along a north-south grid superimposed upon the site. It covered the area between the Four Mile House and the surface remains of the Bee House discovered by Nissley, and then extended to the north of the Bee House in an effort to locate other outbuildings or perhaps remnants of the trail (Fig. 5.33). Using a magnetometer in the city is fraught with difficulties caused by such distractions as electric wires and passing vehicles. However, five major anomalies were recorded and excavated by the University of Denver team. Two of these appear to have been caused by historically interesting features. Anomaly A is in the area of an irrigation ditch. Anomaly E turned out to be a clay floor with large pieces of adobe and nonlocal pebbles. There were no clear artifacts associated with this floor. It was quite small and may have been the entrance into a calf pen or corral, or it may be a prehistoric living surface. The other anomalies appeared to have been caused by more recent trash, metal horseshoes or, in one case, a rotting tree stump.

None of the anomalies appeared to be clearcut historic features. However, some more subtle information was gleaned through these investigations. Although archaeologists hope to find clear architectural data, structural evidence can also be found in the form of individual artifacts. Twelve trenches were excavated in the field north of the Bee House and the Four Mile House. The depth and location in the trench was noted for each artifact uncovered. Nelson (1979b) anticipated that items that were part of dwellings (window glass, brick, and nails) and domestic items that could be expected to be found within them (dishes and bottles) would be located in the vicinity of dwellings. Outbuildings not used for living space would be represented by items like nails, horseshoes, and horseshoe nails. Plotting artifacts in each trench begins to show us such variation. The nails were found predominantly in the A trenches, in H, and in E. The A trenches are near the Working House. Trenches E and H may be near a single building, or could be indications of two buildings. Glass is also widespread, but tends to be concentrated near the Working House and in Trench E. There is a possibility that an outbuilding in this vicinity had window glass. Horseshoes and horseshoe nails were found exclusively in the two northernmost trenches, while sherds were found predominantly near the Working House.

A few statistical tests were run to see whether the patterns of artifact locations were random or statistically significant. Artifacts were grouped into those that were identified as household related and outbuilding/corral related. A scatterplot of the data shows differences between the trenches and a chi-square test of the same data proved to be significant at the 0.05 level.

To cross-check these differences, trenches were grouped into "yard" and "corral" designations. Included in the "yard" group were A1, A3, K, L, and M, which are within the fence indicated on a 1956 aerial photograph and confirmed by the finding of a fence post in Trench K. The others, trenches B, C, D, E, H, and J, were grouped together as the "corral." Six classes of artifacts (bones, glass, metal fragments, nails, horseshoes and horseshoe nails, and sherds) were tested for randomness of distribution. A chi-square test of the resulting grouping was highly significant, indicating that the probability that

HISTORIC ARCHAEOLOGY | 195

this artifact distribution happened by chance was very low. In general it appears that these areas differed in their historic use.

The proton magnetometer survey was not the only archaeological investigation conducted by the University of Denver that summer. The Working House and the Bee House were also excavated, at least in part, by archaeology graduate students.

The Bee House was constructed in 1866. The structure was a simple one-and-one-half-story front gable frame house covered, like the original wing of the Four Mile House, in wooden clapboard. An 1880 photograph of the structure shows the north side of the building (Fig. 5.34). Originally constructed as a residence, it was later used primarily as an outbuilding for Millie Booth's apiary. An 1890s photograph shows the

Figure 5.34. The Bee House, winter 1880. Photograph courtesy of Four Mile House Historical Park.

Figure 5.35. Bee hives at the Bee House, 1890s. Photograph courtesy of Four Mile House Historical Park.

Bee House as it looked at the height of its beekeeping days (Fig. 5.35). It appears that after Millie's death the house was again used as a dwelling. Records indicate it was occupied when it burned in 1939. Like the Working House, the location of the Bee House was identified by surface manifestations. The recovered material culture gives us clues not only about the construction and decoration of the house, but also about the diet of those who lived and worked in the house and the articles they lost. Since the University of Denver investigations, the Bee House has been reconstructed, its location based on this archaeological investigation. Although the interior has not been reconstructed (the building is used as an office and a museum store), the items recovered would aid in such an effort if it were to occur.

The Working House, located to the north of the Bee House, was a single-story frame house with a two-story brick addition on the north forming the top part of a T-shaped structure (Fig. 5.36). Holbrook Working indicated that the frame portion of the Working House was built in 1897, with the brick addition built in 1901 (Nelson 1979b). The house was demolished in the 1960s, but excavations revealed details of construction. The house was built with plaster and lath. Several of the color schemes

Figure 5.36. The Working House. Photograph courtesy of Four Mile House Historical Park.

were evident in the plaster portions collected. Wood and wood moldings were painted to match the plaster, and pieces of wallpaper were recovered. Linoleum was used in the house, which was plumbed for both water and sewer and had electricity. If a decision were made to rebuild the Working House, such detailed information would be a valuable guide for accurate reconstruction.

The Anthropology Department of the Metropolitan State College of Denver Anthropology department conducted a series of investigations at the Four Mile House in 1989 and 1991, excavating a series of trenches as well as collecting and recording artifacts from a waterline excavation. As part of their original research design (Kent 1989), the team gathered all the data from previous excavations and plotted the locations of all known excavations. Jonathan Kent, who directed the investigations, has produced a series of interim reports (Kent 1989, 1991). All the artifacts from those excavations have been cataloged and entered into a database. In addition, a number of students have completed in-depth analysis of several artifact categories retrieved from both excavations. A volume documenting their work is currently in preparation (Kent, Bandy, and Walsh n.d.)

In 1989 Metropolitan State College excavated a series of trenches, numbered 25–30, to the southeast of the Four Mile House. The main purpose of these trenches was to locate the remains of the Smoky Hill/Cherokee Trail as it passed through the site. Historic maps of the area indicate that the Smoky Hill Trail ran parallel to the northeast bank of Cherry Creek. The Colorado State University excavations had indicated that a gravel trail runs northeast from the Four Mile House. Metro's trenches were placed in an area previously unexcavated. In general the results in each ten-by-two-foot trench were similar. The top six inches appear to be a plow zone, with artifacts dating from the last 50 years. Trench 28 contained two parallel wheel tracks which excavators hoped were remnants of the trail. But they turned out to be tractor impressions, interpreted by tread in the imprints as well as evidence of plowed material underneath. No other anomalies indicative of a trail or road were encountered in the trenches. What the trenches did reveal is a particular effect of approximately a century years of plowing on the Plains. At the base of the plow zone (ranging from 6 to 10 inches in depth) there was a hardpan that extended down to about 15 inches below present ground surface. It appears that minerals and finer soil particles percolate through the constantly churned and thus less consolidated plow zone, settling into the consolidated soil below and creating a hardened, high clay content level. Below the hardpan no cultural deposits were found.

After the disappointing results in trenches 25–30, another three trenches (31–33) were excavated in the grove area nearer the Four Mile House, in an attempt to locate any previously unrecorded outbuildings or features. To this end, researchers drove a metal probe into the ground in portions of the grove area not previously disturbed by utility lines. Places where the probe encountered solid material were flagged. These trenches turned out to be very productive. Trench 31 revealed small pieces of pipe and a rotting tree stump. Excavation among and below the tree roots revealed what appears to be a buried prehistoric living surface at about two feet below the present ground surface. The component is indicated by a scatter of lithic debris, a side scraper of petrified wood, and occasional fragments of charcoal. Square nails were also recovered from the surrounding deposit, however. This juxtaposition probably indicates disturbance of the soil by the tree roots and perhaps animals, although it could indicate a contact-period aboriginal site. The lack of any marked contact-period material culture (beads, iron artifacts, etc.) seems to indicate that this is not the case, but the small sample of the pit (1.5 x 5 ft) may be inconclusive. Trench 33 revealed the top of a circular cement encasing wall about 4 feet in diameter. This appears to be a previously unknown well. The contents of the well were not explored.

In 1991 Metropolitan State College excavated two ten-by-two-foot hand-dug trenches 34 and 35, located in the area between the Four Mile House and the Bee House (Fig. 5.34). The area was first probed with a metal rod to locate any foundation stones. An area that appeared to contain a row of stones was identified and bisected by the trench. Trench 35 was located between trench 34 and the Four Mile House. Trench 34 did reveal an alignment of rocks approximately 2 ½ feet wide running northwest at the same angle as the Four Mile House. The artifacts recovered from this trench include structural items such as window glass, brick, and nails. Domestic items included a complete perfume bottle and ceramics. Charcoal flecking was common in the eastern end of the unit, with a number of charred bones coming out of a lower level. Three lithics were also recovered: a chert flake, a petrified wood flake, and a utilized flake.

The foundation revealed in trench 34 did not continue in trench 35, which is nearer the Four Mile House in an area that has been repeatedly disturbed. After going through a number of soil lenses mixed with modern artifacts, the excavators encountered a level of angular gravel with very little soil at all. Below this level they encountered a high number of artifacts, including glass, nails, and burned and unburned butchered bone. This artifact-rich level was located between 6 and 11 inches below present ground surface. The faunal analysis (Gay n.d.) indicates that trench 35 contains the highest number of both burned bone items (Fig. 5.37) and butchered bones of any Metro excavation unit (Fig. 5.38). Interestingly trench 34 contains less overall bone than 35, but more unburned bone. It appears that this area was at one time some type of a kitchen dump. The relatively clean gravel covering the deposit was probably intentionally dumped there to cover the trash after the dump was no longer used.

Metropolitan State College has performed the most extensive artifactual analysis of any Four Mile House researchers. A number of students have completed analysis of the artifacts recovered during the excavation, including faunal and floral remains, gun cartridges, barrels, and bottle glass. Analysis of cartridges at the site revealed a number of interesting pieces of data (Winters 1992). The cartridges ran the full range from .22 short-range guns to 12-gauge shotguns. A variety of pistols, rifles, and shotguns were used at the Four Mile House. All the cartridges are designed for short range use, accurate only at about one hundred yards. The bullet size and range limitations seem to indicate that guns were probably used for game birds and other small game, as well as the elimination of vermin. They could also have been used for personal protection or target practice. The absence of large, long-range cartridges suggests that hunting of large game (elk or deer) did not occur here. One might think that such game would not have been present, but Grace Booth Working recalls herds of antelope watering near the site (*Rocky Mountain News* 1956). The dates of cartridges fall mostly between 1890 and 1934. It appears that the encroachment of the city of Denver curtailed shooting at the Four Mile House. The majority of the cartridges were recovered from trenches 36 and 37, located between the Working House and the river, a much more suitable spot for shooting than the area between the Four Mile House and the Bee House (trenches 34 and 35).

The floral remains analyzed at the Four Mile House come from dry screening, and are thus dominated by larger seeds. Smaller remains that might be recovered by flotation, for example grass seeds, are not represented. The floral analysis is contextualized by a survey of the plants currently located on the site (Otto 1989). The majority of seeds recovered from the Metro excavation are Russian olive. Russian olive is a transplant to the Denver area, used for ornamentation; it was removed from Four Mile Historic Park in the 1970s when the site was restored. The next three most common seeds, bulrush, thistle, and cottonwood, are all still present on or near the site. They thrive in the riparian area near Cherry Creek.

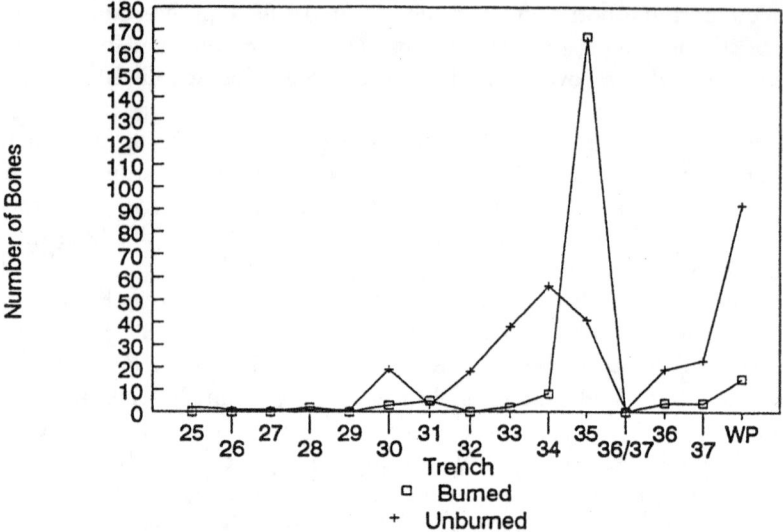

Figure 5.37. Results of faunal analysis at the Four Mile House. From Patrick Gay, Faunal Analysis at Four Mile House: Excavations of Field Seasons in 1989 and 1991 (Department of Anthropology, Metropolitan State College of Denver); reproduced by permission.

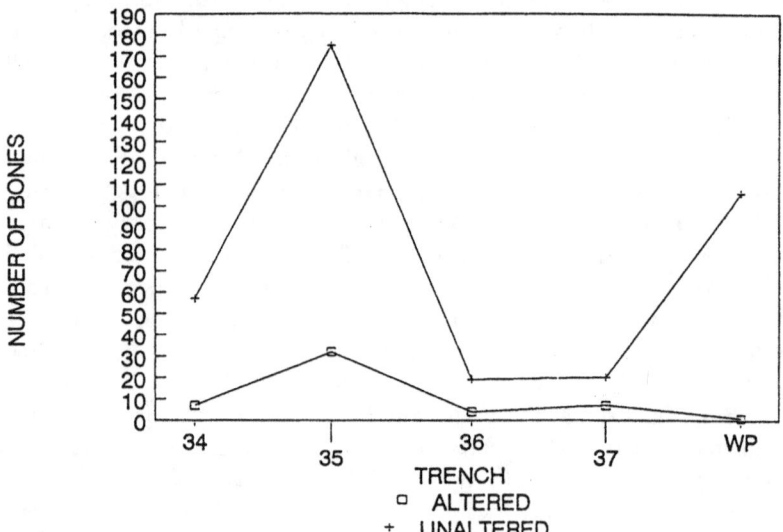

Figure 5.38. Results of altered versus unaltered bone analysis at the Four Mile House. From Patrick Gay, Faunal Analysis at Four Mile House: Excavations of Field Seasons in 1989 and 1991 (Department of Anthropology, Metropolitan State College of Denver); reproduced by permission.

Other seeds recovered include crabapple, hackberry, chokecherry, and peach. Peach pits have been noted by many excavators. One of the pits analyzed by Bob Rowe (Rowe n.d.) bore cut marks, probably from someone who cut the peach in half before eating it. The peaches could have been purchased, but were probably grown on the site, perhaps in Millie Booth's orchard. The crabapple may have been grown as an ornamental plant as well as being used to make jelly. Hackberry is indigenous to this area, often found along canyons and arroyos (Weber 1976). The seeds recovered from excavations came either from hackberry growing along Cherry Creek or from Chinese elm, a relative of hackberry currently growing at the site. Chokecherries are in fact the source of the name for Cherry Creek and grow wild along its banks. Rowe observed that the majority of the chokecherry pits have been gnawed, indicating they were deposited on the site by rodents rather than human inhabitants. Chokecherry can also be used for jelly and may have been processed on the site, as well. There are no chokecherries currently located onsite, although there are probably some along the creek.

One of the most interesting finds was eleven yucca seeds. Yucca is native to this area and can still be found in remnant areas of short-grass prairie. Culturally, however, it is associated with deserts. One cannot imagine the residents of the Four Mile House living with such plants for long. Indeed, the yucca seeds came from the bottom two levels of trench 37, which yielded predominantly native plants. In fact level 4 contains only cottonwood, bulrush, and yucca seeds, and probably reflects the flora of the area when it was first inhabited. Unlike cottonwood and bulrush seeds, yucca seeds disperse very near the mother plant (within 5–8 feet). It appears that there was once a yucca very near Trench 37.

Analysis of the bottle glass from the Metro excavations indicates differential deposition of specific types of artifacts. However, before presenting the analysis, it is critical to know a little more about the contents of bottles recovered from the site. Penny Nelson (1992) divided bottle glass into functional categories based on color, bottle design, and maker's marks. The categories included liquor, medicinal, perfume, bitters, topical (including balm, tooth powder, and ink), and unidentifiable.

Proprietary medicines, also known as patent medicine, bitters, and sarsaparillas, were heavily consumed commodities between the 1850s and the 1920s. These products often included narcotics such as morphine, anesthetics like cocaine, and other substances now controlled, like cannabis. They invariably had a high alcohol content, and sometimes contained ingredients considered poisons, like arsenic and mercury. The 1870s to about 1900 was the height of this era, fueled by advertising and made more profitable as bottle production became more automated. Social reformers and doctors led crusades against the abuse of these medicines. Even popular magazines such as *Harper's Weekly* wrote exposés on opium in medicine. In 1906 the Pure Food and Drug Act for the first time regulated such products, making them display their contents and outlawing the advertisement of "cures."

The bottles recovered from the Metropolitan State College Four Mile House excavations provide good examples of this type of product. The bitters bottles, Log Cabin and Warner's Safe, were both marketed by the same company. Warner began selling his "Safe" cures and bitters in 1879 and introduced the Log Cabin line in 1886. Warner heartily believed in name recognition. He spent "a small fortune on promotion"

(Wilson and Wilson 1971:144) and each line had a distinctive, easy to recognize bottle. Even given the fragmentary nature of the bottles at the Four Mile House, Nelson was able to identify them. The Warner's Safe Cure line included kidney and liver cure, Nervine, rheumatic cure, diabetes cure, and bitters. The Log Cabin remedies included hair tonic, liver pills, cough and consumption remedy, and sarsaparilla extract. According to the advertising, Warner's Log Cabin Sarsaparilla "positively" cured a host of diseases including scrofula, syphilis, "humors of a cancerous nature," scald head, boils, rheumatism, ulcers, female weakness, dyspepsia, and "all diseases caused by impure blood" (Wilson and Wilson 1971:96). The medicine bottle identified by Nelson (1992) was Davis Vegetable Pain Killer. The original formula of the painkiller was gums of myrrh, opium, benzoin, guaiac, camphor, and capsicum; by 1880 the opium had been taken out. It was advertised as "A safe and sure remedy for rheumatism, neuralgia, cramps, cholera, diarrhoea, dysentery, sprains & bruises, burns & scalds, toothache & headache" (Wilson and Wilson 1971:31).

As part of her analysis Nelson plotted the location of bottle remains by functional category. The majority of alcohol and bitters bottles were located on the perimeter of the settlement, while household items such as perfume, topical, and medicinal bottles were located between the Four Mile House and the Bee House. Although the sample size is extremely small, it is interesting that bitters bottles, which were advertised along with proprietary medicine bottles, were deposited along with the alcohol bottles. Various archaeological studies have shown that bitters and tonics were often consumed as an alternative to alcohol (Beaudry, Cook, and Mrozowski 1991). It has been suggested that the "medicinal" properties of bitters made Victorian consumers feel better about indulging in alcohol (Wilson and Wilson 1971:6). This was especially true of women who were discouraged from drinking alcohol, particularly in public. Not until Prohibition, when all drinking was illegal, was it common practice for men and women to drink together (Lanza 1995). The Victorian woman who pushed for temperance during the day but took to her tonics at night is something of a stereotype. Still the material record can be indicative of just such a scenario. At the Four Mile House the pattern is somewhat different, with medicines and bitters separated in their disposal areas. An analysis of alcohol, bitters, and medicine consumption at the Four Mile House would require a more in-depth study of all the collected bottles and perhaps additional excavation. The data to date present us with only a fragmentary, tantalizing glimpse into this element of life at the site.

## Reflections on the Archaeology of the Mile Houses

The investigations at the The Mile Houses, especially the Four Mile House, illustrate the challenges of archaeology as an approach to historical inquiry. Field studies were able to answer some architectural questions. Locations of the Bee House, the pump house, the privy, and the corral area were all established. Other questions, including the purpose of the stone alignment between the Four Mile House and the Bee House and the location of the original Smoky Hill/Cherokee Trail, were not answered. Still, excavations provided information about building techniques and materials as well as changing site technology. The archaeology of the Four Mile House has illuminated aspects of life not available from the written record, including gun use and alcohol and bitters consumption.

One of the main interpretive themes of the park is women's history. The excavation of the area adjacent to the kitchen is a testament to how technology changed the lives of women at this site. During Millie Booth's time at the Four Mile House it acquired two important innovations, running water and gas. Once those were in place the water no longer needed to be fetched, the wood chopped, the stove tended. Certainly this changed Millie Booth's life. Historians of domestic technology remind us that innovations often do not so much save time as redistribute it (Cowan 1974). For example, washing machines lowered the amount of time spent washing a load of clothes, but raised the level of expectation for how clean clothes should be. One should not just assume that running water and gas made Millie Booth's life easier. It is possible that the majority of the woodchopping and water fetching was done by children, grandchildren, or a hired hand. Certainly she no longer had to tend the fire in the stove or sweep out the ashes. Perhaps it was these innovations that allowed her to spend more time pursuing beekeeping. Regardless, it serves as a material reminder of how life in the Denver Basin has changed.

Like all social and field scientists, archaeologists often do not find what they are looking for. The most celebrated period of Four Mile House history is probably the frontier, pre-railroad era. Very little of the material culture of that period has been recovered. This is very often the case at sites occupied for a long time. Continued use of the area destroys the early materials. There may be another, very simple reason that the early material is hard to find—there wasn't that much of it. As exemplified by the Four Mile House itself, the material culture of that era was local, or, if imported, expensive, hard to come by, and very often reused. The bottles and kegs used to hold the drinks sold in Mary Cawker's tavern were precious. They were probably carefully saved and reused. Food was grown onsite, or if purchased was bought either on the hoof or in reusable packaging, such as bushel baskets or cloth sacks. Items (like the barrel in trench 36) were repaired when possible and only discarded after they were no longer of any conceivable use. The arrival of the railroad began an escalation of material goods and the packaging required for long-range shipping that now fills the dumpsters of the alleys of Denver. At the Four Mile House the earlier goods are conspicuous by their absence, especially when compared to the Tremont House. The Tremont House indicates that before the arrival of the railroad goods could be had if people were willing to pay the price. At the Four Mile House it appears they may have not been willing.

In some ways the history of Denver is the history of its waterways. The water and game of Cherry Creek and the Platte River drew Native Americans here. In 1858, the discovery of gold in those same rivers brought the Anglo settlers here. They followed the waterways to get to the city, and then settled along it to raise crops and families. Eventually the growing city enveloped Four Mile House. This one-time ranch, named for and defined by it presence *outside* the city, has been enveloped, its previous activities, grazing cattle, growing alfalfa, shooting game, no longer possible.

It is its presence along and dependence on the creek that makes the Four Mile House typical of the prehistory and history of this region. One critical and often overlooked aspect of Four Mile House archaeology is the presence of Native American materials in every excavation that has occurred here. The Four Mile House site has been a nice place to live for a long time. The Booths and those who lived there before them took advantage of the location as a good spot to either procure or grow food.

Many of the aboriginal materials here probably date back thousands of years. Some, perhaps those in trench 31, may date to the contact period when this was contested land. This is a real possibility given the documentary evidence. Not only was Cherry Creek a favorite camping place for historic Indians, documentation of other Mile Houses often mentions transactions with local Native Americans. The Ute had a well established camp only "a couple hundred yards" from the Twelve Mile House (Harvey 1935). The excavations here, driven by questions about Anglo settlers, raise questions about those who came before them as well. Certainly they illustrate the very real possibility of intact prehistoric or ethnographic sites buried in the first terrace of Cherry Creek and the Platte.

## Life on the Periphery

Historical archaeology in the subregions around Denver's urban core provides insight into the lives and experiences of people living on the immediate periphery of an urban area. These people were in some instances pushed there by political and economic strategies emanating from the urban core. The historical archaeology of the Denver urban periphery reflects agricultural activities before 1940 and primarily military activities after 1940—these being the two most prevalent Euro-American land use themes in this part of eastern Colorado (Tucker, in Stone 1997). This section briefly reviews some studies of historic sites in Denver's urban periphery, and then details recent archaeological work at the Rocky Mountain Arsenal as a way to illustrate the research potential of historic archaeology.

One of the most important historical sites related to the agricultural development of Greater Denver was recorded by Frank Eddy and collaborators (Eddy et al. 1981) in Castlewood Canyon State Park in Douglas County, part of the Black Forest subregion. This site is Castlewood Dam, constructed in 1889–90. The dam was instrumental in supplying irrigation water to farmers in the Cherry Creek Valley until it collapsed in 1933. Other surveys (Mutaw and Tate 1990; Shields 1993) have located house foundations, farm equipment, and trash dumps related to agricultural activities throughout the Streams and Plains subregions. Most of the sites located by these surveys lacked good archaeological integrity and thus had limited research potential. On the other hand, Richard Carrillo's (1986) excavations at the Big Dry Creek Cheese Ranch at Highlands Ranch in Douglas County produced good data to allow clear identification of economic shifts among area residents over time, in this case a shift from hunting to more cash-economy oriented activities (such as dairying) between 1879 and 1940.

Several surveys have located sites sensitive to both the agricultural and military histories of Greater Denver. Marcia Tate and Paul Friedman (1986) recorded several agricultural homesteads before and after 1909 in the area of the Senec Dam site in Arapahoe County. These homesteads were all abandoned by 1940 when the Lowry Bombing Range was established in the area. Many armaments relating to Lowry's bombing activities were located by the survey. A subsequent survey of the Buckley Air National Guard Base in Arapahoe County by Tate and her collaborators (Tate et al. 1990) located one pre-1940s farmstead and a dozen military-related sites. Tammy Stone and her collaborators (Stone 1997) recorded sites sensitive to agricultural and military history in their survey of the Plains Conservation Center, Arapahoe County. Finally, Nelson's (1980) survey at South Table Mountain near Golden recorded several features—including an amphitheater and stone bridge—associated with Camp George West, a Colorado National Guard camp. They date to around 1933, when they were built by the WPA.

Recent archaeological research at another military installation—the Rocky Mountain Arsenal located about ten miles northeast of Denver (Fig. 5.5)—perhaps best illustrates the promise of urban periphery sites for answering questions relating to the themes of this book. The rest of this chapter focuses on Arsenal work.

## Rocky Mountain Arsenal

The Rocky Mountain Arsenal was created in 1942 when the U.S. Army purchased approximately 20,000 acres of farmland from some 474 individual property owners. The property acquired contained 1,440 buildings and structures. Some residents were allowed to remove buildings to other locations. Except for about 80 buildings, the army demolished what remained. Later all but 22 of those buildings were also destroyed. The Arsenal continued to be active throughout the Cold War as a munitions and chemical weapons plant. After wartime operations ceased the Arsenal was leased to Shell Oil, which used it to manufacture pesticides until 1982. Operations at the Arsenal by both Shell and the U.S. Army were concentrated in the center of a 28-square-mile area. In 1987 portions of the Arsenal were designated a Superfund site by the U.S. Environmental Protection Agency and remediation efforts began. The army estimates completion in approximately the year 2006.

In 1994 a local environmental firm called SWCA Inc. contracted with the U.S. Fish and Wildlife Service to perform a cultural resources survey of the Arsenal. SWCA archaeologists recorded a total of 213 cultural resources with a historic component. Of these, 89 were isolated finds, locations without intact features or structural elements; 81 maintained enough integrity to be considered sites. Another fourteen sites had both a historic and prehistoric component. In addition to the archaeological sites, four historic irrigation features, two canals and two reservoirs, were recorded. The archaeological resources are sensitive to a number of issues, including ethnic coresidence, the roles of women, land and resource relationships, and processes of displacement.

> Box 5B. Effects of Survey on the Archaeological Record
> The majority of the sites in our database were recorded by cultural resource managers performing studies in connection with some type of government project. When

> an undertaking involves either federal or state land or money, the potential impact of that project on archaeological resources must be taken into account. Phase 1 is an intensive on-the-ground survey for archaeological sites; phase 2 is ground testing of surveyed sites; phase 3 is site excavation. We know much more about areas that have been intensively surveyed than about those that have not. This causes a spottiness in our data about the past.
>
> The Rocky Mountain Arsenal is a very good example. Before the SWCA survey of the Arsenal, there had been only a handful of sites recorded (Fig. 5.39). After the survey was completed, the number of sites, both prehistoric and historic, grew exponentially (Fig. 5.40). Many of the areas in the Denver Basin that appear to be lacking or devoid of sites have just not been surveyed. In many other areas the build-up of the city has created historic sites and destroyed prehistoric ones. It is important to remember that our ideas about Greater Denver archaeology will keep changing as more sites are recorded and excavated. It is also sobering to think that each newly developed area that is not surveyed may have a site density like the Arsenal.

## *Archival Record*

The archival record for the Rocky Mountain Arsenal is rich. James Ayres, the historical archaeologist who performed the archival research, calls the information on Arsenal properties "one of the largest and best documented collections of information about rural architecture in the western United States" (Clark 1997:49). A sixteen-volume history of the Rocky Mountain Arsenal was compiled by the U.S. Army (U.S. Army 1945). Four of the volumes give detailed information about the properties acquired for the Arsenal, including the owner's name and an inventory of all buildings, structures, and other improvements on each parcel acquired, along with their sizes, building materials, roof-covering material, foundations, and a statement as to the condition of each. The descriptive report is accompanied by photographs of each building on each of the parcels acquired. The work done to date at the Arsenal has focused on the remains of these buildings.

Analysis of the documentary record at the Arsenal outlines a story of the settling of the plains, one that is perhaps typical of agricultural areas on the periphery of larger cities. The Bureau of Land Management tract books indicate that 63 properties on what became the Arsenal were acquired through homesteading, scrip, or cash between 1871 and 1916. The applications hit a high in the years 1879 and 1880, when seventeen patents were recorded. Homesteading quickly dropped off after that, with only occasional patents through the mid- to late 1890s, 1900s, and 1910s.

These homesteaders were part of the tremendous farming boom that occurred on the plains during the late 1880s. These were particularly wet years and both dry farmers and farmers who irrigated had bumper crops. But the wet cycle came to an end in 1890. Many farmers hung on for a while, but the national economy collapsed in 1893 and a mass exodus from the plains occurred at that point (Mehls 1984a). It appears that the farmers at the Arsenal followed the national pattern. Of the 62 properties recorded in the Government Land Office plats for the Arsenal, only five were patented after 1896.

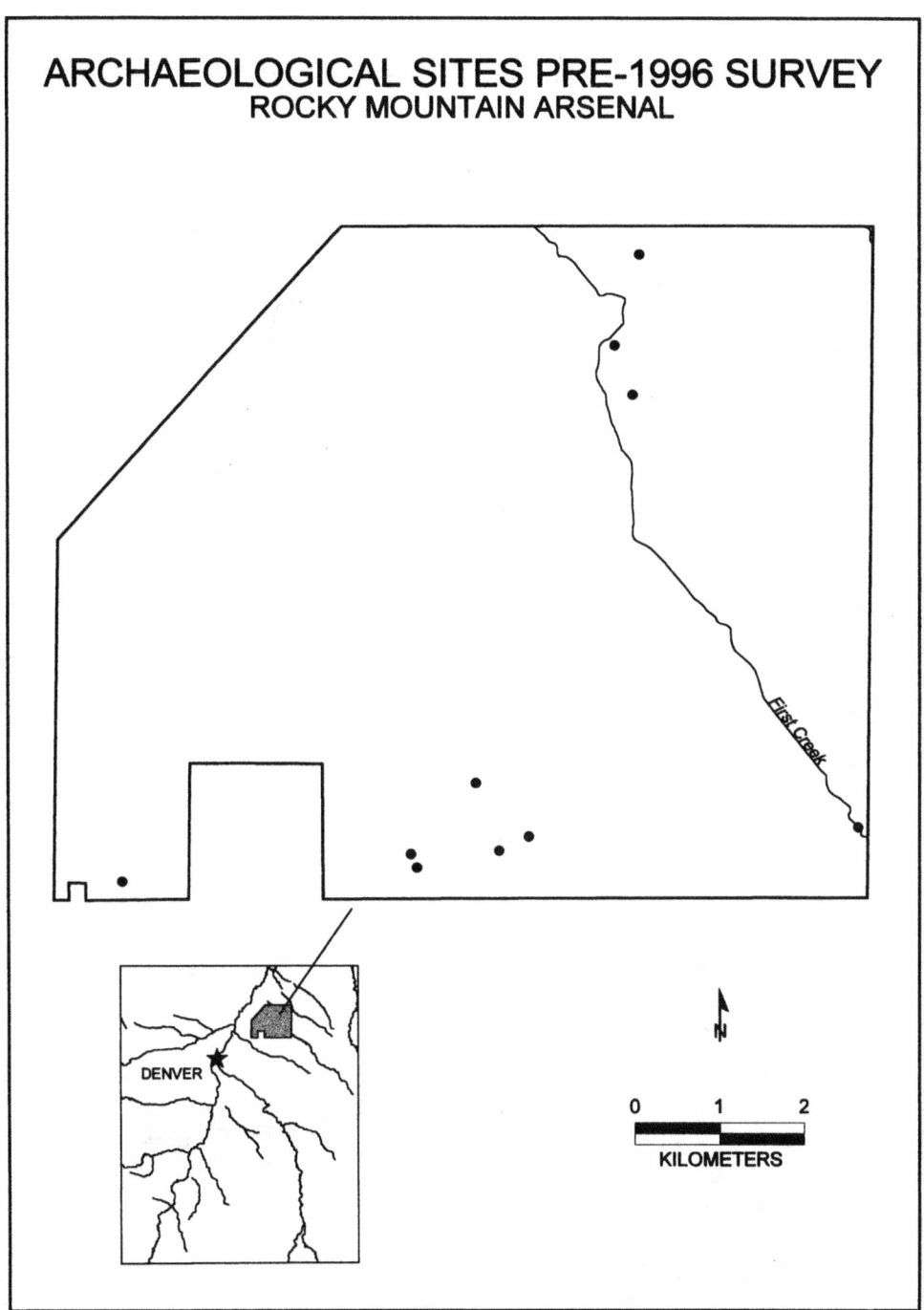

Figure 5.39. Pre-1996 survey sites at Rocky Mountain Arsenal. Francine Patterson.

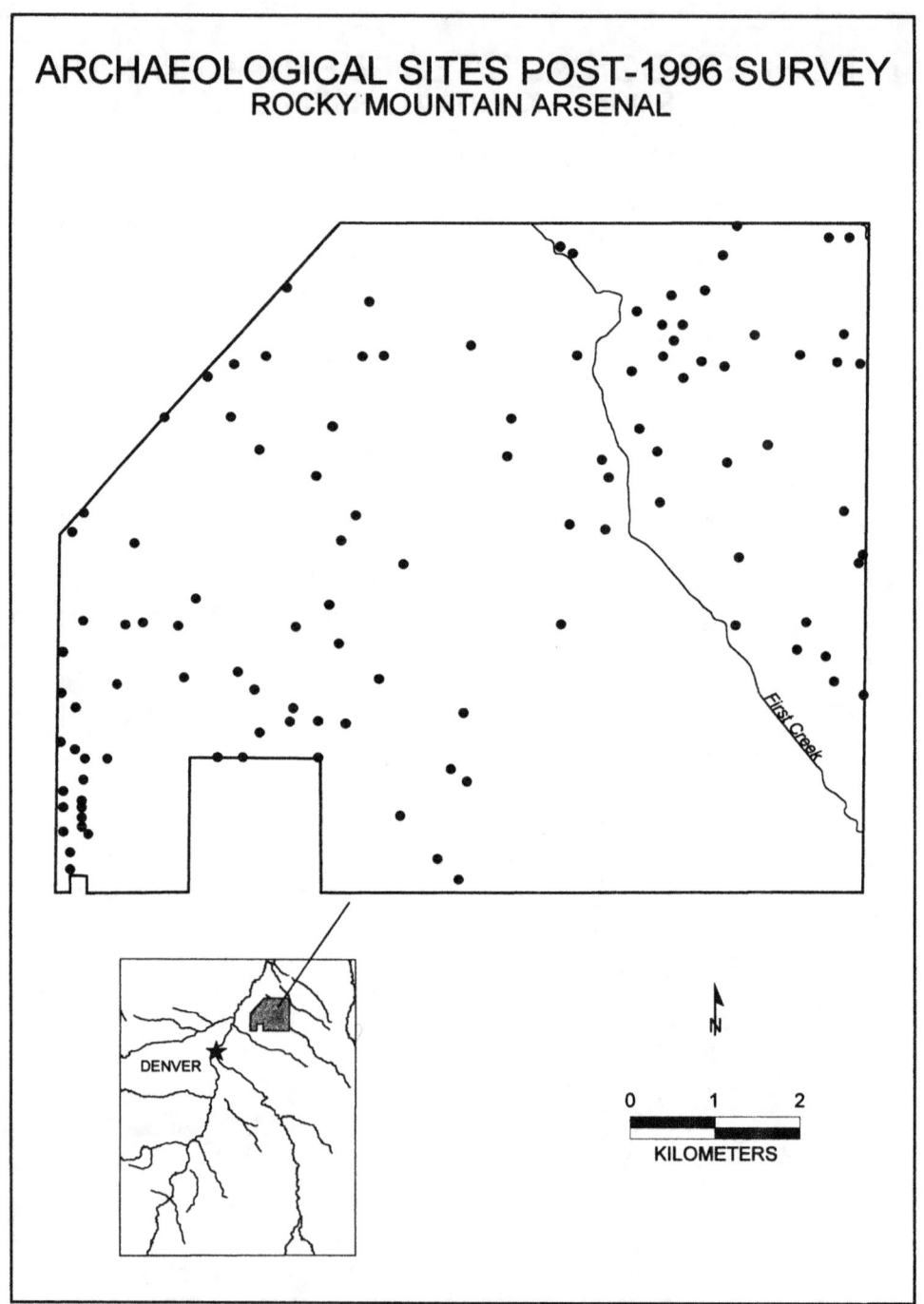

Figure 5.40. Post-1996 survey sites and Rocky Mountain Arsenal. Francine Patterson.

By 1941 there were 231 properties with improvements recorded by the Army. The region was home to a number of settlements, some successful, some not. Irondale and Derby, both settled in 1889, were stations on the Burlington Northern Railroad. The building of the railroads through this area, like the homesteading, was in part due to the farming boom of the 1880s.

Berlin, located along the Colorado Eastern Railroad, was planned as a railroad town. A guide to Colorado ghost towns indicates that it had a few residents between 1887 and 1890 (Eberhart 1986). But the land on which Berlin is located was part of a quarter section homestead that was not patented until 1890. In addition, the Army records do not record any improvements in what was the Berlin townsite, and none are visible on a 1937 aerial photograph of the Arsenal area. If there ever were residents of Berlin, they left very little trace of their short sojourn.

By 1906 the Arsenal area subdivisions and communities included the First Addition to Irondale (including East Irondale and South Irondale); the Second Addition to Rose Hill; Kohnville; Munroe Park; Berlin; and Northern Swansea (Fig. 5.41). Like the townsites, the subdivisions varied in their success; most of them never lived up to their original plans. For example, East Irondale was planned as an area of nine city blocks with 48 lots on each, a total of 432 lots. According to army records, no improvements were ever made on any properties in East Irondale. Northern Swansea, which was divided into 10½-acre plots, was never improved. When the army purchased the land it was owned by Adams County, probably through tax default. Of the early subdivisions only two were successful, Kohnville and the Second Addition to Rose Hill. As opposed to Berlin and the various additions to Irondale, which were divided into city lots, usually 125 ft. by 25 ft. (.07 acre), Kohnville and Rose Hill were divided into five-acre lots. This was essentially the pattern that would be followed for later subdivisions in the Arsenal.

A number of other subdivisions were in existence in 1942 and most were purchased in their entirety by the government when the Rocky Mountain Arsenal was created. For the most part, these were developments of five-acre lots in the southern portion of the Arsenal. Many of the names conjure up a pastoral image—Blueberry Hill, Bryan Gardens, Desmond Gardens, Kincora Gardens, Ormond Gardens, Eire Gardens, Ossian Gardens, and Independence. They were platted at various times over a long period, for example, Rose Hill in 1884, Northern Swansea in 1894, and Avoca City in 1922 (Shaffer 1978:19).

If not for the creation of the Arsenal, other subdivisions would certainly have followed. Indeed, the quarter section near Derby appears on army maps of the Arsenal subdivided into 32 plots of 5 acres each. The inventory for that area indicates, however, that the only landowner was Albert Gerlits, whose farm was located there. This area appeared to have been ripe for change. Although there may have been land passed down through daughters, a comparison of the names of those who homesteaded in what would become the Arsenal with the landowners bought out by the army indicates only one property still definitively in the hands of the original family. In 1942 the army purchased from Mary Bollers the same 160-acre tract her late husband Bernard Bollers patented in 1890.

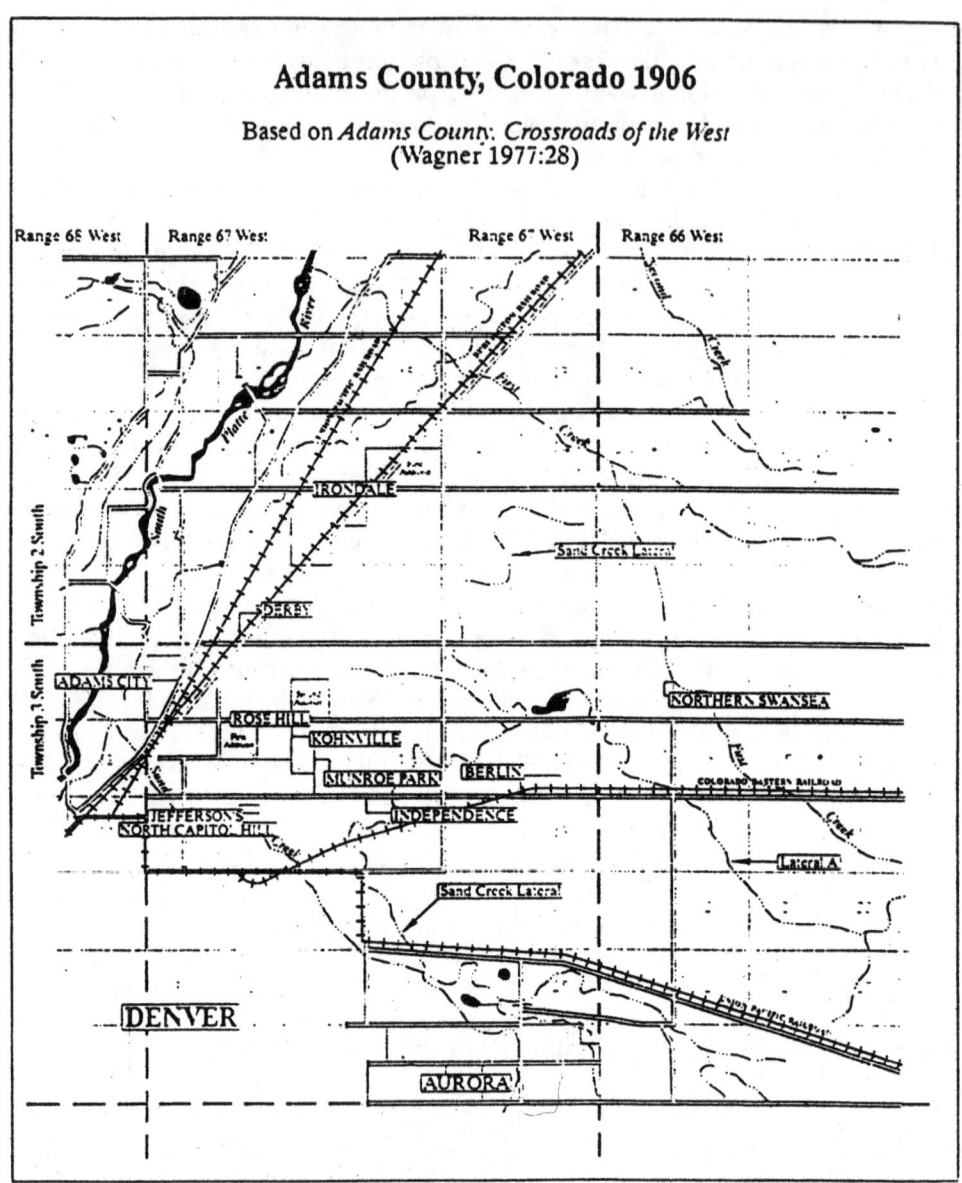

Figure 5.41. Adams County, Colorado, 1906, showing the Arsenal area subdivisions and areas. From Bonnie J. Clark, ed., Archaeological Investigations and Cultural Resources Management Plan for the Archaeological Resources of the Rocky Mountain Arsenal, 1997, based on A. Wagner, *Adams County: Crossroads of the West*; reproduced by permission.

## Demographics

When the army purchased the Arsenal, land parcels ranged in size from half an acre to over 1,500 acres. Only five property owners—three individuals and two companies—held plots over 360 acres in size. Mainly as a result of the heavy subdivision of the area, the majority of the holdings, approximately 70 percent, were 20 acres or smaller, with about 40 percent only 5 acres or smaller. Parcels of less than 80 acres could not have supported a family engaged in growing wheat, raising cattle, or similar activities, but the small holdings might have provided a living for truck farming or dairying raising or chickens or pigs. The information on these parcels indicates that the majority of the residents of the Arsenal area had buildings and structures whose function it was to house chickens, pigs, and dairy cattle on their properties. Of the 232 parcels that had buildings and structures on them, 179—or 77 percent—had facilities for raising chickens (U.S. Army 1945:3840–5567). Of these, 42 had horse-raising facilities and only 29 were specifically listed as having a dairy component. There was some overlap of these three animal groups, but only five farms had all three. Clearly chickens were the most important farm animal raised by the Arsenal area residents. Horses, nondairy cattle, turkeys, and rabbits also were kept.

It is likely that many residents did not derive a living from their properties. Some worked as salaried employees or wage laborers in Denver and surrounding towns. Area resident Gunner Herskind recalled that one reason there were more subdivisions in the southern portion of the Arsenal was its proximity to Denver. "The fathers might commute to Denver for work while the women ran the farms" (*Eagle Watch* 1992).

## Women at the Arsenal

The archival records for the Arsenal area give us information not just about the land, but also the people who lived on it. Forty-two properties, or 18 percent, were owned by women. Women's holdings ranged from 5 to 560 acres in size and were scattered throughout the Arsenal area. Of the 42, only six women shared a family name with other property owners. In some cases, such as Bertha Toedtli, who owned 8.1 acres, it is probable that the woman was related to local property owners, in Bertha's case William and Amelia Toedtli. In other cases, where the woman's surname is more common, such as Porter or Carter, a family connection is not as dependable an assumption. All 42 of the woman-owned properties were working farmland, and all but four had buildings on them. Most of the properties were small—61 percent were 10 acres or less—but 20 percent were over 150 acres.

The presence of so many female landowners on the Arsenal property is an interesting historical puzzle. It is known that many women homesteaded. A study based on land office records in Lamar, Colorado and Douglas, Wyoming from 1887 to 1908 found that 11.9 percent of the homestead claims were filed by women. Proportionally more women than men "proved up" their claims (Jones-Eddy 1992). In order to file a homestead, one needed to be the head of the household, so married women would not have been able to file. It has been suggested by researchers that when women successfully homesteaded they almost always sold their land, often using that money to improve their chances for marriage (Fink 1992). Homesteading records for the Arsenal indicate only four women homesteaders, none of them still in possession of their land in 1942.

Certainly a number of the woman-owned farms were owned by widows. The census data indicate two, Mary Bollers and Mary Christian, who were heads of household in 1920. A widowed woman often retained control of a farm using either the labor of her children or hired help (Fink 1992). U.S. Department of Agriculture records indicate that women engaged in what were thought of as "secondary" farming enterprises, for example, raising chickens, growing fruit, and making honey and cream. Field crops and large livestock were almost always tended by men (Fink 1992). At the Arsenal, however, this was often not the case, as indicated by the small size of the parcels. Indeed, the fact that chickens were the most common animal raised indicates these were the types of operations in which "women's" farm work was the primary endeavor. These farms could have been easily run by female heads of household who were nonetheless acting within socially accepted task boundaries.

Archaeology also speaks to the roles of Arsenal women. Home canning is evidenced at a number of the sites. Of the 70 sites that were historic habitations, 33 (47 percent) had definitive evidence of canning (identifiable pieces of canning jars, porcelain liners for zinc canning jar lids, etc.). Many of those without overt markers had a number of clear or aqua jars that were probably from canning. The archaeological record clearly demonstrates that home canning was an important subsistence activity at the Arsenal.

To say that many of these households engaged in canning appears pedestrian enough. However, the ability to put up food could make the difference between a lean winter and a more comfortable one. That job fell almost exclusively to women. They were very invested in following the changing technologies of home canning. This letter, written by a woman homesteader in Wyoming to her family back east, exemplifies how involved women were in home canning:

> August 1, 1922 We have been canning beans—17 quarts today—all canned with meat. We like them that way so much more than plain. I have long been wanting some of the spring glass top jars so I would not have to monkey with these old Mason jars that take so much time and effort to get sealed. Today John told me that while I was east he had ordered 15 dozen Lightning jars. My, that is a nice surprise! He brought me a dozen of the Kerr lids today to try. What with them and the new spring top jars that are to arrive in a few days, I will have a picnic with the rest of my canning. I wish I had got the Kerr lids sooner. I had so much trouble with the cherries opening, and had enough spoil to pay for several dozen lids. My Mason lids are old and do not fit well any more, and the edges are getting so soft they will not stay put. I think that is the main trouble. (quoted in Hendricks 1986)

Perhaps future researchers could compare the canning remains at the Arsenal with those in suburban, rural, and urban areas. Such a study may indicate whether the high participation in canning at the Arsenal is more indicative of early twentieth–century sites in general, or of the activities occurring on small and large farms.

*Ethnicity*

Although the 1942 army records do not include information about the ethnicity of individual landowners, it is possible to use other data to get at such information. One of the best sources is census data. In the area that was to become the Arsenal, Germans and Scandinavians were the dominant immigrant groups. In 1910 the census for the two districts covering the Arsenal area indicates that, among the 230 heads of household, 131 (57 percent) were foreign-born. Of these, 32 percent were German, 31 percent were Scandinavian (from Denmark, Sweden or Norway), 16 were from the British Isles or Commonwealth (England, Scotland, Ireland, Canada) and 11 percent were Italian. The area around Brighton had a great influx of Russian Germans, many of whom immigrated expressly to work on sugar beet farms; however, only three families headed by Russian Germans were recorded in the Arsenal area. Other countries represented include Greece (all but one Greek were listed as railroad workers), Japan, and Hungary. There are interesting differences between the two districts. Both census districts have a very similar ratio of foreign-born heads of household (56 and 57 percent), but in First Creek, the district covering the eastern, more agricultural area, the foreign-born population was 56 percent German, compared to the more urban Irondale district in which Germans made up only 27 percent. Almost all the Irish, Italian, and Greek heads of household lived in the Irondale district.

By comparing the detailed census data for the early 1900s with the 1942 army records, it is possible to identify the ethnicity of individuals who lived in the Arsenal area. The details of their paths to the Denver Basin are typical of settlers in the regions that support the urban core. Gottlieb Egli was a German who became a U.S. citizen in 1890. His wife Rose was native born of German parents. His hired hand Fred Kenel was also German. Gottlieb and his sons Henry and Alfred lived on the Arsenal in 1942. Gottlieb Egli's partner was William Toedtli, also German. He, his wife Amelia, and presumably their relative Bertha were living at the Arsenal in 1942. Another relative, Conrad Toedtli, and his wife Katherine, also German, appear on the 1910 census. Conrad became a citizen in 1894 and his wife in 1904. The census lists three Toedtli children, all born in the United States. Ulrich Furrer and his wife Rosina, both German, had two children, a son born in Germany and a daughter born in the United States. Their son William and his wife Emma lived at the Arsenal in 1942, as did Adolph Furrer, who was presumably a relative. There are a great number of other Arsenal residents who do not appear in earlier census data but who have Germanic surnames, for example Liebfried, Scholz, Gerlits, Schwarzenback, and Schoneweis.

A number of immigrants were from the British Isles or the Commonwealth. Mary Bollers was one of the Irish residents of the area. John Mayberry was from Canada; his wife Viola was from Missouri. The census lists 10 children for them, all born in the

United States. Charles and Jessie Black and their son Melvin were living on the Arsenal in 1942. Charles was native born, but his wife Jessie was Canadian of Scottish parents. Their first four children were born in Kansas, the fifth in Colorado. Many Arsenal residents were Scandinavian. Mary Christian, an Arsenal landowner in 1942, is listed along with her husband Samuel in the 1910 census as Danish hog ranchers. Mary Nelson, also a landowner, may have been related to Oskar Nelson and his wife Allice. Oskar was Swedish; his wife was native born in Minnesota of Swedish parents. Others who may have been Scandinavians include Anderson, Jensen, Petersen, Hansen, and Rolsen. A few Italian names were also recorded by the army, including Domenico Strafacia and Angelmaria Tellarico. A small subdivision next door to Strafacia and Tellarico's property, the Scavo, was owned by various members of the Scavo family, who most likely were Italian as well.

The Arsenal was settled during a period of immigration unprecedented in U.S. history. Between 1880 and 1900 nearly 2 million individuals arrived from Germany alone. As opposed to other groups like the Irish, who settled mostly in cities, Germans settled in rural areas, comprising over a third of all foreign-born farmers as early as 1870, before the big wave of immigration (Daniels 1990). In 1900 foreign-born residents accounted for 42 percent of the adults on the census for the Arsenal area; of these, 51 percent were born in Germany. On the 1910 census the percentage of foreign-born residents dropped slightly to 36 percent. This can be compared to a study of a rural farming area in Nebraska where only 15 percent of the population were foreign born (Fink 1992).

The demographic information from the Arsenal provides for us a concrete example of the residents of the Plains before World War II. The myth of the American Heartland is something with which most of us are familiar. Yet here are data that suggest that two of the most vilified aspects of life in the late twentieth century—female heads of households and immigration—were an intrinsic part of life in the heartland in the early portion of that century.

*People and Natural Resources*

Archaeologists, whether prehistoric or historic, are interested in why people choose to live where they do. The prehistoric sites at the Rocky Mountain Arsenal, like those at Denver International Airport, are concentrated along semipermanent waterways, and access to water was equally important during the historic period. A map of water rights compiled by the army indicates that approximately 31 of the properties taken over by the Army received water from the Sand Creek Lateral (Fig. 5.42). Although they represent only 13 percent of the 231 properties with improvements, these properties averaged 80 acres in size. These larger parcels would have been able to sustain activities such as cattle ranching and grain production. In fact, one of the parcels noted on the map is the Victor Ranch and Livestock Company.

The majority of tracts were located in subdivided plots without water rights. In fact, approximately half the improved properties are located in four sections of the southern portion of the Arsenal, an area 20 percent of the size of the whole site. This

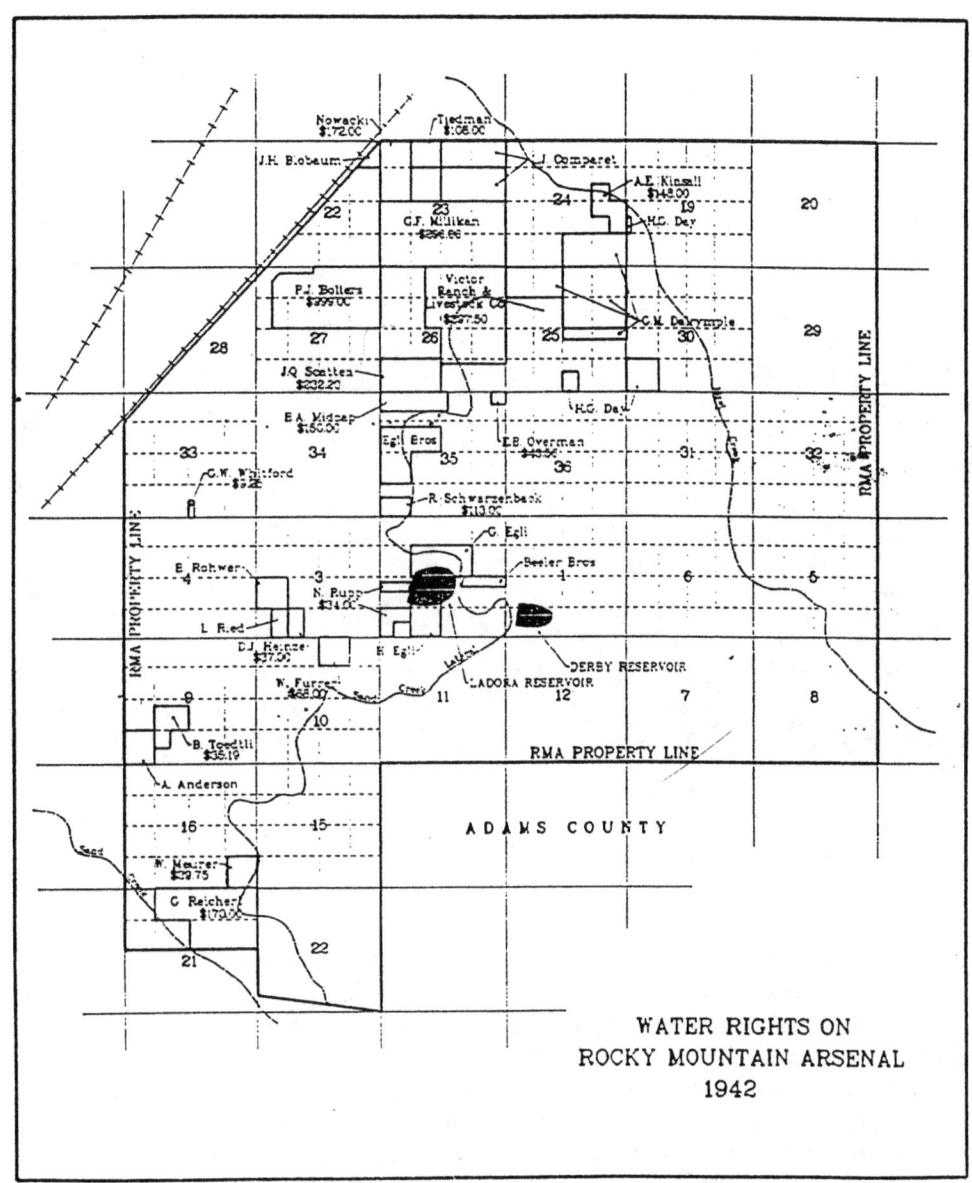

Figure 5.42. Water rights on Arsenal property, 1942. From Bonnie J. Clark, ed., Archaeological Investigations and Cultural Resources Management Plan for the Archaeological Resources of the Rocky Mountain Arsenal, 1997; reproduced by permission.

Figure 5.43. Alignment of trees and locust thickets at the Arsenal. From Bonnie J. Clark, ed., Archaeological Investigations and Cultural Resources Management Plan for the Archaeological Resources of the Rocky Mountain Arsenal, 1997; reproduced by permission.

includes the locations of substantial communities and subdivisions like Rose Hill and Desmond Gardens. It appears that settlers located in a particular area depending on the type of subsistence they intended to pursue—large-scale farmers were located along the waterways, truck farmers on small lots watered by wells.

Writing about military posts as cultural landscapes, Robert Melnick notes, "while settlement communities may encompass buildings, often the more lasting changes occur in the landscape—changes like roads, house locations, and train lines" (1994:108). In those portions of the Arsenal not used for munitions or chemical production the landscape is very much like it was in 1942. The irrigation canals and section-line roads divide up the space. Alignments of trees and locust thickets mark the former locations of houses (Fig. 5.43). In a number of cases other landscaping persists, including lilac bushes and irises. Some of the irises on the Arsenal have been identified as antiques, species not currently in horticultural production.

Although we may tend to look at landscaping as a luxury, for settlers living on the plains the creation of a windbreak was an absolute necessity. For example, when

Figure 5.44. Offset rows of trees at the Arsenal. From Bonnie J. Clark, ed., Archaeological Investigations and Cultural Resources Management Plan for the Archaeological Resources of the Rocky Mountain Arsenal, 1997; reproduced by permission.

asked about their attitude toward their living environment, Nebraska farm women often complained of the ever-present wind (Fink 1992). The residents of the Arsenal used a number of different tree configurations. Especially popular were offset rows of trees (Fig. 5.44), which afforded more protection than either single rows or a double aligned row of trees.

As development in the Denver vicinity increases, landscapes like that at the Arsenal will become increasingly rare. In many ways, the Arsenal represents a fossilized version of 1942 patterns of land use, transportation, irrigation, and landscaping. The northern portion of the Arsenal, which was far less subdivided than the southern portion, reflects the township, section, and range pattern established by the Government Land Office. The mile square grid that seemed ubiquitous on the Plains is becoming less so with increasing urbanization and the use of circular sprinklers. In a region where the involvement of the federal government in land issues is hotly contested, we lose the visual reminders of early government influence at our own risk.

The later settlement pattern, reflected in the small truck farms of the southern Arsenal, is perhaps even more rare. Although subdividing increases at a furious pace, the lots have gotten much smaller. The five- and ten-acre plots at the Arsenal testify to a subsistence pattern that is disappearing in suburban areas. How many people who work in Denver still raise chickens?

## A History of Displacement

Perhaps the most important message of the archaeology of the Rocky Mountain Arsenal is the legacy of displacement in the west. Dozens of prehistoric sites and isolated finds, as well as historic accounts, attest to the utilization of the region by Native Americans. They were removed from the area by the federal government who opened up the region for homesteading.

The removal of subsequent settlers on Arsenal land by the army certainly didn't involve bloodshed, as it had for the Cheyenne and Arapaho. Still, very few wanted to leave land in which they had invested so greatly. A former resident of the Arsenal, Gunner Herskind, had this to say about the situation: "War feelings were such that there was no resistance to the vacate order. We loved the farm and the land. It was beautiful farmland, very rich and flat. But we all remembered what happened at Pearl Harbor" (*Eagle Watch* 1992).

Still, the army did not have any voluntary departures when it came to claiming eminent domain. Instead, the army had to take the residents to court. The Adams County Courthouse books and the Brighton newspaper contain the details of these cases. Herskind recalls, "I don't think we really believed it but once we drove down to our south field and saw the Army trucks dumping lumber in the middle of a ripe wheat field across the street, we realized how fast things were moving" (*Eagle Watch* 1992). It is ironic that the federal government, the same entity that opened this area up for settlement through the various homesteading acts, would turn around and once again invoke their power over place. The forgotten elms and lilacs, the shadows of those farms speak powerfully about those who are gone.

The displacement of some Arsenal families did not stop there. Some of the families moved east into the area that became the Denver International Airport. Historical studies of the airport property involved interviews with some of these families. The Bollers settled along First Creek before 1900. Mary Bollers shows up on the 1900 census as an Irish-born 43-year-old widow, working as a farmer, and the head of a household of eight children. Her land, a 160-acre tract, included a 24-by-40 foot house, a WPA-built toilet, a granary, a barn, a wood silo, and a chicken coop. What is left of her farm was relocated during the Arsenal survey (Clark 1997). One of her sons, Bernard, with his wife Margaret, purchased all the section now just south of the Arsenal. When they were forced off their land, Margaret and Bernard Bollers bought a farm at the corner of Buckley Road and 56th Avenue. They were joined there by their nephew, Kenneth Custy, who was also forced off his family farm at the Arsenal (Friedman 1989). The Bollers farm is now part of Denver International Airport, the construction of which displaced the Bollerses again. This time, however, the government entity was the city of Denver.

Today the trees planted by those former landowners shelter animals pushed out of Denver by increasing urbanism. In fact, there are probably more deer at the Arsenal now than when the Cheyenne and Arapaho hunted there. In addition to the traditional purpose of a National Wildlife Refuge, to protect wildlife, the Rocky Mountain Arsenal has another purpose written into the legislation that created it—to serve as a venue for environmental and land use education. That education will emphasize "the historical interaction between land, people, and technology" (U.S. Fish and Wildlife Service 1996). The archaeological sites of the Rocky Mountain Arsenal tell many stories about that interaction. They also stand as a visual reminder of how humans have written themselves across the landscape of the Denver Basin.

• • •

The archaeological investigations described here, taken together, provide a unique view of Denver's urbanization. In some instances they correct the historical record, in other instances they add to it, in still others they establish new directions for *both* archaeological and historical research. In every instance the archaeology has brought us into intimate contact with remnants of American culture and lifeways beyond the images and perceptions available from written history—images that may, of course, be skewed by the chroniclers writing those histories.

One historian has captured Denver's urban origins by stating that "Denver grew up in a hurry. It was conceived in gold lust and born in the middle of nowhere on a nippy November day" (Noel 1996). Another—Gunther Barth (1988)—lays out more systematically the "instant" quality of Denver's origin and early evolution. The archaeological evidence discussed here (especially from the Tremont House Hotel) broadly corroborates these models of Denver as an "instant city." Witold Rybczynski (1995) has provided a typology of cities that distinguishes "symbolic" cities (e.g., capitals), "practical" cities (e.g., New York City with its regular street grid), and "organic" cities (e.g., Venice, London, and others with medieval origins and sprawling, labyrinthine configurations). Although useful for comparative purposes, such typologies can obscure as much as they illuminate. Certainly, the characterization of Denver as an instant city misses many of the historical dynamics that shaped the subsequent evolution of the city including, perhaps most conspicuously, its skewed downtown street grid. Continued study and, when necessary, preservation of Denver's urban archaeological record promises to illuminate the sociocultural dynamics behind such developments and enhance our understanding of Denver's evolution as a distinctive urban form.

CHAPTER 6

## Conclusion

Greater Denver has been used by various groups probably for as long as humans have lived in the Americas. The area's archaeological record—running the gamut from small prehistoric scatters of lithic material to rockshelters to historic homes and mines (and even including the burial site of the infamous local cannibal Alferd Packer)—has been used to tell a variety of stories about the lives of its occupants. Although this region was used by different groups of people with different cultures, who brought different abilities and expectations to the region, each found some constants: a region a mile high next to the Rocky Mountains, a place of beauty with breathtaking vistas, a land with occasional blizzards tempered by chinook winds that can melt several inches of snow in a day, and hot dry summers with clear blue skies and at least some sunshine for more than 300 days in an average year. No basic resources were lacking. This is a region with permanent water and easy trails in the plains, and accessible tracks, following river and creek valleys, into the mountains. It offers both mountain and plains vegetation and animals within a day's walk of any location.

In this final chapter we revisit some broad themes that have characterized the history of this area for at least 10,000 years. They include, first, Greater Denver as a collection of diverse lifeways and survival strategies, second, Greater Denver as a crossroads of interaction, and third, Greater Denver as a locus of cultural coexistence. We also reflect a bit on how these themes continue to be manifested in Greater Denver and the value of taking a "deep time" perspective on them.

### Diverse Lifeways

Subsistence, or acquiring the ingredients for meals and making them edible and palatable, is basic for all human groups. The archaeology of Greater Denver reveals major differences across our broad time periods in the core components of human diets. However we can also glimpse, in every period, diversity in the strategies that humans used to make a living. Ever since late Archaic times humans in the area have made use of both wild and domesticated resources, although the relative contributions of each to the diet, as well as the value assigned to each, have varied. Wild game, which was a mundane staple in Paleoindian times, became an exotic treat in historic times (as evidenced at the Tremont House) and is even more exotic today as evidenced by the menu at upscale restaurants in the area, such as the Fort. The regional archaeology demonstrates continuities in the use of other strategic resources. The stone used by prehistoric peoples for their tools was also sought after by the first Euro-American settlers for different purposes (especially buildings), and the clay sources that had been used for pottery were also useful to Euro-Americans for bricks.

The Paleoindian peoples that ranged through the basin are almost unknown from direct evidence. From the fact that their projectile points are found throughout the region, we may deduce that they came to this area following herds that fed on High Plains grasses—primarily mammoth in Clovis times and bison during the Folsom and Plano eras. The other edible animals of the region, both large and small, probably were not neglected. Mule deer, bighorn sheep, antelope, rabbit, and even possibly prairie dog found their way into these earliest diets. The emphasis archaeologists place on big game hunting in Paleoindian times is based on scarce remains, and these have been interpreted almost exclusively in terms of a "man the hunter" model of subsistence. We can only speculate about the rest of their lives, but it is almost certain that they collected plants, divided labor and tasks among men and women, looked at the stars, told stories about the way the world began, and mourned when a member of the group died. But most of the details about these irreducibly social and cultural aspects of their lifeways so far elude us.

Archaic peoples continued to use the atlatl as a way to enhance spear throwing accuracy and distance. Perhaps related to their skill with atlatls (but also likely as a function of climate change that influenced their subsistence strategies) is the fact that they left a greater variety of animal bones in their sites. Occasional dry caves in the other parts of the North American West allow glimpses into a wider use of plants as well. Basketry, for example, is found at a number of sites. Baskets or other containers would have been necessary to collect the many weedy species such as goosefoot and pigweed whose remains are found in sites. These seeds were ground on prepared two-part grinding stones (metates and manos), and presumably were used for food. It is interesting to ponder how those small-seeded plants were prepared for consumption without pottery containers. The best guess is stone boiling in basket or skin containers. Plants were probably also collected for their medicinal properties, and for their fibers for basketry. Sandals and perhaps other clothing were made from plant materials as well.

Early Ceramic groups not only made pottery, but also left behind evidence in several sites that they grew maize (corn) and perhaps even squash and beans, although too little direct evidence of these plants is found in the archaeological record. These plants were originally domesticated in Mesoamerica. The combination of wide-mouthed ceramic pots and maize is probably not fortuitous. Flat stones for cooking tortillas are not known in this region (unless the flat metates were used in this way), so we need to look for other methods of cooking. The wide-mouthed pots were needed to make the maize edible by cooking it into porridge or mush, and the pots, unlike baskets, could be set directly in the fire. Weedy plants such as goosefoot and pigweed continued to be eaten, and might have been cultivated as well.

As a consequence of their adoption of agriculture, Early Ceramic peoples established larger, more permanent settlements near valley bottoms. These were located not only beside the larger permanent streams such as Cherry Creek, but also along intermittent streams like Piney Creek. Perhaps because risk of intermittent flooding was known, houses were constructed several meters above the water source. Fields may have been planted nearer to the streams. We know that Early Ceramic people had a variety of types of corn, which suggests that it was a more important part of the diet than the sparse finds otherwise imply.

The developing course toward farming was truncated toward the end of Early Ceramic, perhaps in response to local drought conditions, although there are some sites suggesting continuity of lifeways into Middle Ceramic times. Middle Ceramic farming groups left few traces in the Greater Denver region. Evidence of potmakers from A.D. 1000 to 1300 is still found, but it is much less frequent. Perhaps a temporary drought discouraged the makers of cord-marked pots, causing them to go elsewhere. Another possibility is that the groups grew too large for the erratic nature of the rainfall and temperature in Greater Denver, and finally had to move away. More benevolent environments were subsequently occupied in Nebraska and Kansas, presumably allowing larger settlements, and some of our Early Ceramic occupants may have moved there.

Late Ceramic and historic Native American groups did not farm Greater Denver either. Horses and later guns made hunting buffalo more productive than agriculture. During this period many Plains Indian groups abandoned their earlier farming pursuits to pursue the abundant bison instead. As another strategy, roaming groups on horseback could easily raid the winter stores of settled agriculturalists.

Up to now the reader might get the impression, with all the talk of bones and tools, that the aboriginal inhabitants of Greater Denver were overwhelmingly motivated by economics. But we know from the study of cultural anthropology that aboriginal landscapes are sacred as well as secular. American Indian groups have an intimate relationship to their environment, often endowing it with important spiritual qualities. There is suggestive evidence, such as material offerings (see Chapter 4), that the springs around Greater Denver were recognized as sacred places. Archaeology still has much to teach us about the ways aboriginal occupants of Greater Denver defined their landscapes as sacred places, and the ways in which they reproduced both themselves and the land through ritual and ceremony.

The first European settlers entered a land that was not farmed and which had been proclaimed to be the "Great American Desert" by early explorers (as just noted, the aboriginal characterizations of the landscape were likely a good bit different). But since they came to Denver to serve the mining camps, they must have brought seeds of familiar crops with them to farm the prairies. Although we do not know which grains, fruits, and vegetables were favored in the early days, it was probably the familiar foods they had previously grown in the east or midwest. In semiarid Greater Denver, the rainfall was sufficient in some years and not in others. Even many of those who planted winter wheat gradually gave up the struggle to maintain an adequate water supply. Agriculture was chancy.

There is a pattern to where people live that is based on what they do for a living. The degree to which Indians and Anglos occupied the same locations in Greater Denver is striking. Prehistoric campsites from all time periods tend to cluster around permanent water. Agricultural groups, including the Ceramic period people of prehistory and the Euro-American farmers of history, also tended to live along waterways. The Four Mile House is an apt example of the way Euro-Americans obeyed some of the same environmental and economic dictates as the aboriginal inhabitants. As noted in Chapter 5, every excavation at this historic farm turned up many prehistoric artifacts.

Although ranching and dairying were more suitable to the semiarid climate, farms were homesteaded throughout Greater Denver. A twelve-year-old girl left a diary from 1890, giving us a glimpse of what it was like to live in Valverde, one of the small farming communities around Denver (Shoemaker 1976). These former farms are now turning into golf courses, housing developments, and office parks, irrigated with precious mountain water jealously guarded by the municipalities of Greater Denver. Archaeological research is needed to retrieve more details of the history of these homesteading peoples.

## Greater Denver as a Crossroads of Interaction

From the beginning, the archaeological record of Greater Denver has revealed evidence for the long-distance movements of peoples, goods, and ideas. Indeed, our archaeological history of Greater Denver supports Patricia Limerick's (1987) concept of the West as more a well-established meeting ground than an untamed frontier.

Even in sites that date to the Paleoindian period, raw materials for toolmaking were imported from outside the local area. By Early Ceramic times even decorative items were imported, including Olivella shell from the Gulf Coast. This is direct, powerful evidence that even the earliest human inhabitants of Greater Denver participated in large-scale social networks of exchange and interaction. It is likely they were actively exchanging not only economic resources, but also information about resource distributions, and finding eligible marriage partners.

The earliest transportation was of course on foot, but it is not beyond the scope of archaeology to reveal where the footpaths were. Ancient trackways can be hard-packed, and may someday at least partly turn up in a site and between sites (human behavior, after all, is continuously transacted across space). Sometimes it is possible to guess where human trails went, if we know the origin and destination points. It is very likely that trails followed animal tracks, and went to water, to sources of raw material, and to favored collecting spots for berries, nuts, and other plant food. People needed to cross rivers, and fords or shallower spots probably had prehistoric trails leading to them. The tracks across the prairie and into the mountains must have remained the same for millennia. However, the invention of the travois, at first for dogs to pull, perhaps required wider and smoother trails. With the use of horses pulling tent poles four meters long or more, wider paths and shallower river fords were required.

It was certainly such paths that the first Anglo explorers in the West followed, guided by Indians. Francis Parkman tells of coming across a "very large [deserted] camp of Arapahoes" in 1847. He describes their remains further: "The ashes of some three hundred fires were visible among the scattered trees, together with the remains of sweating lodges" (Parkman 1948:255). He notes their trail, in which every footprint could be seen. Such large groups traveling together must have cut a wide swath. It seems likely that the first wagon train, organized by Cherokees and whites from Oklahoma, must have followed an older path along the Smoky Hill Trail, now made wide enough for wagons. Gradually the trails became wider and wider. When hordes of gold seekers headed for the mountains near Denver, even wider trails were needed to transport various supplies, including food. Patricia Limerick (1987) notes that early settlers, and no doubt the miners, too, tended to eat out of cans, and all those cans had to be sent over roads. Other goods noted as having been carried include flour, sugar, bacon, dry goods, and whiskey. "By 1859, organized stage, express, and freight lines were swamped with traffic, and many new outfits sprang into existence. . . . The first stagecoach arrived in Denver in May, 1859, making the trip of 687 miles [from Leavenworth, Kansas] in 19 days" (Poor 1976:4). A network of wagon and toll roads sprang up, especially into the mountains. The first was between Denver and Central City in the spring of 1860. Even today major thoroughfares in Denver—like University Boulevard—meander in places, hinting at their origins as deer trails or human tracks with no need to be straight.

The archaeological record at the Tremont House provides additional kinds of evidence for long-distance relationships. As noted in Chapter 5, diagnostic artifacts from the Tremont House were produced throughout various regions of the United States and as far away as Europe. The assemblage confirms the extensive availability of goods manufactured in faraway places. Recovered objects place the Tremont House within a series of local, regional, national, and international economic networks, and indicate that even the animal-powered transportation system functioned to connect Denver to global markets.

The coming of the railroads brought an unprecedented expansion and solidification of these markets. The Colorado Central was the first railroad in the state. It featured a standard gauge line from Denver to Golden and then to Cheyenne, and a narrow gauge up Clear Creek Canyon. The city of Denver saw to it that Golden, which for a time was the territorial capital, was cut off from the main line by building its own rail to Cheyenne, which became the Denver Pacific Railway. The last railroad built was the Denver, Laramie and Northwestern, conceived with the grandiose plan of laying track all the way to Seattle in competition with the Union Pacific. Starting out from downtown Denver the new line reached Greeley in 1909, but that was as far as it ever got. It stopped running in 1917, a casualty, perhaps, of overambitious expansionism.

Less widely known, and of particular interest from an archaeological perspective, is the large number of short-lived railroads constructed in the early days of Denver. Described by Robert Ormes (1992) as "ghost railroads," these lines ran not only into the mountains to serve the miners, but to the north and east as well. Ormes identifies some thirty of these "ghost railroads" in the Denver area. They reflect bursts of activity, born of competition between towns and local boosterism, to establish a regional center for Denver's developing interaction network. By identifying and mapping these ghost railroads archaeologists can contribute much to the study of Greater Denver political and economic geography and history.

## Greater Denver as a Locus of Cultural Coexistence

Just as Greater Denver has always served as a crossroads of movement and interaction, so too has it served as a locus for the coexistence of different cultural groups opting to settle here. Given its location at the intersection of the Great Plains, Rocky Mountains, and American Southwest—and given its attractive suite of environmental attributes—Denver has been a place where groups typically associated with these different areas come together. The Ute and the Apache, and later the Cheyenne and Arapaho, are pertinent examples. As already noted, prehistoric aboriginal sites provide a record of cultural contact and mixing, with exotic stone and tool styles from sometimes hundreds or even thousands of miles away appearing in local sites. Some of this record is undoubtedly the result of the movement of goods and ideas rather than people, but it is reasonable to suppose that direct physical contact and interaction did occur.

This cultural contact continued into the historic period. One of the features that most characterized early historic Denver was Euro-American and Native American coresidence. A visitor to Denver wrote in 1860, "Before us were the abodes of civilizations while to the right were the smoky wigwams of the Aborigines.... Surely the two extremes had met" (quoted in Barth 1988:117). This juxtaposition, captured in many sketches of early Denver, must have fascinated visitor and inhabitant alike (Fig. 6.1).

Native Americans were not alone in a sea of Euro-Americans, however. Hispanic traders from New Mexico supplied many early Denver residents. The city of Santa Fe had been established for over 150 years when Denver arrived on the scene. The traders of the region were kept busy freighting produce, grain, livestock, and other goods from New Mexico. In fact, the city of Trinidad in southeastern Colorado was established by a Denver-bound New Mexican trader. As Denver grew, the aboriginal and New Mexican presence waned, but Irish, German, Chinese, Italian, Swedes, and many others contributed their heritages to Denver's cultural mix. As discussed in Chapter 5, the archaeology of the Rocky Mountain Arsenal gives us insight into the groups participating in this mosaic.

The dynamic of cultural mixing has not always been a happy one. The "War on the Plains" during the 1860s (which culminated in the infamous Sand Creek Massacre), the riots in Chinatown on Halloween 1880, and the Ku Klux Klan activity of the Stapleton era are notable examples of ethnic tension and conflict. Greater Denver archaeology tells us that we have always been "multicultural," yet we have been slow to appreciate these diverse cultural heritages (Leonard and Noel 1990:477). If there is one defining characteristic of urban existence it is cultural diversity, and a key challenge for those living in or near a city is to learn how to deal with it.

## Same Themes, Different Times

These themes are still relevant today. The lives of contemporary occupants of Greater Denver continue to be governed by them, making for a compelling and instructive link between past and present.

Figure 6.1. Sketch of Denver showing log cabins, covered wagon, and various people including an Indian, around 1859. Courtesy of the Colorado Historical Society.

The inhabitants of Greater Denver continue to pursue diverse economic strategies, albeit ones increasingly removed from the intimacies of collecting plants, cultivating crops, and mining the earth. Service, high technology, telecommunications, and recreation industries rule economic life in Denver today. In keeping with these strategies, Denver continues to be a crossroads of interaction over long distances, evidenced most recently and dramatically by the building of Denver International Airport. Issues of cultural coexistence and ethnic boundary maintenance are continuing struggles, as evidenced by occasional Martin Luther King Day unrest and the arrests during Cinco de Mayo celebrations in 1996.

The ability of archaeology to provide a "deep time" perspective on these processes makes it an important undertaking in today's world. Such a perspective helps us understand what factors are constant, what factors are constraints, and what factors are utterly contingent in shaping the history of an area. It also helps us sort out the enduring problems of life from the quick fix ones. Because of the materiality of the themes discussed here, it should not be hard for future Denver archaeologists to recognize them and extend the story, albeit with new details and different emphases. Still, the constant reshaping of the Denver landscape both creates and obliterates the material remains of the past, ever threatening to deny us access to the details and nuances of this history. This in itself is not alarming, for landscapes, like languages, only remain interesting if they are changing. But there is more we can and should do to see that the still unwritten chapters in Denver history have a chance to be researched, written, and read.

AFTERWORD

# John L. Cotter

The title of this book implies, as the authors intended, that what is written here is based primarily upon what the trowel has revealed in the ground. Yet, as all archaeologists agree, what we really know about the prehistoric past has to be analyzed in the light of what we perceive as demonstrated analogues—we would know nothing whatever of the Paleoindians if we did not have the ethnographic record of living Plains tribal groups. By the same token, the vanished evidence of early Denver can best serve future archaeologists with archival and living references.

What my family witnessed and what I remember vividly as a child and youth in Denver has become the archaeology of Denver—its atmosphere, its distinct character, its vanished or altered notable structures. Sarah Nelson and her group have noted here the cultural change as recorded in ground investigations and historical observations. My family and I have lived them—at least the ones that came after my family arrived in the 1880s, and what I observed for myself after the first decade of the twentieth century.

What archaeology has not yet recorded by excavation is the clear atmosphere of the young city of electric street cars (my mother recalled earlier horse cars and one line that featured a rear platform on which the horse rode down a long hill toward town) (Fig. A1). That was when the automobile spent most of its time in the garage or on the street, awaiting family outings on weekends. The tram was the way to get to work downtown from uptown homes and how housewives got to the many department stores downtown to "shop": Daniels and Fisher, the Denver Dry, Gano's, Joselyn's, and the Golden Eagle down across from D. and F., where "fire sales" offered alluring bargains, and so on including the many specialty shops. Even one that catered decorously to the "old fashioned," where conservative ladies scornful of the latest fashions could find their familiar buttons, gloves, ribbons, and "personal things" still kept in drawers that ranged behind the counter to the ceiling (Fig. A2).

And no archaeologist has evidently unearthed examples of pneumatic tubes in the dry goods stores that sucked up cylinders of cash from the clerk's station and blew them back from the central cashier's booth with change and receipt. And if not the pneumatic tube, the overhead wire that carried baskets with payments to the cashier's box overhead and beyond and back (the clerk sent the basket on its way with a pull cord that gave it a mighty push, which the cashier reciprocated). Thus the marvels of modern merchandising before the cash register gave way to the computer and cash drawer.

Figure A1. An early horse team in Denver, with the horse positioned for the downhill section of the line. Courtesy of the Colorado Historical Society.

Figure A2. A retail store in early twentieth-century Denver. Courtesy of Denver Public Library.

The archaeologist must one day delve into the sites of such industrial landmarks as the old Globe and Grant Smelters and locate their slag dumps long ago broken up for road ballast. I remember the tall Grant Smelter chimney, for many years rising high above the edge of the old cityscape, beyond the other high landmark, the tower of Daniels and Fisher (Fig A3).

The archaeological evidence of so many vanished buildings is mainly in the minds of the very old or in the recorded recollections of the departed. But I can tell you how it was to thrill to the wonder of the new Denver Municipal Auditorium, which could be transformed from a great rectangular hall to a huge theater by lowering a proscenium arch from the center loft and swinging the balconies on either side in on great rollers to meet the proscenium and complete the theater, ready for operas, ballets, recitals, and convocations of all kinds (Fig A4).

Figure A3. Denver smelter, circa 1906. Courtesy of the Colorado Historical Society.

Figure A4. Denver City auditorium annex. Photo by Floyd H. McCall, the Denver Post.

Other great theaters were the Broadway Theater, with its oriental decor, onion-domed boxes, and curtain on which was painted "A Glimpse of India"—a busy city bazaar somewhere in the subcontinent; and the Tabor Grand Opera House (Fig A5) where I saw second-run movies: on special occasions the great painted curtain was rung down and the organ played "Pomp and Circumstance" while I gazed at an idyllic classical landscape of ruins and billowing clouds above the legend, a quote from Charles Kingsley:

So fleet the works of men,
Back to the earth again.
Ancient and holy things fade like a dream.

A fitting reflection for a future archaeologist. Regrettably, the wonderful Tabor Grand with its mahogany and red plush trim has vanished, and with it the memory of many notable musical events when music meant much to Denver and its large German population. The Tuesday Musical Club and the turnvereins of various designations left little material evidence for archaeology; yet they were part of Denver's cultural history, along with much other ephemera.

The sight and scent of the past that the archaeologist cannot evoke is the tang of wood and coal in the air when fireplaces and stoves burned wood and furnaces heated the houses and other buildings with coal, when ash pits, often large receptacles above ground, burned trash to be collected by the ash hauler periodically, before regular trash collection was organized. Also beyond archaeological retrieval are the sight and sound of the horsedrawn "vegetable wagons" that plied the streets and alleys with the driver calling out his wares, and the ice wagons driven by the iceman, who spotted signs in the windows turned to the pounds of ice required for the ice box in the kitchen and cut the lump from the blocks of ice in the wagon, to be carried into the house with pincer tongs.

The downtown streets, teaming with pedestrians, included at some corner the chimney cleaner, who wore the tall pointed hat of his trade and stood with his sooty clothes and brushes and rope, ready to take orders. He characteristically bore the marks of his trade—soot inflamed eyelids. One of the chimney cleaners would have his small boy along in small cone hat and sooty clothes as an additional advertisement.

They are gone, and with them the "violet man" in front of the *Denver Post* (O Justice!), who was blind and sat behind his box of fresh violets for sale. Denver knew his story—he had lost his sight in a misplaced suicide shot to the temple and lived to remain a handsome, gray-haired old man. No amount of digging will discover him, or the little gnome-like cripple on the busiest street corner who was so adept at handing out a folded paper with one hand and collecting 3 cents with the other. When he died, Denver was amazed to find he had saved his money and was quite wealthy for the time.

In the early part of the twentieth century, when the "white plague" of tuberculosis was running through the urban centers of the East, especially among Eastern European immigrants, Denver was the mile-high fresh air mecca for the victims advised by their doctors to seek recovery there. I remember the hospital on Colfax Avenue

Figure A5. Tabor Grand Opera House. Courtesy of the Colorado Historical Society.

Figure A6. Tuberculosis patients at National Jewish Hospital around 1900. Courtesy of the National Jewish Medical Center Archives.

where many tuberculosis patients were treated, which had little open porches off each room, so that patients' beds were half outdoors "in the fresh air" and half inside where it was warm (Fig. A6). The tubercular were required to keep paper cups with them at all times and forbidden to expectorate on the street. Archaeology has nothing to show for this except in the foundations of razed buildings or their standing alterations and the historical records. Historical archaeology spans the gap.

Archaeology must delve carefully to discover the distinctive culture of childhood, its experience, observations, and activities. Recalling my own boyhood of eighty years ago, I find myself running with my companions to the raging flood of Cherry Creek after summer downpours to witness "ocean size" waves coursing between the walls of its concrete channel that passed through the city to the Platte River—a token of the archaeological record of many floods before and since. I also recall how dusty Denver was on dry and windy days before the streets of the residential sections were paved. The admonitions "shut the door quickly and don't let the dust in" came from many a housekeeping mother. In summer the sprinkler wagon, first team-drawn, then motorized, came by to "lay the dust" periodically—until it had to be done over again as the wind blew and the dust flew. Once a month the road grader came along and scraped the surface from gutter to center of the road to maintain the "crown" and drainage.

After that came the woeful experiment with "tarring" the streets with heavy oil sprinkled like water from a tank on wheels. That done, a shoveled scrim of sand was thrown over the fresh oil to "settle" it, and the wheeled traffic did the rest. But woe betide the kid who stepped on fresh oil and tracked it indoors. Motor traffic in the days before modern shock absorbers created the harmonic phenomenon of "washboarding," when oscillating wheels set up a pattern of ripples that sent light cars, notably the Model T Fords, dancing sideways into the gutter to scrape along the curb until car and driver could regain composure. After that, asphalt paving proceeded as quickly as possible in the 1920s and 1930s until the streets were reliably surfaced. Then there was only the problem of snow removal as required. Thus progress and growing came to the city and for all.

Entertainment for children and adults started in the home, but spread to the delights of Elitch Gardens and Lakeside (Fig A7), the recreation parks on the outskirts of the city that opened in summer with their amusements—carousels, roller coasters,

Figure A7. Elitch Gardens. Courtesy of Denver Public Library.

fun houses with things to see and do, and at Elitch's a theater where summer stock companies presented the new show while rehearsing the next two, often giving future stage and screen luminaries like Fredric March, Florence Eldridge, and Lewis Stone their intensive training on stage. Alas, these sites are all archaeological.

On either side of Curtis Street downtown for two wonderful blocks were one dazzling movie after another—the joy of child and adult alike—first-run, vaudeville added for some, and for the best, a "symphony orchestra" always supplemented by the "grand organ," and finally the second-run houses. Every marquee had to be illuminated with as many light bulbs as the frontage allowed—Curtis was indeed a street of lights: "the best lighted street in America," as Thomas A. Edison was said to have said (Fig A8). Everybody knew that. It's all archaeology now; the bulbs are gone. And the movie multiplexes offer only little shoebox halls for viewing just one film at a considerable price. I could get into a Saturday matinee on Colfax Avenue for a dime—feature, serial, news, and comedy, the whole works. Progress.

It didn't cost a kid anything to see the rocking and winking electric signs downtown on building roofs, or marvel at the "Gas and Electric Building," which had clusters of electric bulbs inset in the masonry on two street sides of its corner.

Finally, the archaeology of childhood itself, the most ephemeral of all the past, albeit the culture of childhood, is to be found in all peoples from the Paleolithic to the present. Kids had to be more resourceful in Denver before radio, television, the computer, and organized play and sports. Children, boys in my case, exercised constantly outdoors, on roller skates, racing, wrestling, jumping, playing vigorous games of kick-the-can, and others, propelling Irish mail push-pull carts on which you sat and worked your arms like mad while steering with your feet. The older kids had bikes if their parents could afford them. But any boy could go in with another kid and round up four matched wire wheels, two axles, a platform, and a soap box mounted on it to be pushed, pulled, or propelled by the rider's feet, until a downgrade allowed a free coasting ride. Some boys got a "coaster wagon" for Christmas, and wore out their knickers and their knees kneeling with one leg inside and pushing madly with the other while steering with the pull bar pulled back, with one hand. You didn't have to play football to wreck your knee in those days.

Kids who had no fancy equipment could at least get a hoop of some sort, a light wheel or just a wheel rim, and a stick to keep it rolling along as they ran. Kid marksmen who didn't have water pistols or BB guns (and most did not) could wedge a small stone in the end of a split shingle and throw it with remarkable force, if limited accuracy, at anything—hopefully without disaster. Big boys could make deadly sling shots with a leather thong with a pouch in the middle to hold a stone. The longer the thong and the faster it was swung around overhead, the faster the projectile flew. Many a make-believe Goliath was the target of many a David. More pacifically, boys devised tree houses far up in the few great cottonwood trees that remained in vacant lots along the Cherry Creek bottoms; the climbers found or swiped railroad spikes to hammer into the bark for a foothold, and I observed how the spikes in less than a generation of kids were engulfed by tree growth until they were useless or disappeared entirely (archaeologists finding spikes deep in ancient timber, please note).

AFTERWORD | 239

Boys who hesitated to risk their lives building tree houses could join together in a usually less hazardous enterprise of digging caves in vacant lots (Fig. A9). These were simple rectangular pits about five feet deep roofed over with whatever scrap materials could be scrounged from neighborhood discards of lumber and siding. The cave roof had to be engineered to hold the dirt from the digging, which was carefully placed above and camouflaged. At one end of the cave a fireplace was dug, with a flue to the surface. The real fun was to dig a winding, baffle-filled tunnel from the cave to a hidden entrance. Only a kid who knew where the cave was and where the entrance could be found was a member of the club. In the cool autumn evenings potatoes could be roasted in the embers of the fire in the fireplace. That was living.

Figure A8. Curtis Street at Night. Courtesy of the Colorado Historical Society.

Figure A9. Boys digging "caves." Courtesy of the Colorado Historical Society.

Football didn't figure in those days. Baseball did—softball for the smaller kids, hard baseball for the teenagers, the chief reason being that mitts were hard to come by, and usually were available only to the older boys. Girls never played.

While the girls played hopscotch on the chalked sidewalk or jumped rope (Fig. A10), the boys scratched a circle in the dirt, stomped it flat and smooth, drew an accurate boundary with a string held from the center, got out their individual hoards of marbles, and began the game. Aggies, glassies, and the lowly mig of lead-glazed earthenware were the familiar mainstays of the game. The lucky shooters acquired the ultimate marble, the "steelie," which could only be had by much resourceful poking in the trash in back of repair garages to discover a rare main bearing from the transmission—rumor had it—from a junked Ford T truck. A steelie could split any unlucky marble the accuracy of its shooter could reach. That was a game!

AFTERWORD | 241

Figure A10. Girls on the playground. Courtesy of the Colorado Historical Society.

Finally, the art of top spinning is now lost. An expert kid with a turnip-shaped wooden top with a steel peg for spinning and a good string wound around the top could aim it at a spinning rival, and with good luck or skill or both, split the opponent's top. Game won.

Any archaeologist who encounters a cache of marbles in the cellar floor of an extinct house, or a top, or a hoop, or a set of jacks—those 6-pronged metal things that were cast down as a handful by an adept girl who had to sweep them all up with the same hand that bounced a rubber ball—once—should know what he has found. The boys played the more dangerous game of mumblety-peg with dull pen knives flicked down from the chin between fingers placed on the ground. (I detested this game and suffered scorn and taunts rather than risk my fingers!) Finding a jackknife in a deposit long lost sight of may indicate that story to an alert archaeologist.

Figure A11. Dr. E. B. Renaud and his University of Denver students, John Cotter, Marie Wormington, two unknown students, and Gilbert Bucknum. Courtesy of the Marie Wormington Collection.

So this archaeologist has devoted himself to the remembered and forgotten past of Denver and Philadelphia, and the remote past of the Paleoindian people I encountered at Clovis, New Mexico, and in many Denver and other Colorado collections (Fig. A11). And so on to the Hopewellian mound builders of the beginning of the "Common" (read Christian) era and their successors who built large temple mounds in Mississippi. From investigating historic Jamestown, the first permanent English settlement in Virginia in the 1950s I went on to teach historical archaeology at Penn and explore Philadelphia with colleagues and students.

My coeditor and I salute Dr. Nelson and her colleagues on their achievement, which has been facilitated so generously by my friend and contemporary at the University of Denver, Leo Block '35. We join with pride the University of Pennsylvania Press in offering this volume in tribute to Denver and its university.

# REFERENCES

Abbott, Carl, Stephen J. Leonard, and David McComb
   1982   *Colorado: A History of the Centennial State.* Boulder: Colorado Associated University Press.

Abernathy, Keith
   1982   Cultural Resources Inventory of the Arapahoe Motorized State Recreation Area. Manuscript on file at the Colorado Historical Society Office of Archaeology and Historic Preservation, Denver.

Abert, Lt. J. W.
   1846   *Report on the Upper Arkansas and the Country of the Comanche Indians.* 29th Congress, 1st Session. Senate Executive Document 438. Washington, D.C.: U.S. Government Printing Office.

Abramova, Z. A.
   1967   "Paleolithic Art in the USSR." *Arctic Anthropology* 4(2): 1–179.

Adkins, J. Frank
   1976   "Salvage Archaeology on the Ken Caryl Ranch: Falcon's Nest Site, Progress Report 1976." Paper presented at the 1976 Colorado Archaeological Society Annual Meeting, Montrose.
   1982   "Salvage Archaeology on the Ken Caryl Ranch: Status and Significance of the Crescent II Dig." Paper presented at the 1982 Colorado Archaeological Society Annual Meeting, Durango.
   1993   "Falcon's Nest Site, 5JF211 Ken-Caryl Ranch, Jefferson County, Colorado." In *Archaeological Investigations at the Ken-Caryl Ranch, Colorado,* ed. Richard F. Somer. Vol. 1, Part III. Memoirs of the Colorado Archaeological Society 6. Denver: Colorado Archaeological Society.

Adkins, J. Frank and Florence Irish
   1994   Potsherds. In *Miscellaneous Materials and Records in Falcon's Nest Site (5JF211) Ken-Caryl Ranch, Jefferson County, Colorado. Archaeological Investigations at the Ken-Caryl Ranch, Colorado,* ed. Richard F. Somer. Vol. 6, Part I. Memoirs of the Colorado Archaeological Society 6. Denver: Colorado Archaeological Society.

Adkins, J. Frank and Carolyn M. Kurtz
   1993   "Falcon's Nest Site in Its Time and Place. Falcon's Nest Site (5JF211) Ken-Caryl Ranch, Jefferson County, Colorado." In *Archaeological Investigations at the Ken-Caryl Ranch, Colorado,* ed. Richard F. Somer. Vol. 1, Part III. Memoirs of the Colorado Archaeological Society 6. Denver: Colorado Archaeological Society.

Adovasio, J. M.
   1999   Basketry from Franktown Cave (L:9:31), Douglas County, Colorado. Manuscript on file at the Department of Anthropology, University of Denver.

Albanese, J.
 1990 Geomorphological Studies at Isolated Finds 5AM428, 5AM431, and 5AM434, New Denver International Airport, Denver County, Colorado. Submitted to Dames and Moore, Golden, Colorado.

Albert, Lois E. and Don C. Wyckoff
 1984 "Oklahoma Environments: Past and Present." In *Prehistory of Oklahoma,* ed. Robert E. Bell. New York: Academic Press.

Anderson, Jane L.
 1985 "Projectile Points." In *A Chronological Framework of the Fort Carson Pinion Canyon Maneuver Site, Las Animas County, Colorado,* ed. C. Lintz. U.S. Army Fort Carson Pinion Canyon Cultural Resources Project, Contribution 2. Center for Archaeological Research, University of Denver.

Anderson, Jane L., Lawrence C. Todd, Galen R. Burgett, and David J. Rapson
 1994 *Archaeological Investigations at the Massey Draw Site (5JF339): Archaic Occupations Along the Rocky Mountain Front Range, Jefferson County, Colorado.* Colorado Department of Transportation Archaeological Research Series 3. Denver: Colorado Department of Transportation.

Annand, E. R.
 1967 "A Description and Analysis of Surface Pottery from the Collbran Region, Colorado." *Southwestern Lore* 33(2).

Apple, Rebecca McCorkle and Andrew L. York
 1993 Kern River Gas Transmission Company Kern River Pipeline, Cultural Resource Data Recovery Report California. Submitted to Federal Energy Regulatory Commission, San Diego by Dames and Moore, Golden, Colorado.

Armstrong, David M.
 1972 *Distribution of Mammals in Colorado.* Ed. William E. Duellman. Monograph of the Museum of Natural History, University of Kansas 3. Lawrence: University of Kansas Printing Service.

Athearn, Frederic J.
 1985 *Land of Contrast: A History of Southeastern Colorado.* Denver: Bureau of Land Management.

Athearn, Robert G.
 1962 *Rebel of the Rockies: A History of the Denver and Rio Grande Western Railroad.* New Haven, Conn.: Yale University Press.
 1971 *Union Pacific Country.* Chicago: Rand McNally.
 1976 *The Coloradans.* Albuquerque: University of New Mexico Press.

Baker, Steven G.
 1978 "Historical Archaeology for Colorado and the Victorian Mining Frontier: Review, Discussion and Suggestions." *Southwestern Lore* 44(3).
 1983 "The Railroad and the American Victorian Cultural Horizon: An Archaeological Perspective from Colorado." In *Forgotten Places and Things: Archaeological Perspectives on American History,* ed. Albert E. Ward. Pp. 239–50. Contributions to Anthropological Studies 3. Albuquerque, N.M.: Center for Anthropological Studies.

Baltensperger, Bradley H.
 1979 Agricultural Adjustments to Great Plains Drought: The Republican Valley, 1870–1900. In *The Great Plains: Environment and Culture,* ed. Brian W. Blouet and Frederick C. Luebke. Pp. 43–59. Lincoln: University of Nebraska Press.

Bark, L. Dean
    1978    History of American Droughts. In *North American Droughts,* ed. Norman J. Rosenberg. Pp. 9–23. Boulder, Colo.: Westview Press.

Barth, Gunther
    1988    *Instant Cities: Urbanization and the Rise of San Francisco and Denver.* Albuquerque: University
    [1975]  of New Mexico Press.

Baskin, O. L. and Company
    1880    History of the City of Denver, Arapahoe County, and Colorado. Denver: O. L. Baskin and Company.

Beaudry, Mary C., L. J. Cook, and Stephen A. Mrozowski
    1991    "Artifacts and Active Voices: Material Culture as Social Discourse." In *The Archaeology of Inequality,* ed. Randall H. McGuire and Robert Paynter. Pp. 150–91. Oxford: Blackwell.

Bender, S. J. and Gary A. Wright
    1988    "High-Altitude Occupations, Cultural Process, and High Plains Prehistory: Retrospect and Prospect." *American Anthropologist* 90(3): 619–39.

Benedict, James B.
    1973    "Chronology of Cirque Glaciation, Colorado Front Range." *Quaternary Research* 3(4): 585–99.
    1979    "Getting Away from It All: A Study of Man, Mountains, and the Two-Drought Altithermal." *Southwestern Lore* 45(3): 1–12.
    1981    *The Fourth of July Valley: Glacial Geology and Archeology of the Timberline Ecotone.* Research Report 2. Ward, Colo.: Center for Mountain Archeology.
    1985    *Arapaho Pass: Glacial Geology and Archeology at the Crest of the Colorado Front Range.* Research Report 3. Ward, Colo.: Center for Mountain Archeology.
    1992a  "Footprints in the Snow: High-Altitude Cultural Ecology of the Colorado Front Range, U.S.A." *Arctic and Alpine Research* 24(1): 1–16.
    1992b  "Sacred Hot Springs, Instant Patinas." *Plains Anthropologist* 37(138): 1–6.

Benedict, James B. and Byron L. Olson
    1978    *The Mount Albion Complex: A Study of Prehistoric Man and the Altithermal.* Research Report 1. Ward, Colo.: Center for Mountain Archaeology.

Berry, Joseph W.
    1968    "The Climate of Colorado. In *Climates of the United States.*" Pp. 595–98. New York: Office of the National Oceanic and Atmospheric Administration, U.S. Department of Commerce, Water Information Center.

Berthrong, Donald J.
    1963    *The Southern Cheyenne.* Norman: University of Oklahoma Press.

Binford, Lewis R.
    1981    *Bones: Ancient Men and Modern Myths.* New York: Academic Press.

Black, Kevin D.
    1991    "Archaic Continuity in the Colorado Rockies: The Mountain Tradition." *Plains Anthropologist* 36(133): 1–29.
    1992    A Cultural Resources Inventory at Dinosaur Ridge, Jefferson County, Colorado. Colorado Historical Society Office of Archaeology and Historic Preservation, Denver.
    1994    *Archaeology of the Dinosaur Ridge Area.* Denver: Friends of Dinosaur Ridge.

Bolton, Ralph P.
1964 *Spanish Borderlands: A Chronicle of Old Florida and the Southwest*. Norman: University of Oklahoma Press.
[1921]

Bowden, Martyn J., Robert W. Kates, Paul A. Kay, William E. Riebsame, Richard A. Warrick, Douglas L. Johnson, Harvey A. Gould, and Daniel Weiner
1981 "The Effect of Climate Fluctuations on Human Populations." In *Climate and History: Studies in Past Climates and Their Impact on Man,* ed. T. M. L. Wigley, M. J. Ingram, and G. Farmer. Pp. 479– 513. Cambridge: Cambridge University Press.

Boyle, Susan Calafate
1994 *Comerciantes, Arrieros, y Peones: The Hispanos and the Santa Fe Trade. Southwest Cultural Resources Center*. Professional Papers 54. Southwest Cultural Resources Center, Southwest Regional Office, National Park Service, Santa Fe, N.M.

Brasser, Ted J.
1982 "The Tipi as an Element in the Emergence of Historic Plains Indian Nomadism." *Plains Anthropologist* 27(98) (Part. 1): 309–21.

Brumbach, Hetty Jo and Robert Jarvenpa
1997 "Ethnoarchaeology of Subsistence Space and Gender: A Subarctic Dene Case." *American Antiquity* 62(3): 414–36.

Brunswig, Robert H., Jr.
1992 Geoarchaeology at the Dent Mammoth Site in the Northeastern Colorado High Plains. Manuscript in possession of author, Greeley, Colorado.
1995 "Apachean Ceramics East of Colorado's Continental Divide: Current Data and New Directions." In *Archaeological Pottery of Colorado: Ceramic Clues to the Prehistoric and Protohistoric Lives of the State's Native People*. CCPA Occasional Papers 2. Colorado Council of Professional Archaeologists, Denver.

Brunswig, Robert H., Bruce A. Bradley, and Susan Chandler, eds.
1995 Archaeological Pottery of Colorado: Ceramic Clues to the Prehistoric and Protohistoric Lives of the State's Native People. Colorado Council of Professional Archaeologists.

Bryant, Bruce, Robert D. Miller, and Glen R. Scott
1973 Geologic map of the Indian Hills Quadrangle, Jefferson County, Colorado. Denver: U.S. Geological Survey.

Buckles, William G.
1968 "Archaeology in Colorado: Historic Tribes." *Southwestern Lore* 34(3): 53–67.

Buckles, William G., George H. Ewing, Nancy Buckles, George J. Armelagos, John J. Wood, James D. Haug, and John H. McCullough
1963 "The Excavation of the Hazletine Heights Site." *Southwestern Lore* 29(1): 1–37.

Burney, Michael S., Thomas J. Lennon, Mark E. Sullivan, and Charles W. Wheeler
1979 A Cultural Resource Inventory of the Highlands Ranch. Prepared for the Jack G. Raub Co. by Western Cultural Resource Management Inc., Boulder, Colorado.

Burney, Michael S. and Stephen F. Mehls
1987 A Cultural Resource Survey of Two Parcels Near Second and Third Creeks Within the Study Area of the New Denver Airport in Western Adams County, Colorado. Prepared for Greiner Engineering Sciences, Inc., Denver by J. F. Sato and Associates, Denver. Manuscript on file at the Colorado Historical Society Office of Archaeology and Historic Preservation, Denver.

Butler, William B.
- 1980 "Comments on a Research Design for the State Historic Preservation Plan: Eastern Colorado." Paper Presented at the March 1980 Meeting of the Colorado Council of Professional Archaeologists. Manuscript on file at the Colorado Historical Society Office of Archaeology and Historic Preservation, Denver.
- 1981 "Eastern Colorado Radiocarbon Dates." *Southwestern Lore* 47 (3): 12–30.
- 1986 "Taxonomy in Northeastern Colorado Prehistory." Ph.D. dissertation, Department of Anthropology, University of Missouri, Columbia.
- 1988 "The Woodland Period in Northwestern Colorado." *Plains Anthropologist* 33(122): 449–65.
- 1990 "Reinterpreting the Magic Mountain Site." *Southwestern Lore* 56(3): 8–21.

Butzer, Karl W.
- 1983 "Human Response to Environmental Change in the Perspective of Future Global Climate." *Quaternary Research* 19(3): 279–92.

Carrara, P. E., W. N. Mode, Meyer Rubin, and S. W. Robinson
- 1984 "Deglaciation and Post–Glacial Timberline in the San Juan Mountains, Colorado." *Quaternary Research* 21: 42–55.

Carrillo, Richard F.
- 1986 Archaeological, Architectural and Historical Research of the Big Dry Creek Cheese Ranch (5DA221) at Highlands Ranch, Douglas County, Colorado. With E. Anderson, S. Anderson, D. Mullineaux, and M. A. Van Ness. Submitted to Mission Viejo Company, Denver.
- 1987 Evaluation of Old Las Animas (5BN176), a Late Nineteenth-Century Town on the Arkansas River, Bent County, Colorado. With Amy C. Earls, Nick Trierweiler, and John C. Acklen. Prepared for U.S. Army Corps of Engineers, Albuquerque District by Mariah Associates, Inc., Albuquerque, New Mexico.
- 1989 Historical Archaeology at the Site of the Tremont House (5DV2954), an Early 1860's Denver Hotel: Results of Testing and a Proposed Data Recovery Plan. Unit, Archaeological and Colorado Department of Highways.
- 1990 "Historical Archaeology Research Design." In *An Introduction to the Archaeology of Pinon Canyon, Southeastern Colorado,* vol. 3, ed. William Andrefsky, Jr. Submitted to National Park Service, Rocky Mountain Regional Office, Denver, by Larson-Tibesar Associates, Inc., Laramie, Wyoming and Centennial Archaeology, Inc., Fort Collins, Colorado.
- 1991 An Historical Archaeology Survey Along the Proposed Route of the 20th Street Viaduct Replacement Project, Denver, Colorado. Prepared for Zimmer-Gunsul-Frasca Partnership, Portland, Oregon.
- 1996 "Archaeological Sites on El Rio de Purgatorio: Hispanic New Mexican Influences in the Historical Archaeology of Southeastern Colorado." Paper presented at the 58th Annual Meeting of the Plains Anthropological Conference, Laramie, Wyoming.

Carrillo, Richard. F., Bonnie J. Clark, Pamela K. Cowen, and Philip L. Petersen
- 1997 Four Features at the Prowers House: Historical Archaeology at Boggsville Historic Site (in preparation).

Carrillo, Richard F. and Daniel A. Jepson
- 1995 *Exploring the Colorado Frontier: A Study in Historical Archaeology at the Tremont House Hotel, Lower Downtown Denver.* Denver: Colorado Department of Transportation and Federal Highway Administration, U.S. Department of Transportation.

Carrillo, Richard F., Renee Johnson, and Margaret A. Van Ness
- 1987 Historical Archaeology Along the Proposed Speer Viaduct Replacement Route in Denver, Colorado. Prepared for CRS Sirrine Civil Engineers, Inc., Denver.

Carrillo, Richard F., Sarah J. Pearce, Stephen Kalasz, and Daniel A. Jepson
  1993  *The Tremont House (5DV2954): Historical Archaeological Investigations of an Early Hotel in Denver, Colorado.* Colorado Department of Transportation Archaeological Research Series 1. Denver: Colorado Department of Transportation.

Carrillo, Richard F., Christian J. Zier, and Andrea M. Barnes
  1991  The Documentation of Stone City (5PE793): Historical Archaeology at the Fort Carson Military Reservation, Pueblo County. Prepared for National Park Service, Branch of Interagency Services, Denver by Centennial Archaeology, Inc., Fort Collins, Colorado.

Cassells, E. Steve
  1983  *The Archaeology of Colorado.* Boulder, Colo.: Johnson Books.

Catts, Wade P.
  1993  "Review of *The Buried Past: An Archaeological History of Philadelphia* (John L. Cotter, Daniel G. Roberts, and Michael Parrington)." *American Anthropologist* 95(4): 10–14.

Chandler, Susan M.
  1989  Archaeological Studies at the New Denver Airport, Phase II, Long Range Development. Alpine Archaeological Consultants, Montrose, Colorado.

Chandler, Susan M., Alan D. Reed, and Jonathan C. Horn
  1989  Archaeological Studies at the New Denver International Airport, Phase II Long Range Airport Development, Denver County, Colorado. Alpine Archaeological Consultants, Inc. and Colorado Montrose. Submitted to Dames and Moore, Golden, Colorado.

Chorley, Richard J., Stanley A Schumm, and David E. Sugden
  1984  *Geomorphology.* London and New York: Methuen.

Chronic, Halka
  1980  *Roadside Geology of Colorado.* Missoula, Mont.: Mountain Press Publishing Company.

Churchill, Ward
  1992  *Fantasies of the Master Race: Literature, Cinema, and the Colonization of American Indians.* Boulder, Colo.: Westview Press.

Clark, Bonnie J.
  1994  "Order and Disorder in the Queen City of the Plains: A Material Cultural Study of the Denver City Layout." Paper presented at Society for Historical Archaeology Annual Meeting.

Clark, Bonnie J., ed.
  1986  Prehistoric Archaeological Sites in and Near the Hogback Valley West of Denver, in Douglas and Jefferson Counties, Colorado. Manuscript on file at the Colorado Historical Society Office of Archaeology and Historic Preservation, Denver.
  1997  Archaeological Investigations and Cultural Resources Management Plan for the Archaeological Resources of the Rocky Mountain Arsenal, Adams County, Colorado, vol. 1. Submitted to National Park Service, RMR-AC. Denver: SWCA, Inc. Environmental Consultants. Colorado Archaeological Society, Denver.

Clark, Bonnie J. et al.
  1993  An Historical Archaeology Survey Along the Southwest Corridor Alternative Route, Regional Transportation System (RTD), Denver, Arapahoe, and Douglas Counties, Colorado. Submitted to Hermsen Consultants, Littleton, Colorado.

Clark, Bonnie J., Lori E. Rhodes, and Richard F. Carrillo
  1994  Cultural Resource Investigations for the 120th Avenue Extension Project Adams County, Colorado. Submitted to Dames and Moore, Golden, Colorado.

Collins, Susan M.
- 1979 "Appendix: Test Trench." In F. A. Patterson, *A Cultural Resource Survey of the Proposed C-Line Realignment, Lower Downtown Combined Sewer Separation.* Cultural Resource Consultants, Denver.
- 1993 Introduction to Richard F. Carrillo, Sarah J. Pearce, Stephen Kalasz, and Daniel A. Jepson, *The Tremont House (5DV2954): Historical Archaeological Investigations of an Early Hotel in Denver, Colorado.* Colorado Department of Transportation Archaeological Research Series 1. Denver: Colorado Department of Transportation.

Colorado Archaeological Society
- 1986 Prehistoric Archaeological Sites in and Near the Hogback Valley West of Denver, in Douglas and Jefferson Counties, Colorado. Compiled by members of the Colorado Archaeological Society. Manuscript on file at the Colorado Archaeological Society, Denver.

Covington, James W.
- 1953 "Ute Scalp Dance in Denver." *Colorado Magazine* 30 (2): 119–24.

Cowan, Ruth Schwartz
- 1974 "A Case Study of Technological and Social Change: The Washing Machine and the Working Wife." In *Clio's Consciousness Raised: New Perspectives on the History of Women,* ed. Mary S. Hartman and Lois Banner. Pp. 245–53. New York: Harper and Row.

Cressey, Pamela J. and J. F. Stephens
- 1982 "The City-Site Approach to Urban Archaeology." In *Archaeology of Urban America: The Search for Pattern and Process,* ed. Roy S. Dickens. Pp. 41–61. New York: Academic Press.

Csikszentmihalyi, Mihaly and Eugene Rochberg-Halton
- 1981 *The Meaning of Things: Domestic Symbols and the Self.* Cambridge: Cambridge University Press.

Cummings, Linda Scott
- 1994 "Pollen and Macroflora." In Jane L. Anderson, Lawrence C. Todd, Galen R. Burgett, and David J. Rapson, *Archaeological Investigations at the Massey Draw Site (5JF339): Archaic Occupations Along the Rocky Mountain Front Range, Jefferson County, Colorado.* Colorado Department of Transportation Archaeological Research Series 3. Denver: Colorado Department of Transportation.

Cummings, Linda Scott and Thomas E. Montoux
- 1997 "Appendix J: Stratigraphic Pollen Analysis at the Crescent site (5JF148), Jefferson County, Colorado." In *Archaeological Investigations at the Ken-Caryl Ranch, Colorado,* ed. Richard F. Somer. Memoirs of the Colorado Archaeological Society 6. Denver: Colorado Archaeological Society.

Dames and Moore
- 1991 Cultural Resources Class III Survey of the Department of Energy Rocky Flats Plant, Northern Jefferson and Boulder Counties, Colorado. Submitted to EG&G Rocky Flats.

Daniels, Roger
- 1990 *Coming to America: A History of Immigration and Ethnicity in American Life.* New York: HarperCollins.

Davis, Leslie B., Stephen A. Aaberg, James G. Schmitt, and Ann M. Johnson
- 1995 *The Obsidian Cliff Plateau Prehistoric Lithic Source, Yellowstone National Park, Wyoming.* Division of Cultural Resources Selections 6. Denver: National Park Service, Rocky Mountain Region.

Deetz, James
- 1967 *Invitation to Archaeology.* Garden City, N.Y.: Natural History Press.

1977 "The Archaeology of Early American Life." In *Small Things Forgotten: An Archaeology of Early American Life.* New York: Doubleday.

DeSart, Dennis J.
1981 Auraria Archaeological Project, Interim Report, Summer 1981. Copy on file at the Colorado Historical Society Office of Archaeology and Historic Preservation, Denver.

Dick, Everett Newfon
1937 *The Sod House Frontier, 1854–1890: A Social History of the Northern Plains from the Creation of Kansas and Nebraska to the Admission of the Dakotas.* New York: Appleton Century.

Dorsett, Lyle
1977 *The Queen City: A History of Denver.* Denver: Pruett Publishing Company.

Downing, Barbara James
1981 "A Re-Appraisal of Old Archaeological Collections: The Renaud Collection." Master's thesis, Department of Anthropology, University of Denver.

Eagle Watch
1992 Historical Issue, August. Denver.

Eberhart, Perry
1986 *Ghosts of the Colorado Plains.* Athens, Ohio: Swallow Press.

Eckerle, William
1992 "Geoarchaeological Assessment." In *Two Cultural Resource Studies for the Questar Pipeline Company Near Flaming Gorge Reservoir.* Pp. 50–55. Research Paper 4. Phoenix: Dames and Moore Intermountain Cultural Resource Services

Eddy, F. W., C. Jurgens, P. D. Friedman, and T. R. Farmer
1981 A Cultural Resources Inventory of the Castlewood Canyon State Park, Douglas County, Colorado. Manuscript on file at the Colorado Historical Society Office of Archaeology and Historic Preservation, Denver.

Eighmy, Jeffrey L.
1984 Colorado Plains Prehistoric Context. Manuscript on file at the Colorado Historical Society Office of Archaeology and Historic Preservation, Denver.

Ellwood, Priscilla B.
1983 Mee Whole Vessel Description. Manuscript on file at the Colorado Historical Society Office of Archaeology and Historic Preservation, Denver.
1987 "Bayou Gulch (5DA265) Ceramics." *Plains Anthropologist* 32(116): 113–39.

Elwood, Priscilla B. and D. R. Parker
1995 Rock Creek (5BL2712) Ceramics. Appendix B in Peter J. Gleichman, Carol L. Gleichman, and Sandra L. Karhu, *Excavations at the Rock Creek Site: 1990–1993.* Boulder, Colo.: Native Cultural Services.

Emmons, David M.
1971 *Garden in the Grasslands: Boomer Literature of the Central Great Plains.* Lincoln: University of Nebraska Press.

Felch, Richard E.
1978 "Drought: Characteristics and Assessment." In *North American Droughts,* ed. Norman J. Rosenberg. Pp. 25–42. Boulder, Colo.: Westview Press.

Fink, Deborah
1992 *Agrarian Women: Wives and Mothers in Rural Nebraska, 1880–1940.* Studies in Rural Culture. Chapel Hill: University of North Carolina Press.

Fischer, John W.
  1992  "Observations on the Late Pleistocene Bone Assemblage from the Lamb Spring Site, Colorado." In *Ice Age Hunters of the Rockies,* ed. Dennis J. Stanford and Jane S. Day. Niwot: University Press of Colorado.

Five Points Business Association
  1994  Five Points Walking Tour. Prepared by City and County of Denver, Planning and Development Office.

Fletcher, Jack E. and Patricia K. A. Fletcher
  1995  "The Cherokee Trail." *Overland Journal* 13 (2): 21–33 (Independence, Mo.: Oregon-California Trails Association).

Ford, David
  1983  "Three-Dimensional Computer Graphic Determination of Occupation Surfaces: A Beginning Assessment. Crescent Site I, 5JF148." Master's thesis, Department of Anthropology, University of Denver.

Friedman, Paul D.
  1985  Final Report of History and Oral History Studies of the Fort Carson-Pinon Canyon Maneuver Area, Las Animas County, Colorado. Submitted to National Park Service, Rocky Mountain Regional Office, by Powers Elevation Co., Inc., Aurora, Colorado.
  1989  Historical Studies at the Proposed New Denver International Airport Denver County, Colorado. Vol. 2, Site Forms. Submitted to City and County of Denver New Denver Airport Office by Dames and Moore, Golden, Colorado.

Frison, George C.
  1978  *Prehistoric Hunters of the High Plains.* New York: Academic Press.
  1991  *Prehistoric Hunters of the High Plains.* 2nd ed. San Diego: Academic Press.

Garrard, Lewis Hector
  1955  *Wah-to-Yah and the Taos Trail.* Norman: University of Oklahoma Press.
  [1850]

Gay, Patrick
  n.d.  Faunal Analysis at Four Mile House: Excavations of Field Seasons in 1989 and 1991. Manuscript on file at the Department of Anthropology, Metropolitan State College of Denver.

Geismar, Joan H.
  1993  "Where Is the Night Soil? Thoughts on an Urban Privy." *Historical Archaeology* 27(2): 57–70.

Gero, Joan M.
  1991  "Genderlithics: Women's Roles in Stone Tool Production." In *Engendering Archaeology: Women and Prehistory,* ed. Joan M. Gero and Margaret W. Conkey. Pp. 163–93. Oxford: Blackwell.

Gifford, Diane P. and A. Kay Behrensmeyer
  1976  "Observed Depositional Events at a Modern Human Occupation Site in Kenya." *Quaternary Research* 8: 245–66.

Gifford-Gonzalez, Diane
  1993  "Gaps in Zooarchaeological Analyses of Butchery: Is Gender an Issue?" In *From Bones to Behavior: Ethnoarchaeological and Experimental Contributions to the Interpretation of Faunal Remains,* ed. Jean Hudson. Pp. 181–99. Carbondale: Southern Illinois University at Carbondale Center for Archaeological Investigations.

Gifford-Gonzalez, Diane P. et al.
  1985  "The Third Dimension in Site Structure: An Experiment in Trampling and Vertical Dispersal." *American Antiquity* 5(4): 803–18.

Gillio, David and Douglas Scott
  1971  "Archaeological Tests of the Forney Site, Denver, Colorado." *Colorado Anthropologist* 3(2): 24–34.

Gilmore, Kevin P.
  1989  "Archaeology and Holocene Stratigraphy at the Foot of the Front Range." *Southwestern Lore* 55(3): 12–30.
  1991  "Bayou Gulch: Geoarchaeology of a Multicomponent Site in Central Colorado." Master's thesis, Department of Anthropology, University of Colorado, Boulder.
  1999  "Late Prehistoric Stage." In *Colorado Prehistory: A Context for the Platte River Basin,* ed. Kevin P. Gilmore, Marcia J. Tate, Mark L. Chenault, Bonnie J. Clark, Terri McBride, and Margaret Wood. Colorado Council of Professional Archaeologists.

Gleichman, Peter J., Carol L. Gleichman, and Sandra L. Karhu
  1995  *Excavations at the Rock Creek Site: 1990–1993.* Boulder, Colo.: Native Cultural Services.

Goetz, Liesel
  1996  The Olson Site. Manuscript on file at the Department of Anthropology, University of Denver.

Graham, Carole L.
  1996  Test Excavations at 5AH552, 5AH741, and 5AH747, Three Prehistoric Sites Located in the E-470 Right-of-Way and a Treatment Plan for 5AH741, Arapahoe County, Colorado. Prepared for Centennial Engineering, Inc., Arvada, Colorado by Metcalf Archaeological Consultants, Inc., Eagle, Colorado.

Greeley, Horace
  1964  *An Overland Journey from New York to San Francisco, in the Summer of 1859.* New York: Knopf.
  [1860]

Green, Harvey
  1983  *The Light of the Home: An Intimate View of the Lives of Women in Victorian America.* New York: Pantheon.

Greiser, Sally Thompson
  1985  "Predictive Models of Hunter-Gatherer Subsistence and Settlement Strategies on the Central High Plains." *Plains Anthropologist* Memoir 20.

Gregg, Josiah
  1954  *Commerce of the Prairies.* Reprint Norman: University of Oklahoma Press.
  [1844]
  1962  *Commerce of the Prairies.* Vol. 1. Reprint Philadelphia: Lippincott.
  [1844]

Grinnell, George Bird
  1962  *Cheyenne Indians: Their History and Ways of Life.* Vol. 1. New York: Cooper Square.

Gunnerson, James H.
  1968.  "Plains Apache Archaeology: A Review." *Plains Anthropologist* 13(41): 167–89.
  1987  *Archaeology of the High Plains.* Cultural Resource Series 29. Denver: Bureau of Land Management.

Gunnerson, James H. and Dolores A. Gunnerson
  1988  *Ethnohistory of the High Plains.* Cultural Resource Series 26. Denver: Bureau of Land Management.

Guthrie, Mark R.
- 1979 A Proton Magnetometer Survey of a Specified Area Within Four Mile Historic Park, Denver, Colorado. Manuscript on file at Four Mile Historic Park, Denver.
- 1983 "The Aurora Burial: Site 5AH244." Paper presented at the fifth annual meeting of the Colorado Council of Professional Archaeologists, Denver.

Guthrie, Mark R., Powys Gadd, Renee Johnson, and Joseph J. Lischka
- 1984 Colorado Mountains Prehistoric Context. Colorado Historical Society, Denver.

Hansen, W. R., J. Chronic, and J. Matelock
- 1978 *Climatography of the Front Range Urban Corridor and Vicinity, Colorado.* Geological Survey Professional Paper 1019. Washington, D.C.: U.S. Government Printing Office.

Harper, F.
- 1994 "Colorado's Forgotten Airbase: The Original Lowry Field." *Colorado Heritage* (Autumn): 2–11.

Harrington, H. D.
- 1967 *Edible Native Plants of the Rocky Mountains.* Albuquerque: University of New Mexico Press.

Harvey, James
- 1935 "The Twelve Mile House, Recollections of Mrs. Jane Melvin as Related to James Harvey." *Colorado Magazine* 12(5): 173–78.

Haviland, William A.
- 1983 *Cultural Anthropology.* 4th ed. New York: Holt Rinehart.

Heinrich, Paul V.
- 1984 "Petrographic Analysis of Jasper from 5CF84, Chaffee County, Colorado." Appendix C in Collette Chambellan, Margaret Kadziel, Thomas J. Lennon and Eliza K. Wade, *A Cultural Resource Evaluation of Site 5CF84, Salida Ranger District, Pike and San Isabel National Forest, CO.* Pp. 97–104. Boulder, Colo.: Western Cultural Resources Management. Manuscript on file at the Colorado Historical Society Office of Archaeology and Historic Preservation, Denver.

Hendricks, Celia H.
- 1986 *Letters from Honeyhill: A Woman's View of Homesteading, 1914–1931.* Boulder, Colo.: Pruett Publishing Company.

Hermsen, Gail
- 1990 Survey Report 23rd Street Viaduct Replacement. Prepared for Colorado Department of Highways by Hermsen Consultants, Littleton, Colorado.

Hicks, Dave
- 1971 *Englewood from the Beginning.* Denver: A-T-P Publishing.

Hodder, Ian
- 1982a *The Present Past: An Introduction to Anthropology for Archaeologists.* London: Batsford.
- 1982b "Theoretical Archaeology: A Reactionary View." In *Symbolic and Structural Archaeology,* ed. Ian Hodder. Pp. 1–16. Cambridge: Cambridge University Press.

Hoebel, E. Adamson
- 1960 *The Cheyennes: Indians of the Great Plains.* Case Studies in Cultural Anthropology. New York: Holt.

Hoig, Stan
- 1989 *The Cheyenne: Indians of North America.* New York: Chelsea House.

Holliday, Vance T.
 1987 "Geoarchaeology and Late Quaternary Geomorphology of the Middle South Platte River, Northeastern Colorado." *Geoarchaeology* 2(4): 317–29.

Hollon, W. Eugene
 1966 *The Great American Desert.* New York: Oxford University Press.

Hunt, Charles B.
 1953 *Pleistocene and Recent Deposits in the Denver Area.* U.S. Geological Survey Bulletin 996-C. Washington D.C.: U.S. Government Printing Office.

Hurt, Wesley
 1939 "Indian Influence at Manzano." *El Palacio* 46: 245–54.

Husted, Wilfred M.
 1978 "Excavation Techniques and Culture Layer Analysis." Chapter 6 in *The Mummy Cave Project in Northeastern Wyoming,* pp. 50–132. Cody, Wyo: Buffalo Bill Historical Center.

Hyde, George E.
 1959 *Indians of the High Plains.* Norman: University of Oklahoma Press.

Irwin, Henry T. and Cynthia C. Irwin
 1959 "Excavations at LoDaisKa Site." *Denver Museum of Natural History Proceedings* 8. Denver: Denver Museum of Natural History.
 1961 "Radiocarbon Dates from the LoDaiska Site, Colorado." *American Antiquity* 27(1): 114–15.

Irwin-Williams, Cynthia C. and Henry T. Irwin
 1966 "Excavations at Magic Mountain: A Diachronic Study of Plains-Southwest Relations." *Denver Museum of Natural History Proceedings* 12. Denver: Denver Museum of Natural History.

Irwin-Williams, Cynthia C., Henry T. Irwin, George Agogino, and C. Vance Haynes
 1973 "Hell Gap: Paleo-Indian Occupation on the High Plains." *Plains Anthropologist* 18(59): 40–53 (Eastern New Mexico University).

Jennings, Jesse D.
 1968 *Prehistory of North America.* New York: McGraw-Hill.

Jepson, Daniel A.
 1990 Archaeological Inventory of 17 Miles of U.S. Highway 85 Between Castle Rock C-470, Douglas County, Colorado. Submitted to Colorado Department of Highways by Centennial Archaeology, Fort Collins, Colorado.

Jepson, Daniel A. and O. D. Hand
 1994 *Archaeological Excavations at a Portion of the Dutch Creek Site (5JF463), A Multicomponent Camp in Jefferson County, Colorado.* Transportation Project CY 11–0470–13, C470 at Dutch Creek (bikepath structure). Colorado Department of Transportation Archaeological Research Series No. 4. Denver: Colorado Department of Transportation.

Johnson, Ann Mary and Alfred E. Johnson
 1998 "The Plains Woodland." In *Archaeology on the Great Plains,* ed. W. Raymond Wood. Lawrence: University of Kansas Press.

Johnson, A. M., J. F. Adkins, C. Beal, F. Irish, R. D. Lyons, H. Quinn, F. Rathbun, D. Rhodes, A. Sands, M. J. Tate, W. H. Tate, and J. Mobley-Tanaka
 1997 *Archaeological Investigations at the Ken-Caryl Ranch, Colorado.* Ed. Richard F. Somer. Memoirs of the Colorado Archaeological Society 6. Denver: Colorado Archaeology Society.

Jones, W. and K. Forrest
 1985 *Denver: A Pictorial History.* 2nd ed. Boulder: Cambridge University Press.

Jones-Eddy, Julie
　1992　*Homesteading Women: An Oral History of Colorado, 1890–1950.* Oral History Series 7. New York: Twayne Publishers.

Jorgensen, Joseph G.
　1972　*The Sun Dance Religion: Power for the Powerless.* Chicago: University of Chicago Press.

Joyner, Kathryn L.
　1988　Final Report of Cultural Resource Inventory for the Proposed E-470 Corridor, Douglas, Arapahoe, and Adams Counties, Colorado. Prepared for the State Historic Preservation Office by Engineer 470 Partnership and E-470 Authority, Aurora, Colorado.
　1989　Final Report of Test Investigations at Sites 5AH417, 5AH422, 5AH428, and 5AH258 Along the Proposed E-470 Corridor in Arapahoe County, Colorado. Submitted to Engineer 470 Partnership Denver.

Kainer, Ronald E.
　1976　"Archaeological Investigations at the Spring Gulch Site (5LR252)." Master's thesis, Department of Anthropology, Colorado State University, Fort Collins.

Kalasz, Stephen et al.
　1994　Historic Archaeological Investigations Associated with the 20th Street Viaduct Replacement Project, Downtown Denver, Colorado. Manuscript on file at the Colorado Historical Society Office of Archaeology and Historic Preservation, Denver.

Kalasz, Stephen, Bridget M. Ambler, Linda Scott Cummings, Michael McFaul, Kathryn Puseman, Wm. Lane Shields, Grant D. Smith, Karne Lynn Traugh, and Christian J. Zier
　1995　Report of 1994 Archaeological Excavations at the Magic Mountain Site (5JF223) in Jefferson County, Colorado. Centennial Archaeology, Inc., Golden Landmarks Association, City of Golden, Colorado.

Kalasz, Stephen, Mary W. Painter, Stephen A. Brown, Michael McFaul, Grant D. Smith, Christian J. Zier, Bridget M. Ambler, Jan Saysette, Kathryn Puseman, and Thomas E. Moutoux
　1996　Excavation of Prehistoric Archaeological Site 5AH416 Arapahoe County, Colorado. Prepared for MK Centennial, Arvada, Colorado and E-470 Highway Authority, Greenwood Village, Colorado by Centennial Archaeology, Inc., Fort Collins, Colorado.

Kehoe, Alice B.
　1990　"Points and Lines." In *Powers of Observation: Alternative Views in Archaeology,* ed. Sarah M. Nelson and Alice B. Kehoe. Pp. 23–28. Archaeological Papers of the American Anthropological Association 2. Washington, D.C.: American Anthropological Association.

Kehoe, Thomas F.
　1960　*Stone Tipi Rings in North-Central Montana and the Adjacent Portion of Alberta, Canada: Their Historical Ethnological, and Archaeological Aspects.* Smithsonian Bureau of American Ethnology Bulletin 73, Anthropological Paper 62. 421–73. Washington, D.C.: U.S. Government Printing Office.

Kennedy, Lawrence Michael.
　1967　"The Colorado Press and the Red Men: Local Opinion About Indian Affairs, 1859–1870." Master's thesis, University of Denver.

Kenner, Charles L.
　1969　*A History of New Mexican-Plains Indian Relations.* Norman: University of Oklahoma Press.

Kent, Jonathan
　1989　Proposal for Archaeological Investigations at Four Mile Historic Park, 1989. Manuscript on file at Four Mile House Historic Park, Denver.

1991 Four Mile House Historic Park Excavation Research Design. Manuscript on file at Four Mile House Historic Park, Denver.

Kent, Jonathan, Ruth Bandy, and Meichell Walsh
n.d. Historical Archaeology at a Denver Mile House: Archaeological Investigations of the Four Mile House (5DV7), Denver, Colorado. Metropolitan State College of Denver. In progress.

Keyser, James D.
1979 "Variations in Stone Ring Use at Two Sites in Central Montana." *Plains Anthropologist* 24(84) (Part 1): 133–43.

Kindig, Jean Matthews
1987 "An Evaluation of an Ethnohistoric Account of a Plains Indian Communal Hunt in the Boulder Valley, 1862." *Southwestern Lore* 53(4): 17–27.

King, Dale Stuart
1931 "Archaeology of the Central Highlands of Eastern Colorado." Master's thesis, Department of Anthropology, University of Denver.

Kroeber, Alfred L.
1902 *The Arapaho* American Museum of Natural History Bulletin 8. New York: American Museum of Natural History.

Kunstler, J. H.
1993 *The Geography of Nowhere: The Rise and Decline of America's Man-Made Landscape.* New York: Simon and Schuster.

Lanza, Joseph
1995 *The Cocktail: The Influence of Spirits on the American Psyche.* New York: St. Martin's Press.

Larson, Mary Lou
1990 "Early Plains Archaic Technological Organization: The Laddie Creek Example." Ph.D. dissertation, Department of Anthropology, University of California, Santa Barbara.

Lavender, David
1954 *Bent's Fort.* Lincoln: University of Nebraska Press.

Lawson, Merlin Paul
1976 *The Climate of the Great American Desert: Reconstruction of the Climate of the Western Interior United States, 1800–1850.* Lincoln: University of Nebraska Press.

Leach, Larry L.
1966 "Excavations at Willowbrook, a Stratified Site near Morrison." *Southwestern Lore* 32(2): 25–46.

Lecompte, J.
1978 *Pueblo, Hardscrabble, and Greenhorn: Society on the High Plains, 1832–1856.* Norman: University of Oklahoma Press.

Lee, W. C. and H. C. Raynesford
1980 *Trails of the Smoky Hill: From Coronado to the Cow Towns.* Coldwell, Idaho: Caxton Printers.

Leonard, Stephen J. and Thomas J. Noel
1990 *Denver: Mining Camp to Metropolis.* Niwot: University Press of Colorado.

Leone, Mark P. and Paul A. Shackel
1987 "Forks, Clocks, and Power." In *Mirror and Metaphor: Material and Social Constructions of Reality*, ed. Daniel W. Ingersoll and Gordon Bronitsky. Lanham, Md.: University Press of America.

Leone, Mark P. and Neil Asher Silberman
 1995 *Invisible America: Unearthing Our Hidden History.* New York: Henry Holt.

Lewis, G. Malcolm
 1965a "Three Centuries of Desert Concepts of the Rocky Mountain West." *Journal of the West* 4: 457–68.
 1965b "Early American Exploration and the Rocky Mountain Desert, 1803–1823." *Great Plains Journal* 5: 1–11.
 1966 "Regional Ideas and Reality in the Rocky Mountain West." *Transactions of the Institute of British Geographers* 38: 135–50.
 1979 "The Cognition and Communication of Former Ideas about the Great Plains." In *The Great Plains: Environment and Culture,* ed. Brian W. Blouet and Frederick C. Luebke. Pp. 27–42. Lincoln: University of Nebraska Press.

Liestman, Terri L. and Kris J. Kranzush
 1987 Dancing Pants Shelter: Prehistoric Occupation of the South Platte Canyon Below Cheesman Dam. Prepared for the Denver Water Department by Engineering Science, Denver.

Limerick, Patricia Nelson
 1987 *The Legacy of Conquest: The Unbroken Past of the American West.* New York: W. W. Norton.

Lockeretz, William
 1981 "The Dust Bowl: Its Relevance to Contemporary Environmental Problems." In *The Great Plains: Perspectives and Prospects,* ed. Merlin P. Lawson and Maurice Baker. Pp. 11–31. Lincoln: University of Nebraska Press.

Lockley, Martin G.
 1990 *A Field Guide to Dinosaur Ridge.* Denver: Friends of Dinosaur Ridge and the University of Colorado at Denver Dinosaur Trackers Research Group.

Long, Margaret
 1943 *The Smoky Hill Trail: Following the Old Historic Pioneer Trails on the Modern Highways.* Denver: W. H. Kistler Stationery Co.

Lower Downtown District
 n.d. *Lower Downtown Walking Tour.* Brochure. Project funded by a State Historical Fund Grant from the Colorado Historical Society. Denver, Colorado.

Madole, Richard F.
 1978 Geology of Archeological Sites in Middle Cottonwood Creek Valley and Taylor Park, Chaffee and Gunnison Counties, Colorado. U.S. Geological Survey Open File Report 87-78.

Madole, Richard F. and Meyer Rubin
 1984 "Reinterpretation of Holocene Alluvial Chronology in Major Valleys of the Northern Colorado Piedmont." In *American Quaternary Association: Program and Abstracts of the Eighth Biennial Meeting.* P. 76. Boulder: University of Colorado.

Malde, Harold E.
 1964 "Environment and Man in Arid America: Geologic, Biologic, Archeologic Clues Suggest Climatic Changes in the Dry Southwest in the Last 15,000 Years." *Science* 34: 123–29.

Mantz, Charles W.
 1973 The Analysis of Flaked Stone from Colo. L:9:31. Manuscript on file at the Department of Anthropology, University of Denver.

Marsh, Charles S.
  1982  *The Utes of Colorado: People of the Shining Mountains.* Boulder, Colo.: Pruett Publishing Company.

Martorano, Marilyn A.
  1988  "Culturally Peeled Trees and Ute Indians in Colorado." In *Archaeology of the Eastern Ute: A Symposium,* ed. Paul R. Nickens. CCPA Occasional Papers 1. Colorado Council of Professional Archaeologists.

Mayo, Dan
  1978  Preliminary Report on Excavations Conducted Within Four Mile Historic Park. Manuscript on file at Four Mile House Historic Park, Denver.

McNees, Lance
  1989  Addendum to: The Archaeological Investigations at the Dutch Creek Site-5JF463, Jefferson County, Colorado. Denver: Colorado Department of Highways, Archaeological Unit.

Medina, Douglas
  1974  "Excavations at Ken Caryl Ranch, 1973 and 1974, Report on Bradford House III Site." *Southwestern Lore* 40(4): 46–47.
  1975  "Preliminary Report on the Excavation of the Bradford House III Site—Ken Caryl Ranch." *Southwestern Lore* 41(4): 51–56.

Mehls, Steven F.
  1984  *Colorado Plains Historic Context.* Denver: Colorado Historical Society.
  1992  Denver International Airport Historic Resources. Multiple Property Listing. OAHP.
  n.d.  Archaic Period Architectural Sites in Colorado. Multiple Property Listing. OAHP.

Mehls, Steven F. and C. J. Carter
  1984  *Colorado Southern Frontier Historic Context.* Denver: State Historical Society of Colorado.

Melnick, Robert Z.
  1994  "Military Posts as Cultural Landscapes." In *Settler Communities in the West: Historic Contexts for Cultural Resource Managers of Department of Defense Lands.* Denver: National Park Service, Rocky Mountain Region.

Mendoza, Ruben G.
  1993  Archaeological Investigations at the Crescent Rockshelter Locality (Site 5JF148): The 1992 Field Season. Submitted to the State Archaeologist of Colorado, Denver.

Metcalf, Michael D. and Kevin D. Black
  1991  Archaeological Excavations at the Yarmony Pit House Site, Eagle County, Colorado. Denver: Bureau of Land Management, Colorado State Office, Cultural Resource Series 31.

Miller, Mark and Kathleen Wasson Fiero
  1977  An Archaeological Survey of the Proposed Parker Road Expansion Between State Highway 88 and Franktown. Colorado Department of Highways Project Number FC 083–1(7). Highway Salvage Report 19.

Monmonier, Mark S.
  1995  *Drawing the Line: Tales of Maps and Cartocontroversy.* New York: Henry Holt.

Montgomery, John
  1984  An Archaeological Overview and Management Plan for the Rocky Mountain Arsenal, Adams County, Colorado. Submitted to National Park Service, Atlanta by Woodward-Clyde Consultants, Walnut Creek, California.

Moore, J. L.
  1992 "Spanish Colonial Stone Tool Use." In *Current Research on the Late Prehistory and Early History of New Mexico,* ed. Bradley J. Vierra. Pp. 239–44. Special Publication 1. Albuquerque: New Mexico Archaeological Council.

Moorhead, Max L.
  1958 *New Mexico's Royal Road: Trade and Travel on the Chihuahua Trail.* Norman: University of Oklahoma Press.
  1968 *The Apache Frontier: Jacobo Ugarte and Spanish-Indian Relations in Northern New Spain, 1769–1791.* Norman: University of Oklahoma Press.

Morris, Ralph C.
  1926 "The Notion of a Great American Desert East of the Rockies." *Mississippi Valley Historical Review* 13: 190–200.

Mullen, Frank
  1977 "History Lies Under Auraria." *Auraria Times,* February 28.

Mulloy, William T.
  1958 *A Preliminary Historical Outline for the Northwestern Plains.* University of Wyoming Publications in Science 22(1). Caspar: University of Wyoming.
  1960 "Late Prehistoric Stone Circles." *Southwestern Lore* 25(4): 1–3.

Mumen, Nolie
  1942 *Early Settlements of Denver.* Glendale, Calif.: Arthur H. Clark.

Mutaw, Robert J. and Marcia J. Tate
  1990 A Cultural Resource Inventory of the Pine Ridge Ranch, Arapahoe County, Colorado. Aurora, Colo.: Powers Elevation Company, Inc.

Neighborhood Cultures of Denver
  n.d. Program brochure. Lawrence Street Center. Colorado Center for Community Development, Denver.

Nelson, Charles E.
  1966 "Excavation of Graeber Cave, North Turkey Creek." *Southwestern Lore* 32 (2).
  1967 "The Archaeology of Hall-Woodland Cave." *Southwestern Lore* 34(4): 85–106.
  1969 "Salvage Archaeology on Van Bibber Creek, Site 5JF10." *Southwestern Lore* 34(4): 85–106.
  1971 "The George W. Lindsay Ranch Site, 5JF11." *Southwestern Lore* 37(1): 1–14.
  1981 "Cherry Gulch Site (5JF63): A Projectile Point Study." *Southwestern Lore* 47(2): 1–27.

Nelson, Charles E. and Bruce G. Stewart
  1973 "Cherokee Mountain Rock Shelter." *Plains Anthropologist* 18(62): 328–35.

Nelson, Penny
  1992 An Analysis of the Glass Bottle Assemblage of 5DV7. Manuscript on file at Department of Anthropology, Metropolitan State College of Denver.

Nelson, Sarah Milledge
  1979a Archaeological Investigations in the Chatfield Reservoir, Colorado. Department of Anthropology, University of Denver. Submitted to Heritage Conservation and Recreation Service, U.S. Department of the Interior.
  1979b Excavations at Four Mile Historic Park, 1979. For the Colorado State Historic Preservation Office. Manuscript on file at the Colorado Historical Society Office of Archaeology and Historic Preservation, Denver.
  1980 South Table Mountain Archaeological Survey. Submitted to Bradley, Campbell and Carney, Golden, Colorado. Manuscript on file at the Colorado Historical Society Office of Archaeology and Historic Preservation, Denver.

    1993    *The Archaeology of Korea.* Cambridge: Cambridge University Press.
    1997    *Gender in Archaeology: Analyzing Power and Prestige.* Walnut Hills, Calif.: Alta Mira Press.

Nelson, Sarah Milledge, Myron Plooster, and David L. Ford
    1987    "An Interactive Computer Graphic Technique for Identifying Occupation Surfaces in Deep Archaeological Sites." *Journal of Field Archaeology* 14: 353–58.

Newberry, Gregory S. and Marcia J. Tate
    1994    City of Aurora Evaluative Site Testing-5AH48, Arapahoe Meadows, Arapahoe County, Colorado. Prepared for City of Aurora Golf Department.

Nickens, Paul R., ed.
    1988    *Archaeology of the Eastern Ute: A Symposium.* CCPA Occasional Papers 1. Denver: Colorado Council of Professional Archaeologists.

Nissley, Claudia
    1976    Progress Report #1, Four Mile House. Manuscript on file at Four Mile House Historic Park, Denver.
    1979    Four Mile House Narrative. Site documentation on file at the Colorado Historical Society Office of Archaeology and Historic Preservation, Denver.

Noel, Thomas
    1996    "The Mark of History." *Denver Post,* October 13.

Okladnikov, A. P.
    1967    "Ancient Population of Siberia and Its Culture." In *The Peoples of Siberia,* ed. M. G. Levin and L. P. Potapov. Chicago: University of Chicago Press.

O'Neil, Brian P. and Marcia J. Tate
    1986    Evaluative Testing of Archaeological Sites at the Proposed Senac Dam Sites, Arapahoe County, Colorado. Submitted to CH2M Hill, Englewood, Colorado by Powers Elevation, Inc., Denver.

O'Neil, Brian P., Marcia J. Tate, Paul D, Friedman, and Robert J. Mutaw
    1988    Data Recovery Program at Site 5AH380 for the City of Aurora Proposed Senac Dam Sites, Arapahoe County, Colorado. Submitted to the City of Aurora by Powers Elevation Co., Denver.

Ormes, Robert
    1992    *Tracking Ghost Railroads in Colorado.* Colorado Springs: Green Light Graphics.

Otto, N. E.
    1989    Taxonomic Identification of Plants & General Vegentational Types Occurring on the Four Mile House Archaeological Study Site. In Historical Archaeology at the Four Mile House, Denver, Colorado. First Interim Report by Jonathan D. Kent, Submitted to the Colorado Historical Society Office of Archaeology and Historic Preservation.

Overton, Richard C.
    1953    *Gulf to Rockies: The Heritage of the Fort Worth and Denver-Colorado and Southern Railways, 1861–1898.* Austin: University of Texas Press.

Parker, Watson
    1964    "Wading to California: The Influence of the Forty-Niners on the Notion of a Great American Desert." *Great Plains Journal* 3: 35–43.

Parkman, Francis
    1948    *The Oregon Trail.* Garden City, N.Y.: Doubleday.
    [1849]

Pascoe, Peggy
   1991  "Western Women at the Cultural Crossroads." In *Trails: Toward a New Western History*, ed. Patricia Nelson Limerick, Clyde A. Milner II, and Charles E. Rankin. Pp. 40–58. Lawrence: University of Kansas Press.

Patterson, Floyd A.
   1977a  Report on Monitoring Activities on the Site of the Denver Sulphite and Fibre Co. Mill. Cultural Resource Consultants, Denver.
   1977b  A Cultural Resource Survey of Selected Areas in the Union Station Neighborhood, Denver, Colorado. Cultural Resource Consultants, Denver.
   1979  A Cultural Resource Survey of the Proposed C-Line Realignment, Lower Downtown Combined Sewer Separation, by F. A. Patterson. Cultural Resource Consultants, Denver.

Patterson, Floyd A. and Virginia Garcia
   1977  A Cultural Resource Survey Along the Platte River II Interceptor Sewer. Cultural Resource Consultants, Denver.

Peters, Bette D.
   1976  Footnotes and Bibliography for the Park People Brochure Containing the History of the Four Mile House. Manuscript on file at Four Mile House Historic Park, Denver.
   1980  *Denver's Four Mile House*. Denver: Junior League of Denver for Four Mile House Historic Park.

Pettit, Jan
   1990  *Utes, the Mountain People*. Rev. ed. Boulder, Colo.: Johnson Books.

Plessinger, Patricia
   1985  "Lithic Debitage: A Computer Study." Master's thesis, Department of Anthropology, University of Denver.

Poor, M. C.
   1976  *Denver South Park & Pacific, Memorial Edition*. Denver: Rocky Mountain Railroad Club.

Powell, Nena
   1990  "Tipi Rings and Nomadism in the High Plains." Master's thesis, Department of Anthropology, University of Denver.

Prown, Jules David
   1996  "Material/Culture: Can the Farmer and the Cowman Still Be Friends?" In *Learning from Things: Method and Theory of Material Culture Studies*, ed. W. David Kingery. Washington, D.C.: Smithsonian Institution Press.

Pustmueller, Helen M.
   1977  "Notched Projectile Points from Franktown Cave: Classification and Traditional and Statistical Analyses." Master's thesis, Department of Anthropology, University of Denver.

Radspinner, Judy
   1977  Report on Wooden and Fibrous Artifacts, COLO L:9:31. Manuscript on file at Department of Anthropology, University of Denver.

Rancier, James, Gary Haynes, and Dennis Stanford
   1981  "1981 Investigations of Lamb Spring." *Southwestern Lore* 48(2):1–17.

Rathbun, Fred C.
   1977  "Progress Report: Lithic Materials Analysis, Falcon's Nest Site, 5JF211." *All Point Bulletin* 14(4).

Renaud, Etienne B.
　1931　First Report. Archaeological Survey of Eastern Colorado. University of Denver
　1932　Second Report. Archaeological Survey of Eastern Colorado. University of Denver
　1933　Third Report. Archaeological Survey of Eastern Colorado. University of Denver
　1935　Fourth Report. Archaeological Survey of Colorado. University of Denver

Rhodes, Lori E.
　1990　Results of Cultural Resource Investigations at Site 5AH416 within the E-470 Project Area. Prepared for the E-470 Authority, Aurora, Colorado by Dames and Moore.

Richardson, Rupert Norval
　1933　*The Comanche Barrier to South Plains Settlement.* Glendale, Calif.: Arthur H. Clark.

Rick, John W.
　1976　"Downslope Movement and Archaeological Intrasite Spatial Analysis." *American Antiquity* 41: 133–44.

Riefler, Roger F.
　1978　"Drought: An Economic Perspective." In *North American Droughts,* ed. Norman J. Rosenberg. Pp. 63–77. Boulder, Colo.: Westview Press.

Rocky Mountain News
　1956　"Denver Woman, 88, Recalls Early Four Mile House." September 16: 4.

Rood, Ronald J.
　1991　"Archaeofauna from the Yarmony Site." Chapter 8 in *Archaeological Excavations at the Yarmony Pit House Site,* ed. Michael D. Metcalf and Kevin D. Black. Pp. 157–78. Colorado Cultural Resource Series 31. Denver: Bureau of Land Management.

Rothschild, Nan A. and D. diZerega Rockman
　1982　"Method in Urban Archaeology: The Stadt Huys Block." In *Archaeology of Urban America: The Search for Pattern and Process,* ed. Roy S. Dickens, Jr. Pp. 3–18. New York: Academic Press.

Rowe, Bob
　n.d.　Floral Analysis of 5DV7, the Four Mile House. Manuscript on file at Department of Anthropology, Metropolitan State College of Denver.

Royce, Charles C.
　1899　*Indian Land Cessions in the U.S.* 18th Annual Report of the Bureau of American Ethnology, 1896–97, part 2. Washington, D.C.: U.S. Government Printing Office.

Rudolph, Gerald
　1964　"The Chinese in Colorado, 1869–1911." PhD dissertation, University of Denver.

Ruffner, James A. and Frank E. Bair
　1985　*The Weather Almanac.* Detroit: Gale Research Company.

Rybczynski, Witold
　1995　*City Life: Urban Expectations in a New World.* New York: Touchstone.

Sanders, John E., Alan H. Anderson, Jr., and Robert Carola
　1976　*Physical Geology.* New York: Harper and Row.

Satersmoen, Carol
　1990　"Cultural Change Among the Northern and Southern Utes as Represented by the Beadwork Collections of the Colorado Historical Society." Master's thesis, Department of Anthropology, University of Denver.

Sayres, James G.
　1984　"Work: An Experiment with Energy at Franktown Cave." Master's thesis, Department of Anthropology, University of Denver.

Schiffer, Michael B.
   1987   *Formation Processes of the Archaeological Record.* Albuquerque: University of New Mexico Press.

Schroeder, Albert H.
   1965   "A Brief History of Southern Utah." *Southwestern Lore* 30(4): 53–78.

Scott, Douglas D.
   1988   "Conical Timbered Lodges in Colorado or Wickiups in the Woods." In *Archaeology of the Eastern Ute: A Symposium,* ed. Paul R. Nickens. CCPA Occasional Papers 1. Denver: Colorado Council of Professional Archaeologists.
   1993   "Preliminary Analysis of Location Strategies of Plains Woodland Sites in Northern Colorado." *Southwestern Lore* 39(3): 1–11.

Scott, Douglas D. and E. Charles Adams
   1973   A Report on the Feature Behind the Molly Brown House. Report on file at the Colorado Historical Society Office of Archaeology and Historic Preservation, Denver.

Scott, Douglas. D. and D. A. Gillio
   1973   A Report on the Archaeological Impact of the Proposed "Foothills Project" of the Denver Board of Water Commissioners. Manuscript on file at Colorado Preservation Office, Denver.

Scott, Glenn R.
   1963   *Quanternary Geology and Geomorphic History of the Kassler Quadrangle, Colorado.* Geological Survey Professional Paper 421-A. Washington D.C.: U.S. Government Printing Office.
   1982   *Paleovalley and Geologic Map of Northeastern Colorado.* U.S. Geological Survey Miscellaneous Investigations Series, Map I-1378. Washington D.C.: U.S. Government Printing Office.

Scott, Glenn R. and Arnold M. Withers
   n.d.   Archaeological sites in the Kassler and Littleton quadrangles, Colorado. Manuscript on file at the Department of Anthropology, University of Denver.

Semenov, S. A.
   1964   *Prehistoric Technology: An Experimental Study of the Oldest Tools and Artifacts from Traces of Manufacture and Wear.* New York: Barnes and Noble.

Shaffer, Ray
   1978   *A Guide to Places on the Colorado Prairie, 1540–1975.* Boulder, Colo.: Pruett Publishing Co.

Shields, W. Lane
   1993   The E-470 Re-Alignment Survey and Limited Testing in Adams, Arapahoe and Denver Counties, Colorado. Prepared for Centennial Engineering, Arvad, Colorado by Metcalf Archaeological Consultants, Eagle, Colorado.

Shimkin, Demetri Boris
   1940   "Shoshone-Comanche Origins and Migration." *Pacific Congress Proceedings* 6(4): 17–25.

Shoemaker, Debra
   1976   "Social Relationships Within the French Family of Valverde, Colorado 1890." Master's thesis, Department of Anthropology, University of Denver.

Short, Susan K. and Loreen K. Stravers
   1981   Pollen Analysis, Parker, Colorado: Comparison of Modern Pollen Deposition and Archaeological Soil Samples. Manuscript on file at the Colorado Department of Highways.

Simmons, Alan H. and Douglas D. Dykeman
  1989  "The Protohistoric Period: 1300–1539." In *Human Adaptations and Cultural Change in the Greater Southwest*. Arkansas Archaeological Survey Research Series 32. Fayetteville: Arkansas Archaeological Survey.

Simmons, Marc
  1983  "Carros y Carretas: Vehicular Traffic on the Camino Real." In *Hispanic Arts and Ethnohistory in the Southwest,* ed. Marta Weigle, Claudia Larcombe, and Samuel Larcombe. Pp. 352–84. Santa Fe, N.M.: Ancient City Press.

Smith, Anne Milne
  1974  *Ethnography of the Northern Utes.* Papers in Anthropology 17. Santa Fe: Museum of New Mexico Press.

Smith, Craig S., Lance M. McNees, and Thomas P. Reust
  1995  "Site Structure of Two Buried Stone Circle Sites, Southern Wyoming." *Plains Anthropologist* 40(151): 5–21.

Smith, Henry Nash
  1950  *Virgin Land: The American West as Symbol and Myth.* Cambridge, Mass.: Harvard University Press.

Stanford, Dennis J.
  1979  "The Selby and Dutton Sites: Evidence for a Possible Pre-Clovis Occupation of the High Plains." In *Pre-Llano Cultures of the Americas: Paradoxes and Possibilities,* ed. R. L. Humphrey and Dennis J. Stanford. Washington, D.C.: Anthropological Society of Washington.

Stanford, Dennis J., Waldo R. Wedel, and Glenn R. Scott
  1981  "Archaeological Investigations of the Lamb Spring Site." *Southwestern Lore* 47(1): 14–27.

Stapp, Darby
  1977  A Study of Manos and Metates from Franktown Cave. Manuscript on file at the University of Denver.

Stark, J. T. et al.
  1949  *Geology and Origin of South Park, Colorado.* Geological Society of America Memoir 33. New York: Geological Society of America.

Stieghorst, Junann J. and Betty Bennett
  1983  "Salvage Archaeology at Golden Site 5JF12." *Southwestern Lore* 39(1): 13–17.

Stewart, Omer C.
  1966  "Ute Indians: Before and After White Contact." *Utah Historical Quarterly* 34(1): 38–61.

Stoffle, Richard W., Henry F. Dobyns, Michael J. Evans, and Omer C. Stewart
  1984  Toyavita Piavuhuru Koroin, "Canyon of Mother Earth": Ethnohistory and Native American Religious Concerns in the Fort Carson-Pinon Canyon Maneuver Area. University of Wisconsin–Parkside, Kenosha, Wisconsin. Submitted to USDI National Park Service, Rocky Mountain Regional Office, Denver, Contract No. CX 1200-3-A006.

Stone, Tammy
  1997  An Intensive Archaeological Survey of the Plains Conservation Center, Arapahoe County, Colorado. Western Central High Plains Archaeological Research Project Survey. Submitted to the Colorado Historical Society Office of Archaeology and Historic Preservation by the Department of Anthropology, University of Colorado at Denver.
  1999  *The Prehistory of Colorado and Adjacent Areas.* Salt Lake City: University of Utah Press.

Stone, Tammy and Ruben Mendoza
   1994   Excavations at the Crescent Rockshelter, 1993 Field Season. Manuscript on file at the Office of Archaeological and Historical Preservation, Colorado Historical Society, Denver.

Studenmund, Sarah J.
   1976   "Description of the Pottery from Franktown Cave." Honors thesis, Department of Anthropology, University of Denver.

Sullivan, Donald G.
   1992   "From Plains to Peak: Mount Evans Biogeographic and Geomorphic Transect, Front Range Colorado." In *Interdependece in Geographic Education, Colorado Field Studies: The International Geographical Union's Commission on Geographical Education Symposium,* ed. A. David Hill. Pp. 27–36. Boulder, Colo.: Center for Geographic Education, Department of Geography, University of Colorado at Boulder.

Swadesh, Frances L.
   1966   Hispanic Americans of the Ute Frontier from the Chama Valley to the San Juan Basin 1694–1960. Research Report 50. Tri-Ethnic Research Project, University of Colorado, Omer C. Stewart, director.
   1974   *Los Primeros Pobladores, Hispanic Americans of the Ute Frontier.* Notre Dame, Ind.: University of Notre Dame Press.

Tannehill, Ivan Ray
   1947   *Drought: Its Causes and Effects.* Princeton, N.J.: Princeton University Press.

Tate, Marcia J.
   1979   *A Cultural Resource Inventory of Roxborough State Park.* Denver: Colorado Historical Society.
   1984   The Cherry Creek Mile Houses. Manuscript in possession of the author.
   1987   Additional Cultural Resources Inventory at the Senac Dam Site, Arapahoe County, Colorado. Manuscript on file at the Office of Archaeological and Historical Preservation, Colorado Historical Society, Denver.
   1989   Archaeological Studies at the New Denver Airport. Vol. 1, Technical Report. Powers Elevation Company, Inc., Aurora.
   1991   Moffitt Property Cultural Resources Inventory, Adams County, Colorado. Submitted to City of Aurora, Aurora History Museum.

Tate, Marcia J. and Paul D. Friedman
   1986   A Cultural Resources Inventory of the Proposed Senac Dam Site, Arapahoe County, Colorado. Submitted to CH2M Hill, Englewood, Colorado by Powers Elevation/Archaeology Department, Denver.

Tate, Marcia J., Lloyd J. Glasier, Robert P. Ryan, and David R. Stuart
   1979   Archaeological Investigation at the Twelve Mile House. Manuscript in possession of the author.

Tate, Marcia J., Robert J. Mutaw, and Paul D. Friedman
   1989   A Cultural Resources Inventory of the Proposed Betts Ranch, Douglas County, Colorado. Archaeology Department, Powers Elevation Co., Aurora, Colorado.

Tate, Marcia J., Robert J. Mutaw, Cheryl A. Harrison, R. Laurie Simmons, and Christine Whiteacre
   1990   Final Report, a Cultural Resources Inventory of the Buckley Air National Guard Base, Arapahoe County, Colorado. Prepared for PAHL, PAHL, PAHL, Architects/Planners, Denver by Powers Elevation Co., Aurora, Colorado.

Tate, Marcia J., Brian P. O'Neil, Robert J. Mutaw, and Gordon C. Tucker, Jr.
 1989 Archaeological Studies at the New Denver International Airport Phase 1, Denver County, Colorado. Prepared for Dames and Moore, Golden, Colorado by Archaeology Department, Powers Elevation Co., Aurora, Colorado.

Taylor, Bayard
 1867 Colorado: A Summer Trip. New York: Putnam.

Taylor, R. C.
 1963 *Colorado South of the Border.* Denver: Sage Books.

Thompson, Gerold D.
 1956 The Archaeology of the Cherry Creek Canyon Area: A Study of Woodland Culture Remains. Manuscript on file at the Department of Anthropology, University of Denver.

Trenholm, Virginia Cole
 1970 *The Arapahoes, Our People.* Norman: University of Oklahoma Press.

Trimble, Donald E. and Michael N. Machette
 1979 Geologic Map of the Greater Denver Area, Front Range Urban Corridor, Colorado. U.S. Geological Survey Miscellaneous Investigations Series, Map I-856-H. Washington D.C.: U.S. Geological Survey.

Trimble, Donald E., G. R. Scott, and Wallace R. Hansen
 1984 *Mountains and Plains: Denver's Geologic Setting.* Popular Publications of the U.S. Geological Survey. Washington, D.C.: U.S. Geological Survey.

Tucker, Gordon C., Jr.
 1990 Monaghan Camp (5DV3041): Results of Data Recovery Efforts at a Prehistoric Site at the New Denver International Airport, Denver County, Colorado. Prepared for Dames and Moore, Golden, Colorado by Archaeology Department, Powers Elevation Co., Aurora, Colorado.
 1994 The Moffitt Site (5AM631): A Multi-Component Campsite in Adams County, Colorado. Prepared for Colorado Historical Society, Denver, by City of Aurora.

Tucker, Gordon C., Jr., Marcia J. Tate, and Robert J. Mutaw
 1992 Box Elder-Tate Hamlet (5DV3017): A Multicomponent Habitation Site at the New Denver International Airport, Denver County, Colorado. Prepared for Dames and Moore, Golden, Colorado by Archaeology Department, Powers Elevation Co., Aurora, Colorado.

Tweto, Ogden
 1979 Geologic Map of Colorado. U. S. Geological Survey. Washington, D.C.: U.S. Geology Survey.

Upton, Dell
 1992 "The City as Material Culture." In *The Art and Mystery of Historical Archaeology: Essays in Honor of James Deetz,* ed. Anne Elizabeth Yentsch and Mary C. Beaudry. Pp. 51–73. Boca Raton, Fla.: CRC Press.

U.S. Army
 1945 *History of the Rocky Mountain Arsenal, Denver, Colorado.* 16 vols. Denver: Army Service Force, Chemical Warfare Service, Rocky Mountain Arsenal.

U.S. Fish and Wildlife Service
 1996 Rocky Mountain Arsenal National Wildlife Refuge, Comprehensive Management Plan.

Utley, Robert M.
 1984 *The Indian Frontier of the American West, 1846–1890.* Albuquerque: University of New Mexico Press.

Veblen, Thomas T. and D. C. Lorenz
   1991   *The Colorado Front Range: A Century of Ecological Change.* Salt Lake City: University of Utah Press.

Wadley, Lyn
   1997   "The Invisible Meat Providers: Women in the Stone Age of South Africa." In *Gender in African Archaeology,* ed. Susan Kent. Walnut Creek, Calif.: AltaMira Press.

Wagner, A.
   1977   *Adams County: Crossroads of the West.* Brighton, Colo.: Adams County Commissioners.

Wallace, G. W. and J. P. Friedman
   1985   Seismotectonic Assessment Alluvial Terrace Investigation, North Fork South Platte River and Horse Creek, East-Central Front Range, Colorado. In Geologic and Seismotectonic Investigations East Central Front Range, Colorado. Denver: Report B of Second Interim Report, Denver Water Department.

Walsh, Meichell
   n.d.   Field Report, Trenches 34 & 35, 5DV7, Four Mile House Historic Park. Manuscript on file at the Department of Anthropology, Metropolitan State College of Denver.

Warrick, Richard A. and Martyn J. Bowden
   1981   "The Changing Impacts of Droughts in the Great Plains." In *The Great Plains: Perspectives and Prospects,* ed. Merlin P. Lawson and Maurice E. Baker. Pp. 111–37. Lincoln: University of Nebraska Press.

Weber, David J.
   1971   *The Taos Trappers.* Norman: University of Oklahoma Press.
   1982   *The Mexican Frontier, 1821–1846: The American Southwest Under Mexico.* Albuquerque: University of New Mexico Press.

Weber, Kenneth R.
   1980   "Ecology, Economy, and Demography: Some Parameters of Social Change in Hispanic New Mexico." *Social Science Journal* 17(1): 53–64.
   1990   "Ethnohistory of the Pinon Canyon Maneuver Site." In *An Introduction to the History of Pinon Canyon, Southeastern Colorado,* ed. William Andrefsky, Jr. Submitted to NPS-RMRO, Denver by Larson-Tibesar Associates, Inc., Laramie, Wyoming and Centennial Archaeology, Inc., Fort Collins, Colorado.

Weber, William A.
   1976   *Rocky Mountain Flora.* Boulder: Colorado Associated University Press.

Wedel, Waldo
   1959   *An Introduction to Kansas Archeology.* Smithsonian Institution Bureau of American Ethnology Bulletin 174. Washington, D.C.: U.S. Government Printing Office.
   1961   *Prehistoric Man on the Great Plains.* Norman: University of Oklahoma Press.

Weigle, Marta
   1970   *The Penitentes of the Southwest.* Santa Fe, N.M.: Ancient City Press.

Wendland, Wayne M.
   1978   "Holocene Man in North America: The Ecological Setting and Climatic Background." *Plains Anthropologist* 23: 273–87.

Wenger, Gilbert R.
   1956   "An Archaeological Survey of Southern Blue Mountain and Douglas Creek in Northwestern Colorado." Master's thesis, Department of Anthropology, University of Denver.

West Colfax Neighborhood Plan
 1987 Denver Planning and Community Development Office.

West, E.
 1991 "A Longer, Grimmer, But More Interesting Story." In *Trails: Toward a New Western History*, ed. Patricia Nelson Limerick, Clyde A. Milner II, and Charles E. Rankin. Pp. 103–11. Lawrence: University of Kansas Press.

West, Steven
 1991 Report on Bayou Gulch. Manuscript on file at Historic Franktown, Inc.

Wilmsen, E. and F. H. H. Roberts
 1978 *Lindenmeier, 1934–1974: Concluding Report on Investigations.* Smithsonian Contributions to Anthropology 24. Washington, D.C.: Smithsonian Institution Press.

Wilson, Bill and Betty Wilson
 1971 *19th Century Medicine in Glass.* Eau Gallie, Fla.: 19th Century Hobby & Publishing Co.

Winters, Ron
 1992 An Analysis of Metallic Firearm Cartridges from the 1989 and 1991 Field Seasons at Four Mile House. Manuscript on file at the Department of Anthropology, Metropolitan State College of Denver.

Withers, Arnold M.
 1954 "Reports of Archaeological Fieldwork in Colorado, Wyoming, New Mexico, Arizona, and Utah in 1952 and 1953: University of Denver Archaeological Fieldwork." *Southwestern Lore* 19(4): 1–3.

Wolf, Eric
 1982 *Europe and the People Without History.* Berkeley: University of California Press.

Wood, J.
 1967 "Archaeological Investigations in Northeastern Colorado." Ph.D. dissertation, Department of Anthropology, University of Colorado, Boulder.

Wood, W. R.
 1971 "Pottery Sites near Limon, Colorado." *Southwestern Lore* 37(3): 53–85.
 1998 *Archaeology of the Great Plains.* Lawrence: University of Kansas Press.

Working, Holbrook
 1975 Letter to Bette D. Peters, May 25, 1975. Report number DVL6F2. Manuscript on file at the Colorado Historical Society Western Central High Plains Archaeological Research Project Survey, Denver.

Wormington, Hannah Marie
 1957 *Ancient Man in North America.* Popular Series 4. Denver: Colorado Museum of Natural History.

Windmiller, R. and Frank W. Eddy
 1975 Two Forks: An Archaeological Study of Aboriginal Settlements and Land Use in the Colorado Foothills. National Park Service report. Manuscript on file at the Colorado Historical Society Office of Archaeology and Historic Preservation, Denver.

# INDEX

alder, 49–50, 108
altithermal, 43, 52, 55–56, 75, 80
amaranth, 50, 74, 80–81, 85, 94, 107
amateur archaeologist, 8, 10, 72
American Fur Company, 119
animal bone, 50, 72, 75, 83, 92, 100–101, 107, 222
Arapahoe County, 10, 85, 205
archaeological sites: Bat Cave, 104; Bayou Gulch, 39, 42, 53, 55–56, 66, 73–74, 78, 80–82, 85–87, 92, 100, 106–7; Bee House, 186, 190, 194–96, 198–99, 202; Box Elder, 81–82, 85, 87, 100, 104; Bradford House III, 74, 80, 82–83, 87, 92, 105; Cedar Point, 117; Cherokee Mountain, 120; Cherry Creek Canyon, 80, 87, 100, 106; Cherry Gulch, 80, 83, 92; Crescent, 73, 80, 83–84, 92, 106; Dancing Pants, 57, 80–81, 85; Falcon's Nest, 80, 83, 93; Four Mile House, 48, 58, 153, 180–95, 197–204, 224; Franktown Cave, 8, 15, 52, 65, 69, 74, 77, 80, 87, 90–91, 94–96, 100, 104–6, 108, 120; Graeber Cave, 69, 120–21; Hall Woodland Cave, 93, 106; Hatch, 117, Hazeltine Heights, 8, 69, 74, 88, 102; Jarre Creek, 93; Lamb Spring, 54, 72, 82; Lindenmeier, 65, 70, 72; LoDaisKa, 9, 73–74, 79–80, 84–85, 92, 104–5; Magic Mountain, 9, 15, 53, 66, 73, 78–81, 83, 87–88, 90, 93, 100, 105; Massey Draw, 34, 49–50, 53, 56–57, 80, 87; Moffitt, 74, 87, 106; Monaghan Camp, 52, 81, 85, 87; Olson, 84; Rainbow Creek, 90–91, 93; Rock Creek, 51, 53–54, 69, 78, 81–82, 86, 92, 104, 107; Senac Dam, 51–52, 55, 73, 77; Swallow, 73, 75, 80, 87, 93, 104; Tremont House, 19, 44, 142, 144, 153–71, 203, 219, 221, 225; Twelve Mile House, 180–83, 204; Van Ness, 102, 105; White Cat, 116; Willowbrook, 92, 106; Yarmony, 51, 78, 81
Archaic: Early, 37, 53–54, 56, 66, 78, 80–81, 85; Middle, 66, 82–86; Late, 55–56, 66, 75, 80, 83, 86–88, 95, 104, 107–8, 221
Arkansas River, 5, 21, 33, 113, 123–25, 130, 177
Army, U.S., 68, 125, 130, 181, 205–6, 209, 211, 213–14, 218. *See also* military
Auraria, 58, 142, 145–46, 152–53, 156, 159, 161, 171–72. *See also* West Denver

basket, 15, 58, 61, 80, 82, 85, 94–95, 96, 99, 109, 203, 222, 229
Bayou Gulch. *See* Archaeological sites
Bee House. *See* archaeological sites
Berlin, Colorado, 209
bison, 46–48, 50–52, 56, 61, 65, 68, 70, 72, 77, 80, 82, 87–88, 93, 95, 99–101, 104, 107, 116, 118, 120, 123, 135–27, 170, 222–23
bitters, 201–3
Black Forest, 5, 9, 21, 32–33, 35, 38–39, 42–43, 48–49, 52, 54–56, 67, 72–73, 78, 80, 82, 85–87, 93, 106, 120, 136–37, 204
Booth, Millie, 186, 195–96, 201, 203
bone grease, 50, 61, 75, 81, 102
bottle, 151, 162, 164, 169, 183, 190, 193–94, 199, 201–3
bow and arrow, 65, 88, 95
Bradford House III. *See* Archaeological sites
Brantner, Samuel and Jonas, 185
brickyard, 142
Buffalo Creek, 38
buffalo hide, 119, 124–25, 128
butcher, 49–51, 67, 80, 82, 101, 199

camp, campsite, 3, 9, 10, 13, 23, 29, 34–35, 49, 53, 55–56, 62–63, 68, 72, 75, 77, 80, 85–86, 101, 113–14, 116–17, 119–20, 122–24, 126–29, 131, 133–34, 136, 146, 204–5, 223–24. *See also* archaeological sites: individual names
Castlewood Dam, 204
cattle, 45, 148, 158, 170, 203, 211, 214
Cawker, Mary 185–86
caves, 40, 67, 82, 84, 93–94, 121, 222, 239–40; Colorow Cave, 84, 121. *See also* archaeological sites: Franktown Cave, Graeber Cave, Hall Woodland Cave; rockshelter
cellar, 151, 162, 164–65, 183, 186, 190–91, 241
Ceramic period: general, 51, 53–54, 69, 83, 88–89, 93, 105, 107, 224; Early, 10, 12, 53–55, 61, 65–66, 69, 74, 77, 81, 84, 86–88, 92–95, 103–4, 106–8, 222–24; Middle, 65–66, 69, 85, 92, 95, 100–101, 103–4, 106–8, 121, 223; Late, 70, 120, 123, 132, 137, 223
Chatfield Reservoir, 42–43, 48, 54, 74
chenopod, *Chenopodium,* 50, 74, 80–81, 85, 94, 101, 107–8
cheno-am, 50–52, 56, 85, 102
Cherry Creek, 1–2, 5, 9, 29, 31, 33, 38, 42–45, 48, 55, 58, 61, 67, 73, 77, 80, 87, 93–94, 100, 103–4, 106, 130–31, 139, 142, 151–52, 154, 161, 172, 177, 179, 180–82, 184, 186, 190, 198–99, 201, 203–4, 223, 236, 238
Cherry Creek Canyon. *See* archaeological sites
chicken, 170, 190, 211–12, 218
Chinatown, 149–50, 165, 226
Chinese, 149–50, 165, 226
ciboleros, 124–26
Civil War, 125, 170
Clovis, 65–66, 68, 72, 222, 242
collectors, modern, 8, 10, 17, 79, 86, 93
Colorado Archaeological Society, 8, 81, 85, 91, 117
Colorado Springs, 5, 21, 23
Colorado State University, 191, 198
Colorow, 84, 121, 123, 135. *See also* archaeological sites; caves
Colorow Cave. *See* caves
comancheros, 124–25
Contact period, 65, 70, 111–13, 115, 135–36, 204
Continental Divide, 53, 122

coprolites, 52
corn, 45, 52, 86, 104–5, 126, 222–23. *See also* maize
Coronado, 113
cottonwood, 48–49, 52, 58, 95, 100, 106, 131, 142, 186, 199, 201, 238
cultural contact, 226

dairying, 204, 211, 224
Dancing Pants shelter. *See* archaeological sites
deer, 47–49, 51–52, 67, 75, 77, 80, 82–83, 85, 87–88, 93, 95, 101, 107, 199, 219, 222, 225
Denver Pacific railway, 175, 225
desert, 36, 41, 48, 58–59, 148, 201, 223
diary, 224
diet, 47, 50, 86, 93–94, 102, 104, 106 196, 221–23
digging stick, 95, 129
dinosaur, 23, 34, 58, 123
Dismal River aspect, 114, 116–17
dog, 72, 82, 93, 107, 115, 131, 162, 224
drought, 12, 44, 55–56, 58, 82, 148, 223
dune, 41, 56–57
Dutch Creek, 50, 53, 57, 84, 87

earth lodge, 69
ecological zones, 2
ecosystem, 5
electric street car, 229
electricity, 148, 197
Elitch Gardens, 232, 238
erosion, 12, 21, 23, 25–26, 35, 39, 41–42, 44–45, 54–55, 77
ethnicity, 19, 213
Euro-American, 2, 3, 16, 19, 43–44, 70, 109–11, 118–20, 124–26, 128, 131–32, 134–35, 137, 204, 222, 224, 226
Excelsior Mill, 148

farm, 3, 5, 19, 126, 186, 205, 209, 211–13, 218, 224
faunal remains, 50–51, 72, 85
fire of 1863, 148, 158
fish, 23, 48, 67, 129, 169–70
Five Points, 177
flood, 12, 31, 44–45, 81, 161, 236; of 1864, 151, 158, 161, 186; of 1875, 159; of 1876, 151; of 1878, 161, of 1885, 151; of 1912, 151–52,

161–62, 164–65; 1933, 44, 190; of 1965, 44–45
Folsom, 65–66, 68, 70, 73, 222
fort: Bent's, 129; Collins, 73; Kearny, 130; Laramie, 130; Leavenworth, 179; Lupton, 131; St. Vrain, 131; Wise, 130
Four Mile House. *See* archaeological sites
Franktown Cave. *See* archaeological sites
Front Range, 21–22, 24–26, 28, 34, 37, 39, 42, 47, 52–53, 55, 67, 117, 131, 137
frontier, 1–3, 13, 18–19, 111, 119, 121, 123–25, 139, 142, 172–73, 176–77, 186, 203, 224
fuel, 50, 52, 87, 100, 106–8
fur trade, 118–19, 130

gender, 19, 128
Geographical Information Systems. *See* GIS
geology, 1, 18, 20–22, 33–34. *See also* individual periods
German, 49, 149, 153, 213–14, 226, 234
ghost railroad, 225
GIS (Geographical Information Systems), 7
glacier, 21, 26, 57
glass, 126, 142, 146, 148, 165, 169, 190–91, 194, 198–99, 212; bead, 16, 113, 119, 131
gold, 39, 57–58, 117, 130, 139, 142, 146, 148, 173–74, 177, 179, 203, 219, 225
gold rush, 57, 171
goosefoot, 50, 74, 80, 85, 100, 106–7, 222. *See also* chenopod; cheno-am
Grant Smelter, 232
Greeley, Horace, 58, 132–33
Greek, 213
Greek Revival style, 156
Green Mountain, 25, 28, 37–38, 73
grid, 172–74, 176–77, 183, 194, 217, 219. *See also* streets
grinding stone, 10, 35, 47, 67–68, 75, 77–79, 82, 87–88, 93–94, 104–5, 109, 222
gun, 113, 118–19, 157, 199, 202

hide working, 15, 51
Highline Canal, 7, 148
Hispanic, 118, 124, 126, 226
Hispano, 124
Hogback subregion, 23, 26–28, 33–34, 37–39, 43, 49–50, 53–54, 56–57, 73, 93, 120, 132

homestead 9, 12, 131, 172, 204–6, 209, 211–12, 218, 224
horse, 47, 49, 52, 68, 70, 72, 113, 118–19, 126–28, 133, 145, 180, 185, 211, 223–24, 229–30, 234
hotel, 139, 145–46, 149, 155, 157, 161–62, 176–77, 180, 185. *See also* archaeological sites, Tremont House

immigrant, 130, 149, 151, 161, 171–72, 177, 213–14, 234
Irish, 149, 213–14, 218, 226, 238
Irondale, 209, 213
Irwin-Williams, Cynthia, 8, 15, 37, 78, 81, 87, 100

Jewish, 149, 177, 236
juniper, 49, 52, 55, 95, 106, 122

Kemper, Ernst, 10, 12

Limerick, Patricia, 3, 224–25
lithic scatter, 11, 73, 77, 80, 86, 101, 113, 120
LoDaisKa. *See* archaeological sites

Magic Mountain. *See* archaeological sites
mail, 148, 180, 238
mammoth, 47, 49, 61, 65, 68, 70, 72, 222
manifest destiny, 16, 129
Masonic lodge, 150
medicine, 50, 68, 80–81, 107–8, 128–29, 190, 201–2
men, 61, 65, 108, 111, 128–29, 133, 135, 146, 151, 202, 211–12, 222, 234
Metropolitan State College, 83, 153, 197–99, 201
mica, 39, 114
military, 13, 204–5, 216. *See also* Army
mining, 13, 146, 148, 171, 176, 223, 227
Molly Brown House, 153
mountain men, 111

National Register of Historic Places, 155
Native American, 3, 15, 19, 23, 34, 48, 107, 109, 111, 113, 118–20, 125–26, 132, 134, 137, 139, 177, 191, 203–4, 218, 223, 226
newspaper, 133, 155, 158, 161, 171, 175, 193, 218

OAHP (Office of Archaeology and Historic Preservation), 5, 7
obsidian, 36, 74, 103, 108; obsidian hydration, 35–36

Paleoindian, 42, 53–54, 61, 65–66, 68, 70–73, 75, 78, 82, 221–22, 224, 229, 242
petrified wood, 9–10, 37–38, 73–74, 198–99
Pike, Zebulon, 58
Piney Creek, 10–11, 42–43, 49, 54, 93, 223
pithouse, 78, 81, 85, 97, 102, 117
Plains subregion, 10, 30, 35, 48, 51–52, 55, 77, 132, 137, 204
Platte River, 1, 9, 125, 139, 161, 172–73, 203, 236
Pleistocene, 26, 41–42, 47, 67–68, 72
Plum Creek, 42–44, 48, 72, 75, 102, 116
pollen, 8–9, 46–47, 55–56, 85, 87, 93–94, 104, 106
preservation, 5, 41, 46, 79, 84, 102, 153–54, 176, 219
privies, 151, 183, 190–91, 193
projectile point, 9, 15, 35, 47, 65–66, 68, 70, 73–75, 77–84, 86, 88, 92–93, 95, 99–102, 104, 106–8, 113, 117, 120, 131–32, 222
pronghorn, 48, 51, 77, 87, 101–2
Protohistoric, 55, 111, 114–15
Public Land Survey System, 172
Purgatoire River, 113, 125

quarry, 35, 37, 39, 53, 62, 74, 77, 185
quartzite 10, 37–39, 74, 107

railroad, 129, 147–49, 151–52, 161, 171, 174–76, 180, 186, 203, 209, 213, 225, 238
Ralston Cemetery, 139–41
ranches: Betts, 77; Big Dry Creek Cheese, 204; Cherokee, 120; Davidson, 10; Esser, 10; Evernut, 10–11; Victor, 214
Red Rocks Park 23, 34, 49, 83
removal, 3, 51, 124, 218. *See also* displacement
Renaud, Etienne, 8–9, 92, 242
reservation (Indian), 16, 126, 130, 135
road, 10, 26, 44, 77, 80, 90, 145, 154, 180, 192, 198, 216, 218, 225, 232, 236; Smoky Hill Road, 10; Parker Road, 77, 90; Jimmy Camp Road, 177, 179; Buckley Road, 218

rockshelter, 19, 23, 29, 34–35, 39–40, 57, 67, 78, 80, 83–85, 99, 120–21. *See also* cave; archaeological sites
Rock Creek. *See* archaeological sites
Rocky Mountain Arsenal, 19, 81, 90, 100, 140–42, 144, 204–10, 214–19, 226
*Rocky Mountain News,* 133, 135, 145–46, 157–61, 174, 180, 185, 199
Roxborough Park, 23, 28, 34, 37, 74, 77, 81

Salt Lake, 3, 113
saltbush, 52, 56, 100–101, 106, 108
Sampson Gulch, 10, 12
Santa Fe, New Mexico, 118, 130, 180, 226
Sargent, Nelson, 157–58, 161
scalp dance, 135
Scandinavians, 213–14
scarred tree, 122–23
sheep, 49, 51, 53, 72, 77, 85, 100, 126, 130, 170, 222
shell, 15, 35, 49, 52, 61, 67, 73–74, 102, 108, 224
Silk, Mattie, 151, 153
silver, 58, 148
site formation, 39–40
Smoky Hill tradition, 92
South Platte River, 2, 5, 21, 25–26, 29, 33, 42–45, 57–58, 61, 67, 72–73, 77, 82, 102, 125, 127, 130–31, 134, 149, 151, 153–54, 174, 177
Spanish, 113–15, 118, 123–25
stage (coach), 145, 147, 179–80, 185–86, 225
state capitol (Denver), 149, 161, 173
stone circle, 81–82, 113, 132, 137
stratigraphy, stratigraphic, 8, 40, 42, 86, 93, 183
Streams subregion, 29, 31, 33, 42, 49, 51, 54, 57, 82, 86, 88
street: Arapaho, 148; Blake, 148–49, 151, 169; Colfax, 148, 177, 234, 238; Curtis, 161, 238–39; Fifteenth, 148; Fourteenth, 148, 151, 180; Front, 155; Larimer, 148–49, 152, 161; Leetsdale, 185; Market, 147–49; Speer 149, 153–54; Thirteenth, 149, 152, 155, 169; Walnut, 152; Wazee, 149, 152–53
Sun Dance 129, 131
surveys 8–10, 12, 19, 73, 77, 85, 92, 101–2, 120, 122, 172, 147, 182–83, 193–95, 204–8, 218

tanning, 15, 79, 129, 132

tepee, 2, 93, 117, 128–29, 131–32, 134, 137
trade goods, 16, 116, 119–20, 125, 131
trail, 3, 7, 10, 70, 123, 145, 177–80, 183, 186, 192, 194, 198, 221, 224–25; Cherokee, 177, 179–80, 190–92, 198, 202; Overland, 177, 180; Santa Fe, 124, 177; Smoky Hill, 11, 179–80, 190–92, 198, 202, 225
treaty, 124–25, 130, 134
Tremont House. *See* archaeological site
tribe: Apache, 70, 111, 113–18, 123–24, 137, 226; Arapaho, 3, 10, 25, 42, 70, 113, 124–27, 129–31, 133, 218–19, 224, 226; Cheyenne, 3, 16, 70, 113, 124–32, 135, 175, 218, 225–26; Comanche, 113, 118–19, 123–24, 127; Crow, 125; Kiowa, 125; Lakota, 119; Osage, 123; Pawnee, 114, 125–27; Pueblo, 114, 118, 124; Shoshone, 69–70, 105, 118, 120–21, 123; Sioux, 119, 125, 127; Ute 16–18, 70, 111, 113, 117–25, 132–37, 180, 204, 226
truck farm, 19, 211, 216, 218
tundra, 49
Twelve Mile House. *See* archaeological sites

Ulibarri, Juan de, 118, 123
University of Colorado, 8, 83, 102, 190
University of Denver, 7–8, 10, 12, 74, 77, 81–83, 93–94, 106, 117, 126, 132, 193–96, 242
Upper Republican, 69, 92, 102–3, 104–7, 120

urbanization, 137, 140, 142, 153, 161, 170, 180, 217, 219
Ute Council tree, 123

Victorian, 128, 148, 162, 170, 176, 202

wagon train, 147, 225
warehouse, 148, 151, 161, 171
water, 10, 26, 35–36, 43–45, 50, 74, 78, 82, 87–88, 101, 104, 123, 127, 145, 147–48, 161, 169, 186, 194, 197, 203–4, 214–15, 221, 223–24, 238
Wazee Market, 152
well, 145, 186, 191–92, 198, 214, 216
West Denver,146, 151, 156–61, 171. *See also* Aurora
wheat, 48, 211, 218, 223
wickiup, 120, 122
widow, 129. 185, 212
windbreak, 34, 216
women, 3, 15, 19, 61, 108, 128–29, 135, 151, 202–3, 205, 211–12, 217, 222
Woodland period, 12, 43, 69, 77, 81, 88, 90, 92–94, 100–101, 103, 107
Wormington, Marie, 8, 68, 242
WPA, 205, 218

yucca, 15, 48, 52, 95, 97, 101, 139, 201

www.ingramcontent.com/pod-product-compliance
Lightning Source LLC
Chambersburg PA
CBHW082335300426
44109CB00046B/2486